WRITING AGAINST REVOLUTION

Conservative culture in the romantic period should not be understood merely as an effort to preserve the old regime in Britain against the threat of revolution. Instead, conservative thinkers and writers aimed to transform British culture and society to achieve a stable future in contrast to the destructive upheavals taking place in France. Kevin Gilmartin explores the literary forms of counterrevolutionary expression in Britain, showing that while conservative movements were often inclined to treat print culture as a dangerously unstable and even subversive field, a whole range of print forms – ballads, tales, dialogues, novels, critical reviews – became central tools in the counterrevolutionary campaign. Beginning with the pamphlet campaigns of the loyalist Association movement and the Cheap Repository in the 1790s, Gilmartin analyses the role of periodical reviews and anti-Jacobin fiction in the campaign against revolution, and closes with a new account of the conservative careers of Robert Southey and Samuel Taylor Coleridge.

KEVIN GILMARTIN is Associate Professor of English Literature at the California Institute of Technology. He is the author of *Print Politics: The Press and Radical Opposition in Early Nineteenth-Century England* (Cambridge, 1996) and the editor, with James Chandler, of *Romantic Metropolis: The Urban Scene of British Culture, 1780–1840* (Cambridge, 2005).

This series aims to foster the best new work in one of the most challenging fields within English literary studies. From the early 1780s to the early 1830s a formidable array of talented men and women took to literary composition, not just in poetry, which some of them famously transformed, but in many modes of writing. The expansion of publishing created new opportunities for writers, and the political stakes of what they wrote were raised again by what Wordsworth called those "great national events" that were "almost daily taking place": the French Revolution, the Napoleonic and American wars, urbanization, industrialization, religious revival, an expanded empire abroad and the reform movement at home. This was an enormous ambition, even when it pretended otherwise. The relations'between science, philosophy, religion, and literature were reworked in texts such as *Frankenstein* and *Biographia Literaria*; gender relations in *A Vindication of the Rights of Woman* and *Don Juan*; journalism by Cobbett and Hazlitt; poetic form, content, and style by the Lake School and the Cockney School. Outside Shakespeare studies, probably no body of writing has produced such a wealth of response or done so much to shape the responses of modern criticism. This indeed is the period that saw the emergence of those notions of "literature" and of literary history, especially national literary history, on which modern scholarship in English has been founded.

The categories produced by Romanticism have also been challenged by recent historicist arguments. The task of the series is to engage both with a challenging corpus of Romantic writings and with the changing field of criticism they have helped to shape. As with other literary series published by Cambridge, this one will represent the work of both younger and more established scholars, on either side of the Atlantic and elsewhere.

For a complete list of titles published see end of book.

WRITING AGAINST REVOLUTION

Literary Conservatism in Britain, 1790–1832

KEVIN GILMARTIN

California Institute of Technology

CAMBRIDGE
UNIVERSITY PRESS

CAMBRIDGE UNIVERSITY PRESS

Cambridge, New York, Melbourne, Madrid, Cape Town, Singapore, São Paulo

Cambridge University Press

The Edinburgh Building, Cambridge CB2 2RU, UK

Published in the United States of America by Cambridge University Press, New York

www.cambridge.org

Information on this title: www.cambridge.org/9780521861137

First published 2007

Printed in the United Kingdom at the University Press, Cambridge

A catalogue record for this publication is available from the British Library

ISBN-13 978-0-521-86113-7 hardback
ISBN-10 0-521-86113-6 hardback

For Susan and Raymond

Contents

Illustrations

Acknowledgments

The study of counterrevolutionary expression has consistently led me into unfamiliar literary and historical terrain, and I am immensely grateful to the many friends, colleagues, and institutions who have supported and assisted my work on this book.

Above all Jim Chandler has remained an extraordinarily generous scholar and friend, reading and responding to many portions of this book as it was written, and sensitively guiding me through a number of challenges along the way. Working on conservatism has made me all the more aware of the remarkable community of historians and literary scholars who share my interest in romantic-period radical culture, and I want to acknowledge the support of Saree Makdisi, Jon Mee, Iain McCalman, James Epstein, John Barrell, and David Worrall. Particularly in the early stages of the research, Marilyn Butler was a generous host in Cambridge, and I am indebted to her as well for expert guidance through the byways of romantic literature and culture.

Southern California possesses a generous community of scholars with an interest in British romantic literature, and in their regular gatherings at Anne Mellor's UCLA Romantic Studies Group, they have heard and responded to some of the earliest versions of this project; I am particularly indebted to Anne Mellor, Julie Carlson, Margaret Russett, Alan Liu, Bob Essick, Reg Foakes, and Bob Maniquis. Other colleagues near and far have responded generously to my work and my enquiries through the years, including Orrin Wang, Michael Gamer, Jon Klancher, Neil Fraistat, Andy Franta, Jerome Christenson, Peter Manning, Alan Bewell, Theresa Kelley, Jeffrey Cox, Anne Janowitz, Greg Dart, Ian Haywood, and Paul Keen. Closer to home, I have benefited from the support of colleagues at the California Institute of Technology, particularly Cindy Weinstein, Cathy Jurca, Mac Pigman, John Sutherland, and John Brewer.

A key phase of the research and writing of this book took place during a summer in which I co-directed with Saree Makdisi a Mellon Foundation seminar at the Huntington Library, on the topic "British literature and culture in the 1790s." I am grateful to the Mellon Foundation for funding this program, and to the seminar participants who made it a memorable summer: Tone Brekke, Sibylle Erle, Frank Mabee, Kelli MacCartey, Matthew Mauger, Suzie Park, Willis Scilacci, and Joanne Tong. The establishment of the seminar program was the work of Bill Deverell, now a former Caltech colleague but thankfully still a near neighbor and friend.

Research for this book has been supported at every stage by the Division of the Humanities and Social Sciences at the California Institute of Technology, and I am grateful to its staff and administration, particularly John Ledyard, Jean Ensminger, and Susan Davis. Barbara Estrada provided expert support throughout the research and writing of this book. Judy Nollar, the humanities research librarian at Caltech, has assisted with a range of electronic and print resources, and I have relied as well on the Interlibrary Loan staff at Caltech's Millikan Library. The Huntington Library in San Marino, California, has been a second institutional home, and I am particularly grateful to the director of research, Roy Ritchie, to the curator of rare books, Alan Jutzi, and to the curator of historical prints, Cathy Cherbosque. Other libraries whose staff and collections have assisted my research include the British Library and its newspaper library at Colindale, the Bodleian Library, the Cambridge University Library, and the Sutro Library in San Francisco.

Versions of the first two chapters appeared in *ELH* and in *The Journal of British Studies*, and I am grateful to the publishers for permitting me to reprint that material here.

List of Abbreviations

ADB   Ann Thomas, *Adolphus De Biron. A Novel. Founded on The French Revolution*, 2 vols. (Plymouth, [1795])

AE   Jane West, *The Advantages of Education, Or, The History of Maria Williams, A Tale for Misses and Their Mamas, By Prudentia Homespun*, 2 vols. (London, 1793)

AJ   *The Anti-Jacobin; or, Weekly Examiner*

AJR   *Anti-Jacobin Review and Magazine*

AP   Association for Preserving Liberty and Property against Republicans and Levellers, *Association Papers*. Part I: *Proceedings of the Association* and *Publications Printed by Special Order of the Society*. Part II: *A Collection of Tracts Printed at the Expence of the Society* (London, 1793)

BEM   *Blackwood's Edinburgh Magazine*

BC   *British Critic*

CG   *Christian Guardian*

CL   *Collected Letters of Samuel Taylor Coleridge*, ed. Earl Leslie Griggs, 6 vols. (Oxford: Clarendon Press, 1956–1971)

CW 3   Samuel Taylor Coleridge, *Essays on His Times in the Morning Post and The Courier*, ed. David V. Erdman, 3 vols., Vol. 3 of *The Collected Works of Samuel Taylor Coleridge* (Princeton: Princeton University Press, 1978)

CW 4   Samuel Taylor Coleridge, *The Friend*, ed. Barbara E. Rooke, 2 vols., Vol. 4 of *The Collected Works of Samuel Taylor Coleridge* (Princeton: Princeton University Press, 1969)

CW 6   Samuel Taylor Coleridge, *Lay Sermons*, ed. R.J. White, Vol. 6 of *The Collected Works of Samuel Taylor Coleridge* (Princeton: Princeton University Press, 1972)

CW 7   Samuel Taylor Coleridge, *Biographia Literaria*, ed. James Engell and W. Jackson Bate, 2 vols., Vol. 7 of *The Collected*

Introduction: Reconsidering counterrevolutionary expression

This is a study of the literary forms and rhetorical strategies involved in British counterrevolutionary and anti-radical print expression from the first reaction to the French Revolution through the Napoleonic era to the Reform Act of 1832. The specific provisions of the 1832 bill for reform – a rationalization and limited extension of the franchise, and redistribution of parliamentary seats away from pocket boroughs in favor of populous towns and counties – by no means answered radical expectations. But taken together with a significant erosion of the constitutional position of the Church of England in the late 1820s, through the repeal of the Test and Corporation Acts and Catholic relief, electoral reform and the middle-class political ascendancy it facilitated served to shift the ideological and social terms in which a defense of the establishment was conducted over the course of the rest of the nineteenth century. While my own rationale for historical coverage has to do with developments in political expression, the years marked out for this study coincide with the notional boundaries of the British romantic period, less often insisted upon in recent literary scholarship perhaps, but still evident in a field now constituted by a critically productive tension between the old romantic canon and an influx of competing aesthetic movements and recovered writers and texts. The argument of this book is not intended to reground romanticism in conservative terms. But in drawing on recent historical scholarship that insists upon the productive role of conservative movements in the political culture of the period, it will challenge the tendency for a leading strand of romantic studies to identify literary expression and the life of the imagination, whether by way of positive affiliation or more ambiguous dislocation and displacement, with some primary sympathy for the French Revolution, and to privilege the progressive affiliations of literature and of print culture more broadly.[1]

1

And yet any account of a counterrevolutionary culture that was itself obsessed with the print sources of subversion must grant some measure of the romanticist tendency to associate literary expression with radical social change, particularly where revolution was itself understood in mediated terms. It is certainly striking how often in British literature of the romantic period disruptive political energies seem to arrive through the written or printed word. This was partly a matter of experience, as revolution became for British culture and society what Ronald Paulson has suggestively termed "a secondary French reality – history at second hand in written reports."[2] But there is also evidence here of a kind of ideological defense mechanism, and literary expression offers a particularly acute register of the way the threat of subversion was consistently displaced from England to republican France, to North America, and to Ireland, with the trauma of political change getting relayed and reported as news, rumor, and correspondence. In her important study of British fictional reworkings of the sentimental plot of Rousseau's *La Nouvelle Héloïse*, Nicola J. Watson has shown how, as "the Revolution was read and reread, written and rewritten" in these years, the sentimental device of intercepted correspondence came to figure transgressive energies,[3] and similar relays for revolution can be found throughout the literature of the period. In the conservative imagination, patterns of discursive transmission were complicated by a symptomatic ambiguity about the geography of subversion. Complaints about foreign contagion were common enough, but so too were opportunistic reprisal campaigns against at least a century of indigenous liberal and Enlightenment tendencies, blamed for sapping the moral and spiritual foundations of political stability. And alarmist responses to dissident forces at home were concerned to justify repressive measures by drawing a short line from the London radical press to diffuse manifestations of popular discontent. "What think you of a club of Atheists meeting twice a week at an ale-house in Keswick, and the landlady of their way of thinking" (*SLC* 4: 210), Robert Southey wrote from his remote rural home to a London correspondent in 1816, and discoveries of this kind only served to reinvigorate his furious *Quarterly Review* campaign against William Cobbett and the London radical press.

To identify Robert Southey and other hostile commentators on the transmission of radical unrest as *counterrevolutionaries* itself merits some reflection. One paradoxical assumption of this book is that a programmatic defense of the unreformed constitution and the established

Church in this period can be considered "counterrevolutionary," and that there are reasons to prefer this term to a defensively construed conservatism, even though the British state did not experience a political transformation that could be said to enlist a "counter-revolution" in the strict sense of "a revolution opposed to a previous revolution."[4] The anti-radical arguments and print forms of expression treated in this book were often not simply retrospective nor committed to preserving "things as they are," but were instead involved in a more enterprising and potentially compromised literary-political project that itself contributed to the transformation of the established order, in part by systematically engaging a subversive enemy on its own compromised literary and public terrain. They were counterrevolutionary in the sense that they were unapologetically committed to a project of social renovation, and to intervening in present conditions even to the point of adjusting inherited arrangements, in order to block revolutionary designs. To raise this issue about the term "counterrevolution" is not to overlook a historical record of political violence and conspiracy that extends in this period from the naval mutinies of 1797, the Irish rising of 1798, and the Despard plot of 1802 through the Luddite disturbances of 1811 and 1812, the Pentridge rising of 1817, and the Cato Street conspiracy of 1820.[5] But it is to recognize that the scale of events in England did not approach that of revolutionary France, so that the tendency to figure catastrophic political change in mediated terms – and particularly through the production, circulation, and reception of print – was to some extent a matter of experience. At the same time, geographical displacements of revolutionary energy can be more critically evaluated, as a determined result of loyalist efforts to discredit dissent of any kind as essentially alien, disloyal, and extreme, present in Britain only as the phantasmal consequence of overheated speculation and unreliable print transmission. There is reason, then, to be alert to the risk that we sustain a conservative polemic when we recapitulate displaced conceptions of revolution in our own interpretive discourse. From at least the founding of *The Anti-Jacobin; or, Weekly Examiner* in 1797, the term "anti-Jacobin" was itself a politically calculated self-identification, meant to gather a host of dissident political, social, and cultural forces under the ominous sign of a Jacobinism whose real sympathies lay abroad.

Within British romantic studies, revolution as a matter of literary and print intervention is a familiar pattern, though it manifests itself in the first instance as an Enlightenment inheritance, and what David

Simpson has identified as the belief among "radicals of the 1790s, like Godwin, Paine and Thelwall, and some of their French precursors, . . . that print would be the agent of world revolution."[6] It was arguably in its *negative* form that this belief in the disruptive power of the printed word acquired its more distinctive romantic inflection, above all in Edmund Burke's "mastery of the semiotics of revolution" in the *Reflections on the Revolution in France* (1790), a text shot through with anxieties about the subversive work of newspapers, pamphlets, reprinted sermons, paper currency, and a shadowy conspiracy of the political men of letters at home and abroad.[7] Advanced, examined, and contested through the early phases of the revolution controversy and the campaign against domestic radicalism, the connection between revolution and the printed word found emblematic as well as casual expression throughout canonical romanticism. In *The Excursion* (1814), William Wordsworth identifies one source of the Solitary's postrevolutionary disaffection in a copy of Voltaire's *Candide*, although any sense of a compelling political threat is mitigated by the cavalier dismissal of Voltaire's text – "dull product of a scoffer's pen" – and by its discovery among the ornaments of a child's playhouse.[8] A similar pattern of print transmission is more ambiguously underscored in Jane Austen's *Northanger Abbey* (1818) through the telling error by which Eleanor Tilney mistakes Catherine Morland's anticipation of a "very shocking" gothic novel due out in London for news of a "dreadful riot."[9] And again towards the end of the period, with a dialectical precision born of his own uneasily sustained radical commitments, William Hazlitt brought the legacies of Paine and Burke together in his *Life of Napoleon Buonaparte* (1828, 1830) when he wrote that "the French Revolution might be described as the remote but inevitable result of the invention of the art of printing,"[10] a claim made more provocative by Hazlitt's insistence on tracing the critical and democratizing effects of print back through a native revolutionary inheritance to the impact of the English Reformation.

The anxious intersection of print and subversion has long made romantic studies fertile ground for interpretive theories of a revolution in language, aesthetics, or consciousness, and in recent decades, for the more materially and institutionally grounded theories of social transformation that have entered literary studies through Jürgen Habermas' account of the structural development of a political public sphere.[11] In this regard, the talismanic year 1789 has proven a fluid and even unpredictable literary-historical marker. It persists as a point of departure for British romanticism less from any strictly causal claim about the relation between politics and the arts, between France and Britain, but rather as a potent (if often unexamined) figure for the way writers responded to, identified with, or repudiated a whole range of social, psychological, and aesthetic transformations conjured by events in France. To be sure, the perception that British literature and culture were undergoing changes not directly related to revolutionary events in Paris was available to late eighteenth- and early nineteenth-century commentators on the right and on the left, particularly where a longer view of the Enlightenment was possible, and where liberating (or corrupting) changes in taste, morality, and manners were found to be at work. And while this book is certainly interested in the way that subversion in all its forms was felt to circulate through literature and society, it will generally take the view that programmatic conservative anxieties about the threat of revolution were dictated by political concerns for monarchy, constitutional government, Church establishment, and social hierarchy.

This is not to deny that over the course of the 1790s a revolution controversy tended to spill over from political and constitutional principle to manners, mind, and morality, so that any strict distinction between politics and literature become increasingly hard to sustain, nor is it to dismiss such celebrated episodes in the literary politics of the period as the assault of the *Anti-Jacobin* on Robert Southey's early radical verse or the strictures of *Blackwood's Edinburgh Magazine* on the Cockney School of poetry. Instead, it is to keep in mind that the campaign against subversion was chiefly conducted on other fronts, with the *Anti-Jacobin* establishing a sense of proper authority by constituting itself within the periodical framework of a single parliamentary session, and *Blackwood's* developing its sense of festive embattlement primarily with respect to the Whig opposition and plebeian unrest rather than Cockney versification. Extreme fears continued to circulate around extreme outcomes: insurrection, regicide, the leveling of property rights and class privilege, and a sectarian dissolution of the Anglican establishment. Jane West certainly betrayed a common counterrevolutionary sentiment when she claimed, in her 1799 novel *A Tale of the Times*, that "the annihilation of thrones and altars" was the work not of arms but of "those principles which, by dissolving domestic confidence and undermining private worth, paved the way for universal confusion"(*TT* 2: 275). But the force of this argument lay precisely in its warning that any compromises in matters of domesticity, manners, and taste would precipitate the fall of governments and "universal confusion." A crucial exception can be found among Evangelical moral reformers, for whom the crisis of the 1790s was, as David Eastwood has written, a crisis "in the realm of public morality rather than in the world of politics."[12] Even here, however, the urgent new political threat was seized upon by Evangelical activists as an opportunity to extend the base of support for a moral reform campaign had once seemed suspiciously revisionist, and contaminated with its own Puritan revolutionary associations.

Within the framework of a counterrevolutionary imagination that traced the alarming movement of subversive energies back and forth from nation to nation, and from politics and religion to manners, taste, and judgment, the printed word was subject to heightened scrutiny because it was understood to mediate the threat of revolution, anticipating in its own disruptive historical development a traumatic break with inherited forms, and conditioning the reception of cataclysmic events through the "rapid communication of intelligence" that Wordsworth famously entered in his catalogue of debilitating modern developments.[13] For radicals and liberals, the alignment of print with social change was readily understood in progressive terms. Thus Hazlitt extended his discussion of the revolutionary consequences of print through a series of conventional Enlightenment distinctions between "the diffusion of knowledge and inquiry" on the one hand and the stubborn remnants of "barbarous superstition" and "the feudal system" on the other.[14] For those inclined to defend the established Church and the unreformed constitution, the situation was altogether more difficult, not least because such defenses were characteristically expressed in print. Nor was it easy to renounce altogether the progressive assumptions bound up in an identification of print culture with radical change. The British constitution had long been celebrated, by contrast with Continental absolutism and Eastern despotism, for its capacity to accommodate new social and political energies, of the kind manifestly evinced in the career of a politician and writer such as Edmund Burke. And the commitment to social and economic advancement was a widely shared inheritance among eighteenth-century British elites. One of the challenges facing counterrevolutionary movements was to sustain a qualified commitment to progress while distinguishing the reformist designs of present-day radicals from earlier constitutional revisions by which the English state had legitimately accommodated the Reformation and the rise of commercial society.

With the ambiguities of an enterprising and resourceful conservatism in mind, it is important to acknowledge that the shock of 1789 did often yield a straightforward logic of reaction: in blunt defenses of monarchy, social hierarchy, and economic inequality as a providential dispensation; in unyielding and often contorted accounts of the benefits of an unreformed electorate; in a repudiation of the skeptical, speculative, and cosmopolitan tendencies of the eighteenth century; and in a commitment to social forms that were conceived (however notionally) in local, rural, and oral terms. For literary and cultural studies, this nostalgic structure of feeling has long served as the dominant framework for romantic-period conservatism, against which to measure the political inclinations of particular writers, texts, and movements. And while this deep conservatism – often identified as "Burkean," though Edmund Burke is at best an imperfect type – was certainly crucial to the defense of Church and state in the period, it does not tell the whole story. The *Reflections* routinely betrays competing counterrevolutionary energies, for example, in the way Burke sets out from an implicit contrast between his own reluctantly published private correspondence and Richard Price's promiscuously reprinted sermon in support of the French, even as he then proceeds to hunt down an ominous "predecessor" for Price in the figure of Hugh Peter, the Puritan era divine notorious for having preached at the execution of Charles I. Mixture is of course a favorite Burkean figure, and his own mixed rendering of Price's offensive communication – is it characteristically printed or spoken? a betrayal of foreign or indigenous sympathies? an alarming present departure or an echo of past transgressions? – suggests how a counterrevolutionary discourse could remain alert to the transmission of stabilizing and destabilizing tendencies back and forth between print and speech. While the *Reflections* did partly encode its political suspicions as a matter of literary form, with Burke's own unsystematic private correspondence pitted against calculated conspiracies in print, it became increasingly clear to counterrevolutionary activists over the course of the 1790s that an effective challenge to the threat of revolution would have to engage directly with those modes of public organization and print communication that were associated with radical protest.

As an account of the challenges involved in this kind of mixed conservative print campaign *against* the rise of radicalism in print and in public opinion, the present study can be said to draw its concerns from the nervously imperfect rhetorical organization of the *Reflections*,

rather than from the more usual romanticist identification of Burke
with conservative principles of organic development, generational
inheritance, and immediate local attachment as the precondition for
national feeling. Given the prominence Burke has long enjoyed within
British romantic studies, a field that has not easily accommodated
topical prose, his diminished presence in the chapters that follow
deserves some explanation.[15] The fact that literary scholarship has
paid far less attention to other leading social and political writers of the
period (Thomas Malthus, David Ricardo, Jeremy Bentham, Robert
Owen, and even Thomas Paine) can certainly be traced to the
impressive rhetorical force of the *Reflections*, to the way Burke's anxieties
about the politics of sentiment, theater, sublimity, and domesticity get
played out elsewhere in the literature of the period, and to his influence
on such leading poets and essayists as William Wordsworth and William Hazlitt.[16] In this sense, there is no reason to challenge the
canonical status of the *Reflections*, and my decision not to devote a
chapter of this book to Burke is a recognition of the range and quality
of existing scholarship.[17] What is more problematic, however, is the
tendency for literary scholarship to make the ideological disposition
of the *Reflections* a simple index of conservatism, in the way Paine's
Rights of Man or "English Jacobinism" once stood for a radical culture
that we now correctly understand to have been more complex and
internally differentiated, extending through a range of native, cosmopolitan, constitutionalist, Dissenting, infidel, feminist, and economic idioms of protest.[18] And in many respects Burke was a far less
representative man of the right than Paine was of the left. In a
perceptive account of how the *Reflections* came to achieve its status "as
a conservative classic," J. G. A. Pocock reminds us that Burke
remained through much of his late career "a lonely and distrusted
figure," by no means a prime mover of conservative thought and
action in a decade that has since been identified with his impact:
"The counterrevolutionary associations which were formed in and
after 1793 seem to have relied less on Burke for their polemics than
on William Paley, Hannah More, and other authoritarian elements
lying deep in Whig and Tory tradition."[19] The appearance after the
Reflections of such contrarian polemics as *An Appeal from the New to the
Old Whigs* (1791) and *A Letter to a Noble Lord* (1796) serves to underscore the development of his counterrevolutionary writing amidst the
disintegration of the Whig corporate identities he had once sustained,
as well as his unwillingness or inability to bring his animosity towards

the French Revolution to bear upon secure collective affiliations. In an astute survey of the pamphlet literature of the 1790s, Gregory Claeys has further complicated Burke's situation by challenging the very framework of a "Burke-Paine debate" as a way of understanding the British controversy over the French Revolution, on the grounds that conflict "was waged in terms not immediately given in the two major combatants' main texts," particularly once loyalism became fixated with a misleading charge of social and economic leveling advanced against *Rights of Man*.[20]

Successive scholarly formulations of a "Burke problem" suggest that, in accounts of his own work, the tendency has been to acknowledge a complex and distinctive achievement.[21] Yet an ambivalence about matters of party, property, national identity, and literary profession-alism tends to get overlooked where Burke comes to stand for a reflex counterrevolutionary traditionalism. While there is no arguing against the need for interpretive shorthand in literary and ideological analysis, the effect here has been both to misrepresent Burke and to flatten out the range and complexity of conservative positions in an age of revo-lution. The growing body of work in romanticism that identifies radical expression with a range of dissident traditions has not been accom-panied by a similar appreciation of the diversity and resourcefulness of conservative movements.[22] While historians and political theorists such as H. T. Dickinson, Ian R. Christie, Frank O'Gorman, Mark Philp, Gregory Claeys, David Eastwood, James J. Sack, Don Herzog, and Emma Vincent have undertaken a substantial critical reassessment of conservatism in this period,[23] their work has yet to be felt in the political framework for romantic studies. Again, the effect is doubly distorting, making some of Burke's distinctive idioms and concerns a measure of British conservatism, while reserving a formally and stylistically engaging response to the French Revolution for the magnificent prose of the *Reflections*. In drawing upon recent historical scholarship, my aim is to recover for literary studies the range and complexity of counter-revolutionary expression, and to demonstrate the enterprising and pro-ductive (rather than merely negative or reactive) presence of counterrevolutionary voices in the culture of the romantic period.

It is worth being clear at the outset about the limits of this study. My interest lies with an articulate, self-conscious, and interventionist conservatism in print, rather than with sporadic outbreaks of "Church and King" violence, or with those more implicit and deeply embedded habits of deference and national feeling that undoubtedly contributed to the prevention of revolution in Britain.[24] Nor do the chapters that follow substantially engage visual and theatrical forms that were increasingly brought to bear upon political controversy in this period.[25] In adhering to deliberate counterrevolutionary verbal expression in print, my aim is to bring into focus some of the constitutive tensions that make this a distinct body of writing: tensions between revision and tradition; between a desire to confront radicalism on its own terms, and a deep-seated skepticism about the political legitimacy of print culture and public opinion; between an unyielding confidence in the viability of the old regime, and a realization that new social forces and cultural forms must be enlisted in its defense. And of course conditioning every dimension of the response to radical protest there is a framing tension between counterrevolutionary public expression and coercive state action. No account of an enterprising conservatism in this period can afford to ignore the repressive network of spies, gagging acts, and criminal prosecutions that went into "Pitt's terror" and subsequent government campaigns against popular unrest. Yet here too it is important not merely to construe such repression as a distinct outer limit upon free expression, an approach that tends to reinforce straightforward identifications of print culture with liberating social change. Loyalist civic associations and government sponsored periodical forms were designed to align counterrevolutionary public expression with state repression and legal restriction, and conservatives strenuously denied that there was anything inappropriate or inconsistent about this kind of collaboration. Contrary to the liberal assumptions that often guide our histories of the institutions of criticism, this book suggests that aggressive critical practices developed in the late eighteenth and early nineteenth centuries on both sides of a sustained debate over the legitimacy of the old regime in Britain.

I have already suggested that "conservative" can be a misleading term for counterrevolutionary expression if it is construed in a narrowly retrospective or defensive sense. Semantic difficulties do not end here, as James J. Sack has suggested in his study of the ideological development of "reaction and orthodoxy" in Britain from the 1760s to 1832. Where the term "Jacobite" was clearly passing out of relevant usage in these decades, the alternative "Tory" was factionally contested and inconsistently applied; "Pittite" entered the field in the 1790s in honor of the Prime Minister William Pitt's decisive leadership against the French and against domestic radical protest, but the term then became embroiled after his death in 1806 in rival commitments among the Pitt Clubs, particularly over the rights of Roman Catholics. The political application of "conservative" was for the most part a later nineteenth-century development, anticipated in the 1810s by Robert Southey and others, but not decisively claimed by the Tory party until a *Quarterly Review* article of 1830. "Counterrevolutionary" was similarly emerging in the period, again with assistance from Southey.[26] To frame his own study, Sack chooses the terms "right" and "right-wing," on the pragmatic grounds that they were not in use in England before 1832, and are therefore unencumbered by contemporary meanings or shifts in meaning.[27] While my own local terminology in the chapters that follow is (like Sack's) somewhat eclectic, in preferring "counterrevolutionary" to frame my argument I have the advantage of setting out from the years after 1789, when Sack's "right-wing" positions were vividly shaped by the campaign against Jacobin principles and popular radical organization. At the same time, the period framework for this book is not meant to refute the argument by Sack and others that the British reaction to the French Revolution involved important continuities with the earlier eighteenth century. In particular, my first two chapters consider the ways in which the Cheap Repository and the Association for Preserving Liberty and Property against Republicans and Levellers drew on available traditions of civic enterprise and Evangelical moral reform.

As part of the case for an enterprising and productive counter-revolutionary culture, this book joins other recent revisionist accounts of the history of the right in suggesting that the conservative structure of feeling that emerged in the period of the late Enlightenment and the American and French Revolutions was a feature of modernity as well as a reaction to it, and should not simply be assigned to outmoded institutions and residual social forms. Darrin M. McMahon puts the point succinctly in his study of the French counter-Enlightenment, when he describes how the "distinctly new ideological culture" of the early French Right took shape *within* the emerging institutions of the political public sphere: "Its defense of tradition was not traditional, its reverence for history was a historical departure, and its arguments for the family and patriarchal power were a response to novel threats both real and perceived."[28] In the early formation of British conservatism, the prominent role played by politicians, writers, and intellectuals with reformist impulses and affiliations – Burke of course, but also William Pitt, George Canning, and Samuel Taylor Coleridge – should by itself suggest the inadequacy of a merely defensive or nostalgic conception of conservatism. And conservatives constructively engaged new modes of public communication and persuasion not only to combat their enemies, but also to negotiate differences among themselves. There were controversies within broadly loyalist and anti-radical political movements over slavery and empire; over the balance of authority between crown and parliament; over poor law reform and education for the lower orders; over the rights of Roman Catholics, the rise of Methodism and Evangelical piety, and the ascendancy of the Church of England; over agricultural improvement, the merits of commerce and industry, and the relative responsibilities of landed and commercial elites; and over the rights of women and the propriety of female public agency. As a result, it is not always easy to define the social and political order that counterrevolutionary activists were concerned to defend, and in the campaign against subversion, there were invariably shifting and competing definitions of the establishment. Evangelical moral reformers were particularly concerned to answer radical theories of natural right with a new language of social duty that enlisted all ranks and classes, so that popular subordination came to depend reciprocally on the moral probity of elites. And very often in counterrevolutionary discourse, the authority of the public writer entered the political equation as a potential challenge to the inherited privileges of the landed classes. The strains at work in brokering such power relations were evident in the anti-Jacobin novel and in the writings of Southey and Coleridge, though again, Evangelical moral reform offers the most vivid case of a kind of contractualism in counterrevolutionary expression, with a range of rewards held out to readers of every class in exchange for their strict piety and renewed moral discipline.

The relevance of organic theories of formal and aesthetic development to literary theory certainly helps explain the prevailing emphasis within romantic studies on traditionalist elements of conservatism. However, to assign conservative thought and action to a straightforward preservation campaign is to accept uncritically one of conservatism's own legitimating mythologies. In fact strategies that were not consistent with an announced resistance to social change were routinely justified through an appeal to the urgent and extraordinary threat of subversion. To acknowledge that counterrevolutionary movements were to some extent a concerted social fabrication should reinforce rather than diminish our sense of their profound impact upon the literature and culture of the period. In the sustained atmosphere of crisis that extended from the Jacobin threat of the early 1790s through the furious agitation for reform in the years leading up to 1832, it was never enough for conservatives to mobilize existing social and cultural resources, nor to remind disaffected subjects of their shared stake in an inherited constitution. As Linda Colley has observed, in accounting for a reconstruction of the monarchy and the ruling classes that accompanied the emergence of British national identity, "active commitment to Great Britain was not, could not be a given" in this period: "It had to be learnt; and men and women needed to see the advantage in learning it."[29] The challenges faced by counterrevolutionary activists in fashioning a familiar and acceptable countenance for newly acquired commitments will be a central concern of this book. Certainly, the idea that loyalty and subordination might be transmitted without benefit of formal instruction – in effect eliding the education that Colley describes – remained a powerful conservative ideal. And a condition of natural attachment to established social forms was nowhere more aggressively advanced than where its premises were manifestly belied, in vernacular loyalist addresses to the lower orders. Thus the principal correspondent in William Jones' loyalist Association tract of 1792, *John Bull's Second Answer to His Brother Thomas*, is made to ask: "Does [Paine] and his brothers think that we shall be as easily gulled as the French? and that Britons, who enjoy more liberty and property, than any nation under Heaven, will change it for their foolish equality?" (*AP* II, 2: 6–7). Paine and his brothers aside, the anxieties of William Jones and his loyalist collaborators were palpable enough as the "John Bull" series of tracts and handbills extended through a flurry of fictional correspondence between the patriotic brothers and their stridently patriotic cousins and countrymen.[30]

Literary analysis can contribute signally to our understanding of the emergence of modern conservatism by coming to terms with a paradoxically revisionist response to the threat of revolution. The chapters that follow are linked above all by their sustained attention to a pervasive rhetorical and literary dilemma: the resistance of counterrevolutionary expression to what might be termed *achieved* form, a defense of established powers that is fully and stably vested in the compromised terrain of print culture and public opinion, and that issues from an untroubled sense of the political authority of the public writer. For this reason, "form" will be an important and critically flexible conception throughout the book, as an account of a range of counterrevolutionary printed forms and literary genres – pamphlets, broadsheets, narrative and ballad tracts, vernacular dialogues, periodical reviews, magazines, satirical novels, domestic romances – registers the pressure that polemical exigencies brought to bear upon literary form, and the way distinct strands of counterrevolutionary sentiment (vernacular, satirical, Evangelical) came to be invested in different forms of expression. Given the prevailing attention of romantic literary studies to radical and oppositional expression, this book cannot do justice to the whole range of neglected counterrevolutionary forms. My focus has been determined in part by an interest in the constitutive tension between aggressive counterrevolutionary enterprise and a reluctance to extend the authority of print culture, between active intervention in the public sphere and a desire to contain similar radical interventions. There is an emphasis too on texts that achieved their counterrevolutionary vocation through a heightened reflexivity about their own rhetorical devices. So for example Hannah More undertook in her Cheap Repository Tracts (1795–8) to represent the process by which Cheap Repository Tracts took effect, and the leading counterrevolutionary critical reviews scrutinized other critical reviews as well as the wider field of new publications. If reflexive form has long interested literary scholarship, these instances are instructive and challenging because they were driven not by internal considerations about aesthetic organization but rather by a desire to achieve greater leverage on the social world. In its sequence of chapters, this book traces a general course of historical development from the 1790s through the early nineteenth century, yet formal considerations are relevant here as well. An opening pair of chapters considers the new modes of disciplinary print expression that were unleashed by the leading counterrevolutionary publishing operations of the 1790s, John Reeve's loyalist Association and Hannah More's Cheap Repository. A second pair of chapters then considers two major literary (or quasi-literary) forms, the periodical review and the novel, that helped extend counterrevolutionary expression through a wider social and cultural field. I then close with the late conservative careers of Robert Southey and Samuel Taylor Coleridge, considered less as a default on early radicalism (a leading concern within romantic studies) than as an extension and deliberate redirection of existing counterrevolutionary impulses.

The first chapter, "In the theater of counterrevolution: loyalist association and vernacular address," analyzes the close relationship between the language of counterrevolutionary pamphleteering and the organizational imperatives of John Reeves' Association for Preserving Liberty and Property against Republicans and Levellers, in order to show how vernacular dialogues and polemical tracts came to realize the impressive potential of counterrevolutionary public expression even as they embodied its underlying tensions and ambiguities. The discussion is framed by a reading of William Paley's pivotal Association pamphlet, *Reasons for Contentment* (1792), as a compelling preliminary effort to theorize and resolve the challenges involved in writing, publishing, and reasoning against revolution. Hannah More's *Village Politics* (1792) was another early Association pamphlet, and it remains the most widely known and reprinted of the era's demotic loyalist tracts. Yet it was in her subsequent Cheap Repository Tracts that More came to shape a distinctive Evangelical contribution to counterrevolutionary print culture. Chapter Two, "'Study to be quiet': Hannah More and counterrevolutionary moral reform," shows how the energy at work in the circulation of these tracts was invariably recapitulated in their complex narrative form. Though committed to social hierarchy, More had a far less divided conception of counterrevolutionary labor than did her counterparts at the loyalist Association, and her Cheap Repository tracts imagine a self-reforming polity knit together by the collaborative energies of model clergymen, enterprising charitable women, munificent gentry, and redeemed common people. If her writing for the poor is often loosely identified with a timeless rural world, More herself was committed to middle-class enterprise and resourceful literary production as a way of rescuing Britain from the twin threat of religious infidelity and political subversion.

By the end of the 1790s, deliberate counterrevolutionary expression had worked its way through the entire print register, from newspapers and magazines to satirical prints and verse, history, travel writing, conduct books, and works of devotion. For my purposes here, the novel and critical review merit close study: both involved comprehensive social ambitions and a rich tradition of formal experimentation, and taken together they disclose the possibilities and the characteristic inconsistencies of counterrevolutionary print expression. Chapter Three, "Reviewing subversion: the function of criticism at the present crisis," shifts attention from the pamphlet controversies of the 1790s to the ongoing periodical engagements of the nineteenth century, while also serving as a hinge between the social movements that absorb the first half of the book and the more familiar literary material of the second half. To manage the sheer range of periodical forms, the chapter advances from a preliminary overview of titles and formats to a closer analysis of conservative reviewing, where the aim was to offset all manner of subversion through what one reviewer suggestively termed "the regular inspection of a strict literary police" (*QR* 2 [1809], 146). The sequence of "anti-Jacobin" publications, extending from the first weekly *Anti-Jacobin* through the monthly *Anti-Jacobin Review and Magazine* (1798–1821) to a range of compilations and annual digests, captures the antagonistic resourcefulness of counterrevolutionary periodical expression and brings into focus the habit of reviewing other reviews as a way of establishing effective periodical surveillance. The anti-Jacobin movement through weekly, monthly, and annual formats also suggests a distinctive temporal organization, and while counterrevolutionary reviews resisted apocalyptic radical expectations, they were similarly guided in their periodical appearance by an acute sense of crisis. Editors and publishers met specific challenges with ephemeral print forms, even as the *Quarterly Review* (1809–) and *Blackwood's Edinburgh Magazine* (1817–) became controversial fixtures on the periodical landscape.

If the rise of counterrevolutionary reviewing was shadowed by a contempt for the expansion of print culture, a similar paradox haunted the development of the anti-Jacobin novel, as longstanding conservative doubts about the morality of popular fiction were reinforced by political concerns about the novel's subversive commitment to social mobility, individual gratification, and sexual transgression, to say nothing of the specific threat posed by English Jacobin fiction. Chapter Four, "Subverting fictions: the counterrevolutionary form of the novel," considers the way Elizabeth Hamilton, George Walker, Henry James Pye, Jane West, and others brought the design of the novel to bear upon the campaign against revolution, while simultaneously striving to redeem popular fiction from its suspect moral associations. While there was no single solution to this problem, my analysis focuses on a hybrid form of the counterrevolutionary novel, composed from two strands of fictional tradition, the domestic romance and the picaresque or rogue's tale. The anti-Jacobin picaresque typically mapped the progress of its subversive rogue along the circuits of print communication and social mobility that haunted the counterrevolutionary imagination in this period – bookshops, coffee-houses, newspapers, taverns, dining clubs, and stagecoaches. By contrast, domestic interiors offered a refuge from corrupt public life, and an emblem of everything that revolutionary desire put at risk. And yet the most compelling anti-Jacobin novels were not content with a crude polarization of social forces. I explore the development in these fictions of a more complex form of counterrevolutionary domestic agency, shaped by conversation and rational deliberation, and oriented outward from the home toward the public threat of revolution. Interestingly, there was a clear reluctance to deploy this engaged domesticity against the threat of revolution in any direct way, a reticence that was reinforced in skeptical treatments of female charitable agency. In the end, the anti-Jacobin novel typically purged its Jacobin rogue through the *deus ex machina* of state repression rather than through any countervailing agency shaped within its own narrative design.

Chapter Five, "Southey, Coleridge, and the end of anti-Jacobinism in Britain," considers the conservative careers of Robert Southey and Samuel Taylor Coleridge as an extension and critical reassessment of the counterrevolutionary enterprise. While both writers insisted that domestic revolution remained a clear threat through the post-Napoleonic era, they felt it was important to work beyond the immediate crisis toward a more self-sustaining social order, and in doing so they proved unusually willing to reimagine the established order as an order that must somehow involve their own literary authority. Though furiously anti-democratic, Southey's contributions to the *Quarterly Review* sustained a revisionist conservatism by insisting that radical discontent was exacerbated by economic conditions and by maintaining that only new legislation instituting a national system of elementary schools under Church auspices could permanently avert the threat of revolution. Always resourceful and pragmatic in his own professional practice, Southey nevertheless intimated more utopian premises for conservative intellectual enterprise in his vision of a revitalized Anglican clergy. Coleridge's own contradictory project of social renovation and retrospection similarly hinged upon the Church, notably in the ambitious constitutional theories of *On the Constitution of the Church and State* (1829). Although critics have sometimes portrayed Southey as an extreme reactionary in order to argue Coleridge's supposed moderation, the fact is that Southey was no less reformist on matters of education and political economy, and was arguably more sympathetic to the plight of the poor. The difference between the two writers can be found in the terms through which they negotiated their competing reactionary and revisionist impulses, not in the relative strength of those impulses. Like Southey, Coleridge wanted to reach beyond his own present remedial discourse to envision a social order permanently secured by the conciliatory role of the Anglican clergy. Yet he was reluctant to achieve this through new legislation, and his constitutional theorizing represents an effort to set the future on secure historical foundations. Through their contributions to debates over parliamentary representation, religion, poverty, and education in the years leading up to 1832, both writers substantially reworked the counterrevolutionary concerns of the 1790s even as they transmitted them into the later nineteenth century.

CHAPTER 1

In the theater of counterrevolution: Loyalist association and vernacular address

In the writing of history as well as in literary studies, conservative movements have generally played a negative role in accounts of the history of political expression in Britain during the period of the French Revolution. Where E. P. Thompson and others on the left tended to identify radicalism with the disenfranchised and with a struggle for the rights of free expression and public assembly,[1] conservative activists have been associated with state campaigns of political repression and legal interference. Indeed, conservatism in this period is typically conceived in negative terms, as anti-Jacobin or counterrevolutionary feeling. If this has been the view of hostile commentators, it is consistent with a more sympathetic mythology that sees nothing novel about the conservative principles that emerged in late eighteenth- and early nineteenth-century Britain.[2] They represent an establishment response to foreign and novel challenges. Even where conservatives set about mobilizing the resources of print, opinion, and assembly in a constructive fashion, the reputation for interference has endured. John Reeves' Association for Preserving Liberty and Property against Republicans and Levellers is an instructive case in point, since it managed in its brief but enterprising history to combine fierce anti-Jacobinism with the later eighteenth century's rising tide of voluntary civic activism. The Association came together at the Crown and Anchor Tavern when a group of self-professed "private men" decided "to form ourselves into an ASSOCIATION," and announced their intentions through the major London newspapers in November and December of 1792. The original committee then called upon others "to make similar exertions in their respective neighbourhoods," forging energetic local associations that would be linked by regular correspondence with the central London committee (*AP* I, Proceedings, 1: 5, 10). In this way, the loyalist movement grew with astonishing speed. By the early months of 1793, it included perhaps a thousand local affiliates (the London committee claimed over two thousand),[3] all engaged in the business of corresponding with other societies, circulating conservative pamphlets, issuing loyal addresses, and exposing the threat of Jacobin conspiracy. Though the Association maintained a high public profile in all these areas, its repressive legal campaign against the radical press and the London Corresponding Society has attracted the most notice. According to one historian of extra-parliamentary organization, "the Association, with Reeves in command, had one object. Its mission was repression . . . . The campaign against subversion was swift, vindictive, and unrelenting."[4]

Yet even a "one object" assessment of the Association need not exclude a variety of means. Loyalists were flexible in conceiving their own activity, and they endorsed approaches to public enterprise that ranged from repression and opposition ("against") through conservation ("preserving") to more autotelic energy ("exertions") and even a kind of self-invention ("to form ourselves into"). The complex historical possibilities expressed by conservative activism have been more fully acknowledged in recent years by H. T. Dickinson, Ian Christie, Robert R. Dozier, and others, who have sought to rehabilitate the intellectual credibility and popular appeal of a loyalist defense of the British state in the 1790s.[5] This body of scholarship clearly suggests a less negative understanding of conservatism with respect to public opinion and print expression, in part through the basic claim that radical discontent was put down not by extreme methods of state repression ("Pitt's reign of terror"), but rather by relatively ordinary mechanisms of public deliberation and civic enterprise. In defending "the strength of conservative ideas and opinion," Dickinson proposes that "the radicals were defeated by the force of their opponents' arguments and by the climate of conservative opinion among the politically conscious, not simply by the recourse to repressive measures and the forces of order."[6] The credible presence of counterrevolutionary sentiment in public life is reinforced, in this view, by the fact that conservative principles, broadly understood as a resistance to social change and a commitment to British constitutional traditions, were in place well before the outbreak of the French Revolution.[7] So too were the practices of civic association and public expression through which loyalism took hold, and even historians not committed to a defense of conservatism have identified enterprises like Reeves' Association and the later volunteer movement with "a growing civic-mindedness and voluntary endeavour" which, far from being narrowly repressive in its aims and impact, "contributed significantly to the building of civic cultures in a period when these were starting to shed their old exclusiveness and becoming more public and self-consciously communal."[8]

Yet the case for a more sympathetic treatment of loyalism has its critics. Revisionist claims about "the genuine popularity of the loyalist cause among all ranks in society,"[9] and about the credibility and persuasiveness of arguments against reform, have come in for particular scrutiny. In a wide-ranging response to Dickinson and others, John Dinwiddy argued that while "in some areas the conservatives were able to counter radical arguments quite cogently, there were other areas where they had to resort either to evasiveness, or to misrepresentation, or to some fairly transparent special pleading."[10] Challenges have also been mounted to the idea that counting up the sheer number of tracts published on each side of the revolution controversy reveals a conservative advantage in public opinion, and this has led to a more critical treatment of the material and institutional procedures for loyalist expression. Dinwiddy makes the case along the axis of production as well as reception, observing that "many writers on the conservative side were place-holders or place-hunters," and that "many conservative tracts, especially at the popular end of the spectrum, were purchased in bulk for free distribution," so that "their extensive circulation said far more about upper-class anxiety to instill anti-Jacobin views than about the lower-class appetite for them."[11] In what is likely to remain the most searching critique, Mark Philp grants loyalist address more force than Dinwiddy and others, but raises questions about the direction it would have moved ordinary readers. Philp identifies Reeves' Association with a "vulgar conservatism" that disrupted the established terms of political debate by challenging Edmund Burke's view that "the vulgar were the object of conservative thinking, not intended participants in it." In directing political arguments, however inflexibly and coercively, to a class of readers once felt to lie below the threshold of public opinion, Association pamphleteers like William Paley and Hannah More "breached the traditional boundaries of the political nation and thereby advanced a process of mass participation which they had come into existence to prevent." From the 1790s onward, according to this analysis, ordinary subjects were incorporated into public life by radical and reactionary writers alike, through the sheer force and range of printed works addressing them as political agents. Even where conservative activists relied upon the stabilizing effects of a British national identity forged in the wars with France, they were courting an interest in political participation that had unpredictable ideological consequences.[12] Philp's analysis complicates a polarized historiographical debate by challenging straightforward claims about the popularity of conservatism while reinforcing a sense of the Association's constructive impact on popular political consciousness.

Philp's shrewd interpretive reversal has important methodological implications as well, forcing us to consider the gap between the enterprising production and reactionary content of loyalist discourse, and to dwell more closely upon the rhetorical features of a crucial episode in British political history. In this chapter, I want to revisit loyalism as a rhetorical crisis, precipitated in part by the Association's effort to align counterrevolutionary argument with the ordinary reader *and* with the authority of the government. While my treatment of the loyalist enterprise is indebted to Philp's account of a movement that "mirrored radicalism's transgression of the traditional boundaries between the elite and the common people,"[13] I extend this line of enquiry and qualify its implications by exploring some of the ways in which the Association understood and managed its own contradictory premises. Closely scrutinized by the government, faced with public criticism from the right as well as the left, and goaded by a contempt for the illegitimacy of radical protest, Reeves and his allies became obsessed with the legitimation of their own enterprise. They were acutely aware of the difficulties involved in mobilizing opinion *against* radical opinion, and tried to create procedures that would facilitate public expression in order to limit the political change it effected. To be sure, this kind of self-management was imperfect, and Philp is right to stress the intractable challenge posed by any democratization of print forms of political address in the 1790s. Yet it is important to recognize that the management of unintended consequences was no casual afterthought or latent effect, but rather a constitutive feature of conservative enterprise, evident in the earliest efforts to manage a popular response to the French Revolution.

My main concern here will be with the way loyalism constituted itself as a mode of public argument and political organization, and not with the distinct question (too casually treated in some revisionist accounts) of whether loyalist activists effectively represented the political views of most ordinary British subjects. As A. V. Beedell has recently observed in this regard, "popular loyalism, like popular radicalism, is difficult to interpret," and evidence about the vast circulation of Association pamphlets or the quantity of signatures collected for a loyalist address is typically compromised by the quasi-official framework of public organization within which such events took place.[14] While a more finely grained interpretation of loyalist discourse cannot resolve the problem of representativeness, it does clarify some of the ways in which representative status was first negotiated, and in doing so it tends to complicate our understanding of "the British avoidance of revolution."[15] Among those who were convinced that "avoidance" required civic activism, how was public opinion mobilized in defense of a regime committed to limiting the political force of public opinion? It is not enough to insist, with Robert Dozier, that loyalism "was not a conservative reaction" but rather "an attempt to maintain the most liberal constitution in Europe,"[16] since loyalists were quite clear about the need to preserve that constitution's limits and exclusions along with any of its more "liberal" features. The paradox of loyalist activism, deeply embedded in its discursive organization, involves the effort to combat radicalism through a set of political strategies (vernacular argument, civic assembly, public correspondence) with evident radical associations. To be sure, Reeve's Association and the London Corresponding Society were sufficiently distinct in their political aims and social foundations to prevent them from being easily confused; yet both derived their authority from the same rapidly changing terrain of popular expression and civic organization. In developing a public profile for counterrevolutionary activism, through contested strategies of association, assembly, and correspondence, loyalism shifted the terms of political participation and transformed the public arenas in which it operated, even as it committed itself to identifying and combating radical transformations of the same terrain. In this sense, Reeves and his allies typify a contradictory type of *counterrevolutionary enterprise*, aggressive in its designs upon the political sentiments of ordinary people, but concerned to project a kind of public spirit that was subordinate to government and the law.

Although my argument turns upon loyalist efforts to manage the unintended consequences of a conservative appeal to ordinary readers, it is worth being clear at the outset about a second constitutive tension in loyalist rhetoric, involving the relationship between government and organized conservative opinion. Set in sharp relief by the development of the Association, it is an issue that will return later in the book in discussions of Evangelical moral reform, periodical criticism, and even the narrative form of the anti-Jacobin novel. Commentators have long remarked on the limited and imperfect policing powers available to the eighteenth-century British state, and while the threat of English Jacobinism would seem to have invited a considerable expansion of those powers, the underlying structure of the revolution controversy made this an unappealing option. The attack on French revolutionary principles was itself a defense of the distinctive history and style of English liberty. In an important analysis of the complex relationship between loyalism and the British state, David Eastwood has observed that, however energetic the official mobilization of the 1790s might have been, "the essentially defensive nature of conservative ideology explicitly precluded the possibility of major institutional reform in response to any real or imagined revolutionary threat." Yet ambiguity about the springs of conservative authority ran both ways. Given the perceived immediacy of the threat, and the limits of their own resources, government ministers had no choice but to rely upon what Eastwood terms "a new public energy" from without: "When effectively harnessed, voluntary endeavour could constitute a major augmentation of the state's power and resources; giving government both at national and local level new capacity and new power without in any serious sense subverting the existing structure of authority within the state."[17] If this approach underscored official anxieties about French institutional innovation, it also created difficulties for those individuals and groups who were prepared to act "out of doors" in support of the government. Expressions of public opinion relied for authority upon their perceived *public* character, which implied some degree of independence. As a matter of polemical practice, loyalists had to develop arguments on behalf of the state that did not appear to issue from the state, and they had, furthermore, to provide an apology for official government obstruction of radical versions of their own methods – public assembly, pamphlet distribution, and national networks of correspondence and political organization.

As we will see, perceptions that the Association emerged in close collaboration with government ministers threw its advocates on the defensive, and precipitated some of loyalism's clearest reflections on its own public character. The underlying dilemma has been sustained in the historiographical record. Where E. P. Thompson dismissed as a "fiction" the idea that loyalist campaigns were "the work of 'voluntary' associations of 'private' citizens," more sympathetic recent accounts have been concerned to show that a public campaign "encouraged" by government ministers prevailed because of "the popularity of conservative opinions among many in the middling and even the lower orders of society."[18] The dilemma of close ministerial affiliation was intensified by the Association's powerful sense of its own conservative mission ("preserving") with respect to an unprecedented radical challenge. The threat of Jacobinism seemed so subversive and conspiratorial as to require thorough elimination. The more the Association appeared as a result to seek a monopoly on public expression, through a systematic campaign of legal harassment developed in concert with the government, the more it could be viewed as a dangerous innovation rather than a legitimate extension of longstanding (and in national terms, essentially disorganized) traditions of civic association in support of government policy.

MANAGING THE SPECTACLE OF REVOLUTIONARY ENVY

The role of government intervention in loyalism's understanding of itself as a public enterprise will become clearer in the second half of this chapter, which considers the development of the Association movement in the years 1792–3, with particular emphasis on its founding and on the *Association Papers* (1793), a published compendium of the records of the London Association and the tracts it made available for national distribution. But in order to bring the rhetorical dimensions of this historical episode into sharp focus, I want to begin with a close analysis of William Paley's *Reasons for Contentment; Addressed to the Labouring Part of the British Public* (1792), one of the Association's earliest and best known pamphlets, and to my mind its most serious and sustained reflection on the ambiguities of counterrevolutionary popular address. As Archdeacon of Carlisle and fellow of Christ's College, Cambridge, and author of *The Principles of Moral and Political Philosophy* (1785), which became the standard text on the subject for Cambridge students well into the nineteenth century, Paley entered the political controversies of the 1790s with an impressive public reputation. *Reasons for Contentment* and a related dialogue tract brought out by the Association in 1793, *Equality, As Consistent with the British Constitution*, have been described as the "zenith" of his reactionary career,[19] but the disposition of Paley's thought up to 1789 was by no means a reliable predictor of subsequent conservatism. His sound rejection of contractual theory proved consistent with later attacks on Paine, but the leading feature of the *Principles* was a theological utilitarianism that frustrates political categorization.[20] Robert Hole has recently positioned Paley "at the extreme 'liberal' end of the Anglican spectrum," particularly in his utilitarian commitment to "a secular view of the source of authority and obligation," an attitude that drew sharp criticism from Evangelicals, and made Paley an enemy in Samuel Taylor Coleridge's campaign to reconstruct the constitutional position of the Church.[21] Though his social views were broadly conservative well before the 1790s, Paley famously set up the analysis of poverty in the *Principles* with a pointed comparison between the existing social order and "a flock of pigeons in a field of corn," where ninety-nine gather everything "but the chaff and refuse" for the benefit of one, "and that the weakest perhaps and worst pigeon of the flock."[22] The gambit earned him the nickname "Pigeon Paley," and reportedly led to the King's refusal to appoint him Bishop of Gloucester.[23]

If there were ambiguities about Paley's political reputation, they did not appear to trouble the Association. *Reasons for Contentment* figured prominently in the *Association Papers* among a select group of works "Printed by Order of the Society" (*AP* I, 6: 1–10), and the London committee and its regional affiliates brought out a number of cheap editions. The tract reappeared in later episodes of political crisis, notably in 1819 and 1831.[24] However, unlike many works in the Association's core catalogue, *Reasons for Contentment* was not written for Reevesite distribution, having first appeared under the independent auspices of its author in 1792, in an edition which was then picked up by the Association movement's Carlisle branch, and recommended to Reeves and the London committee.[25] This provenance suggests that the tract held a status prior to, and arguably outside of, the network of national organization and ministerial influence that has often been said to compromise the more systematic public activities of loyalism. To be sure, any claim about Paley's personal independence would have been disputed by reformers on the grounds of his multiple church appointments,[26] and his archdeaconry was prominently displayed on the title page of some versions of the tract. Yet the prior publication of *Reasons for Contentment*, along with the philosophical credentials Paley brought to loyalism, serve to reinforce an impression left by a reading of the tract: that this is an unusually distanced and self-conscious polemic, one that provides a bridge between the Association and the pre-existing political culture it sought to preserve and transform. Where Paley's later pamphlet, *Equality, as Consistent with the British Constitution*, contained elements of the dialogue form and contrived vernacular idiom that became standard in elite appeals to ordinary readers, *Reasons for Contentment* proceeded in a more reflective, probing, and even skeptical manner. Indeed, the tract sometimes reads like a proleptic meditation on the conceptual foundations of loyalism, and it is possible to condemn its condescending principles while still admiring the frank way it wrestles with the conditions under which its putative audience, "the Labouring Part of the British Public," might be safely made available for thoughtful political address. If in the end Paley seems to fail in bringing his "Reasons" to bear upon the condition of ordinary British subjects, particularly those attracted by *Rights of Man*, this in part because his argument reveals the hazards of a vernacular discourse that would simultaneously acknowledge and neutralize its audience as a political entity.

Reasons for Contentment begins by comparing social order with the experience of the theater, in a philosophically ambitious figure that seems calculated to address the anxieties of the author rather than the reader. It is symptomatic of his difficult rhetorical position, at the historical opening of an elite counterrevolutionary address to common readers, that Paley does not immediately set about reasoning his audience into contentment, but instead develops the theatrical figure in order to reflect upon the conditions under which such an enterprise might take place. Though less controversial than his earlier "flock of pigeons," Paley's enlightenment version of the ancient *theatrum mundi* has a clear political lineage, having figured centrally in British moral philosophy and social theory over the course of the eighteenth century.[27] The opening paragraph sets the parameters for a sustained reflection upon the challenges of counterrevolutionary address:

Human life has been said to resemble the situation of spectators in a theatre, where, whilst each person is engaged by the scene which passes before him, no one thinks about the place in which he is seated. It is only when the business is interrupted, or when the spectator's attention to it grows idle and remiss, that he begins to consider at all, who is before him, or who is behind him, whether others are better accommodated than himself, or whether many be not much worse. It is thus with the various ranks and stations of society. So long as a man is intent upon the duties and concerns of his own condition, he never thinks of comparing it with any other; he is never troubled with reflections upon the different classes and orders of mankind, the advantages and disadvantages of each, the necessity or non-necessity of civil distinctions, much less does he feel within himself a disposition to covet or envy any of them. He is too much taken up with the occupations of his calling, its pursuits, cares, and business, to bestow unprofitable meditations upon the circumstances in which he sees others placed. And by this means a man of a sound and active mind has, in his very constitution, a remedy against the disturbance of envy and discontent. These passions gain no admittance into his breast, because there is no leisure there or vacancy for the trains of thought which generate them. He enjoys therefore ease in this respect, and ease resulting from the best cause, the power of keeping his imagination at home; of confining it to what belongs to himself, instead of sending it forth to wander amongst speculations which have neither limits nor use, amidst views of unattainable grandeur, fancied happiness, of extolled, because unexperienced, privileges and delights. (*RC* 3–4)

From the outset, Paley narrows the range of theatrical possibilities. What absorbs his attention is neither the dramatic activity on stage, nor its impact upon the audience, nor even the architecture of the theater itself, but rather "the situation of spectators" with respect to each other. The fragile attention of these spectators, as they are distracted by relative privilege, comes to stand for the fragility of a hierarchical social order.

Interestingly, such a response accords less with the traditions of political discourse than with Henry Fielding's development of the *theatrum mundi* as a set piece in the first chapter of Book VII of *Tom Jones* (1749), "A comparison between the world and the stage." As Ronald Paulson has suggested, Fielding's contribution to the theatrical metaphor was to divert attention "from the stage . . . to the audience, its divisions, different responses, and tendency to confuse actor and role. The audience becomes the most important part of the metaphor."[28] Yet for Fielding this shift did not exclude other theatrical possibilities. Though he wanted to restore the audience's "claps and shouts" to a tradition that had long developed theatrical resemblances "from the stage only," Fielding still insisted upon the orientation of his spectators toward some dramatic action, and his mock-heroic references to "the scenes of this great theatre of Nature" preserved comic traces of the figure's ancient comprehensiveness.[29] There is, by contrast, very little sense of the stage in Paley's *theatrum mundi*, and this constricted attention yields a double fragmentation, separating individual spectators from each other and from the spectacle they have come to observe. Like the "remiss" readers he would correct, this 1790s pamphleteer seems too concerned with the "civil distinctions" represented by a theater audience to notice what takes place on stage, or to account for its potential significance within his unfolding figure.

Treatments of the French Revolution as a dangerous theatrical distraction suggest that the eclipse of the stage from *Reasons for Contentment* may be a concerted act of suppression. William Wordsworth traced depraved popular taste and the degenerate condition of "the literature and theatrical exhibitions of the country" to a "degrading thirst after outrageous stimulation" brought about in part by "great national events" like the French Revolution, and Edmund Burke similarly condemned the "taste" and "moral sentiments" of those who responded sympathetically to the Revolution: "There must be a great change of scene; there must be a magnificent stage effect; there must be a grand spectacle to rouze the imagination."[30] Yet Paley's theatrical figure is overdetermined, and our sense that a revolution (or a revolutionary attention to spectacle) may be repressed in this opening paragraph should not prevent us from recognizing what Paley has achieved with his prevailing orientation toward the audience. In diminishing the scope of the *theatrum mundi* (Fielding's "great theatre"), and in seeming to cut off his audience from what might be taking place on stage, Paley generates a more manageable type of public subjectivity. The figure of theater works here to advance the curious suggestion that the ideal spectator should be self-absorbed: insulated from the "unprofitable meditations" that interrupt ordinary "business," Paley's "man of sound and active mind" will never succumb to revolutionary "envy and discontent."[31] John Rieder has observed that "the crucial problem" in *Reasons for Contentment* is "the way the poor become aware of their place in society."[32] If so, Paley's first solution to the problem is simply to eliminate the social dimensions of popular consciousness.

In this sense, the opening meditation on the fraught spectacle of public life does not so much account for Paley's own public intervention as it does imagine a world in which such intervention would be unnecessary: subjects who lack a capacity for social comparison do not need to be reasoned out of any discontent with their place in the world. The figure of theater has therefore become an aid *against* reflection, even as it curiously mimics the trajectory of a reflecting mind in its disciplinary return from extravagant outward "speculations" to the narrow parameters of the individual's "own condition" and "imagination." Paley's magisterial shift from the initial figure to its political import ("It is thus with the various ranks and stations of society") requires an equally deliberate shift away from expansive social theater to the narrower "duties and concerns" of each individual. As a result, any conclusion tends to defeat the collective point of the initial resemblance. Put another way, the three terms established by "the situation of spectators in a theatre" ("spectator," "scene," and "situation") are substantially reworked in the "remedy against the disturbance of envy and discontent" that follows: scene and situation collapse upon the figure of the spectator, who becomes absorbed in a "confining" loop of individual attention to individual "pursuits, cares, and business." If the hierarchical idiom ("ranks and stations," "classes and orders") suggests a frank acknowledgment of the actual social heterogeneity of the late eighteenth-century London theater,[33] it is important to recognize that differences are noticed only so they can be overlooked or repressed, through the subject's salutary "power of keeping his imagination at home." This treatment of the mind as "home" reinforces the shift from public to private concerns, just as an interest in the "very constitution" of the individual seems calculated to defuse an explosive public debate in the 1790s over the constitution of the British state.

Given Paley's hasty retreat from risky social theater to a secure private condition, it is worth emphasizing that social envy had not always seemed an unqualified hazard. On the contrary, Adam Smith's *Theory of Moral Sentiments* (1759) developed a more mixed response to the spectacle of elite privilege, insisting on its inevitability and on the ambiguity of its social effects: "This disposition to admire, and almost to worship, the rich and the powerful, and to despise, or, at least, to neglect persons of poor and mean condition, though necessary both to establish and to maintain the distinction of ranks and the order of society, is, at the same time, the great and most universal cause of the corruption of our moral sentiments."[34] By 1792, Paley substitutes a "disposition to covet or envy" for Smith's "disposition to admire," and does not credit such a disposition with even a partial tendency to secure hierarchy. The case against revolution becomes a case for a popular "imagination" that is so thoroughly privatized and domesticated, and so devoid of social considerations, that the individual can be a spectacle only to himself, "intent upon the duties and concerns of his own condition." In refusing the figure of theater, the opening paragraph of *Reasons for Contentment* refuses the very principle of an internalized moral sense, understood by Smith and other eighteenth-century moralists to emerge reflexively, through a complex process of observing others and imagining oneself being observed in return by them.[35] As a framework for developing the public profile of counter-revolutionary activism, then, Paley's dramatic figure seeks to short-circuit rather than rework the concerted theatricality of the British moral tradition. And while it may be tempting to coordinate the opening paragraph of *Reasons for Contentment* with the theatrical displays of state power that have recently absorbed the attention of historians of eighteenth- and nineteenth-century Britain, the occlusion of stage effect in favor of individual self-regard suggests that Paley is not anticipating subsequent efforts to deploy public spectacle and pageantry for patriotic ends.[36] The social space of theater is introduced here so that it can be *refused* as an appropriate conservative figure for political life and public attention in 1792 – refused precisely because it risks disclosing those matters of social difference and economic inequality that were the object of radical protest.

Yet *Reasons for Contentment* remains compelling in part because it fails to sustain this initial containment of a threatening new form of political subjectivity. Paley's effort to arrest the figure of theater is itself arrested, as his second paragraph begins the uneasy transition from a reflective prose (directed against reflection) to a more conventional didacticism that would manage and direct, rather than foreclose, the wayward attention of the working poor:

> The wisest advice that can be given is, never to allow our attention to dwell upon comparisons between our own condition and that of others, but to keep it fixed upon the duties and concerns of the condition itself. But since every man has not this power; since the minds of some men will be busy in contemplating the advantages which they see others possess, and since persons in laborious stations of life are wont to view the higher ranks of society with sentiments which not only tend to make themselves unhappy, but which are very different from the truth, it may be an useful office to point out to them some of these considerations, which, if they *will* turn their thoughts to the subject, they should endeavour to take fairly into account. (*RC* 4–5)

As abruptly as he first closed down the theater of social difference, Paley here reopens it with himself in the role of director or theater manager, a "useful office" that allows him to "point out" considerations that mitigate inequality. The dramatic gesture accords with the governing stage figure, and with the impression of a theater that is peculiarly absorbed in the attention of its audience. It also suggests something distinctive about Paley's rhetorical construction of "the Labouring Part of the British Public." Loyalist pamphleteering normally registered the presence of this readership through the use of vernacular idioms, proverbial wisdom, or a hastily sketched framework of humble life, and this is Paley's practice too later in the tract. But the nominal working-class audience first arrives here in the more abstract guise of a distinctive point of view within the theater of social relations, and specifically, as a dangerous affective response to the hierarchical ordering of those relations. The point could not be made in a more blunt fashion: "persons in laborious stations of life are wont to view the higher ranks of society with sentiments which . . . make themselves unhappy." This pivotal Smithian insight leads directly to Paley's own authorial "office," and to the real work of reasoning the plebeian reader into contentment. By 1792, "busy" minds are in fact busy "contemplating the advantages which they see others possess," and for this reason the fall into a (potentially) revolutionary self-consciousness about inferior social position cannot simply be reversed or wished away. The new conditions for public life that result are nowhere more vividly instantiated than in Paley's own political address to a "Part of the British Public" once felt to lie outside the political nation.

From here, *Reasons for Contentment* proceeds through a sequence of "considerations" meant to demonstrate the relative "advantages of those laborious conditions of life, which compose the great portion of every human community" (*RC* 8). A didactic turn makes itself felt in the tract's increasingly rudimentary and disaggregative style of announcement, suggesting that the abstract presence of the ordinary reader has given way to a more direct address:

Another article, which the poor are apt to envy in the rich, is their *ease*. Now here they mistake the matter totally. They call inaction ease, whereas nothing is farther from it. Rest is ease. That is true. But no man can rest who has not worked. Rest is the cessation of labour. (*RC* 16)

The stylistic contrast with the tract's opening meditation could not be more sharply drawn. Yet Paley's tendency to isolate his subject and fragment and simplify the argument in order to distribute elementary (not to say meager) rewards is undermined by the fact that estimates about the politics of envy do involve more coordinated and socially relative considerations. In the sentence immediately following this passage, the desire to assign "ease" exclusively to "labour" is suddenly undone, along with a crude declarative prose, by the recognition that a somatic state of "rest" only becomes a pychosocially desirable condition of "ease" through the alchemy performed by the differential gaze of another: "The rich see, and not without envy, the refreshment and pleasure which rest affords to the poor, and chuse to wonder that they cannot find the same enjoyment in being free from the necessity of working at all" (*RC* 16). In orchestrating this kind of envious regard, *Reasons for Contentment* becomes an increasingly complex and convoluted exercise in the manipulation of collective forms of attention. The project remains essentially theatrical, and Paley secures his point with a tableau that encourages ordinary readers to achieve contentment by appreciating the "envy" to which privileged observers are driven by the spectacle of their own modest lives:

I have heard it said that if the face of happiness can any where be seen, it is in the summer evening of a country village. Where, after the labours of the day, each man, at his door, with his children, amongst his neighbors, feels his frame and his heart at rest, every thing about him pleased and pleasing, and a delight and complacency in his sensations far beyond what either luxury or diversion can afford. The rich want this; and they want what they must never have. (*RC* 16–17)

To flatter the poor with the impression they make upon their jealous superiors is by itself a simple enough gesture, and it would prove the stock in trade of anti-Jacobin argument. Paley's rural vignette was translated into dialogue form in subsequent Association tracts like *The Labourer and the Gentleman*, where the complaint of a restless Labourer – "I envy the 'Squire every time I hear his dinner bell" – was answered by a Gentleman's soothing mediation of social extremes: "It was only yesterday he told me he envied you" (*AP* II, 3: 10). Yet the crude reversal of class advantage proves more compelling in relation to Paley's theatrical assessment of the epistemological conditions under which relative deprivation becomes intelligible to ordinary subjects. The "face of happiness" in a "country village" may be a widely available spectacle ("can anywhere be seen"), but the enjoined popular response is not possible within the framework of unreflective self-absorption recommended in first paragraph of this tract. A wholly self-contained imagination cannot possibly know what others want. In its underlying logic, then, the counterrevolutionary contentment that Paley reaches later in the tract is a postlapsarian condition, the result of a revolutionary fall into public consciousness, and it therefore requires the more knowing "kaleidoscope of reflections and representations" at work in Adam Smith's *Theory of Moral Sentiments*.[37] The same can be said of Paley's own rhetorical enterprise. To restore popular subordination through public argument is to encourage a densely mediated and essentially *social* (rather than private or "confining") act of reflection, in which readers come to understand their own relative privilege through an informed appreciation of the jealous regard of others. This effort to reverse rather than interrupt the course of public resentment indicates just how far Paley has traveled from his early strictures against envy, and from his initial suspicion of theatricalized social relations. As *Reasons for Contentment* unfolds, revolutionary envy of another is reworked as counterrevolutionary appreciation of another's envy: "The rich want this; and they want what they must never have." Within the framework of the revolution controversy, this recuperation of social jealousy is a striking and risky gesture. Paley has added envy to the list of intractable facts about human nature and the human condition that conservatives were fond of marshalling against their speculative Jacobin enemies.

In some respects, this kind of counterrevolutionary theorizing reinforces the tract's initial preference for the mind at "home," since Paley leaves no doubt about where the laboring man should look for the contentment denied his superiors. "One . . . constant spring of satisfaction, and almost infallible support of chearfulness and spirits, is the exercise of domestic affections" (*RC* 18). As in the tract's opening sequence, however, any suppression of a destabilizing social theater proves imperfect. *Reasons for Contentment* deftly accommodates its own public purposes, as rhetorical performance and political argument, by making domestic stability available through the author's "useful office" of instruction. This requires an attentive subject, one whose "power of keeping his imagination at home" has so fully eroded that he now regards "every thing about him," including the regard of others. For this reason, it is worth considering the exact position Paley assigns his contented village laborer with respect to the wider community. In his immediate social relations ("with his children, amongst his neighbours"), this figure accords with Edmund Burke's principle of the "little platoon we belong to in society," that "first link" in the anti-Jacobin "series by which we proceed towards a love to our country and to mankind."[38] The liminality of the laborer's attitude is no less striking ("in the summer evening," "after the labours of the day," "at his door"), and this suggests another way of aggregating individuals, one more closely governed by the tract's Smithian moral logic. A complacent inferior can only witness the jealousy of his superiors if he occupies a position that is at once domestic yet out of doors, self-possessed yet available to others. Where the initial orientation of the figure of theater toward audience relations created a gap in distracting stage effect, that gap is filled here by a closely mediated and reduplicated spectacle: the author directs the reader to observe an observer and to find himself and his own contentment in the discontented eyes of another.

In this way, counterrevolutionary argument is fully implicated in the relentless logic of publicity that shadows *Reasons for Contentment*.

Tempting as it might have been to propose a wholly domestic solution to the public crisis of the 1790s, Paley cannot help but place the laboring subject "at his door," rather than safely indoors, if he expects that subject to be available to public argument. The open cottage door remained a pervasive feature of anti-Jacobin pamphleteering, particularly in Hannah More's *Cheap Repository*, where it made the lives of the rural poor available to charitable middle-class interference. Recall for the purposes of comparison the related triangle in *The Labourer and the Gentleman*, when the Gentleman called the Laborer's attention to the envious gaze of the 'Squire: "It was only yesterday he told me he envied you." In preparing the way for just this kind of schematic loyalist dialogue, and for his own subsequent pamphlet, *Equality, As Consistent with the British Constitution*, Paley had to establish and occupy the pivotal position of the Gentleman, a third party responsible for managing and defusing volatile encounters between rich and poor. Again, the postlapsarian approach to contentment as a politically constructed and polemically enforced condition contains an implicit challenge to more nostalgic or retrospective varieties of conservatism. If the "face of happiness" can be observed "in the summer evening of a country village," this is not because summer evenings or English country villages have any inherent power to guarantee civic order, but rather because "William Paley, M. A. Archdeacon of Carlisle" has, as the title page indicates, undertaken to provide "the Labouring Part of the British Public" with "Reasons" for their contentment, in a penny tract that was subsidized and distributed, often for free, by the London Association and its national affiliates.[39]

This acknowledgment that communities are secured from revolution by interjected political argument, not by their own internal structure, completes Paley's departure from the confined terms of his opening theatrical figure. As *Reasons for Contentment* winds to a close, one late maxim sums up the more complex pedagogical assumptions that underlie a interventionist vulgar conservatism: "To learn the art of contentment is only to learn what happiness actually consists in" (*RC* 18).[40] Far from being a matter of inherent self-possession ("in his very constitution"), the laboring man's counterrevolutionary "power of keeping his imagination at home" is an acquired and *transmitted* "art," one that requires the speculative comparison across class lines that so troubled the first paragraph. Even the author's own detached sense of rhetorical mastery takes shape within a complex order of social relations. While the rehearsed formulas that govern key turns in the argument ("Human life has been said to resemble . . . ," "I have heard it said that if the face of happiness can any where be seen . . .") are broadly characteristic of a didactic mode, they serve here to identify knowledge as a mediated and communicated phenomenon. And far from evincing embedded forms of vernacular wisdom, these proverbs are regularly subject to authorial elaborations that depart from the terms of the original formula: the theater of human life is no longer a place where individuals can safely ignore the situation of their fellow spectators; summer evenings in a country village betray the frustrations of the rich rather than the happiness of the poor. To become effective, Paley's counterrevolutionary "reasons" have to be witnessed by others, and assisted by dramatic gestures ("to point out") that implicate the author in his own theatrical figure. Contentment is restored to the 1790s when the potentially Jacobinized working man is joined on the political landscape by an equally novel figure, the didactic author of conservative political tracts for the poor. *Reasons for Contentment* closes with a final warning that social change invariably undermines human happiness, a tenet that is rescued from reflex conservatism by the striking manner in which it gets introduced: "If to these reasons for contentment the reflecting husbandman or artificer adds another very material one, that changes of condition, which are attended with a breaking up and sacrifice of our ancient course and habit of living, never can be productive of happiness . . ." (*RC* 22). The vivid conjuring of an acute common reader again reverses Paley's early injunction against popular "reflections" and "speculations," and orchestrates a dramatic clash between a Burkean commitment to "our ancient course and habit of living" and the more disruptive reactionary claim of the tract's title: popular contentment now depends upon the general public exercise of political reason, rather than inherited constitutional benefits or the salutary ignorance of the poor. The "reflecting husbandman or artificer" has turned out to be the unexpected remainder of loyalist discourse.

"ASSOCIATE TO COUNTERACT": ORGANIZING CONSERVATIVE OPINION

What distinguishes *Reasons for Contentment* from the great mass of "popular" counterrevolutionary writing that appeared in the 1790s is the sophistication it betrays about its own status as political argument and public performance. Though initially reluctant to imagine and enter upon a political address to ordinary readers, Paley soon accepts the fall into a theater of social difference, and then attempts to work through its implications for conservative argument. The result is a counterrevolutionary didacticism that attends not only to what the poor should be made to believe, but also to the conditions and forms of attention that make such beliefs possible. The point is not that Paley transcends his fellow pamphleteers, nor that he misses their mark; instead, he anticipates and frames similar polemical efforts, and in fact his own later tract, *Equality, As Consistent with the British Constitution*, more closely follows loyalist norms. In tracing a sequence of attitudes toward reactionary popular address, *Reasons for Contentment* delivers in unexpected ways on the promise of its title, and offers a public reasoning through of the conditions for political discourse in 1792. As the psychically confined subject of the first paragraph gives way to "the reflecting husbandman or artificer," Paley confirms Mark Philp's account of an inclusive vulgar conservatism, and dramatizes the considerations that led its author away from a simple defense of the established order, and into a more complex and potentially compromised political address to the common reader. The burden of the figure of theater as it unfolds in *Reasons for Contentment* is first to underscore the appeal (among conservatives) of a society that holds its ordinary subjects just below the threshold of political consciousness, and then to demonstrate the futility of imagining such a society after 1789. Once reciprocal spectatorship in a heterogeneous social order is allowed, envy and resentment need to be organized rather than suppressed.

What is missing from *Reasons for Contentment*, and what was not yet possible at the time of its composition, was an account of the mechanisms of civic organization and subsidized distribution through which "these reasons" could be made available to "the Labouring Part of the British Public," and other reasons (Paine's for example) effectively discountenanced and proscribed. If Paley's tract aired the logic of a conservative address to the working poor, the Association forged the necessary institutional framework. At the same time, the frankness with which Paley reasoned through his own rhetorical difficulties, even as he reasoned his audience into contentment, suggests that vulgar conservative argument was capable of acknowledging and managing its own tensions and inconsistencies. For what is finally striking about *Reasons for Contentment* is not just that it concedes the political consciousness of "the Labouring Part of the British Public," but that it does so after allowing its preference for a pre-political and pre-public subjectivity – the social imagination of the laboring man confined "to what belongs to himself." Paley's determined orchestration of the reciprocal gaze between rich and poor was soon vigorously reinforced by the Association movement, whose repressive designs belie the abstract spectacle and idealized domesticity that alternately frame *Reasons for Contentment*. When it was picked up and reprinted by the London committee and regional loyalist affiliates, the tract entered a catalogue of similar publications and a range of public enterprises, which extended from political meetings and national correspondence to a vigorous campaign of criminal prosecution against the radical press. If vulgar conservative address did invite ordinary readers to join a discussion of national affairs, the invitation was heavily qualified, and came with rules, as it were, for the conduct of deliberation within a hierarchically organized political public sphere.

Chief among these rules was the government supervision of public assembly and print expression, a layer of official control that can be understood as a coercive frame upon Paley's didactic "office" of managing the restless attention of the poor. Historians have disagreed about the extent of this supervision, and the debate often hinges on whether the establishment of the Association in late 1792 was an independent or state-sponsored event. Though they shared ministerial connections and government incomes, Reeves and his fellow projectors insisted that they were acting as "private men," and that "none of the King's Ministers knew or heard of this Association, till they saw the first advertisement in the public prints" in November 1792 (*AP*, Preface, iv).[41] One leading historian of eighteenth-century associational practices rejects this disclaimer, and argues instead that "the decision to act was coordinated in advance with the ministry."[42] Others have maintained that the evidence is less clear, since government support for the Association fell into place after Reeves' first meetings, and since there is evidence that some regional loyalist clubs remained independent of the London committee.[43] The stakes of the debate for recent efforts to rehabilitate conservative opinion are clear, since careful government engineering of the Association would cast a shadow over any popular support it achieved.

In the most important recent contribution to the debate, Michael Duffy has drawn on newly uncovered correspondence to clarify ministerial involvement, and to provide the clearest account yet of how the Association operated within a wider sphere of counter-revolutionary opinion and enterprise. As might be expected, Duffy's careful reconstruction of events indicates neither absolute government control nor spontaneous public initiative, but rather a more complex and compromised series of transactions between the two. He shows that by late 1792 the government was under considerable pressure to act against the increasing confidence of radical societies, with the foreign secretary Grenville going so far as to complain that "we are called upon on all sides for counter associations." While ministers did signal their interest in civic initiatives that would strengthen their hand, Duffy concludes that Reeves' enterprise "was not preconcerted with the ministers," but was instead selected for official support after the first advertisements appeared in the London press. Pitt himself bluntly assessed the value of ministerial engagement with public initiative, remarking that enthusiasm for Reeves' advertisements "shews that there is a Spirit and Disposition to Activity which if We give it at the outset a right Direction may be improved to very important purposes." Improvement and "right Direction" were necessary in part because members of the government were sensitive to the terms of Philp's paradox, especially the way that "counter associations" involving public correspondence through regional affiliates risked mirroring the structure of radical associations. "It is a very delicate point," the home secretary Henry Dundas wrote, "for Government in the present moment to invite Associations of one kind, when they will be called upon soon to condemn so many others."[44]

Ministerial "Direction" over the emerging loyalist movement turned out to be a less abstract exercise than Paley's "pointing out." Beyond government patronage in the form of newspaper advertisements and free postage, there were disciplinary revisions to the Association's charter that suggest a concerted policy of state intervention in the political public sphere. Ministers concerned, as one put it, "to uphold rather than weaken the Authority of regular Government," were not happy with Reeves' original plan for a broad-based movement involving large meetings several times a week. Instead, they formulated a program by which tractable committees would supervise smaller and less frequent public gatherings. "In this Way We hope to avoid the Inconvenience of much public Discussion at Numerous Meetings," Pitt explained, "and yet have the Impression and Effect of Numbers on our Side."[45] Duffy usefully distinguishes between two published plans for the Association, the first drawn up by Reeves and his collaborators at a November 20th meeting at the Crown and Anchor Tavern, the second issuing from a subsequent meeting on November 24th.[46] Ministerial revisions to Reeves' original plan were incorporated into the second version of an Association charter:

It should seem, that the business of such Societies should be conducted by a Committee, and that the Committees should be small, as better adapted for dispatch of business; for it should be remembered, that these are not open Societies for talk and debate, but for private consultation and real business. The society at large need not meet more than once a month, or once in two or three months, to audit the accounts, and see to the application of the money. (*AP* I, Proceedings, 1: 7–8)

In its first public pronouncement, before Pitt's intervention, the Association had struck a keynote of free and open assembly: "We do, as private men, unconnected with any Party, . . . think it expedient to form ourselves into an ASSOCIATION" (*AP* I, Proceedings, 1: 5). This spirited sense of private men associating for public purposes came to ring hollow as the movement closed the ranks of an exclusive "Committee," and devolved the work of association from open "talk and debate" to a form of "consultation" that remained "private" (in the sense of closed) even after its appearance on the public stage. As it turned out, committee structure reinforced social hierarchy. Even historians who insist upon the movement's broad appeal have concluded that, while the common people may well have attended meetings and participated in demonstrations and addresses, committee membership was restricted to men of property, especially "the gentry and substantial farmers in rural areas, and the leading merchants, manufacturers and professional men in the towns."[47]

The structural resistance of loyalist association to unregulated deliberation ("these are not open Societies for talk and debate") was reinforced by the *negative* mission statement that immediately followed the key resolution about limited public meetings:

The object of such Societies should be to check the circulation of seditious publications of all kinds, whether newspapers or pamphlets, or the invitations to club meetings, by discovering and bringing to justice not only the authors and printers of them, but those who keep them in shops, or hawk them in the streets for sale. (*AP* I, Proceedings, 1: 7)

In the published reports of the November 24th meeting, this repressive "object" preceded even the narrowly defined positive purpose of "circulating cheap books and papers" to "undeceive those poor people who have been misled by the infusion of opinions dangerous to their own welfare and that of the State" (*AP* I, Proceedings, 1: 7–8). Although it would be a mistake to ignore the steady stream of elementary political tracts that soon flowed from Association presses, the reduplication of negative terms ("undeceive," "misled") betrays a reluctance to approach political opinion in wholly constructive terms. Making popular loyalist opinion was essentially a matter of unmaking popular radicalism – of undeceiving the deceived.

Just as *Reasons for Contentment* invoked "the Labouring Part of the British Public" as a class of readers in order to blunt its political impact, so the Association followed inconsistent lines of development. On the one hand, loyalism displayed a surprising willingness to organize itself under the sign of opposition, as *counter association*, even where it was most closely aligned with the purposes of the state. In this sense, the crisis of the early 1790s was a signal episode in the antithetical history of political expression in Britain. While Terry Eagleton and others have rightly discovered the radical origins of a counterpublic sphere in the era's "whole oppositional network of journals, clubs, pamphlets, debates and institutions,"[48] it is important to understand that radical reform had no monopoly on the heady politics of resistance. Reactionary movements spawned by the same crisis were not simply a rearguard defense of some hegemonic arena of exchange, but instead represent a calculated and historically ambiguous response to radical counterpublicity. Again, to assign conservatism exclusively to residual social forms is to accept its own mythology. At the same time, the government's decisive role serves to remind us that the Association was no spontaneous act of public resistance to the threat of revolution. Even Reeves, who has been described as a "more radically reactionary" figure than Edmund Burke,[49] first conceived a more dynamic public enterprise than the government was prepared to allow. In this sense, the whole Reevesite moment can be understood as a critical episode in a state campaign to reorganize public opinion in light of its threatening contemporary development. Through the Association, the rapidly changing institutions of the political public sphere would be favorably disposed toward the unreformed constitutional state, at the precise moment when that state faced a critical challenge to its own legitimacy. Of course, we should not exaggerate the novelty or the efficacy of this development. Loyalist association rested upon long-standing traditions of voluntary initiative in support of government, and fell well short of exercising absolute control over print expression and public opinion. It is not easy to describe the exact combination of state policy and public initiative that the Association involved, and historians have long wrestled with imperfectly qualified

terms: "semiofficial organs of government," "a respectable and offi-
cially-sanctioned campaign," "a kind of ideological outrigger to a conservative state."[50] What is clear is that, in its systematic organization and
national scope, the Association effectively transformed available practices of civic enterprise in support of government policy.[51]

The steady stream of reports that were subsequently gathered in the
Association Papers did not hesitate to account for loyalism as a public
enterprise directed *against* radical opinion *within* limits sanctioned by
the state. In a significant echo of the Burke of the 1770s, the report of
the November 24th meeting invoked the "seditious" presence of
radical "Clubs and associations" to justify the Association's call upon
like-minded persons to "form similar Societies in different parts of the
town": "Good men associate to counteract those evil designs" (*AP* I,
Proceedings, 1: 7–8). At the same time, the London committee set
clear limits on the counterrevolutionary activism it was prepared to
sanction, and warned that "it should be a part of the original compact
of every such Society, that in what they mean to do, they shall always
act in subordination to the Magistrate and the Executive Government"
(*AP* I, Proceedings, 1: 8). Given the prevailing terms of the controversy
over the French Revolution and Paine's *Rights of Man*, the contractual
language is striking, and again suggests a concerted antithetical design.
The radical implications of an "original compact" are neutralized as
soon as they are invoked: in calling itself into being as a public, this
loyal public announced its incapacity to challenge the power of the
state. Throughout the Association's founding discourse, subordination
to government and the law serve to distinguish reactionary public
enterprise from its radical opposite:

To associate in the forms in which *they* do (as appears by their printed papers
exhibited to this Society) is always seditious, and very often treasonable: they
all appear to be offenders against the law. To meet, as is now proposed, for
suppressing sedition, for propagating peaceable opinions, and for aiding the
magistracy in subordination to the direction of the Magistrates – the law
allows it, and the time requires it. (*AP* I, Proceedings, 1: 8)

Even this straightened understanding of the range and authority of
public opinion was cautiously handled by the Association, as a
regrettable aberration demanded by "the time" and by the critical
threat of revolution. The anxieties of loyalist organization derive in
part from the movement's compromised and contested understanding
of its own activity.

Even where the early rhetoric of loyalism approached some wider theoretical self-justification, this tended to arrive by way of apology rather than political manifesto:

The Society, after full consideration of the nature of private meetings, formed with a design to take cognisance of what is transacted by the Executive and the Legislative Powers of the country, are of the opinion, that all such meetings are irregular. Such distinct and unharmonized centers have the effect of intercepting and drawing around themselves some of that force, and confidence of the people, which should pass on to their only true center, the constituted Executive and Legislative Authorities of the State. But where such an irregularity has been once permitted, and the balance of the system seems to be affected by it, the equilibrium perhaps cannot be more naturally restored, than by placing a counterpoise of the same sort on the other side. (*AP* I, Proceedings, 1: 8)

Here, the paired principles of radical "irregularity" and conservative "counterpoise" provide a check upon the scope of counterrevolutionary publicity, and they serve notice too that the antithetical and crisis-bound logic of "counter association" does not follow ordinary models of party antagonism. On the contrary, loyal opinion operates within a field of forces that is at once polar ("counterpoise") and centripetal ("center"). Faced with the disruptive or "intercepting" influence of radical protest, the Association offered itself as the appropriate conduit through which the whole "force" of popular opinion could return to its "only true center, the constituted Executive and Legislative Authority of the State." Yet the ambiguities of loyalism were firmly embedded in the rhetoric of its early development. For in working to subordinate public deliberation to state power, Reeves and his allies exercised judgments normally assigned to government and the law: the Association's expressed "opinion" about sedition resulted from a "full consideration of the nature of private meetings" and an examination of "printed papers exhibited to this Society." When the members of the London committee disbanded in June 1793, on the grounds that the crisis of the previous winter had passed, the announcement combined an almost obsessive desire to record and publish their own activities with the reaffirmation of a straightened understanding of public opinion. "They associated on a special occasion, and for a defined purpose; and when that occasion was passed, and that purpose was served, they suspended their proceedings" (*AP*, Preface, iii). By 1794, most regional branches had followed suit, though the public energy they represented soon surfaced again as the volunteer movement mobilized against the threat of a French invasion.[52]

THE ARCHIVE OF COUNTERREVOLUTIONARY ASSOCIATION

The tendency to understand print expression and public assembly as inferior extensions of ministerial authority was critically reinforced when the Association filled out its catalogue with documentary evidence of state controls upon political opinion. Recent reconstructions of conservative opinion have tended to overlook the way that loyalism manifested itself, even beyond the courtroom, as an implacable expression of the power to silence. At the same London meeting where Pitt achieved restrictions on loyalist assembly, and just before the sanctioned appearance of Paley's *Reasons for Contentment*, the Association announced that its first printed work would be the "CHARGE delivered by Mr. JUSTICE ASHURST [*sic*] to the Grand Jury in the Court of King's Bench this term" (*AP* I, Proceedings, 1: 6), a charge that originated in the government's legal assault on radical organization. The status of this courtroom transcript as a political pamphlet bears some consideration. Made available by the Association through a number of London and provincial publishers, in formats ranging from cheap pamphlets to handbills and broadsides, the charge acquired a calculated afterlife in the same arena of printed opinion that its first oral delivery was intended to police. Justice Ashhurst anticipated later reiterations of his speech, and endorsed the Association's collaborative logic, by calling to "public service" those jurors in "a private station" as well as those "invested with the office of Magistracy," and by launching a broad defense of the right of government to extend its "coercive" and "restraining hand" against publications "in which the Author disclaims all ideas of Subordination." In passing these instructions along to the nation, with the insistence that they "must be read with Heart-felt Satisfaction by every true ENGLISHMAN," *Mr. Justice Ashhurst's Charge* in effect reconstituted the reading public as a jury, in ways that complement Ashhurst's initial treatment of the jury as public. Gathered by the Association with ministerial support, readers of the pamphlet were enjoined to witness and countenance the law, and to follow the government's lead in condemning "seditious and unconstitutional doctrines" (*AP* I, 1: 1, 3–5).[53] Ashhurst's speech was soon joined in print by other judicial charges, and the Association then extended this strategy to other official expressions, including the Royal Proclamation of May 1792 against seditious writings, Lord Loughborough's speech in the House of Lords on the Alien Bill, Grenville's circular letter to local magistrates, and the Lord President's anti-Jacobin address "in the Name of the Court, Magistrates, and Council of Edinburgh."[54] As the litany of official controls and sanctions grew, the rhetoric of Association pamphleteering was sometimes reduced to the list of repressive authorities that could be gathered on a single title page, as for example in one eight page tract circulated by the East-Kent and Canterbury Association in 1792: *Judge Ashhurst's Charge to the Grand Jury of Middlesex. II. Proclamation of May, 1792. III. Proclamation of Nov. 1792. IV. Lord Grenville's Circular Letter. V. Thanks of the Common Council of London, To the Lord Mayor. VI. Resolutions of the Corporation of London.*[55]

This kind of publication made legal sanction an intrinsic feature of print expression, rather than its mere external limit, in ways that have important interpretive consequences. Historians have disagreed over the extent to which the Association actually waged, rather than threatened, a legal campaign against the radical press, and the recent tendency to align the movement with broad public support has corresponded with efforts to distance it from the courtroom, on the grounds that prosecutions were relatively infrequent and limited in their impact. Yet as Mark Philp observes, it may be enough that the law was sometimes used against the radical press: "Scholars who have insisted upon the relatively moderate scale of prosecutions of radicals miss the point that loyalists' arguments about the limits of legitimate discourse *were* backed up by sanctions – without those sanctions their claims would have been little more than sound and fury."[56] The point is reinforced by the facility with which evidence of legal sanction was put before the reading public, in order to reinforce and amplify its effect. The printed version of *Mr. Justice Ashhurst's Charge* entered the Association catalogue along with *A Protest against T. Paine's Rights of Man* and *Short Hints upon Levelling,* but it could be recommended above these ordinary polemics because it breathed "the SPIRIT of the ENGLISH LAW," and was therefore "well suited to CURB the LICENTIOUS SPIRIT of the TIMES" (*AP* I, 1: 1). If in principle the Association did invite ordinary subjects to join a national conversation about politics, those subjects immediately confronted the intimidating premise that public "cognisance" of the "Executive and Legislative Authorities of the State" was "irregular" and therefore illegitimate. They then found themselves in a political arena that was collaboratively organized by the government, closely integrated with its purposes, and saturated with evidence of legal limits upon expression – that is, as far as can be imagined from "the state of confrontation between government and the press" that Jürgen Habermas has theorized for the classical public sphere of the early eighteenth century.[57]

The Association's preference for government initiative over voluntary enterprise did not entirely subvert the collaborative structure of loyalism. By facilitating state intervention in the political public sphere, Reeves and his colleagues ingratiated themselves with the Pitt ministry, and established networks of mutual reinforcement that implicitly advanced the claims of public opinion on the political process. This was powerfully brought home by Justice Ashhurst in a subsequent grand jury charge, which called the work of the Association in evidence to support his own judicial proceedings. With his earlier charge already in print, urging readers to follow jury guidelines, Ashhurst pressed ahead by instructing jurors to "persevere in the same line of conduct" pursued by the loyalist Association movement:

> The zeal and spirit which has been shewn by the different societies in this metropolis, has warmed and pervaded the most distant parts of this kingdom; and the several useful publications which have been dispersed abroad, have enlightened the deluded minds of the lower classes of the people, which had been deceived and practiced upon by the diabolical artifices of crafty and designing men. (*AP* I, 7: 2–4)

As the Judge warmed to his task, the charge became a concerted defense of loyalism against those who discovered a threat to British liberty in the systematic campaign against radical expression. Unwilling to let this endorsement languish in a courtroom, the London Association completed the circuit of collaboration when it brought out a pamphlet version of the charge.

By locating itself at the critical intersection of public assembly, print expression, and state power, the Association became – in its own assessment – a semi-official organ of political legitimation. This was signaled in Ashhurst's judicial commendation, and then reinforced in June 1793 with the appearance of the full archive of *Association Papers* in a format that drew crucial distinctions within the printed record. The most authoritative pamphlets appeared in a first part, "Publications Printed by Special Order of the Society"; these included extracts from sermons, courtroom charges, and parliamentary speeches, as well as historical material from Lord Bolingbroke and Soame Jenyns. Less fully sanctioned works were bound in a second part, containing "A Collection of Tracts, Printed at the Expence of [the] Society." The distinction accorded with the Association's hierarchical ordering of political opinion, and with its elite sense of responsibility for managing the emergence and development of ordinary political sentiment. *Reasons for Contentment* was among the few works addressed to common readers that made its way into the fully sanctioned first part of the collected papers, reinforcing the importance of Paley's epistemology of popular discontent. A number of more widely reprinted tracts, including Hannah More's *Village Politics* and William Jones' "John Bull" letters, were not similarly privileged. The subordinate second part of the collection served as a grab bag for pseudo-popular ballads like "King and Constitution," "The Happy Man," and "The Revolution Quack," and for vernacular dialogues that endlessly restaged simpler versions of Paley's vexed encounter between rich and poor.

Despite their secondary position within the printed record, these demotic tracts offer perhaps the clearest record of the range of public deliberation and the depth of political consciousness that the Association was prepared to grant ordinary subjects. Yet commentators have disagreed about what this record means. In *The Politics of Language*, Olivia Smith argues that the Association's pervasive "anti-intellectualism" lowered the tone of political debate for a generation, stifling the example of Paine's ambitious vernacular until popular radical fortunes revived during the later phases of the Napoleonic wars: "It was not only radical ideas which the Association wanted to keep from its readers but also any type of political thinking."[58] In challenging this kind of wholesale critique, Mark Philp finds that the transgressive possibilities of vulgar conservatism were most fully realized in "the rhetorical complexities and ambiguities of the dialogue form" as it was deployed by the Association. Dialogue tracts for ordinary readers become "instructive instances of the difficulties of characterizing the voice of the labouring man, and of the costs of doing so successfully," since a counterrevolutionary conversation across class lines involved a "simultaneous appeal to, and exclusion of, members of the lower orders."[59] The point is characteristically shrewd, and again suggests that the trajectory of political discussion under official auspices in the 1790s may represent something other than a stifling anti-Paineite consensus. Yet the catalogue of reactionary dialogues that actually betray a measure of ambiguity turns out to be disappointingly thin. The credible characterization and vigorous argument of Hannah More's *Village Politics* make it a paradigmatic instance of rhetorical complexity, and I will discuss it in more detail in the next chapter, yet Philp concedes that More's treatment of a discussion between two laboring men is exceptional.[60] The more common practice was to reinforce hierarchy by representing vertical interchange, as in *The Labourer and the Gentleman* or *A Dialogue between Mr. T–, a Tradesman in the City, and his Porter, John W–*. Such tracts tend to involve transparent fantasies of successful elite intervention in an arena of plebeian politics that has only been superficially corrupted by radical delusions, and they prefer a facile rhetoric of assent to genuine deliberation across class lines. While not devoid of Paley's interest in the conditions that frame public discourse, such dialogues tend to reduce those conditions to the inexorably legitimating force of national prejudice, material contentment, and class deference.

In *The Labourer and the Gentleman*, for example, the plebeian figure John has been exposed to "the Rights of Men" by a shadowy stranger, whose anonymity figures two related conservative anxieties: the conspiratorial designs of English Jacobin culture, and the dislocated abstraction of a print public sphere. As we will see, this character makes a more sustained and threatening appearance in the anti-Jacobin novel. Here, the Gentleman interlocutor immediately seeks to enforce loyalty in part by reminding John that, while "you know nothing of that fine spoken gentleman" nor of the source of his radical pamphlets, "you and I have known one another many years." The intimacy of hierarchical identification is supposed to supersede a radical bid for horizontal class solidarity, yet the absence of anything like Paley's effort to develop the conceptual terms in which an ordinary reader might be made available for this kind of conscription cannot conceal the rhetorical ironies of a vernacular counterrevolutionary address. This appeal to local and longstanding sentiment takes place within a nationally distributed pamphlet, one that appeared in the *Association Papers* as part of the managed process by which the London committee made approved literature available to regional affiliates without regard to local circumstance. And the fact that a tract like *The Labourer and the Gentleman* affords little room for an active response on the part of the ordinary reader it targets is evident in the sequence of formulaic concessions – "Yes, Master," "No Master, to be sure not," "Why that's true, Master," "Right, Master" – that lead inexorably to the chastened laborer's conversion: "Good day, Master, and thank you for all you have said, which has made me quite easy again" (*AP* II, 3: 8–12). In this sense, dialogue has degenerated into catechism. A stock type of plebeian consciousness, which must be taken to stand for the reader, voluntarily exchanges a deluded Jacobinism (which is at least briefly his own) for "all *you* have said." As it happens, the Association did include two catechisms in its catalogue, and the rhetorical and intellectual limits of these tracts ("Q. Do you possess . . . *Liberty*. A. I do") confirm a tendency within loyalist discourse to reduce political debate to a crude formula of elite prescription and popular assent.[61]

This is not to say that the smooth course of loyalist interchange was never interrupted. On the contrary, efforts to manage the emergence of Paley's "reflecting husbandman or artificer" did from time to time yield vigorous and even violent gestures of exclusion or silencing within the spare narrative framework of these tracts. Where such gestures exceeded the straightened rhetoric of the catechism or the catechism passed off as dialogue, they further undermined any credible rendering of popular contentment as the result of considered political deliberation. Interestingly, serious interruptions of civil exchange tend to occur when these tracts made some effort to represent their own transmission and reception, a concern that would be more fully and engagingly developed in Hannah More's Cheap Repository. The narrator and putative author of *Poor Richard; Or, The Way to Content in These Troublesome Times* identifies himself as "an old man, and . . . formerly an Almanack-maker," an occupation that implicitly harkens back to the expectations of a pre-Jacobin popular print culture:[62]

[I have] in the course of my business . . . calculated many Eclipses and Comets, and other strange Revolutions of the Skies; but I must fairly own that many most extraordinary events have happened lately upon this our Planet the Earth, that were far beyond my abilities to calculate, or, I believe, those of the shrewdest Almanack-maker in the trade. (*AP* II, 12: 12)

The reining in of a millennial style of announcement in the subtitle of the tract ("The Way to Content in These Troublesome Times") only hints at the unsettled radical print expressions that were in danger of supplanting the almanac and its maker. Yet there is a more decisive acknowledgment of a potential break from the past in the setting of the main incident related in *Poor Richard*: an ordinary "public-house," with "ten or twelve people sitting round a table on one side of the room, . . . conversing upon the late transactions of France, and the state of things in this country." Within this prototypical arena of revolutionary sociability, the narrator sets about ordering "a sober pint of porter" and "reading the newspaper that lay before me," but then finds himself distracted from this routine by an extraordinary conversation "upon a public subject" (*AP* II, 12: 13). One young man, "more ignorant as well as more petulant than the rest," offers an "intemperate" defense of the French Revolution, and the manifest "disapprobation of the rest of the company" (*AP* II, 12: 13) nearly affords a credible treatment of political exchange within a vividly realized setting. Before this can take place, however, the episode is "interrupted" by "a plain neat old man with white locks" (*AP* II, 12: 13) whose stern repudiation of Jacobin principles immediately assumes an unequivocal authority within the tavern and the tract. A barrage of Ben Franklin's proverbial wisdom replaces tavern dialogue, with interchange reduced in the old man's speech to the spurious form of an anticipated objection: "Methinks I hear some of you say . . ." (*AP* II, 12: 16). The deterioration of dialogue into monologue is formally registered in the way the main body of the tract, the old man's uninterrupted speech, unfolds within an extended and continuous sequence of single quotation marks, in effect supplanting the Almanac maker's narrative, let alone any credible rendering of tavern conversation within it. The final paragraph offers little more than a perfunctory return to the framing dramatic situation: "Thus the old Gentleman ended his harangue. – The rest of the company applauded his doctrine, and the young man to whom in particular it was addressed, seemed much abashed, and soon took his hat and left the room – I hope much edified with what he had heard." (*AP* II, 12: 20). The closing gesture is entirely characteristic of Association discourse, and it anticipates a number of similar purging devices that develop within the picaresque form of the anti-Jacobin novel. Loyalist principle emerges rhetorically as a venerable pronouncement, with the ordinary subject delineated as a listener who is entitled to just two responses: enthusiastic assent or silent and abashed departure.

Other tracts suggest how political interchange might be further undermined by irregular versions of the official coercive authority embodied in Ashhurst and the published charge. William Jones provides a useful case study of this effect, since his "John Bull" series of tracts exemplified the loyalist effort to intervene in prevailing modalities of political expression: irregularly serial, sponsored by clubs and associations, and cast as a political correspondence, these tracts were often brought out in broadsheet format to facilitate street distribution and display. In *One Penny-worth More, or, A Second Letter from Thomas Bull to his Brother John*, the rootless tavern demagogue of *Poor Richard* returns in the more cynical form of "one of those Fellows who are hired to go about with *Tom Pain's* Books." He is readily silenced, but not without a clear warning that native resistance to alien radical opinion is prepared to exceed verbal force. Had this "London Rider" dared to produce any portion of his radical library, "we should have put them into a *Pitch-Kettle*, and stirred them about well, and then burned the Pitch and Books together." Having exposed the hazards of tavern sociability for radicals and reactionaries alike, the tract goes on to imagine a more controlled arena for distributing political opinion. Our correspondent, Thomas Bull, recommends the practice of a local minister who "takes us all now and then, rich and poor, to dine with him," and allows ordinary conversation "about common Things" to unfold until, with a loud "Rap upon the Table," he enforces "Attention" and unleashes the real business at hand, a spirited anti-Jacobin harangue.[63] If these local gestures of interruption, enforced silence, and threatened violence served to undermine dialogue, they also reinforced the Association's commitment to a political field that referred every public sentiment back to its "only true center," the "Executive and Legislative Authorities of the State." Attempts to represent reactionary argument within a familiar social space were therefore consistent with broader Association strategies. Transferring discussion from the tavern to the vicarage facilitated official supervision, just as the threat of "Pitch and Books" burned together vividly extended the coercive force of the courtroom charge or royal proclamation into the more unruly and violent fringes of the Church and King mob.

Yet as the effort to align public opinion with government authority worked its way through loyalist discourse, difficulties arose, particularly where the collaborative enterprise envisioned by Reeves and his allies suggested that some portion of counterrevolutionary agency might pass from the state into the less predictable arena of public opinion. To begin with, reciprocity of this kind invariably opened reactionary enterprise to a corrosive radical scrutiny. Court proceedings against the radical press triggered an especially spirited public debate, in part because they allowed opponents of the government, otherwise vulnerable to charges of disloyalty in this period, to invoke English libertarian traditions on their own behalf. Critics complained that loyalism enforced a perilously broad understanding of sedition, and exceeded anything like the normal tradition of civic association for the purpose of criminal prosecution.[64] What is striking about this kind of criticism is that it issued in a formal counter association, the Friends to the Liberty of the Press, organized by Thomas Erskine (the celebrated defense attorney for Paine and Thomas Hardy) at a series of London meetings in December 1792. In some respects, this was an unimpressive organization, a "brief and futile effort to challenge Reeves" that dissolved under the twin pressures of external repression and internal dissension.[65] Yet the Friends to the Liberty of the Press were able to launch a vigorous if short-lived print campaign against the Association, the force of which was attested to by the equally vigorous loyalist response.[66] Here reactionary activism did not mark an outer limit of public debate, but instead became one link in a serial logic of antagonistic political organization and expression. In this sense, the Association offers a paradigmatic instance of the "principle of disseminatory limitation" that Alan Liu has proposed to describe the treason trials of the 1790s. In Liu's account, meant to challenge a containment model of discursive power, the radicals and reactionaries of the 1790s were engaged in "limitary contests of legitimation" that did not simply define subversion, but instead allowed its diverse forms to be played out in an "open system" that crossed political boundaries, and extended through a number of discursive arenas – print, law, assembly, opinion.[67] The Association's ironic origins as a state-sponsored "counter association" were therefore reiterated in its counter attack upon the Friends to the Liberty of the Press: loyalists engineered the defeat of an organization they had called into being.

Where this dialectical framework became explicit, political differences tended to be more closely argued, restoring the kind of theoretical self-consciousness that characterized Paley's *Reasons for Contentment*. In their preliminary resolutions, the Friends to the Liberty of the Press defined sedition narrowly as "a design to excite the People to resist the Civil Magistrate," and insisted that the government was adequately "entrusted with powers" to prosecute any such challenge. This approach was calculated to undermine the founding principles of loyalism:

> We have therefore seen with uneasiness and alarm the formation of certain societies, which, under the pretence of supporting the executive magistrate, and defending the Government against sedition, have held out general terrors against the circulation of writings, which without describing them, they term seditious; and entered into subscriptions for the maintenance of prosecutions against them; a proceeding doubtful as to its legality, unconstitutional in its principle, oppressive in its operation, and destructive of the Liberty of the Press.[68]

In *An Answer to the Declaration of the Persons Calling Themselves, Friends of the Liberty of the Press* (1793), the prolific anti-Jacobin John Bowles vigorously defended the Association's understanding of the relationship between public opinion and state authority, and rejected the notion that "the power of accusation against offenders who have violated the laws is confined to the supreme executive magistrate." On the contrary, according to Bowles, not only did "every individual, . . . in his private capacity, and in the character of a prosecutor," have the right "to call for the execution of the laws upon those who have violated them," but "the executive power" had a reciprocal duty "to lend its agency to every one who demands it in the pursuit of so important an object" (*AP* I, 4: 2).[69] This prosecutorial circuit, leading out from an offended private individual through the state and back to an offending private individual, was not only permitted by the constitution, it was positively enjoined by the crime of sedition, which had (according to Bowles) the peculiar effect of restraining vigorous state initiative by making the state an interested party in any criminal case. Where the offense seemed "more immediately leveled at the government of a country," the appropriate response was a "train of prosecution" initiated by those who are "unconnected with the offices of government" (*AP* I, 4: 4). As in the Crown and Anchor meetings that first organized loyalist sentiment, the sphere of voluntary civic enterprise is conceived as a collaborative arena where repressive "agency" circulates back and forth between individual subjects and the state. Far from allowing that this might compromise loyalist opinion, Bowles claimed that Association support for the government was the purest form of public expression: "The general, spontaneous, and independent voice of the people has been expressed with a fervour and an unanimity beyond the example of any former period" (*AP* I, 4: 4, 8). Yet the "independent" status of this voice accords uneasily with the provisional manner in which loyalism was first theorized as a regrettable "counterpoise" to radical transgression, suggesting that *An Answer* had become, through the dialectics of counter sedition, both a defense and a revisionist extension of the Association's founding principles. Bowles' unusually detailed and closely argued analysis of the conditions for civic enterprise implies that, in times of crisis, the state cannot do without the assistance of those who are "the most unconnected with the offices of government." In this sense, a radical threat does wind up advancing the authority of public opinion in its loyalist form. Yet any new legitimation of civic enterprise still takes place within strict limits. Bowles vigorously reinforces the Association's tendency to locate free expression in repression, since "the people" discover their "independent voice" in a demand "for the execution of the laws" against radical protest.

It is worth returning by way of conclusion to the figure of theater with which I opened this chapter, in order to reflect again upon the appearance of *Reasons for Contentment* in the catalogue of Association Papers. If Paley emerges in my analysis as an unusually close theorist of his own rhetorical enterprise, the Association should be understood as a further frame upon that enterprise, and specifically, upon the network of social relations mapped in Paley's idyll of counterrevolutionary contentment. Beyond the spectacle of cottage life, beyond the elite spectator's observable envy, and beyond Paley's own deployment of this kaleidoscopic spectacle for the benefit of the common reader, the Association worked to organize and police the terms within which reasoning with ordinary readers about popular contentment would enter the discourse of public life. Just as his dramatic figure lost sight of events on stage in its concern for audience relations, so Paley never really considered the contours of his theatrical polity. It was left to Reeves and the founders of the Association, acting in concert with the government, to organize the arena within which "the Labouring Part of the British Public" would be permitted to achieve political self-awareness. If the typical loyalist pamphlet was less ambitious than Paley's *Reasons for Contentment*, this was in part because the Association had effectively separated out his simultaneous task of addressing the poor and managing the terms in which that address took effect. Reeves and his allies did not expect to accomplish what Paley deemed impossible, the suppression of political feeling among ordinary subjects, and historiographical debates about the effectiveness of the Association tend to founder upon the counterfactual it helped ordain: a revolution that never took place. Yet by restricting radical argument and radical organization, and by making pamphlet evidence of that restriction part of the public record, the Association guaranteed that the experience of coming to politics in the 1790s involved bearing extensive witness to the repressive authority of the state. If *Reasons for Contentment* flattered its ordinary readers by rhetorically incorporating them into a politically relevant "British Public," those same readers learned from pamphlets like *Mr. Justice Ashhurst's Charge* the fate of those who did not find reason enough for contentment.

CHAPTER 2

"Study to be quiet": Hannah More and counterrevolutionary moral reform

Although not as widely known and anthologized as *Village Politics*, Hannah More's *History Of Tom White the Postilion* (1795) and its sequel, *The Way to Plenty*, are in many respects more typical of the kind of writing through which her Cheap Repository Tracts (1795–8) achieved a leading role in the anti-radical and counterrevolutionary campaigns of the later 1790s.[1] For this reason, *Tom White* can provide a useful preliminary map of More's reactionary fiction, and of the challenge it presents to our understanding of the literary history of romantic-period Britain, particularly the impact that counterrevolutionary movements had upon cultural politics in an age of revolution. The *Tom White* series is typical, to begin with, in its heterogeneous narrative structure (the dialogue of *Village Politics* is less characteristic of More's work), and in the pressure it brings to bear upon the social world More believed her readers inhabited. Like many of the Cheap Repository Tracts, *Tom White* serves up a moral parable that rests in the first instance upon a precisely situated sense of rural virtue:

Tom White was one of the best drivers of a post-chaise on the Bath road. Tom was the son of an honest labourer at a little village in Wiltshire: he was an active industrious boy, and as soon as he was old enough he left his father, who was burthened with a numerous family, and went to live with farmer Hodges, a sober worthy man in the same village. He drove the waggon all the week; and on Sundays, though he was now grown up, the farmer required him to attend the Sunday-school, carried on under the inspection of Dr. Shepherd, the worthy vicar, and always made him read his Bible in the evening after he had served his cattle; and would have turned him out of his service if he had ever gone to the ale-house for his own pleasure. (*WHM* 5: 219–20)

While a sober employer and the weekly round of labor and piety would seem to be adequate security for Tom's virtue, the attractions of the nearby "Bath road" soon lure the young hero from the simple discipline of the wagon to a more glamorous career as a post-chaise driver, and from there to the Black Bear public house and a litany of corrupt habits: "oaths and wicked words," "drunkenness," "fives, cards, cudgel-playing, laying wagers, and keeping loose company" (*WHM* 5: 221–4). Taverns and public houses, strung out along the arteries of transport and communication that linked village and metropolitan life, occupy a critical position in the distinctive cultural geography of the Cheap Repository Tracts. In the Black Bear of reality and imagination, the residue of morally offensive popular recreations catalogued in *Tom White* met emerging patterns of popular literacy and radical organization, which More had noticed earlier in *Village Politics*, in the form of the "mischief" introduced by the Paineite Tim Standish when he threatened to "corrupt the whole club" at the Rose and Crown tavern (*WHM* 1: 347).[2] For this reason, antipathy to the plebeian tavern underworld provided Hannah More with a ready meeting point for her own Evangelical moral reform project and the more narrowly political campaigns of loyalist organizations like John Reeves' loyalist Association.[3] If Tom White's departure from village honesty begins at the Black Bear, it culminates at another public house, when a "foolish contest" among the young post-chaise drivers to see who "would be at the Red Lion first – for a pint" (*WHM* 5: 225) ends in catastrophe. Tom emerges from the wreck with a broken leg and a chastened conscience, and the period of his recuperation at a London charity hospital brings to a close the tract's initial sequence of lively incidents, opening up a "space for repentance" (*WHM* 5: 230) that affords very different narrative as well as spiritual developments. As his early Sunday School education returns to him with the added force of experience, "Tom began to find that *his strength was perfect weakness*," and remorse quickly yields conversion and reform. From London, he retraces the course of his decline, returning first to the Bath road, where as "*careful Tom*" he "soon grew rich for one in his station," and then "to his native village," where he purchases a farm and marries "a young woman of excellent character, who had been bred up by the vicar's lady" (*WHM* 5: 235, 238). By the end of the first part of the tract Tom has returned to Dr. Shepherd's fold and become the respectable Farmer White.

Thus far, the parable of fall and redemption that forms the core of *The History of Tom White* only implies the range of moral categories and social controls that More would extend to her characters and her readers, yet this is by no means the end of the story. Like most of the ballads, tales, hymns, and allegories that she published over the course of a counterrevolutionary decade, *Tom White* is informed by the serial design of the Cheap Repository, and as the second part, *The Way to Plenty*, more closely engages the immediate famine conditions of 1795, narrative becomes more heterogeneous.[4] The ordered plot of the first part – circular in structure, focusing on the spiritual development of an individual, and punctuated by scriptural quotations and pious reflections – gives way to a less continuous series of separately titled episodes: "The Roof-Raising," "The Sheep Shearing," "The Hard Winter," "The White Loaf," "The Parish Meeting," "Rice Milk," "Rice Pudding," and "A Cheap Stew." The first of these programmatic incidents opens with a perfunctory gesture towards Tom's life and narrative continuity – "Some years after he was settled, he built a large new barn. . . ." (*WHM* 5: 249). But subsequent transitions from section to section convey the tract out of the timeless world of the moral parable, and into a more immediate and circumstantial present day. "The Hard Winter" brings the reader down to "the famous cold winter of the present year, 1795,"[5] and "The White Loaf" then explores the consequences of that disastrous season within the context of a government and social hierarchy contending with unprecedented economic distress and popular discontent:

One day, it was about the middle of last July, when things seemed to be at the dearest, and the rulers of the land had agreed to set the example of eating nothing but coarse bread, Dr. Shepherd read, before sermon in the church, their public declaration, which the magistrates of the county sent him, and which they had also signed themselves. Mrs. White of course was at church, and commended it mightily. Next morning the Doctor took a walk over to the farmer's, in order to settle further plans for the relief of the parish. (*WHM* 5: 265–6)

Eventually, the narrative energy derived from a tale of Tom's spiritual fall and redemption dissipates entirely, and is replaced in the climactic "Parish Meeting" episode by the polemical force of Dr. Shepherd's spirited harangue against the prevailing "bad management" of cottage households, apparently the real reason for popular distress (*WHM* 5: 271). As the logic of the tract becomes increasingly programmatic and pedagogical, More exercises her remarkable powers of discursive assimilation, taking on everything from actual public resolutions about poor relief to Mrs. White's "dainty receipts" for rice milk, rice pudding, and cheap stews and soups (*WHM* 5: 268–9, 277). The nominal hero of the tract series increasingly yields the foreground to his wife and Dr. Shepherd, and in the final episodes he must literally "beg leave to say a word to the men" (*WHM* 5: 278) in order to advance community reform. Ironically, his address to the men neither reaffirms the centrality of his experience nor reclaims his patriarchal authority, but instead provides clear evidence of the way that feminized controls upon household management, the central issue in the tract's denouement, will dissolve the moral risks of his own masculine domain: "If you abstain from the ale-house," he tells the assembled men, "you may, many of you, get a little one-way beer at home" (*WHM* 5: 278). In gesturing from public house to private home, Tom also makes explicit the political stakes of moral reform. His claim that "the number of public houses in many a parish brings on more hunger and rags than all the taxes in it" (*WHM* 5: 279) is a calculated refutation of the radical view that popular misery resulted from the excessive taxation required by corrupt government.

What More has done in the second half of *Tom White*, through the collaboration of vicar, housewife, and husband in organizing locally what the "magistrates" and "rulers of the land" have determined nationally, is to shift her writing away from the narrative conventions of a moral parable, and towards a dense fictional representation of her own public enterprise.[6] Plot gets subordinated to schematic treatments of the material and institutional conditions for moral reform, nowhere more clearly than in the recipe sections ("Rice Milk," "Rice Pudding," "A Cheap Stew") with which *Tom White* concludes. Put another way, where the first part of the tract explored Tom's moral and spiritual experience, with only passing attention paid to the institutional agents (schools, publishers, associations, hospitals) conditioning that experience, the second part is concerned above all with the social mechanisms that frame Tom's newly acquired agency in determining the experience of others, an agency that is increasingly shared out to his wife and the vicar. In More's fictional universe, this condition of having acquired moral influence over the lives of others turns out to be the most reliable index of individual regeneration. To be sure, the concern for personal agency in *Tom White* does sometimes mystify the institutional operations of the Cheap Repository and the Sunday school movement, by fictionally privileging less formal networks for communication and social change. The recipes and household tips that achieve mass circulation through this tract are passed along more casually within it: "I shall write all down as soon as I get home," Dr. Shepherd announces in response to Mrs. White's domestic advice, "and I will favour any body with a copy of these receipts who will call at my house" (*WHM* 5: 277). The tract closes, too, under the nostalgic sign of a popular proverb that valorizes individual initiative and inherited wisdom: "Let us now at last adopt that good old maxim, *every one mend one*" (*WHM* 5: 282). Yet as so often in More's work, such gestures towards the authority of the past and the integrity of the individual or local are overwhelmed by the emphatic positioning of her characters within the present framework of an aggressive national movement to reform the social order. The maxim about individual initiative may be old, but its adoption would evidently count as an innovation, since it is "now at last" achieved through the collaborative and institutionally orchestrated work of the narrative agents of moral reform.

The shift from conventional parable to a more ambitious fictional synthesis of the whole machinery of moral reform involves More in a complex and frankly promotional set of references to her activity. In lending its support to an Evangelical campaign against luxuries like white bread in periods of distress, *Tom White* indexes More's other printed works: "Our blessed Saviour ate barley bread, you know, as we are told in the last month's Sunday reading of the Cheap Repository, which I hope you have all heard" (*WHM* 5: 270). The tract is, significantly, "heard" as part of the comprehensive pastoral care offered by Dr. Shepherd, rather than being privately read, so that this reinsertion of a Cheap Repository tract back into Cheap Repository narrative is not simply a matter of verbal reference: the allusion bears with it the whole assembly of enterprises and institutions entailed in Evangelical moral reform. There is more subtle evidence, too, of the way that informal practices and haphazard village conversations about moral propriety might assume a more organized and disciplinary form, quite unlike the fantasy of a world remade through a casual call at the vicarage for a neighbor's recipe. Dr. Shepherd's "common custom" of visiting the celebrations that follow a wedding ceremony, for example, is recommended as a kind of community surveillance, since "the expectation that the vicar might possibly drop in, in his walks, on these festivities, often restrained excessive drinking, and improper conversation" (*WHM* 5: 239–40). Evangelical enterprise becomes disciplinary again later in the tract, when those cottagers "who wished to buy" rice at the "reduced rates" made possible by subscription "were ordered to come to the farm on the Tuesday evening" for a ritual disbursement. The shift here from the volition of the poor ("wished") to the command of the wealthy ("ordered") indicates with unusual clarity how middle-class provision worked to establish material incentives (in this instance, cheap rice) which, if accepted, implied consent to the revised social hierarchy that Dr. Shepherd and the Whites embody. This glimpse into the contractual foundations of a political economy of charitable relief vividly confirms Dorice Elliott's argument that More treated charity as a form of exchange, in which the female philanthropic benefactor acquires "the right and responsibility . . . to superintend those she relieves."[7] The stakes of any transaction between provider and consumer of relief rise further still when we learn that "Dr. Shepherd dropped in at the same time" as the rice was distributed, no doubt by design, so that "when Mrs. White had done weighing," the ritual of elite provision can be reinforced by a pastoral harangue about domestic management (*WHM* 5: 269). The "fresh subscription" for poor relief promised at the end of the tract guarantees that an updated contract between rich and poor will be renewed, its disciplinary clauses formalized by a strict "rule of giving" which in effect punishes the unregenerate by exclusively rewarding those of steady habits: "We will not give to sots, gamblers, and Sabbath-breakers" (*WHM* 5: 279).

These interventions in the moral comportment of the poor may seem remote from the political considerations familiar to readers of *Village Politics*, but More makes it clear throughout *Tom White* that there is a direct link between political unrest and the complaints that "Amy Grumble" and other characters raise (to no effect) against the discipline of a new domestic economy. Dr. Shepherd begins his climactic sermon on diet and household management with a sharp warning about "idle, evil-minded people, who are on the watch for the public distresses," so that "they may benefit themselves by disturbing the public peace" with "riot and drunkenness" (*WHM* 5: 269). Rice pudding may seem a feeble hedge against Jacobin revolution, but More and her collaborators firmly believed that political unrest is what happens when people are not careful about what they eat, among other bodily and spiritual habits. Her tales of domestic improvement were clearly meant to inoculate the poor against revolutionary discontent, although once again, they mystify the process in order to deflect the perception that the author might be conducting a revolution of her own: the ambitious and highly mediated designs of the Cheap Repository are represented within *Tom White* by relatively informal modes of community intercourse. Rather than appending the final sequence of recipes as a coda at the end of the tract, as she sometimes did, More works to integrate them into the plot, through the device of a spontaneous village discussion inspired by the vicar's carefully staged reprimands about luxury.

The culmination of *Tom White* in a systematic reform of cottage management, which aligns Mrs. White's domestic expertise with Dr. Shepherd's pastoral authority, and with a "public declaration" about diet issued by "the rulers of the land," provides compelling evidence for the case made by a number of feminist scholars that More's decisive intervention in British society was to advance responsible household management, a feminized version of the ancient model of *oikonomia*, as the central principle for the management of national affairs.[8] When these principles of reform are applied to domestic matters, as at the close of *Tom White*, they often arrive under the nostalgic sign of restoring lost or corrupted household practices, in part to mitigate the challenge that a new feminine authority posed to masculine conventions about politics and public life. Yet there were limits to More's accommodating spirit, and in the last analysis the Cheap Repository made little real effort to represent household reform as the recovery of some past phase of cottage life. In the sequence of tracts that opened with *The Cottage Cook, or Mrs. Jones's Cheap Dishes*,[9] the recently widowed middle-class reformer, Mrs. Jones, determines "that baking at home would be one step towards restoring the good old management" among local cottagers, which would in turn allow the community to get through a period of high food prices without popular unrest. However, because "the new bad management" has left most cottages without ovens, Mrs. Jones procures subscriptions for "a large parish oven," and the result looks less like a restoration of the old order than the introduction of a new system of central community provision: "To this oven, at a certain hour, three times a week, the elder children carried their loaves which their mothers had made at home, and paid a halfpenny, or a penny according to their size, for the baking" (*WHM* 4: 342, 347–8). Bread making now begins in the privacy of the laborer's cottage, but is completed within the institutional framework of middle-class moral reform. This hybrid ritual (public and private, common and elite) may seem curious, but it is typical of the way female Evangelical enterprise participated in "the inevitable re-negotiation of the apparently fixed public/private, male/female division,"[10] by intruding its own quasi-public operations into the domestic life of the poor, and by inventing collective rituals which drew that life out into a public arena, making the manners and habits of ordinary subjects regularly available to the inspection and supervision of their superiors.

If the proper management of the domestic household was More's model for national affairs, this was in part because the cottage or home (stipulated now as a domain open to observation) seemed to her the safest place for labor and leisure. The consumption of alcohol provides a revealing case in point: recall the suggestion in *Tom White* that men who ought to "abstain from the ale-house" might with less risk "get a little one-way beer at home." As she and her fictional proxies moved outside the domestic sphere, and targeted riskier public habits, their interventions became more aggressively revisionist and controlling, without even modest gestures towards the authority of the "good old." Here we can usefully return to the career of Tom White himself. I have so far emphasized the way the second part of the tract loses interest in his life, and departs from the conventions of a redemption narrative in order to encompass wider institutional and material considerations (in the form of recipes, sermons, speeches, publications, and subscriptions). Yet the first part of the tract is by no means innocent of the collective conditions for individual development. The role of Tom's Sunday school education in his conversion provides the occasion for the tract's first openly self-promotional gesture, as the author interrupts the tale to call the reader's attention to this "encouragement . . . for rich people to give away Bibles and good books" (*WHM* 5: 230). And while a lineage of rural virtue is no doubt the point of Tom's first appearance as "the son of an honest labourer at a little village in Wiltshire," this rural world has from the outset been penetrated by the enterprising spirit associated with "the Sunday-school, carried on under the inspection of Dr. Shepherd." The entire course of the conversion narrative is determined by More's commitment to cosmopolitan middle-class enterprise as a remedy for the moral lapses of the rural poor. For while the tale is mapped along the metropolitan "Bath road," it is nevertheless clear that moral development cannot simply be gauged by proximity to village or city. Far from marking the depth of corruption into which the hero falls, the metropolitan center serves as a pivot for recovery, since the "space for repentance" lies in "one of those excellent hospitals with which London abounds" (*WHM* 5: 226, 230).[11] If the Bath road transmits the vices associated with the Black Bear and the Red Lion, it is also a conduit for the Evangelical enterprise and charitable capital that flow throughout the narrative. For More, redemption and corruption both depend upon national and local relations. When he returns at last to the village of his birth, Tom does not discover the untainted source of his own virtue, but rather a profoundly compromised social order upon which to unleash his own newly acquired zeal for reform. Before yielding the stage to the collaborative enterprise of Mrs. White and Dr. Shepherd, Farmer White undertakes his own vigorous campaign against the residual evils of rural popular culture:

He had sense and spirit enough to break through many old, but very bad customs of his neighbours. If a thing is wrong in itself, (said he one day to farmer Hodges,) a whole parish doing it can't make it right. And as to its being an old custom, why, if it be a good one I like it the better for being old, because it has the stamp of ages, and the sanction of experience on its worth. But if it be old as well as bad, that is another reason for my trying to put an end to it, that we may not mislead our children as our fathers have misled us. (*WHM* 5: 248–9)

There can be no more compelling expression of the way moral principle trumps historical process in More's fiction. Far from offering a reliable guide for human conduct, the pattern of inherited transmission so venerated by Edmund Burke threatens to "mislead" past, present, and future generations alike.[12] The "Roof-Raising" and "Sheep Sheering" episodes that occur in the early phases of the second part of the tract are suffused with Farmer White's iconoclastic determination "to break through a bad custom," and in each case the communal traditions of "ribaldry, and riot, and drunkenness" associated with the agricultural calendar give way under his strong hand to more "orderly and decent" invented traditions of collective psalm singing and sober feasts for the poor (*WHM* 5: 249–61).[13] It is this aggressive revisionism, rather than any simply nostalgic or conservative response to radical innovation, that distinguishes the political project of the Cheap Repository, and links its treatment of a public, masculine sphere of alehouses and barn raisings with the feminine domain of housekeeping and domestic management.

THE POLITICS OF COUNTERREVOLUTIONARY ENTERPRISE

As counterintuitive as it may seem, the recognition that Hannah More, one of Britain's leading counterrevolutionary propagandists, shared Tom White's reformist determination "to break through many old, but very bad customs," can usefully enrich and complicate our understanding

of the cultural impact of conservative movements during the extended
crisis that has been termed Britain's "long counterrevolution."[14] It has
broad implications, too, for romantic literary studies, where the principle
of a "revolution controversy" staged around the writings of Burke and
Paine has long been used to reconstruct a political spectrum in which the
conservative position was primarily defensive, traditionalist, exclusionary,
and tied to an organic vision of history and society that resisted wholesale
strategies of revision – in a word, Burkean. To be clear, my point is not
that we should substitute Hannah More for Burke as the avatar of
reaction in Britain. The cultural field is too uneven and heterogeneous to
be represented by any single writer or activist. Yet More's career does
usefully shift our attention away from the twin poles of a reconstructed
debate (Burke/Paine), which never really occurred in the way we tend to
imagine,[15] and towards a set of literary texts whose remarkable conditions of production suggest, not abstract ideological positions, but the
social and cultural circumstances under which political expression and
persuasion actually took place. As More herself observed, the French
Revolution occurred at a time when "an appetite for reading had, from a
variety of causes, been increased among the inferior ranks in this country," and the Cheap Repository was designed "to supply such wholesome
aliment as might give a new direction to their taste, and abate their relish
for . . . corrupt and inflammatory publications" (*WHM* 5: vii–viii). If for
romanticist readers the language of this passage brings to mind William
Wordsworth's Preface to *Lyrical Ballads* (1800), where voracious reading
habits and revolutionary upheaval also threaten "the present state of the
public taste in this country," this unexpected intersection of two very
different literary careers should encourage us to reconsider the Cheap
Repository as the most institutionally ambitious, and arguably the most
influential, of the many romantic-period efforts to create the taste by
which a new literature was to be enjoyed.[16]

   Although militant loyalism has figured more prominently than
Evangelical moral reform in revisionist historical treatments of British
conservatism in the 1790s, Mark Philp has included Hannah More in
his treatment of a "vulgar conservative" movement that rejected
Burke's position that "the vulgar were the object of conservative
thinking, not intended participants in it," and that set out instead from
the transgressive assumption that conservatives had no choice but to
address the popular political audience brought into being by the
radical press and radical organization. While Reeves and his allies were
content "to evoke loyalist sentiment amongst the populace," More and

other moral reformers ranged more widely, and pursued "an implicit programme of reform which reached up to the traditional elite as well as down to the common people."[17] The historical ironies at work in a reformist counterrevolutionary culture become more complicated still if we recall that the Cheap Repository was part of a tradition of Christian moral enterprise that went back to the late seventeenth century, and culminated in the 1780s, before the French Revolution had its galvanizing impact upon British radicalism. While there may be little reason to worry here about transgressing one of romantic studies' enduring fictions ("1789"), it does seem curious that reactionary enterprise should in this instance precede the revolution.[18] In her careful study of the development of late eighteenth-century moral reform movements, Joanna Innes offers one clue to this puzzle by invoking an earlier revolution: in her account, Evangelical initiatives like the Society for Carrying into Effect His Majesty's Proclamation against Vice and Immorality, founded by More's friend William Wilberforce in 1787, were in part a result of "the complex effects of the disastrous American war," including economic dislocation, the spiraling cost of poor relief, and a perceived degeneracy in the upper classes and the nation's political leadership. Like Philp, Innes is concerned to show that the moral reform projects of the 1780s, which included the Sunday school movement and prosecution societies directed against a host of petty public vices, were not particularly retrospective nor suspicious of change; instead, they were part of a "patriotic, improving, moralizing" campaign of "project-oriented association," which understood itself progressively, as "helping to create the social and institutional framework within which a more virtuous society might henceforth take shape." Evangelical enterprise was self-conscious enough about its own improving energy to assume a kind of tactical caution where this seemed warranted, in ways that help account for More's decision to present the feminine enterprise of Mrs. White as an alliance with the Anglican Church (Dr. Shepherd), which aimed to enforce directives issued by the state (the "public declaration"). Wilberforce and his associates in the Proclamation Society proceeded cautiously, after cultivating the support of government ministers and the church hierarchy, and in fact they secretly engineered the royal proclamation to which they claimed to respond. All this was designed to remove a "lingering taint of Puritanism and social subversion" and "make the cause of moral reform *respectable*," and to fend off conservative critics who argued that responsibility for morality and public

order belonged to "Church and State" rather than private individuals
or self-constituted societies.[19] Evidently, the conditions for a paradoxically reactionary progressivism predated 1789. Elite anxieties
about any activity, however disciplinary its professions, that was conducted outside the established boundaries of the political nation did not
have to wait upon the French Revolution, with its forcible linking of
political change with new forms of social organization.

It is worth being clear about what I take to be the political
dimensions assumed by a tract like *Tom White* when it seeks a wholesale
reform of rural popular culture, replacing the festive and sometimes
prodigal traditions of communal life with more sober and frugal
practices dictated from above. In a provocative article, Susan Pedersen
has challenged the tendency among historians to understand the
Cheap Repository in narrowly political terms, as an assault on Paineite
radical discourse and the London Corresponding Society. Her argument is compelling in many respects. There is ample evidence that, in
their formal devices and material appearance, the Cheap Repository
Tracts sought to imitate, and thus supplant, a vast body of popular
chapbook and broadsheet literature, which had long been treated with
suspicion by Evangelical reformers, for reasons of moral comportment
that have little to do with the rise of radical reform. According to
Pedersen, Cheap Repository ballads that do follow a narrow anti-
Jacobin model are exceptional cases:

> When one confronts the Cheap Repository as a whole, the political expla-
> nation becomes inadequate. Although the political content of "The Riot" is
> clear, this often-quoted ballad is one of the relatively few explicitly anti-
> Jacobin tracts in the Cheap Repository and is virtually lost among the reams
> of Sunday readings, allegories, and little moral tales that attack vices ranging
> from drunkenness to superstition and that defy a simple political explana-
> tion . . . . The tracts were thus less an attack on Tom Paine than on Simple
> Simon: in their content they made a point-by-point critique of the perceived
> norms of popular culture as revealed by contemporary chapbook literature.[20]

The point is an important one as a corrective to casual assumptions
that *Village Politics*, written and published two years before the institution of the Cheap Repository, became the template for More's later
work, and as a reminder of the cultural density of her writing, its effort
to bring about a wholesale transformation of the labor, learning, leisure, piety, and domestic affairs of the common people. However, it
does not follow, as Pedersen implies, that a political understanding of
More's work needs to be reductive in its grasp of her assault on popular

literature and culture, nor is it the case that the political and moral aims of the Cheap Repository were essentially distinct. On the contrary, as Gary Kelly has argued in a compelling account of the Cheap Repository's campaign against unregenerate chapbook literature, More was convinced that "the shoots of 'Jacobinism'" had their "roots [in] popular culture."[21] There is ample evidence, too, for Olivia Smith's observation that popular educators like Hannah More and Sarah Trimmer made no effort to distinguish between "political quietude and religious learning as reasons for teaching the poor."[22] Campaigns to reform the residual elements of a licentious popular culture, and to prevent the spread of an emerging radical culture, were linked above all by their fierce determination to impose habits of subordination and discipline upon the lowest orders of society. Even if we accept Pedersen's point about the relatively few Cheap Repository Tracts that make Paineite radicalism their primary target, the pervasiveness of More's anxiety about political unrest is evident when we see how even a less stridently political work like *Tom White* was still haunted by the threat of "evil-minded people" who would foment "riot" and disturb "the public peace."

To return to Pedersen's own useful but too strictly dichotomous shorthand, the point would seem to be to understand the way that longstanding middle-class suspicions of the popular chapbook culture of Simple Simon assumed a new urgency under the conditions introduced by Tom Paine. More was certainly not unique among Evangelical activists in her conviction that the available principles and institutions of moral reform could be mobilized against a Jacobin political challenge.[23] For her sense of the close relation between the two campaigns, we have no less an authority than the prefatory Advertisement to the Cheap Repository Tracts in the 1801 edition of her works:

To improve the habits, and raise the principles of the common people, at a time when their dangers and temptations, moral and political, were multiplied beyond the example of any former period, was the motive which impelled the Author of these volumes to devise and prosecute the institution of the Cheap Repository. This plan was established with an humble wish, not only to counteract vice and profligacy on the one hand, but error, discontent, and false religion on the other. And as an appetite for reading had, from a variety of causes, been increasing among the inferior ranks in this country, it was judged expedient, at this critical period, to supply such wholesome aliment as might give a new direction to their taste, and abate their relish for those

corrupt and inflammatory publications which the consequences of the French
Revolution have been so fatally pouring in upon us. (*WHM* 5: vii–viii)[24]

This manifesto neatly expresses the historical paradox of a reactionary
campaign "to improve" a nation under siege from "vice" and "discontent" alike: the dangers faced by the common people of Britain
over the course of a revolutionary decade were both "moral and
political," and the Cheap Repository's effort to "counteract" this twin
threat could, in More's own analysis, be understood only within the
precise framework provided by "the consequences of the French
Revolution." It does not diminish More's counterrevolutionary credentials to concede that this argument had a kind of commercial value
in advancing the circulation of Cheap Repository Tracts. She was
shrewd enough to see that the immediate crisis of the 1790s promised
to expand the constituency for existing Evangelical campaigns to
reform the manners and morals of ordinary British subjects: elites who
in the past saw little to fear in the excesses of tavern culture, and even
disparaged the likes of Tom White and Mrs. Jones for their incursions
upon British liberty, might now be recruited to a campaign to put
down public houses if they could be convinced it challenged Paineite
radical organization.

The historical tensions at work in an improving campaign of conservative enterprise tend to confirm Christine Krueger's recent account
of a politically "complicated – and sometimes contradictory" Hannah
More, and to recall too Philp's point about a vulgar conservatism that
unwittingly "mirrored radicalism's transgression of the traditional
boundaries between the elite and the common people."[25] In projects
like the Cheap Repository and the Association, responsibility for social
order tended to migrate back and forth between the government and
the public sphere, as political initiatives once reserved for the state and
church were absorbed into new or expanded civic institutions
and voluntary practices. This shift precipitated structural changes that
were, in important respects, modernizing and arguably progressive,
even where they involved disciplinary mechanisms directed against the
new political claims of the working poor. Ironically, the threat of
working-class revolution authorized middle-class innovation: Mrs. White
assumed a new social and political authority so that Amy Grumble
would not. To be clear, this claim about the enterprising spirit of
counterrevolutionary culture need not be apologist. Conceding that
More worked to create a different future for Britain, rather than

recover some ancient past or secure the available present, does not mitigate the fact that she vigorously opposed the extension of basic political rights that would soon be taken for granted, and that she supported a vision of social order which granted the middle and upper classes extraordinary powers of surveillance and control over the vast majority of ordinary British subjects, whose inferior status was emphatically ratified in the process. Indeed, approaching conservative enterprise as a social fabrication should reinforce rather than diminish our sense of its transforming impact upon British culture and society in the romantic period, by reminding us that, in the crisis atmosphere of the 1790s, it was never enough to mobilize existing social and cultural resources, nor to remind disaffected subjects of their stake in an available constitution. Instead, a vast amount of political and cultural work – new work – was required to secure loyal opinion and turn back the radical challenge. In this sense, I would distinguish my treatment of the Cheap Repository from that of a number of feminist scholars who have argued, each in distinctive ways, that More's effective redefinition of the possibilities available to women, in her own career and in her influence on others, meant that her project was essentially liberating rather than reactionary or disciplinary in nature. She was, in Anne Mellor's provocative phrase, a "revolutionary reformer."[26] The Hannah More presented here is a more compromised though I hope no less complex figure, a reformer no doubt, but in important respects, a reactionary as well. While I share an interest in the transforming cultural work of the Cheap Repository, and have learned a good deal from these feminist scholars about More's attention to women's work, and her provocative redefinitions of gender, domesticity, education, and public life, it seems to me crucial that we not lose sight of the ways in which the Evangelical enterprise of middle-class women imposed an astonishing range of social, political, and religious controls upon the behavior of men and women alike, and insisted above all upon the rigorous subordination of the lower orders.[27]

CIRCULATION, MEDIATION, AND SOCIAL ORDER

Critics interested in recovering Hannah More's didactic fiction for literary history have tended to stress that these tracts were "drawn from life," and have identified her as a "pioneer social novelist" with an abiding interest in the concrete experience of the rural poor: "Here are hard facts and hard lives," Mitzi Myers has written, "vigorous, racy dialogue and homely domestic detail."[28] While this approach does help situate the Cheap Repository with respect to literary tradition, particularly the rise of a socially reformist strand of realist fiction,[29] it risks overlooking crucial features of More's project. Myers has herself observed that in "transcribing her society's exigent problems into fiction," More's tracts "curiously mingle shrewdly observed social documentary and idealistic moral fable."[30] If fantasy and didacticism inevitably enter the equation, it is also true that the presence of vernacular fact can easily be exaggerated; I am not persuaded, for example, that we have the authentic "language of rat catchers, fortunetellers, post-boys, and shoemakers" in any of these tracts, rather than a middle-class Evangelical fantasy about the way such language might be recuperated for respectable society.[31] Furthermore, categories like fact and experience were central to the British rejection of French Revolutionary theory in this period, an attitude neatly epitomized by Arthur Young in *The Example of France a Warning to Britain*: "We know that English practice is good – we know that French theory is bad."[32] In simply assigning the virtues of fact to the Cheap Repository, we risk uncritically reproducing these ideologically charged terms in accounting for counterrevolutionary discourse. For her own part, Hannah More treated available facts about social conditions as a corrupt and dangerous raw material, to be reworked and reformed through narrative devices that are clearly driven more by her own aims and desires than by any scrupulous fidelity to the way that individuals might actually have thought and felt. Though sometimes eager to pass off their version of English social life as an available fact, More and her collaborators were an ambitious set of counterrevolutionary speculators, actively scripting and marketing their cultural revisions in ever more complex formal and institutional terms. Elements of a kind of social realism are consistently subordinated to reformist purposes, and Anne Stott has astutely remarked that "in the interest of her moral and religious message, More stifled her undoubted potential for writing innovating social novels."[33] Ultimately, this urge to deploy fiction as a means of reworking fact, rather than any scrupulous realism, seems the chief characteristic of the literature of Evangelical moral reform. Indeed, few of the many reformist enterprises at work in the period were so fully expressed in fictional form, and for this reason, we are unlikely to find another category of romantic-period writing that so insistently coordinates a set of fictional representations with a credible design for social and cultural practice. To read the Cheap Repository

Tracts is to discover a project for social change as thoroughgoing and closely reasoned as anything in Jeremy Bentham or Robert Owen, expressed in ballad meter and narrative form.

The Cheap Repository Tracts are important, then, for the way they incorporate within a fictional frame the entire Evangelical project for intervening in the life and literacy of the rural poor, a project which sought to reinforce its ambitions in the sphere of manners and morals with a wholesale effort to change the way that printed texts were distributed to and consumed by ordinary readers. More's prose consistently thematizes her effort to replace the haphazard channels through which print culture unevenly penetrated the English countryside with a controlled national economy of provided texts, and to discipline the irregular reading practices of the working poor by subjecting them to the direct supervision of Sunday schools and related institutions for adult literacy and piety. Here, the enforcement of new relations of obligation and subordination was crucial. Susan Pedersen has suggested that "the real success of More's tracts is to be found less in their conversion of the poor than in their effective recruitment of the upper class to the role of moral arbiters of popular culture,"[34] and while this approach should not distract us from the way that calculations about poor readers continued to figure in the production of these tracts, it does call attention to the crucial role that elites played in the Cheap Repository, as "moral arbiters," financial supporters, and avid readers. In exploring the social work these tracts imagined and performed, we need to keep in mind the multiple audiences they addressed,[35] and the way the expectations of those audiences came to be incorporated within a fictional frame. Where, for example, didactic literature had long invoked experience as the arbiter of proper conduct, the errant youths and wayward rustics of the Cheap Repository are typically rescued, not by any internal exigencies of plot, but rather by the endless supply of proxies for Hannah More that circulate through her prose. Tom's conversion experience in the London hospital is typical in this regard: remorse becomes reform only through his decision to send home "for his Bible and Prayer book, which . . . had been given him when he left the Sunday school," and the whole episode becomes an occasion to encourage "rich people to give away Bibles and good books," and to celebrate the charity available in "a christian country, where the poor, when sick, or lame, or wounded, are taken as much care of as any gentry" (*WHM* 5: 227). The "space for repentance" that Tom discovers in London has been constructed for him by others, not least his author, in the form of Sunday schools, charity hospitals, and Cheap Repository Tracts. In this way, Hannah More fictionalized not just the "hard facts and hard lives" of the rural laborer and smallholder, but the way those facts and lives were being mediated and transformed by the incursion of characters like Farmer White and the widow Mrs. Jones of the *Sunday School* series, whose experience in putting down public houses, setting up Sunday schools, reforming popular morals, gathering subscriptions, and combating the indifference of residual elites, closely followed More's own operations as recorded in her letters and memoirs.[36]

Put in terms of the approach to More's work not as realist fiction but as "popular propaganda for the poor," an interpretive tradition forcefully restated by Robert Hole in his recent edition of More's work,[37] the Cheap Repository Tracts gather a certain formal complexity from their dual attempt to show plebeian readers that revolution along French lines is a bad idea, while persuading middle-class supporters and subscribers that More and her associates represent the most effective machinery for securing England against revolution from below. If under the pressure of self-promotion these tracts sometimes become what Patricia Demers terms a "self-referential exercise," the metafiction involves not so much reading about reading (a pleasure of the imagination), but rather a more rigorous exercise in reading about how reading can secure social order, through disciplinary measures imposed upon the irregular forms of literacy associated with residual popular culture and with an emerging, collective working-class radicalism.[38] Although its propagandistic designs were often quite crude, Evangelical discourse developed increasingly sophisticated and reflexive strategies of self-representation, through complex narrative interpolations of its own conditions of production, and through the careful orchestration and layering of implied audiences. More's impoverished readers met other impoverished readers who reformed their habits and improved their condition by reading Cheap Repository Tracts, in part so they could then lay out the few spare pennies that virtuous habits afforded in the purchase of new tracts; more affluent readers were presented with challenging yet finally reassuring case studies of the way their own commitment to the Cheap Repository, as advocates, subscribers, and distributors, could produce a tractable labor force and neutralize the threat of popular insubordination. Men, women, and children; the propertied and the dispossessed; the rural gentry and the provincial middle class; schools, homes, churches, and shops; public and private spaces – all were knit together by the cooperative activity of reading and circulating a literature of Evangelical reform.[39] In this way, More's fiction normally acknowledged the work that had to be done to counter revolution, and avoided the stunning inconsistencies evident in some of the more secular anti-French propaganda of the early 1790s, where hearty rustics blustered about their native resistance to Paineite principles. To return to the sentiments of the first meeting of John Reeves' loyalist Association, "the new lights and false philosophy of our pretended Reformers . . . can have no influence on the good sense and gravity of Britons, who have been used to the enjoyment of true Liberty" (*AP* I, 1: 4). If so, one is inclined to wonder, why the massive outpouring of counterrevolutionary propaganda? Hannah More's project was less inconsistent, though more complex and potentially compromised, since it tended to concede that the revolutionary desires of the people could only be suppressed through the counterrevolutionary enterprise of their betters.

The heterogeneous structure of the two-part *Tom White*, with its opening narrative of fall and redemption followed by a sequence of more discrete programmatic episodes, certainly yields something less than seamless fiction. Yet taken together, and considered in relation to More's wider project, the series does involve an impressive attempt to encompass within a fictional framework the entire Evangelical reform of manners. This comprehensive scope was a chief feature of the Cheap Repository. If the economy of the Evangelical penny tract was by definition marginal, and its target audience impoverished, More's expectations for it were never modest, and she later boasted of having circulated over two million tracts within the first year of the establishment of the project (*WHM* 5: viii).[40] There is ample evidence within these tracts, and in the letters and memoirs that surround them, of her restless campaign for increased subscriptions and more extensive circulation, and her ambition was evidently contagious. The Religious Tract Society, a cooperative enterprise of Evangelical Anglicans and Dissenters founded on More's model within a year of the termination of the Cheap Repository, accounted for sales of more than four million tracts by 1808, and ten million by 1824, and maintained a regular catalogue of hundreds of tracts in a variety of formats and series throughout the early decades of the nineteenth century.[41] Historians have long recognized More's achievement as a watershed event in the history of print, since it was through the Cheap Repository "that influential middle-class Englishmen got their first experience in the mass production and distribution of reading matter."[42] Yet the tension between the announced modesty of the project ("cheap") and its immodest ambitions could only be managed through the commercial sleight of hand that allowed tracts nominally priced at "one penny" to be distributed in fact through massive charitable subsidy and bulk sales.[43] The peculiar print economy that resulted generated further tensions. Just as Tom White's reform left him eager to reform others, so the print economy of the Cheap Repository was an endless exercise in self-propagation, which seemed always to risk exhausting its own resources. Following the example of the widow Mrs. Jones, who "took care never to walk out without a few little good books in her pocket to give away" (*WHM* 4: 333), rich and poor alike were expected to devote every spare moment, and every spare penny, to the circulation and consumption of a literature of moral improvement. Evangelical principles of thrift, vigorously recommended to the poor within these tracts,[44] were simultaneously unraveled from without, as extravagance became the hallmark of a system of charitable provision that sought to direct an endless flow of excess capital from the rich (as cash subscriptions) to the poor (as printed texts). Where the Cheap Repository did extend to elites the rigorous frugality it preached to the lower orders, the aim was often to shore up the economic foundations of charitable provision – *Hints to All Ranks of People*, for example, advised the wealthy to divert their resources away from "vanity" and "luxury," and bring about a "reduction in your whole establishment," in order to create "a regular fund for your future charity" that would find its natural outlet in supporting Sunday schools and Cheap Repository Tracts.[45]

Given this comprehensive design upon reading audiences ("*All Ranks of People*"), and the sheer scale of the publishing enterprise, one of the most striking rifts within the Cheap Repository involved the tension between a desire to incorporate every reader and every text into a single print economy, and an insistence upon enforcing differences of privilege and function within that economy. While Hannah More proved remarkably dexterous at orchestrating several forms of address within any given tract, she could not help but respond to market conditions that exacerbated social and literary distinctions. In early 1796, in order to continue to reach both elite and ordinary readers, she reorganized the Cheap Repository as a series of octavo (rather than duodecimo) tracts in two formats, distinguished by their paper quality

and price structure. Profits from the more expensive version were used
to subsidize the distribution of cheaper editions, reinforcing the distinct
roles played by different sorts of readers, and suggesting as well that the
structure of a print economy of charitable provision was essentially
circular.[46] As this formal development indicates, the project was
proving more successful on the supply than on the demand side of the
equation. While concrete evidence about the operation of the Cheap
Repository is frequently compromised by self-promotion, it is clear that
More's spectacular ability to enlist the support of elites (at one point
subscriptions came in so fast they had to be declined) was not met by a
similar success in securing the interest of ordinary readers. At first, the
tracts were nominally priced at a penny or halfpenny each, with discounts for bulk sales to two kinds of purchasers: wealthy supporters
who were encouraged to give the tracts away, and hawkers and
chapmen who were offered a financial incentive in the hope that they
would substitute the Cheap Repository for their existing stock of vulgar
popular literature. Yet as G. H. Spinney has observed, despite a
"vigorous campaign . . . to induce the smaller booksellers and hawkers" to stock the tracts, a substantial portion of the achieved circulation was simply "given away at charity schools, workhouses,
hospitals, prisons, and various institutions." "It is hard to say what
proportion was bought directly from hawkers by the poorer people, but
it was probably not very high."[47] Elite provision, through subscription
and subsidy, proved the most effective means of circulating a literature
of moral reform, and this made the recruitment of middle-class and
gentry support a critical element of the project. More's class-inflected
versioning of the tracts, which included annually compiled volumes
that could be bound for libraries, and octavo booklet versions of
broadside ballads, was meant to exploit their appeal among elite
readers, whose motivations for purchasing tracts on their own behalf
were no doubt complex. Beyond their direct interest in a literature of
moral reform which regularly addressed their own condition, and their
desire to support a counterrevolutionary enterprise that promised to
secure their own privileges, there was surely some comfort to be found
in More's vision of a secure social hierarchy in which the responsible
stewardship of elites consistently met with grateful deference from
below.

Whatever the relative successes of her project, More later confirmed
that social distinction was among its premises when, in the 1801
edition of her works, she sorted her longer narrative tracts into two

separately titled volumes, "Tales for the Common People" and "Stories for Persons of the Middle Ranks," and congratulated herself on the opportunity this afforded to present the public with "an enlarged and improved form" of her work (*WHM* 4: iv). Editorial confidence aside, this was a deeply imperfect gesture, its discrete categories undermined by More's enduring Evangelical vision of shared obligations in an interdependent social order.[48] To begin with, this collected edition of her works was itself beyond the economic reach of common readers, and in this sense, the vernacular volume of "Tales for the Common People" was in effect redirected to middle- and upper-class audiences at the very moment it was conceived in an explicitly common form. Further, while some tracts fell naturally into the "common" or "middle" category, and while a third rubric, "Ballads and Tales," was devised to pick up some of the most demotic short works, the distinctions in play were far from clear, in part because More's imagination refused to separate the work of capturing the attention of poor readers, enlisting the support of their superiors, and reforming the lives of both. *Tom White* was included in the "Tales for the Common People," although as we have seen, its various episodes address a range of audiences: if Tom's early life is a parable for common readers about the dangers of corrupt habits, it also signals elites about the importance of subsidizing moral reform; and the more episodic second half comprises both a set of domestic guidelines for the ordinary cottager and a handbook for the middle-class moral reformer. More implicitly conceded the flaws in her categories when she prepared the *Sunday School* series for her collected works: the first two tracts, *A Cure for Melancholy* (the revised version of *The Cottage Cook*, with its practical coda of recipes and domestic advice removed[49]) and *The Sunday School*, were placed in the volume for the "Middle Ranks," while the Second Part of the Sunday School, the two-part *History of Hester Wilmot*, fell into the volume "for the Common People" with a note directing readers back to "the preceding volume" (*WHM* 5: 283). In one sense, the editorial logic here was clear enough: the opening pair of tracts considers the induction of Mrs. Jones, "the widow of a great merchant" (*WHM* 4: 325), into the reformist enterprise of organizing charity schools, putting down public houses, and regularizing the habits and morals of the common people; while the second part addresses the impact one of these Sunday schools has in reforming Hester Wilmot, the daughter "of parents who maintained themselves by their labour" (*WHM* 5: 283). Yet in all the essentials of idiom, presentation, and format that mark a class-specific address, the tracts are indistinguishable, and each one entails narrative and thematic elements designed for both common and middle-class readers. For example, the initial account of Mrs. Jones' activity in *A Cure for Melancholy* contains a long didactic section ("The Informer") targeting ordinary readers, in which a blacksmith is painstakingly disabused of his popular prejudice against informing on corrupt tradesmen. And *The History of Hester Wilmot* subsequently describes at some length Mrs. Jones' strategy for persuading Rebecca Wilmot to allow her daughter to attend the Sunday school, an episode that makes sense primarily as a model for other middle-class reformers who must contend with the resistance of unregenerate cottage parents. Again, More's narrative tracts are distinguished by their effort to serve up a world in which every class of reader joins together as both agent and effect of the shared enterprise of Evangelical reform.

LITERARY AUTHORITY AND THE MEDIA OF MORAL REFORM

The willingness of the Cheap Repository to measure success in the proliferation of millions of printed tracts invites a more pointed interrogation of the whole tract system. Who or what ensured the value of all of this printed material? And particularly for elites enjoined to participate as subscribers and distributors, and to lend their credit to a network of effects they could not possibly witness, where was the guarantee that any of this reading material did any good in the world? In an era in which the threat of a French invasion compelled Britain after 1797 to suspend specie payment, and thus to undertake an anxious, extended experiment with a currency not guaranteed by gold, these questions may have acquired an added urgency, since any scheme for unlimited textual production and circulation risked playing into anxieties about an inflationary currency unmoored from intrinsic standards of value.[50] If pressed for some guarantee of the credit of the entire system, the Cheap Repository had an advantage over its equally prolific but relatively secular counterpart, Reeves' Association, where the production of counterrevolutionary propaganda often stood in tension with a blunt insistence that the British constitution was invulnerable to any challenge. By contrast, More's Evangelical version of a counterrevolutionary project not only assumed the corruption of human nature and the imperfection of human institutions, but could also invoke the primary authority of scripture to underwrite its own print enterprise. Even the formal tendency of Evangelical discourse to stray from narrative sequence into catalogues of scriptural references can be taken to confirm the fundamental authority of the Bible in the organization of these tracts. This was, as Robert Hole has indicated, a position with deep political implications: for all her Evangelical leanings, More shared with her Anglican establishment friends like George Horne, Bishop of Norwich, a "politico-religious" commitment to "the divine authority of the established order" in church, state, and society, which "not only provided them with a Biblical foundation of political obligation, it also sanctified the existing social hierarchy as the work of Divine Providence."[51] Yet as the Cheap Repository perfected a system of charitable provision that multiplied titles, editions, and series, and as it seconded the manageable convention of scriptural allusion with a more unruly network of references to other Cheap Repository Tracts (later editions of these works are particularly thick with promotional self-reference), there was a risk that the project might appear to supersede rather than simply reinforce the original authority of scripture.

It is not surprising, then, that Hannah More was not consistent in her treatment of Biblical authority. "The grand subject of instruction with me is the bible itself,"[52] she once told a correspondent, and while this claim was meant to reassure supporters that Sunday-school literacy would not exceed the limits of Christian piety, it seemed to indicate that scripture could by itself produce orderly, submissive, and industrious subjects. Recommending the Bible to her readers in the opening paragraph of *The History of Hester Wilmot*, More's narrator reflects that "it is a pity people do not consult it oftener. They direct their ploughing and sowing by the information of the Almanack, why will they not consult the Bible for the direction of their hearts and lives?" (*WHM* 5: 284). Yet despite this confidence in scriptural sufficiency, More was keenly aware that available habits of piety and loyalty were not adequate grounds for counterrevolutionary culture, and she spent her career supplementing the Bible as moral almanac with an elaborate system of prayers, catechisms, schoolbooks, devotional tracts, and pious tales and ballads, along with supervised reading practices to manage textual reception. The title character of *The Shepherd of Salisbury-Plain*, a two-part Cheap Repository Tract of 1795, strikes his wealthy interlocutor, Mr. Johnson, as remarkable for having generated a whole program (More's own) of loyalty, subordination, temperance, and industry "without any kind of learning but what he had got from

the Bible," and while Johnson readily endorses the Shepherd's resistance to the "new books" and "new doctrines" of "those men who are
now disturbing the peace of the world" (evidence again of the political
dimensions of Biblical authority), he wonders aloud whether this simple
rustic is eccentric in his desire "to make scripture a thing of general
application" (*WHM* 5: 9, 50).[53] It comes as no surprise, then, that the
Shepherd himself reinforces some portion of Johnson's concern when
he indicates that scripture can easily become the source of moral and
doctrinal error, especially among ordinary readers: "I always avoid, as
I am an ignorant man, picking out any one single difficult text to
distress my mind about, or go build opinions upon, because I know
that puzzles and injures poor unlearned Christians" (*WHM* 5: 46).
More to the point, the Shepherd's isolated piety turns out not to derive
from scripture alone. When Mr. Johnson later visits the Shepherd's
cottage, he discovers that "a large old Bible" is the most "reverently
preserved" of the few possessions "inherited from his father." Yet this
patriarchal transmission from the past has been supplemented by
More's own recent print interventions: "On the clean white walls were
pasted, a hymn on the Crucifixion of our Saviour, a print of the
Prodigal Son, the Shepherd's Hymn, a *New History of a True Book*, and
Patient Joe, or the Newcastle Collier," all broadsheet tracts that were
"printed for the Cheap Repository, price 1/2 d. each," as the author
duly reminded readers in a promotional footnote to collected editions
of her work (*WHM* 5: 37–8).[54] This gesture towards her own activity
registers both the Cheap Repository's compulsive self-referentiality,
and the inflationary pressures of a print economy of charitable provision: though "large" and "old," and "reverently" passed from generation to generation, the Bible is neither sufficient nor complete, and
cottage literacy and discipline are instead vividly framed by More's
own publishing enterprise.

This episode suggests why the broadsheet ballad was such a critical
element of the Cheap Repository. Affixed as they are to "the clean
white walls" of the cottage interior, these single sheet tracts offer a
private, domestic, and orthodox response to the disruptive public
handbills of popular radical culture. The configuration of the Shepherd's (nominally) private space would have allayed conservative
anxieties about the emergence of a plebeian public sphere, to which
More's Sunday schools were sometimes felt to contribute, by containing the counterrevolutionary version of that sphere within the four
walls of a cottage, and limiting it to provided texts. In the same way,

the Shepherd's reclusive scripturalism – "my bible has been meat, drink, and company to me" (*WHM* 5: 12) – releases him from the debased political sociability of the tavern and street assembly. While the domestic sphere is privileged here and throughout More's prose as an antidote to radical publicity, she could not ignore the other spaces in which her readers lived and worked, and the Cheap Repository issued similar monitory print instruments for other arenas of common life: *The Loyal Subject's Political Creed; or, What I Do, and What I Do Not Think*, appeared in broadsheet form with an engraving that suggested tavern reception, and *The Apprentice's Monitor; or, Indentures in Verse, Shewing What They Are Bound to Do* was printed with the indication that it was "Proper to be hung up in all Shops" (Figure 1).[55] Broadsheet tracts of this kind are figures of surveillance, too, scrutinizing and setting standards for the homes and workplaces of the poor as surely as Johnson and other privileged characters in the Cheap Repository eavesdrop on the conversations, prayers, quarrels, and recreations of ordinary people. If the political inscription of the Shepherd's interior cottage walls by Cheap Repository publications seems to turn what we expect of the period's more rigid mappings of public and private space inside out (or outside in), it is important to recognize that in some sense privacy is no longer at issue here, since this potent intersection of the domestic and the political, the very faultline along which More conducted her own career, was wholly managed and provided for the Shepherd by his superiors. The collaborative surveillance of Mr. Johnson and the Cheap Repository Tracts effectively eliminates any credible sense of cottage privacy with respect to the intervention of charitable agency.

There may be no more perfect figure for the circumscribed life More would grant to her reformed subjects than the Shepherd's legible cottage, a domestic arena for ordinary literacy that is clearly meant to dissolve the heady public challenge of radical protest. Yet the design of the work as a whole suggests that there is a deeper irony at work in the circular narrative logic by which this cottage interior becomes available to elite scrutiny and oversight. The first part of the tract, leading up to the climactic visit to the cottage, concludes upon an inward sense of pious wonder at the very existence of so remarkable a figure of rural devotion as the Shepherd: Mr. Johnson has "found abundant matter for his thoughts during the rest of his journey," and is determined to seek out the Shepherd's "poor hovel" upon his return from his present journey (*WHM* 5: 31–2). When

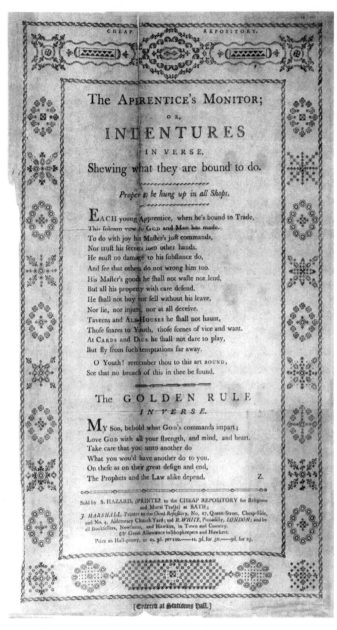

Figure 1. *The Apprentice's Monitor; or, Indentures in Verse* (1795). Reproduced by permission of the Harry Ransom Humanities Research Center, The University of Texas at Austin.

Johnson finally does enter the cottage, however, it turns out that the only real cause for introspective wonder is that he has "found" nothing new at all, but instead confronts modes of piety and discipline that he and the class he embodies have scripted in advance, in the form of "Patient Joe" and other Cheap Repository Tracts. Johnson's odyssey across the "vast plains of Wiltshire" is in this sense a journey of self-discovery, its possibilities (if not its privileges) as limited as the four walls of the Shepherd's cottage. As in *Tom White*, the rural cottage is not the isolated repository of indigenous virtue or loyalty, but rather a conduit through which the commercial enterprise of Evangelical reform can be made to flow. If my emphasis so far has been on the complex structure of the Cheap Repository Tracts, this pattern of elite self-discovery in the work of moral reform – to say nothing of a subtitle like "What I Do, and What I Do Not Think" – provides a salutary reminder of the predictability and crude directness with which Evangelical enterprise would finally dictate and manage popular consciousness. Hannah More often sought to assuage elite fears that access to literacy would radicalize ordinary readers, by insisting that the course of reading in her Sunday schools was limited to the Bible and simple devotional works. Her aim was to control the potential range of discursive effects by making children and the laboring poor consumers but not producers of the written word: "My plan for instructing the poor is very limited and strict. They learn of week-days such coarse works as may fit them for servants. I allow of no writing."[56] Taken alongside the narrative pattern by which characters like the Shepherd of Salisbury Plain discover their own beliefs in texts produced for them by others, this partial dispensation of literacy indicates just how straightened and eviscerated were the kinds of agency made available to the poor by Hannah More and her collaborators.

Nostalgic fantasies of an embedded rural virtue do appear in the Cheap Repository, but they prove to be no match for the author's aggressive revisionism. Indeed, the local or natural in its received form was consistently reworked by More as the product of her own national mission. If the Shepherd of Salisbury Plain is initially recommended to the reader for his rural isolation and embeddedness, a kind of found object, he becomes too perfect a facsimile of More's own reactionary ethos to be allowed to work away in this obscurity. Just as his tale is designed to reach far beyond his remote Wiltshire home, and just as that home discloses evidence of the impressive reach of the Cheap Repository, so the Shepherd himself is finally enlisted in a national campaign of disciplinary literacy. The attitude of pious repose achieved at the close of the first part of the series betrays the inevitability of a sequel, since repose is never the trajectory of these narratives. The second part concludes on a more characteristic note of practical action, as Johnson joins "an excellent institution in London . . . called the Sunday-School Society" (*WHM* 5: 62) in subsidizing a school for the poor under the Shepherd's supervision. Here the reward of virtue, that eternal theme of didactic fiction, has been filtered through More's concern for education, publication, and revision: already shown to be a product of "new books," a category he seemed to disown, the Shepherd is finally extricated from his naive scripturalism and fantastic isolation in order to be incorporated into an advanced economy of reactionary print culture. As Olivia Smith has suggested, the Shepherd's foundation in the real historical figure of David Saunders, who set up a school on his own initiative and was likely paid by his students rather than by outside benefactors, offers a rare opportunity to gauge precisely how More's supposed literary realism was betrayed by her insistence that "the poor exist to be saved by the upper classes."[57] As the agent of this rescue mission, the mobile "charitable gentleman" Mr. Johnson becomes the key figure in refashioning the real as product of Evangelical fantasy. Like the campaign for moral reform, and like the author he represents, Johnson operates without regard for existing geographical boundaries and social hierarchies, through the protean movements of charitable capital and middle-class philanthropy. Title page images reinforce this by consistently distinguishing Johnson's superior position on horseback from the Shepherd's firm grounding in local circumstance (Figure 2). Interestingly, the agent of charitable enterprise achieves his leverage upon the real through a certain personal dislocation: introduced as a traveler, Johnson is distanced from the natural world by an attitude of "serene contemplation" (*WHM* 5: 2), and from the social world by an assumption of privilege that licenses the skeptical interrogation of his inferiors. Responding to the Shepherd's initial professions of piety with the reflection "that no one should be too soon trusted, merely for having a few good words in his mouth," Johnson is rewarded throughout his inquiries by due gestures of subordination: "Indeed I am afraid I make too bold, sir, for it better becomes me to listen to such a gentleman as you seem to be, than to talk in my poor way: but as I was saying, sir, I wonder all working men do not derive as great joy and delight as I do from thinking how God has honoured poverty!" (*WHM* 5: 6, 9–10). The subsequent discovery

CHEAP REPOSITORY.

THE

Shepherd of Salifbury-Plain.

Sold by. J. MARSHALL,
(PRINTER to the CHEAP REPOSITORY) for Moral and
Religious Tracts,) No. 17, Queen-:treet, Cheapfide,
and No. 4, Aldermary Church-Yard, Bow-Lane,
and R. WHITE, Piccadilly, London.
By S. HAZARD,
(PRINTER to the CHEAP REPOSITORY) at Bath ; and
by all Bookfellers, Newfmen and Hawkers, in Town
and Country.
Great Allowance will be made to Shopkeepers and Hawkers.
PRICE 1d. each, or 4s. 6d. per 100.—2s. 6d. for 50.
1s. 6d. for 25.
[Entered at Stationers Hall.]

Figure 2. *The Shepherd of Salisbury-Plain* (1795). Reproduced by permission of the
Department of Special Collections, Young Research Library, UCLA.

of the inscribed cottage walls reinforces the priority of print over speech ("words in his mouth") as evidence of interior spiritual disposition. It also confirms that the Shepherd's bold talk about contentment was all along a subordinate form of listening, since anything he has to say turns out to be the predictable echo of a script that Johnson and his allies circulated in advance.

The Cheap Repository could not have been more deliberate about its departure from localized, contained, or nostalgic approaches to managing the lives of the working poor in the face of revolutionary challenges. The ballad poem *Dame Andrews*, a 1795 Cheap Repository broadsheet that was not written by More, provides a vivid case in point. The opening lines are firmly embedded in a local community – "Near Lechlade Town, in Glostershire, / Upon the Banks of Thame" – but the narrative then conveys its heroine through a series of "mishaps" that require outside intervention. As the impoverished Dame Andrews prepares to feed her children their last loaf of bread, she hears a noise at the door, significantly not a knock, but the rattling of one "who tried to move the pin." Again, the Cheap Repository rescues the dispossessed by opening their private lives and domestic circumstances to the inspection of their superiors. Anticipating relief from a "friendly neighbour," Dame Andrews finds instead a women "lately come / Within this town to live," who turns out emphatically to be a neighbor of another kind – "A friendly Neighbour sure it was!" – by virtue of her willingness to reward virtue by enlisting it in the cash nexus of Evangelical reform: "I an offer to you make / My School-mistress to be; / To teach poor children and for this, / You shall be paid by me."[58] The double substitution here is crucial: as the condition for "neighborhood" shifts from proximity to charitable motive, so a recruitment to Evangelical enterprise replaces bread, alms, or respectability as the reward of virtue. This conscripting mode of recompense allowed More and her collaborators to legitimate their own ambitions by representing the indigenous pious poor and the mobile reformist middle class as interdependent social forces and reciprocal narrative effects.[59] It also sustained the pattern by which a print economy of charitable provision managed its own inflationary pressures by channeling redundant energy (and money) back into further charitable enterprise. The fact that episodes of this kind of reward often occur in a sequel, or in the later phases of a multi-part publication, suggests an important formal consideration: converts to the endless, serial task of moral reform were typically secured where these narratives were supplemented through the device of the sequel or final part.[60] Where conservative reactions to radical protest in this period often involved grub street nightmares of an exploding print culture,[61] the Evangelical economy of print sought to allay such fears by demonstrating an unlimited capacity to recycle its own boundless energy as a kind of discipline. Crudely put, to convert the Shepherd of Salisbury Plain is not to diminish by one the total number of souls to be saved in the world, but rather to multiply by the number of students enrolled in his school the available audience for Cheap Repository Tracts.

The final fact or frame of reference in the Cheap Repository is not the natural resistance of British common life to moral degradation or French revolutionary theory, but rather the ongoing project of revisionist intervention in the life, labor, and learning of the common people. Feminist scholarship has alerted us to the way that More's position as a woman activist and writer informed her qualified commitment to progressive improvement, and it is important to see as well that her willingness to innovate, and to make the counterrevolutionary project a reinvention of popular culture, was predicated on her Christian understanding of a fallen human nature, and the meliorative view of history this implied.[62] If she did not share the deep traditionalism of Edmund Burke, More answered what she took to be a Jacobin spirit of perpetual revolution in pursuit of utopian perfection with a more skeptical view of history. Gratification was deferred to the next life (especially for those who found few privileges in this one), and the world became a scene of permanent reformation, potentially limited only by the nightmarish fear that human corruption or Paineite revolution might somehow triumph. This perspective is succinctly expressed in the Preface to the 1801 edition of her works:

The well intentioned and well principled author, who has uniformly thrown all his weight, though that weight be but small, into the right scale, may have contributed his fair proportion to that great work of reformation, which will, I trust, unless a total subversion of manners should take place, be always carrying on in the world; but which the joint concurrence of the wisdom of ages will find it hard to accomplish. (*WHM* 1: xix–xx)

More's skeptical "trust" about the inveterate challenges she faced was vividly confirmed when the Cheap Repository Tracts were reprinted and made available again during the renewed unrest of the 1810s and 1820s. Revisions that accommodated "the present times," and present enemies like Henry Hunt, signaled a tactical awareness that protean antagonists and the contingencies of history dictated against a fixed or retrospective reform project.[63] The improving energy and incessant meddling of Hannah More and her heroines, who were "always carrying on in the world," was a function of this commitment to permanent reformation, a commitment she projected onto her readers, as readers, laborers, and moral subjects. The serial production of the Cheap Repository Tracts, formalized in May 1795 with the monthly issue of tracts in three distinct formats (one moral tale, one devotional "Sunday Reading," and one broadside ballad), went some way towards countering the perceived radical dominance of popular periodical forms, what Edmund Burke termed the seditious "battery" of "continual repetition."[64] Yet More's higher purpose was to use these regular addresses to readers, along with the Sunday school movement and other charitable incursions into the rhythms of ordinary life, as a means of integrating subordinate forms of work, worship, literacy, and domesticity so thoroughly that each individual life became one "daily lesson of instruction,"[65] leaving no inroad for revolutionary "subversion."

The coordination of reading and conversation with other daily routines was important enough to More that it often served as a framing device for her printed tracts, in title page images that represent pious conversation during labor or leisure, and in titles like *Sunday Reading. On Carrying Religion into the Common Business of Life. A Dialogue between James Stock and Will Simpson, the Shoemakers, as they sat at Work*, to which More later added a sequel, *On the Duty of Carrying Religion into Our Amusements*. These two dialogues formed the last two parts of a six-part series, *The Two Shoemakers*, and in that capacity they drew a particularly suffocating web of daily routine and pious literacy around a more straightforward narrative of spiritual redemption. Introduced on the title page of the tract version by a simple engraving showing two shoemakers conversing as they work, and by a series designation ("Sunday Reading") that situates reception within a similar framework of routine piety (Figure 3), the pattern of integration was systematically intensified throughout the text. "James Stock [the master], and his journeyman Will Simpson, . . . resolved to work together one hour every evening, in order to pay for Tommy Williams's schooling," and these sessions become an occasion for pious conversation about pious conversation, during which the master doubly secures the renunciation of tavern sociability by his "good-natured" but "ignorant" assistant: the arguments against corrupt habits advanced in the dialogue are seconded by the fact that labor and conversation leave no time for dangerous leisure. Meanwhile, all three characters contrive to

CHEAP REPOSITORY.

SUNDAY READING.

O N

CARRYING RELIGION

INTO THE

Common Bufinefs of Life.

A DIALOGUE between JAMES STOCK and WILL SIMPSON, the Shoemakers, as they fat at Work.

Sold by J. MARSHALL,
(Printer to the CHEAP REPOSITORY for Religious and Moral Tracts) No. 17, Queen-Street, Cheapfide; and No. 4, Aldermary Church-Yard; and R. WHITE, Piccadilly, LONDON.

By S. HAZARD, at Bath, and by all Bookfellers, Newfmen, and Hawkers, in Town and Country.

Great Allowance will be made to Shopkeepers and Hawkers.

PRICE ONE PENNY.

Or 4s. 6d. per 100.—2s. 6d. for 50, 1s. 6d. for 50.

[*Entered at Stationers' Hall.*]

Figure 3. *On Carrying Religion into the Common Business of Life* (1796). Reproduced by permission of The Huntington Library, San Marino, California.

support the crippled James Stock, who in turn "requited their kindness, by reading a good book to them whenever they would call in; and he spent his time in teaching their children to sing psalms or say the catechism" (*WHM* 5: 184–6). The sequence of a six-part narrative tract like *The Two Shoemakers* allowed More to unfold these ambitions on a broad canvas, but the same effect could be achieved in a more condensed form through the allegorical design of a short ballad poem. In *Turn the Carpet*, Dick the restless weaver has been misled by the high "price of meat" and "the rich man's state" to doubt God's providence, but his contentment is restored in pious conversation with his fellow weaver, John, and then secured through a conceit drawn from the very fabric they have been laboring to produce. "My own carpet sets me right," Dick exclaims, after John has compared "the whole design" of an inscrutable providence with the two sides of a carpet: "This world, which clouds thy soul with doubt, / *Is but a carpet inside out*" (*WHM* 1: 53–4).[66] Once again, More's own literary authority is never far from the surface. As the weaver discovers a rationale for piety in the material upon which he works, so the author discloses her own craft in a dense figure that draws together her interests in literacy and legibility, in the social work of allegorical representation, and in a selective accessibility of design: like many of the Cheap Repository Tracts, this legible carpet displays different meanings to different readers. Should her patrons worry that busy piety might distract the laboring classes from their essential purpose, working for their superiors, More specified that reading and pious conversation could be managed in "little odd ends and remnants of leisure," without compromising the productivity of a laborer, servant, or child. In the second part of *The Sunday School* sequence, Hester Wilmot has been enrolled in the school set up by Mrs. Jones, but she is forced to read under the watchful eye of an impious mother who "hated the sight of a book." Her recourse is "to learn out of sight" and "to steal time from her sleep," in order that she "would not neglect the washing-tub, or the spinning-wheel, even to get on with her catechism." For the benefit of reluctant parents, cautious patrons, and the unconverted poor alike, More invested Hester's expedient with the force of a general maxim: "It was no disobedience to do this, as long as she wasted no part of that time which it was her duty to spend in useful labor" (*WHM* 5: 297–8).

VILLAGE POLITICS AND NATIONAL ENTERPRISE

The range of Cheap Repository narrative certainly complicates the impression, derived largely from *Village Politics*, of More as a narrowly anti-Paineite polemicist. At the same time, an appreciation of the literary complexity and cultural density of her later work can enrich our understanding of *Village Politics*. This widely reprinted dialogue was arguably her most influential fiction, and in many ways it provides the clearest index of the range of her ambitions, and of the contours she would assign to plebeian life and literacy. From the outset, the conversation "between Jack Anvil, the Blacksmith, and Tom Hod, the Mason" is very much a case of village politics, firmly embedded in English rural life and vernacular idioms, and pitched against the cosmopolitan abstractions of French *"organization* and *function,* and *civism,* and *incivism,* and *equalization,* and *inviolability,* and *imperscriptible,* and *fraternization"* (*WHM* 1: 324). Tom Paine's *Rights of Man* has intruded upon this world, via the intoxicated political sociability of the Rose and Crown tavern, but the radical challenge remains an alien language, both in its French associations and in its remoteness from the concrete experience of village life: the deluded Tom Hod can articulate his discontent only by *"looking on his book"* (significantly, this is the dialogue's first stage direction), and Jack Anvil, who secures the loyalist half of the conversation, considers it "a good sign" that "you can't find out you're unhappy without looking into a book for it!" (*WHM* 1: 323–4). More's effort to weave her later Cheap Repository Tracts into the rhythms of popular life is negatively anticipated here by an attempt to pry the revolutionary script away from the life and experience of its audience. The revolutionary lexicon cited above (*"organization* and *function,* and *civism,* and *incivism* . . .") does not involve a real engagement with republican political theory, since Jack makes no effort to explain or demystify his terms. Instead, the simple act of reiterating the language of revolution within a village dialogue becomes an adequate critique, since the framing rhythms of vernacular speech serve to stigmatize and purge the supposed otherness of revolutionary discourse.

The initial action of the dialogue, Jack's interruption of Tom's reading, announces an apparent ideological pressure in *Village Politics* away from printed texts and towards ordinary speech and immediate experience. Yet as his alertness to "a good sign" indicates, Jack is nothing if not an expert reader of his world, and he shares his author's skepticism that concrete facts or real experiences might by themselves counteract Tom's acquired disaffection. On the contrary, the fundamental aim of the tract, as its full title indicates, is to use the medium of cheap print to make local orthodoxy available on a national scale: *Village Politics. Addressed to all the Mechanics, Journeymen, and Labourers, in Great Britain.* Nor is More content with the well-fed, well-governed logic that informed much of the reactionary discourse of the early 1790s, and issued in such crude dictums as "None but a fool would rebel against beef and pudding" (*AP* II, 8: 14). *Village Politics* is from the outset a text generated out of another text, and Jack's opening gambit, "What book art reading?" (*WHM* 1: 323), is very much the author's own. The tract achieves its orthodox narrative trajectory not by departing from the revolutionary empire of signs for the loyal comforts of "beef and pudding," but rather by succumbing to the inexorable force of other texts and other discourses, which are taken to be more securely embedded in the village world. In a characteristic concession to elites more interested in plebeian industry than orthodoxy, More has Jack confess that his work leaves him "little time for reading," but he goes on to answer Paine's *Rights of Man* with Richard Allestree's *Whole Duty of Man*,[67] and to delineate a series of oral and printed authorities – scripture, sermons, English law, popular songs and sayings, "a story-book from the charity-school" (*WHM* 1: 330) – that leave the village so hemmed in by discursive orthodoxy that there is simply no room for radical expression. The local squire, Sir John, enters the dialogue first as an equal, in Jack's conventional anti-French boast about English equality before the law: "I may go to law with Sir John at the great Castle yonder; and he no more dares lift his little finger against me than if I were his equal" (*WHM* 1: 327). Yet as the discussion proceeds, this leveling gesture loses its force, and the same Sir John becomes the upper limit in a discursive hierarchy that secures the village against revolution. His sayings are local legend, and versions of the formula, "Sir John, who is wiser than I, says . . ." have persuaded Jack, as they will soon persuade Tom, that "the whole [French] system is the operation of fraud upon folly" (*WHM* 1: 340–1). Even the private letters of the Squire contribute to a common network of loyal discourse, as his foreign correspondence filters out through his servants into the village, to expose the bleak reality behind a Jacobin lie: "'Tis all murder and nakedness, and hunger" (*WHM* 1: 340).

If this last claim seems to offer a negative version of the material fact as antidote to revolution (French hunger replaces British beef), my point is to notice also the communicative circuit along which such disenchanting truths are transmitted, so that Tom can make them available to Jack and to the reader: "Sir John's butler says his master gets letters which say . . ." (*WHM* 1: 340). This active exercise of counterrevolutionary orality and literacy, rather than any repressive prohibition of seditious texts, becomes the principal mechanism for contesting and defeating popular discontent in More's fiction. As if to confirm that the stakes here are dangerous reading practices, not dangerous texts, let alone the experience of poverty or injustice, the dialogue closes as Jack first dissuades Tom from burning the book he has agreed to disown – "let's have no drinking, no riot, no bonfires" (*WHM* 1: 348) – and then leads him off to the more important work of breaking up the tavern gatherings that have given rise to his phantom Paineite discontent. The message is clear, and entirely consistent with More's dual role as Sunday school educator and founder of the Cheap Repository: control how books are distributed and where they are read, and there will be less to fear from seditious writers and texts.[68] Tom's rousing chorus of "*The roast beef of old England*," blunt register of material satisfaction and fit accompaniment to a popular riot, gives way in the end to Jack's less nostalgic and subtly revisionist, though still scriptural, motto: "Study to be quiet, work with your own hands, and mind your own business" (*WHM* 1: 347–8).[69] The phrase belies the historical inertia of one of Jack's own earlier anti-French dictums about liberty: "We've no race to run! We're there already!" (*WHM* 1: 335). Instead, "study to be quiet," and work to acquire habits of contentment and subordination. For More, popular loyalty and civil order were neither given conditions nor available inheritances; instead, they had to be aggressively taught and actively learned, through the procedures developed in her educational and publishing schemes, and then relentlessly thematized in her fiction. Again, her willingness to innovate in order to preserve, and educate in order to subordinate, prevented a work like *Village Politics* from sedimenting as a reactionary canon. When it reappeared in 1819 as *The Village Disputants; or, A Conversation on the Present Times*, in an edition priced at "2d. or 25 for 3s. 6d.," the text was revised to meet the distinctive challenge of early nineteenth-century radical reform: a batch of "fine new papers and tracts" replaced the work of Tom Paine, footnotes indicated the latest improving tracts, and there were updated treatments of taxation, war debt, and female reformers.[70]

It is not easy to discover Hannah More's own position in this impressive exercise in counterrevolutionary literacy and acculturation, since *Village Politics* contains no real equivalent to such later authorial proxies as Mr. Johnson or the widow Mrs. Jones. In a sensitive account of the opportunities and challenges that this political dialogue presented for More as a woman writer, Christine Krueger traces the submerged authorial presence to a "dialectical process" that "requires no privileged voice, no hierarchical relation between speaker and listener," yet she observes too that the writer seems not yet to have discovered her distinctive rhetorical powers.[71] This was after all the first of More's popular reactionary fictions. Written at the encouragement of Beilby Porteus, the Bishop of London, and initially printed without the institutional benefit of More's own Cheap Repository, it achieved its remarkable circulation within the advanced network of correspondence, association, and publication provided by John Reeves' Association.[72] In this context, informal nodes of rural gossip within the text are (like Dr. Shepherd's casual conversations about housekeeping) mystified representations of reactionary transmission, a way of insisting that, as a source of knowledge about revolutionary France, loyal association was structurally as well as semantically distinct from the radical corresponding societies. There were good reasons why, for all her literary sophistication, More might want to obscure her own position as author at this early stage in her counterrevolutionary career: not only was she a women writing about public matters, through networks controlled by male authorities like Porteus and Reeves, but she was actively involved in practices of political association and textual production that could appear suspect in an era of acute anti-Jacobin sentiment. In the crisis atmosphere of the 1790s, Sunday schools were themselves suspected of French complicity, and even Hannah More was not immune to the paranoid response. The Blagdon controversy was triggered in 1800 when a local schoolteacher appointed by her was accused of Methodist subversions of the church establishment, and no less a counterrevolutionary authority than the *Anti-Jacobin Review* took a leading role in the print campaign against More and her supporters.[73]

Yet despite the absence of a fully realized self-representation in *Village Politics*, the tract does contain a curious modal shift or rupture that seems to open up the space More would soon visibly occupy. Like much of her counterrevolutionary fiction, this dialogue refused any clear distinction between realistic and emblematic writing by assigning vernacular speech and vivid social circumstance to characters like Jack Anvil, Tom Hod, and Neighbour Snip. However, at the moment when the conversation takes a critical turn towards a direct refutation of Paine's *Rights of Man*, the generic register shifts dramatically from the quasi-realistic to the wholly allegorical. The figure of Sir John, elsewhere rendered in circumstantial detail (he receives letters, entertains visitors, cultivates a garden, and employs village children), becomes an emblem of something else, another "good sign," as Jack spins his refusal "to pull down yonder fine old castle" and remodel it along French lines into an allegory of the "wisdom of [our] brave ancestors" in respecting constitutional government, despite the occasional presence of "a dark closet, or an awkward passage, or an inconvenient room or two in it" (*WHM* 1: 329–30). With this abrupt reminder that we are in the domain of fiction, sharply marked by Jack's formula, "I'll tell thee a story . . ." (*WHM* 1: 329), Hannah More enlists the hermeneutic skills of her reader and discloses the artifice of her own narrative design, and makes both indispensable to the work of counterrevolution. Sir John is reduced from a real source of gentry influence in the surrounding village to a fictional vehicle for the author's more far-reaching professional intervention. Ironically, More's Burkean allegory of the uninterrupted transmission of authority becomes a discursive switch for authority to pass from Sir John's legendary and locally disseminated sayings to her own recently scripted and nationally distributed texts.[74] The point is even more striking if we consider Marilyn Butler's observation that the virtuous patriarch of *Village Politics* cloaks a female villain, the wife whose "fantastical" desire to do "every thing like the French" (*WHM* 1: 329) precipitated the original demand for the destruction of the ancestral English castle.[75] In her fondness for luxury and leisure, this woman of doubtful authority serves as a foil for More's own native industry and thrift. Yet if we recall Tom White's fierce determination "to break through many old, but very bad customs," and take seriously More's reformist designs on the existing social order, there is a sense in which the "fantastical" author of *Village Politics* succeeds in reconstructing "yonder fine old castle" where the misguided wife failed.

The crucial break at this point from vernacular dialogue to allegorical narrative again suggests the limits of an understanding of More's work as a variety of social realism: the point here, and in the Cheap Repository's many allegorical tales, was not the social texture of village life in 1793, but rather the ideological work done upon it by fiction.

If there is an element of what Julie Ellison has called "aggressive allegory" in my reading of the way Sir John is transformed from local authority into national fable, the aggression is not difficult to understand.[76] The rural gentry were frequently implicated in More's comprehensive assault on upper-class corruption, and they tended to figure as obstructions rather than allies in her letters and memoirs.[77] Sir John has his share of successors in More's fiction, but even those who are successfully conscripted to the work of moral reform tend to remain unimpressive or inconsequential figures. The widow Mrs. Jones, for example, succeeds in enlisting gentry subscriptions for her parish oven, but the motives at work are clearly demeaned: "Sir John subscribed to be rid of her importunity, and the squire, because he thought every improvement in oeconomy would reduce the poor's rate" (*WHM* 4: 347). In subsequent Cheap Repository Tracts, as Gary Kelly has observed, "the real leader in rural society, the 'squire, is missing altogether," replaced by a "professionalized" Evangelical clergy and an adjunct committee of women activists and "converted poor" who collectively figure forth More's own energy.[78] At one point in *Village Politics*, when Jack tries to invoke the charity of Sir John and the employment created by his wife's extravagance as a hedge against French leveling (a wholly conventional piece of reactionary political economy for the masses[79]), Tom objects that "there's not Sir Johns in every village." The shift to emblematic status once again diminishes gentry authority, as one particular Sir John loses force in the absence of "Sir Johns." Faced with this challenge, Jack's only recourse is to change the subject: "The more's the pity. But there's other help. 'Twas but last year you broke your leg, and was nine weeks in the Bristol Infirmary, where you was taken as much care of as a lord" (*WHM* 1: 338–9). The institutional associations at work in this abrupt shift from gentry provision to "other help" could not be more sharply drawn. A year later, the prospectus for the Cheap Repository would invoke the same "distinguished" British practice of charitably subsidized "Hospitals, Dispensaries, and Humane societies" in order to fashion a legitimate genealogy for its own fabricated practices.[80] Sir John the inherited figure of social order fades from view, as Tom and his creator turn away from the authority of the landed gentry in an isolated village, and towards the more modern, national, and centralized network of middle-class philanthropy and counterrevolutionary enterprise that the Cheap Repository would soon pioneer.

CHAPTER 3

Reviewing subversion: The function of criticism at the present crisis

In its initial outbreak and enduring impression the revolution controversy in Britain has been considered a pamphlet controversy,[1] precipitated by the dual flashpoints of Burke's *Reflections on the Revolution in France* (1790) and the two parts of Paine's *Rights of Man* (1791, 1792), and driven forward by the pamphleteer's dialectical logic of provocation and response. While such newspapers as *The Times*, the *Morning Post*, the *Courier*, the *Sun*, the *Oracle*, and the *True Briton* were careful observers of contemporary events as well as vigorous participants in controversy, periodical forms have on the whole been less closely identified with the first phase of debate over the French Revolution and domestic radical organization. Periodical expression then breaks through spectacularly with the appearance of the *Anti-Jacobin; or, Weekly Examiner* of 1797 and 1798. In its heterogeneous weekly format, its slashing and reckless satirical manner, and its coterie production by a group of energetic young men associated with the future foreign secretary and prime minister George Canning, this first *Anti-Jacobin* can seem altogether too distinctive to be the inaugural moment for a subsequent lineage of conservative magazines and reviews. Yet it was invoked in just those terms by later writers and editors, and its appearance towards the end of the 1790s, after the effective suppression of the distinctive radical movement associated with the London Corresponding Society, suggests a shift from pamphlet warfare to the sequence of important reviews and magazines that conducted conservative political expression through the early nineteenth century, including the second *Anti-Jacobin Review and Magazine* (1798–1821), the *Quarterly Review* (1809–), and *Blackwood's Edinburgh Magazine* (1817–).[2] In these periodicals, writing against revolution sustained its combative manner of political engagement while working to invest itself in a more sustained and reliable print medium. For literary history, the primary conception of the revolution controversy as pamphlet warfare has much to do with the extraordinary talent marshaled on both sides – Richard Price, Edmund Burke, Thomas Paine, Joseph Priestley, Mary Wollstonecraft, William Godwin, Helen Maria Williams, James Mackintosh, and Arthur Young. Yet it follows too from a tendency to conceive periodical forms as somehow secondary or derivative, and particularly where reviewing is concerned, to privilege a few canonical episodes of judgment and commentary on other primary texts – for the romantic period, these include Francis Jeffrey's treatment of Wordsworth in the *Edinburgh Review*, William Hazlitt's assault on the apostasy of the Lake Poets, and the *Blackwood's* and *Quarterly* attacks on Keats and the poets and essayists of the "Cockney School."[3] Yet conservative periodical expression in response to the threat of revolution and radical reform was a more searching and comprehensive enterprise than this kind of episodic treatment allows.

In a study that extends the history of a broadly "right-wing" press back through the eighteenth century, James J. Sack has shown how in the immediate aftermath of the French Revolution the Pitt administration addressed concerns over unreliable press support by directing substantial attention and subsidy to the daily newspaper press. George Rose, Secretary of the Treasury and a close friend of Pitt, coordinated the establishment of two daily papers, the *Sun* in late 1792 and the *True Briton* in early 1793, both edited by the paid Treasury writer John Heriot and consistently favorable to the administration and hostile to France and domestic radicalism.[4] While it is not clear the extent to which the ministry's role here included direct subsidies, newspapers did continue to benefit from an established practice of assisting well-disposed editors with secret service funds controlled by the Treasury. The historian Arthur Aspinall sets government expenditure on the newspaper press in the early years of the French Revolution at £5000 annually.[5] Of course disaffection with radicalism at home and abroad was not simply purchased by the ministry, nor does it seem likely that the increasingly sharp anti-French tone assumed by such established papers as *The Times* and the *Oracle* depended upon the few hundred pounds they received annually from the government.[6] Newspaper subsidy had long been an uncertain business, and these later years of an old regime were no exception. Sack concludes that for the period after 1800 the *Courier* in the closing years of the Napoleonic wars may represent the one case of a successful ministerial daily paper.[7] Yet the ongoing production of the *Sun*, the *True Briton*, and the *Day*, and the occasional establishment of such new papers as John Stoddart's *New Times* in 1818 and Gibbons

Merle's *True Briton* in 1820 (the first with treasury money and the latter with support from Lord Kenyon), ensured that government views were consistently if not always effectively represented in the newspaper press.[8]

Ministerial dismay at the disaffection of the leading periodical reviews, notably the Dissenting *Analytical Review* and the recently defected *Critical Review*, led to the establishment in 1793 of a staunchly Anglican monthly, the *British Critic*, under the joint editorship of two clergymen, Robert Nares and William Beloe, who were very soon able to compete effectively with the existing reviews, achieving credible circulation figures of around 3,500 per month. While the precise conditions of government support are obscure, Nares received direct Treasury payments in 1792 and 1793, and he and Beloe both subsequently enjoyed ample patronage from the government and the Church. A requisite connection with publishing and bookselling was secured for the new review through its joint ownership by F. and C. Rivington, longstanding publishers to the Society for the Promotion of Christian Knowledge, and reliable promulgators of piety, loyalty, and social order.[9] That the *British Critic* was the one instance of a major new conservative review in the years before the *Anti-Jacobin Review* suggests that the newspapers were considered a more immediate priority. As with the daily press, though, existing periodicals with reviewing content stepped into the breach. Over the course of the first half of the 1790s the annual prefaces to John Nichols' venerable *Gentleman's Magazine* assumed an increasingly sharp and programmatic tone of support for "our Political and Religious Constitution," and contempt for the "strange and heterogeneous philosophy, which has deluged France with blood" (*GM* 63, 1 [1793], iii). Where the *Anti-Jacobin Review* later found ways to respond retrospectively to *Rights of Man* and other seminal radical works, notably in Robert Bisset's ongoing series on "The Rise, Progress, Operations, and Effects of Jacobinism in these Realms,"[10] the prolific *Gentleman's* critic Richard Gough was there to attack Paine's effort "to re-govern the world" from the outset (*GM* 61, 2 [1791], 740). At the same time, the *Gentleman's* suggests the difference between an extension of eighteenth-century periodical routines into the 1790s and the more systematically antagonistic and crisis-oriented reviewing practices of the *British Critic*, the *Anti-Jacobin Review*, and the *Quarterly Review*. Despite regular prefatory reflections on horrific events in France, and a clear editorial line on major political publications (Paine, Price, and Priestley were attacked, while

Burke, Hannah More, John Bowles, and the pamphlets of Reeves' Association were approved[11]), much of the magazine's miscellaneous content remained impervious to the threat of revolution. And at least very early on, there was room for competing views, for example, in a January 1792 letter from the occasional contributor Joseph Mawbey maintaining that the French Revolution had thrown off superstition and despotism, and in a subsequent debate among correspondents over the deprivations endured by the ordinary English laborer.[12]

By the first decades of the nineteenth century, the regular appearance of the *British Critic*, the *Anti-Jacobin Review*, the *Quarterly Review*, and *Blackwood's Edinburgh Magazine* made the monthly or quarterly magazine and review formats among the most reliable print venues in support of established powers. Yet the impact of these well-known publications should not obscure the wider range of antiradical periodical expression. While orthodox Anglican clergymen were active at the *British Critic* and the *Anti-Jacobin Review*, a range of more evangelical Christian views found expression in such works as Sarah Trimmer's quarterly *Guardian of Education* (1802–6), the Clapham Sects' cheap *Christian Observer* (1802–), and the Evangelical monthly miscellany *The Christian Guardian* (1802–). Though not narrowly absorbed by the threat of revolution, these publications advanced loyalty and social subordination along with morality and piety as part of a broad assault on the debilitating effects of radical skepticism. And they supplemented tract production as the leading forum for a disciplinary Evangelical address to the poor. Inspired by the example of Hannah More, Legh Richmond first published narrative tracts that later appeared with the Religious Tract Society as a series in the *Christian Guardian* from 1809 through 1816, in a department entitled "The Poor Man's Friend." These extended the magazine's otherwise elevated address down through to the lower orders.[13] Richmond was responding to a rising tide of popular discontent in the later years of the Napoleonic wars, and as a threat from below intensified, the political orientation of the *Christian Guardian* became more explicit. Contentment and good order were recommended on the firm doctrinal grounds that "a complaining Christian is a disgrace to Christianity" (*CG* 3 [1811], 61), and the vernacular dialogue form of the earlier loyalist Association movement was revived in works that cautioned ordinary readers to prefer the church and scripture to the subversive allure of William Cobbett and tavern reading societies.[14]

What was this kind of writing meant to achieve in a "theological miscellany" whose price and format placed it beyond the reach of impoverished readers? In a pattern that recalls the hierarchically ordered comprehensive social address of Hannah More, the *Christian Guardian* framed its presentation of vernacular literature with promotional addresses to elite readers as potential patrons: factory owners, for example, were urged to sponsor Sunday Schools and tract societies (*CG* 5 [1813], 47–50), and women were called upon as mothers and domestic managers to examine the publications found in their homes and in nearby cottages (*CG* 11 [1819], 493–95). During the alarming first wave of unstamped radical weekly publications in 1817, the *Christian Guardian* reinforced its reproduction of a sample pious tract, *A Word in Season; or, A Dialogue on the Present Times*, with a department entitled "Loyal Tracts," which offered wholesale discounts on cheap reprints of Paley's *Reason's for Contentment* and More's *Village Politics* (updated and retitled *The Village Disputants*), along with such new Hatchard productions as *Church and King* and *My Cottage Is My Castle*. As with More, the case for laying out "a few shillings" in support of this "antidote to the poisonous publications . . . industriously circulated throughout the kingdom" insistently aligned piety and politics: "It becomes every *Christian*, who must of course, or ought to be, a true and loyal subject, to do all he can to counteract by these simple and legal methods, the prevailing disregard for all authority, and the dreadful extension of irreligion and profaneness" (*CG* 9 [1817], 191). If this promotional campaign confirms that cheap tracts remained the main Evangelical instrument against subversion from below, more direct periodical forms of pious vernacular address did begin to appear in these years. Cheap monthly magazines like the *Cottage Magazine; or Plain Christian's Library* (1812–32) and the *Cottager's Monthly Visitor* (1821–) supplemented a steady diet of devotional material and practical domestic and agricultural advice with stern injunctions about living "peaceably and honestly, fearing God and honouring the King," and nightmarish accounts of a French determination to "set fire to our villages" and "abuse our wives and daughters."[15]

Vernacular "anti-Cobbetting" was more characteristically a secular project, and can be taken as evidence of the vagaries of press subsidy, in the sense that the support arranged in 1802 by William Windham (Pitt's former Secretary at War) for the establishment of William Cobbett's *Weekly Political Register* represented an immediate success with disastrous long-term consequences.[16] Staunchly if recklessly "Church and King" through its first few years, and perhaps modeled on the *Anti-Jacobin* weekly of Canning and Gifford,[17] the *Register* did more than any other single publication to establish the weekly newspaper of political comment as an early nineteenth-century periodical fixture. Yet the form was not more widely emulated on the loyalist side until well after Cobbett's radicalization (beginning in around 1806), and his subsequent introduction of a cheap unstamped version of the paper in November 1816. The spate of anti-radical weeklies included *Blagdon's Political Register* (1809–11), *Anti-Cobbett, or The Weekly Patriotic Register* (1817), Gibbons Merle's *White Dwarf* (1817–18), *Shadgett's Weekly Review, of Cobbett, Wooler, Sherwin, and Other Democratical and Infidel Writers* (1818–19), and *The Gridiron, or, Cook's Weekly Register* (1822). Though Merle, Francis Blagdon, and William Shadgett were distinctive political voices in their own right, anti-Cobbetting was for the most part a derivative enterprise. The *Anti-Cobbett* reproduced material from Stoddart's *New Times*, and similar periodicals and pamphlets were often pieced together from embarrassing reprints of Cobbett's earlier loyalist prose. But the response to Cobbett in these weekly publications and in the *Christian Guardian* is important for the way it registers a conservative sensitivity to the social circumstances for radicalization in matters of periodical form and idiom as well as content.

Indeed there had been from the early 1790s a pattern of meeting critical episodes of unrest with occasional periodicals, often vaguely popular in tone, in addition to the usual spate of pamphleteering. Invasion scares and periods of intense Francophobia triggered a number of specialized serials, usually weeklies or monthlies, meant to track the progress of foreign and domestic enemies and encourage a countervailing wave of loyalist feeling. These occasional projects were heterogeneous in their content and imperfectly periodical in their appearance, cobbling together original content with material drawn from other pamphlet and periodical sources, and supplementing news reports of domestic conspiracy and enemy atrocities with patriotic songs and addresses and encouragement to volunteer forces. Few such projects survived beyond a year or two, and their miscellaneous titles often indicate the specific conditions under which they emerged: *The Anti-Gallican Songster* and *The Anti-Levelling Songster* (1793), *The Loyalist: Containing Original and Select Papers; Intended to Rouse and Animate the British Nation, During the Present Important Crisis; And to direct its united Energies against the perfidious Attempts of a malignant, cruel, and impious Foe* (1803), *Ring the Alarum Bell!* (1803), *The Anti-Gallican, or, Standard of British Loyalty, Religion and Liberty, including a collection of the principal papers, tracts, speeches, poems, and songs, that have been published on the threatened invasion : together with many original pieces on the same subject* (1803–4), and the *Anti-Gallican Monitor and Anti-Corsican Chronicle* (1811–17).[18]

It is hard to categorize counterrevolutionary periodicals in part because they extend through so many distinct dimensions of form and organization: there were newspapers, magazines, and reviews, brought out at daily, weekly, monthly, and quarterly intervals; there were coterie and individual projects, incorporating news, commentary, reviews, and furious polemic; there were new titles designed to meet the threat of revolution, and existing ones that assumed an increasingly conservative tenor; there were publications benefiting from direct or indirect government subsidy, and others affiliated with religious groups or civic associations. Nor was this field without internal dissension. Committed counterrevolutionary periodicals were prepared to notice each other as, in the words of the *Anti-Jacobin Review*, "labourers in same vineyard," leagued together against the "subversion of our establishments in church or state" (*AJR* 11 [1802], 428). Yet a sense of common purpose did not prevent the eruption of controversy. So for example the *British Critic* and the *Anti-Jacobin Review* took contrary positions on the Blagdon controversy, which erupted when a schoolteacher appointed by Hannah More at the village of Blagdon was accused by the local curate Thomas Bere of subverting the Anglican establishment.[19] The founders of *Blackwood's* took a dim view of the more plodding methods of the *Quarterly Review*, and when a *Blackwood's* reviewer of Percy Shelley acknowledged, despite abundant evidence of political transgression, that there was genius in the 1816 *Alastor* volume, he took the opportunity to complain that the poet had been "infamously and stupidly treated" in the *Quarterly* (*BEM* 6 [1819–1820], 153).[20] Perhaps more than any other arena of print culture, periodicals render visible competing ideological programs and lines of authority within counterrevolutionary discourse. Indeed, there is very little about conservative expression in this period that was not somehow represented and negotiated in periodical form, as editors set about reporting and responding to foreign and domestic news, reprinting political speeches and pamphlets, announcing and encouraging (or discouraging) political clubs and associations, and reviewing new publications as well as developments in art, music, fashion, and the theater.

My aim here is not an exhaustive study of counterrevolutionary periodical forms. Instead, by focusing on the critical operations of the monthly and quarterly reviews and related magazine formats, the remainder of this chapter will explore how one acutely reflexive type of periodical expression came to map the field of print culture and to develop critical strategies for managing its political risks. After an account of the development of conservative critical reviewing within a framework of perceived crisis, the central section of the chapter traces the sequence of "Anti-Jacobin" titles in order to explore the relationship between shifts in periodical interval and distinct conceptions of the literary and cultural field. The final section then considers counter-revolutionary efforts to engage the traditions of represented periodical sociability. Given the role that periodicals have long played in perceptions about the historical development of public opinion, a central concern of this chapter will be the way the conservative press sought to align itself with the unreformed constitution. Where radical editors and journalists were busy promoting themselves as agents of public pressure for parliamentary reform, conservative periodicals were far more cautious about advancing any direct claim upon established political institutions. Though aggressive and even reckless in their polemical style, they ranged themselves against the idea that the state should become more responsive to public opinion as it was increasingly conditioned and expressed in print.

MEASURES OF CRITICAL SURVEILLANCE

Given their conventional habits of self-reflection and relatively measured period of appearance, the conservative reviews and magazines were often explicit about their desire to raise the threshold of political and literary surveillance.[21] In a retrospective preface for the year 1799, the *Anti-Jacobin Review* framed its own emerging critical enterprise in relation to a much anticipated March 1799 parliamentary report documenting the government's case for the existence of a widespread revolutionary conspiracy. Though based on secret evidence, the sensational committee report was presented to the public, in the words of the Secretary for War Henry Dundas, as the "clearest proof" to date of "a systematic design, long since adopted and acted upon by France, in conjunction with domestic traitors, . . . to overturn the laws, constitution, and government, and every existing establishment, civil or ecclesiastical, both in Great Britain and Ireland" (*AJR* 2 [1799], 413). As a justification for the ensuing Combination Acts of 1799 and 1800, which effectively prohibited collective action and association, this report capped the government's repressive campaign against the radical organizations of the

1790s, and the *Anti-Jacobin Review* seized the occasion to express its own commitment to the same enterprise. The parliamentary report of coordinated schemes for invasion, mutiny, and insurrection had already enlisted attention in the April number of the same volume, where a digest version brought out by Evans and Hatchard, under the title *An Account of the Present English Conspiracy, Taken from the Report of the Secret Committee of the House of Commons*, was favorably if briefly noticed (*AJR* 2 [1799], 403). The Anti-Jacobin office's own sixpenny edition of the report was then more fully extracted and promoted, in a review that concluded by urging "Lords Lieutenants of Counties, Sheriffs, Clergymen, Commanders of Volunteer Corps, and all other friends to their country, in public situations" to "avail themselves of the opportunity afforded by the low price at which this Report is published, to circulate it as extensively as possible" (*AJR* 2 [1799], 419). Revolutionary conspiracy, parliamentary enquiry and report, pamphlet publication, periodical review, parish and local government action, further circulation and reception – the linked sequence of events here, by turns observed and activated by the *Anti-Jacobin Review*, was typical of the way conservative criticism conceived its own role in a wider sphere of counterrevolutionary enterprise. The point of invoking the same committee report in a summary annual preface was to insist that the coordinated activity of central and local government, of pamphlet publishers and periodical reviewers, must not close with the introduction of the Combination Acts. On the contrary, the conspirators were "undismayed by detection" and were already displaying "more caution and prudence in their *means*": "Thus the difficulty of counteraction is enhanced, and the consequent necessity of increased vigilance and circumspection established" (*AJR* 2 [1799], ii). And again there were schemes for future collaborative action, including "a serious admonition to the Clergy of the Established Church" to exercise "unusual vigilance in performing the duties of their stations, and in keeping intruders out of their folds," and grateful acknowledgment to a correspondent whose earlier published letter had first alerted editors to the "truly diabolical effort" of a thwarted Jacobinism to shift its revolutionary designs from open insurrection to the dissemination of revolutionary children's literature (*AJR* 2 [1799], iii–iv, 450–51).

Though imperfect in practice, and vigorously urged in part because even Tory ministers and Anglican clergymen rarely performed up to *Anti-Jacobin* standards, this effort to project a coordinated circuit of political action and scrutiny – extending from Church and state through the critical reviews and enterprising civic associations – was the hallmark of counterrevolutionary periodical reviewing. To be sure, the *British Critic*, the *Anti-Jacobin* and *Quarterly* reviews, and *Blackwood's Edinburgh Magazine* never abandoned the more ordinary enterprise of noticing, categorizing, summarizing, extracting, and evaluating new publications, what John O. Hayden has called "the merest practical function of reviewing."[22] And differences in this regard were conditioned less perhaps by political considerations than by the uneven participation of the conservative press in a decisive historical shift in reviewing practices, triggered in 1802 when the Whig *Edinburgh Review* abandoned the older pattern of briefly noticing and extracting all new publications in favor of a format that offered a limited number of more expansive essays on matters of general public concern.[23] Confronted with this innovation, the *British Critic* and the *Anti-Jacobin Review* continued to pursue the older model of the review as comprehensive "literary register"(*BC* 1[1793], ii). The *Anti-Jacobin* was sufficiently offended by the success of its new Whig rival to issue a mock "Apology," in which it pretended to recommend the free expression of "Northern" genius against "old-fashioned" objections that the *Edinburgh* was not a review at all, but rather "a collection of detached essays, having little connection with the subject under discussion" (*AJR* 33 [1809], 304–5). Yet such recalcitrance should not be taken as evidence of an absolute conservative resistance to formal innovation. Founded in 1809 to challenge the rapid ascendancy of the *Edinburgh*, the *Quarterly Review* was more open to the new method of reviewing, to the extent that Robert Southey could quietly drop the pretense of a list of works under review when he gathered his work for the *Quarterly* in a two-volume essay collection of 1832.[24] *Blackwood's* in its turn sought to inject the venerable form of the magazine or miscellany with a new vitality when it appeared in 1817 to challenge the notion that the staid *Quarterly* could effectively rival the *Edinburgh*. While reviews and notices of new publications routinely appeared in departments committed to that purpose, the politically charged function of counterrevolutionary surveillance spilled over in the heterogeneous pages of *Blackwood's* into a brilliant range of fiction, commentary, authentic and contrived correspondence, and occasional departments.[25]

This diversity of reviewing practices unfolded in conjunction with a shared commitment to align the routine vigilance of periodical expression with a similar vigilance on the part of government, the Church, and the law, so that the counterrevolutionary reviewer was never limited to the role of gatekeeper for the flow of new publications.

Despite its prevailing formal organization as a sequence of numbered review articles, the *Anti-Jacobin Review* incorporated a critical treatment of foreign and domestic news through its regular "Summary of Politics," and in certain respects managed to outstrip the synthetic procedures of the *Edinburgh* through the serial appearance of Bisset's "Rise, Progress, Operations, and Effects of Jacobinism." Launched with a stated intention of more fully applying the conspiracy theories of the Abbe de Barruel and John Robison to the British experience (*AJR* 1 [1798], 110), this ambitious survey of the Enlightenment and Jacobin history of religious infidelity and political subversion allowed the *Anti-Jacobin Review* to extend its critical operations back before the era of its own foundation. Similarly, as editor of the *Quarterly Review*, William Gifford allowed his reviewers to exploit the flexibility of the critical essay to achieve a topical orientation towards matters of general public concern (Church, constitution, political economy, the war), even as his own severe editorial hand ensured a reasonably consistent overall tone. There was no particular innovation about the range of critical attention in these periodicals, since reviewing had developed over the course of the eighteenth century in flexible and miscellaneous periodical formats, a fact sometimes obscured when scholarship tends to extract particular reviews of canonical texts. Yet what is striking about the topicality and comprehensiveness of counterrevolutionary reviewing was that, while the periodical forms themselves preserved a heterogeneous character, the critical impulse was more closely organized, drawing on conspiratorial theories of radical organization to achieve a systematic sense of "vigilance and circumspection." Bisset's history of the "Rise, Progress, Operations, and Effects of Jacobinism" was appropriately serialized over the opening years of the *Anti-Jacobin Review* because it provided an ongoing theoretical commentary that knit together disparate elements of the review, and its assumptions could be found throughout the ordinary business of reporting the news and extracting new publications. If Barruel's particular claims about a covert revolutionary conspiracy of the Illuminati lost their force over the course of the early nineteenth century, anxieties about revolutionary crisis and conspiratorial organization remained a pressing concern through the post-war era for the *Quarterly* and *Blackwood's*. These were *counter-conspiratorial* periodical forms, committed to tracing the influence of subversion through every aspect of print culture and social life, and to linking criticism with other elements of counterrevolutionary enterprise.

The deliberate if often haphazard interlacing of book reviews with observations on national and international affairs heightened the orientation of these periodicals *as periodicals* towards the course of events in the world. In this sense, the conservative periodical in an age of revolution was also an *emplotted* form, acutely sensitive in its temporal dimension, and concerned to align its mission with the fortunes of Church and state. If there are clear ironies about the way this project seemed to require the antagonistic collaboration of the radical press, it is worth distinguishing the ways in which the periodical narrative of counter-conspiracy was shaped by a commitment to the established social order. Radical periodicals in the same era tended to frame their own historical unfolding in relation to political and economic determinants that lay beyond editorial control, and to anticipate their own demise through either the achievement of reform or the triumph of official repression.[26] Counterrevolutionary periodical forms were typically less embattled, and the more successful ones advanced from a founding sense of crisis to an increasingly confident and self-promotional account of their own effectiveness in rooting out subversion. And where cheap radical weeklies negotiated their marginal economic status by resourcefully splitting the difference between newspaper and magazine formats, the monthly and quarterly appearance of the major conservative reviews can itself be understood as a relative privilege, betraying the more secure perspective afforded by a commitment to established powers. Robert Southey vividly conjured different styles of political reading when he struggled to impress upon the polite reader of the *Quarterly Review*, used to taking his newspaper and his coffee at the "breakfast table," the alarming effects that "the weekly epistles of the apostles of sedition" could achieve when they were "read aloud in tap-rooms and pot-houses to believing auditors" and then "discussed over the loom and the lathe" (*QR* 8 [1812], 342).

To be sure, the threat of revolution did pose a risk of counter-revolutionary periodical demise, and military setbacks abroad and renewed episodes of unrest at home typically yielded a darker editorial tone. Nor was the conservative press uniformly successful or triumphant in its development: complacent ministries, unforthcoming patrons and subscribers, and insufficiently alarmed reading audiences were all brought to task for failing to support projects that were, in their own estimation, necessary to the preservation of good order. The demise of the *White Dwarf* in April 1818 with a scathing public letter signed by the editor Gibbons Merle attacking the home secretary Lord

Sidmouth for his failure to deliver "honorable patronage" (*WD* No. 22
[April 28, 1818], 338–42) was only the most spectacular instance of a
periodical project terminating through a lapse in government or public
support.[27] Sack has speculated that "the plaintive and melancholy
wailings of many of the luminaries of the right-wing press" after
around 1812 resulted not only from the straightened economic circumstances of the Liverpool administration, but also from the
increased commercial viability of an "ideologically oriented, high
Anglican, anti-radical press" in these years, a view that seems plausible
if we allow that such a press, as embodied by the *Quarterly Review*, was
often set in motion by government ministers and then staffed by writers
who enjoyed Church and government patronage.[28]

The *Anti-Jacobin Review*'s discovery of subversion in children's literature may betray a paranoid style, but it reflects a widespread conservative assumption about the pervasiveness of revolutionary
impulses. As these reviews undertook to notice parliamentary proceedings, reform agitation, political economy, and military campaigns
alongside new works of fiction, drama, poetry, travel writing, and
scientific enquiry, they did so in part to advance a claim that subversion was migrating from overt political agency to the more elusive front
of mind and manners. There were crucial ambiguities here. A decisive
shift along these lines was identified early in the 1790s, and then
seemed to renew itself through every subsequent phase of acute unrest,
though many conservative commentators were also prepared to trace
intellectual subversion back through the skeptical and speculative
tendencies of the early eighteenth century, treating the Enlightenment
erosion of morality and piety as a precondition for Jacobin politics.
And it remained unclear whether the existence of a cultural front was
to be considered essential evidence of the sinister nature of Jacobinism,
or a secondary consequence of effective legal and critical surveillance.
In any case, counterrevolutionary periodical criticism vested its own
authority in a unique capacity to negotiate the saturated politics of
culture in an age of revolution. To some extent, in conceiving their
enterprise in this way, conservative writers and editors were simply
articulating for themselves a synthetic and comprehensive impulse that
seems embedded in the unconscious, as it were, of periodical expression, and that achieved a kind of apotheosis in this period. It was from
around 1800 that the English word "press," as applied to the art of
printing and the material operation of the printing-press, became as
well a narrower designation for newspapers, magazines, journals, and

reviews, and the OED cites the weekly *Anti-Jacobin*, the *Edinburgh Review*, and Cobbett's *Weekly Political Register* for transitional usages in this sense from 1798 through the early 1820s.[29] And today we still look to the self-reflective (and self-promotional) habits of the periodical press for historical evidence of the rise of print as a symptom of modernity – evidence, for example, of the growth and fragmentation of reading audiences, the commercial erosion of aesthetic values, and the gathering political authority of public opinion. Conservatism has long been identified with a resistance to these developments, in ways that were decisively conditioned in this period by the writings of Burke, Wordsworth, and Coleridge. And while counterrevolutionary periodicals were eager to claim a leading role in the struggle against subversion, they could not help but share an underlying suspicion of the destabilizing impact of print culture. For this reason, conventional habits of periodical self-reflection tended to assume a more ambivalent cast in the conservative press. It was no accident that the first *Anti-Jacobin*'s contribution to a shift in the semantics of the press had negative associations, as the editors issued a farewell address to their readers celebrating the success of a nine-month campaign against subversive newspapers but warning that "the Press" remained a danger because of the ongoing development of subversive reviews and magazines (*AJ* No. 36 [July 9, 1798], 281).

For practical matters of reviewing, this ambivalence meant that conventional hand-wringing about the deluge of new publications was reinforced for conservatives by a conviction that the cause of political stability would be served by some diminishment or more effective management of print culture. The novel was a frequent source of complaint, and attacks on the stage served as a reminder that conservative doubts about popular culture were not restricted to print. Yet the tendency to associate periodical communication with the formation of political opinion, especially radical opinion, made the periodical press a preeminent target of surveillance and complaint. And conservative reviews advanced their own distinctive conception of the periodical press as a privileged conscience for print culture at large by undertaking to review other reviews. This meta-critical impulse informed a number of important programmatic essays, including Bisset's "Rise, Progress, Operations, and Effects of Jacobinism" for the *Anti-Jacobin Review*, Southey's 1816 "Rise and Progress of Popular Disaffection" for the *Quarterly*, and John Gibson Lockhart's 1819 "Reflections Occasioned by Some Late Sins of the Public Prints" for

Blackwood's. It was incorporated into the ordinary routine of periodical expression through such departments as the "The Reviewers Reviewed" in the *Anti-Jacobin Review*, "Periodical Works" in *Blackwood's*, and the "Review of Political Declaimers" in the *National Register* of J. B. Bell and J. De Camp.[30] In the era of the cheap radical weekly it became the primary rationale for entire periodical projects, as indicated in the title of *Shadgett's Weekly Review, of Cobbett, Wooler, Sherwin, and Other Democratical and Infidel Writers*. By demonizing the "seditious press" and the work of "Jacobinical journalists,"[31] this kind of reviewing underscored periodical subversion even as it made periodical surveillance an appropriate means of upholding social order. Appropriate, but not adequate or complete: in their willingness to appeal to government and the law to fulfill their own critical surveillance, counter-revolutionary reviews tended to sustain an underlying skepticism about the political legitimacy of the press and public opinion.

The *Anti-Jacobin Review* offers a useful case in point. In their Prospectus, the editors grimly surveyed a periodical landscape dominated by the "vehicles of JACOBINISM," then advanced the self-promotional view that *"the Press itself"* was the most effective means of "controul": "The press has been too long an engine of destruction, and . . . it ought, at length, to be rendered a means of preservation, and an instrument of protection" (*AJR* 1 [1798], 2, 5). Yet in the months and years to come, the *Anti-Jacobin* routinely registered the limits of its own "controul" by recommending measures beyond its own capacity. There were endorsements of the criminal prosecution of Paine and his publishers as a way of "'chaining up the tongues' of the Jacobins," a vigorous defense of the Vice Society's legal campaign against "irreligious, licentious, and obscene books," and demands for "the active intervention of the magistracy" to suppress the Westminster Forum and other radical debating societies.[32] Given the string of treason trials, gagging acts, and sedition and blasphemy trials that characterized the state campaign against radical protest from the 1790s through the 1820s, it is merely stating the obvious to observe that the development of conservative periodical reviewing as a "means of preservation, and an instrument of protection" was not exclusively, nor even primarily, oriented towards activating a reader's critical reason in an arena of public deliberation. Further evidence of the way counterrevolutionary reviewing developed in conjunction with established networks of state authority can be found in the prominent role played by such Tory politicians and civil servants as George Canning, William Gifford, John

Barrow, Grosvenor Bedford, and John Wilson Croker in the establishment and early history of the *Quarterly Review*, and the less
impressive ministerial patronage enjoyed by a number of regular *Anti-
Jacobin* reviewers, including John Bowles, John Reeves, John Taylor,
and John Richards Green (alias John Gifford).[33]

Regular periodical rhythms served to reinforce the integration of
counterrevolutionary reviewing with the established institutions it
sought to defend. With an uninterrupted history stretching back to
1731, the *Gentleman's Magazine* could itself be construed as a reassuring
counterpoint to revolutionary upheaval, a notion that the fictional
editor, Sylvanus Urbanus, made explicit in a Preface of 1796: "Amidst
all the Horrors which desolate the human Race, and when, from the
Ruins of War, a vain Philosophy, opposing itself to Religion and the
honourable Establishment of Ages, marks a new Æra in the History of
the World; the GENTLEMAN'S MAGAZINE commences a new
Year under the fairest and most promising Auspices." Yet this attitude
served to distinguish the *Gentleman's* from later periodicals conceived
with a counterrevolutionary mission when the same Preface went on to
recommend the magazine's undiminished "Variety" to "Men of deep
reflection and exalted Talents, as a Shelter beneath which they might
repose in literary Ease from the Tumults of the World around them"
(*GM* 66, 1 [1796], iii).[34] At the other extreme, a limit case for crisis-
oriented counterrevolutionary periodicity can be found in the occasional and imperfectly periodical titles that appeared intermittently
throughout this period, from the first appearance of *The Anti-Leveller* in
early 1793 against the backdrop of European war and the trial of
Louis XVI through the late campaign of *The Anti-Infidel, and Christian
Manual of Education and Science* of 1823 to combat a rising tide of radical
freethought by disseminating useful information for the lower orders.[35]

The career of William Blair's *The Loyalist*, a cheap sixteen page
Saturday miscellany that ran through twenty numbers during the
invasion scare of 1803, suggests how an immediate sense of alarm
could be expressed in a periodical format that was, to quote a sympathetic reviewer, "admirably adapted for the times."[36] Published and
distributed by the prolific loyalist and Church of England bookseller
John Hatchard, and made available for bulk purchase ("Price 3d. each
Number, or 2s. 6d. a Dozen") in the manner of More's Cheap
Repository Tracts,[37] *The Loyalist* was haphazardly assembled from the
essays, songs, squibs, speeches, and dialogues that poured out of
Hatchard's Piccadilly shop in pamphlet and broadsheet form, and its

weekly parts were not even dated until the appearance of the seventh number. Yet an anxious attention to the threat of French invasion and to "the Signs and Duties of the Times" (*L* No. 12 [October 15, 1803], 196) burdened the paper with an almost apocalyptic sense of political expectation throughout its brief history. While the habit of extracting pamphlets tended to limit current news content, recent events leading up to the invasion crisis were vividly registered in a harrowing nine-part series of extracts from John Adolphus' pamphlet, *Footsteps of Blood; or, The March of the Republicans*, a sensational geographical and historical tour through "the horrid Cruelties and unexampled Enormities committed by the French Republican Armies in all Parts of the World" (*L* No. 7 [September 10, 1803], 121), from the seizure of Avignon in 1791 down through Napoleon's Egyptian campaign of 1801.[38] The alarmist purposes of the pamphlet were in some respects more fully realized in this periodical version, as competing temporal frames – historical retrospection over ten years, nested within serial publication over twenty weeks – heightened narrative anxiety while pointing ominously ahead to the devastating consequences that would ensue if this bloody republican "March" were to reach British shores. Ephemeral publications of this kind tended to terminate without notice, but *The Loyalist* played out its periodical plot to the end, with the editors surveying the patriotic mobilization that made it safe "to suspend our weekly labours," but warning too that "time and circumstances" would determine "whether it will be necessary hereafter to resume our pen" (*L* No. 20 [December 10, 1803], 334).

Between the extremes marked out by the harrowing brevity of *The Loyalist* and the comforting "Shelter" of the *Gentleman's Magazine*, the main line of counterrevolutionary periodical development was towards more secure and reliable formats that served to manage abundant political energies – relentless antagonism, close surveillance, a slashing style of attack, rising and falling perceptions of a subversive threat – within a periodical routine that itself figured the stability put at risk by revolution. The *Anti-Jacobin* and *Quarterly* reviews were particularly concerned to take the immediate shock of the French Revolution as the occasion for a long-overdue critical reassessment of the subversive eighteenth century, in order to urge more vigilant present and future resistance to the whole range of social and intellectual developments (skeptical, experimental, enlightened, cosmopolitan, dissenting, sectarian, liberal, democratic) that eroded the old regime and prepared the way for Jacobin subversion.[39] As a matter of critical principle, this could involve a rejection of what Marilyn Butler has termed "the more innovatory styles" of the arts in the later eighteenth century, including primitivism, sentimentalism, and even classicism if it appeared suspiciously pagan rather than Christian.[40] In this sense subversion was a protracted condition, and even the most aggressive critical reviewing could not expect its imminent demise. At the same time, threats of popular insurrection remained a core rationale for periodical vigilance, a fact that helps account for the persistence and the fluid application of "Jacobin" as a term of abuse and mobilization well into the nineteenth century. The *Anti-Jacobin Review* arguably fell back on its High Church convictions when it changed its name in 1810 to *The Antijacobin Review, and True Churchman's Magazine*, but it continued to insist that Jacobinism was a present threat, and was by no means eccentric in this regard. Coleridge and Southey both identified the plebeian radicalism of the late 1810s as a more threatening incarnation of Jacobinism even as they sought to distance themselves from the "Church and King" bigotry of the 1790s, and in his 1818 "Reflections Occasioned by Some Late Sins of the Public Prints" Lockhart similarly cautioned readers of *Blackwood's* about the ongoing outrages of the "Jacobin press" (*BEM* 4 [1818–19], 356).

It is tempting to join Cobbett and other early nineteenth-century radicals in dismissing the "cry about Jacobinism" as an outmoded political slander, meant to reduce even legitimate dissent to alien subversion.[41] And as popular radicalism came increasingly to rest on the demand for radical parliamentary reform in the early nineteenth century, the political tenor of a second wave of conservative periodicals – notably the *Quarterly Review* and *Blackwood's* – was perhaps counter-reformist rather than counterrevolutionary. Yet campaigning conservatives were concerned to reverse Cobbett's charge, arguing that the constitutionalist idiom of parliamentary reform was a sinister rhetorical cloak for revolutionary ambition, and that any change at all in electoral procedures would fundamentally compromise established powers, particularly Church and crown. "Radical reform is a safer text than revolution," Southey wrote in the *Quarterly Review* in 1812, "the same sermon will suit either; the same end is effectually furthered by both" (*QR* 8 [1812], 346). In this way conservative periodicals remained in their own estimation counterrevolutionary forms well after the demise of the "English Jacobin" organization of the 1790s, and the *long durée* of subversion – extending back from the French Revolution through the Enlightenment – inevitably cast a shadow forward, indicating the

future persistence of counterrevolutionary periodical forms. If subversion was not likely to pass away, the antagonisms it sustained were
not to be mistaken for legitimate differences between competing political factions or parties. In an 1802 review of a pamphlet by one of its
own regular contributors, John Bowles, the *Anti-Jacobin Review*
approved the claim that recently contested elections by radical can-
didates at Middlesex, Nottingham, and Norwich demonstrated the
existence of a struggle not "between two opposite parties" but rather
"between property and no property, law and no law, justice and no
justice, government and no government" (*AJR* 13 [1802], 280).[42]

The sort of immediate, crisis-oriented expression that absorbed and
then dissolved *The Loyalist* of 1803 tended to make its way into specific
departments or phases of the more enduring periodicals, so that efforts
to address the shifting character and intensity of subversion could
unfold within the framework of a consistent and authoritative critical
mission. In its first monthly "Summary of Politics Foreign and
Domestic," the *Anti-Jacobin Review* offered a harrowing tour of a Europe
overrun by "the tri-coloured standard of SOCIAL REBELLION":
"We are destined to begin our political career, at a period peculiarly
calamitous to all who feel an interest in the welfare of mankind, and
in the preservation of that order of things which is essential to its
existence" (*AJR* 1 [1798], 119). Within the hybrid "Review and
Magazine" format of the *Anti-Jacobin Review*, the movements of
revolutionary armies and regimes abroad were gauged alongside
the subversive critical work of the liberal and Dissenting reviews at
home, and in its Prospectus and "Prefatory Address" the *Anti-Jacobin*
framed its own mission in relation to these antithetical print forms.
A new counterrevolutionary review was urgently needed because
Jacobin control of "the channels of criticism" had "insidiously
contributed to favour the designs of those writers who labour to
undermine our civil and religious establishments" (*AJR* 1 [1798], 2).
Over the course of more than two decades, the *Anti-Jacobin Review*
sustained its critical vigilance – along with its subtitle, "Monthly
Political and Literary Censor" – in the face of shifting challenges to
established powers, and notably incorporated the phrase "Protestant
Advocate" into its full title after 1810 to contend with rising demands
for Catholic emancipation. While the *Quarterly Review* was more strictly
a review, and did not accommodate the *Anti-Jacobin*'s range of news,
correspondence, and controversial matter, its development of the
newer review essay afforded a similar responsiveness to shifting

conditions within a regular order of periodical production. In April 1818, amidst the wave of popular radical mobilization that culminated in the Peterloo massacre and the repressive Six Acts of 1819, Robert Southey urgently framed an ostensible review of four volumes on poverty and education with the claim that the issue at hand, the need for a national system of elementary education under Church auspices, signaled one of the great "critical seasons" in human development, more momentous perhaps than "the restoration of letters and the invention of printing, the reformation in religion and the discovery of India and America" (*QR* 19 [1818], 79). And while not closely attentive to the publications under review, his essay consistently assimilated a range of immediate conditions and controversies (factory labor, urbanization, radical protest, savings banks for the poor, sensational newspapers) within a portentous historical framework that led back from a present deterioration of popular morals and public order to the corrosive impact of the English Reformation on an adequate educational provision for the poor.

The postwar era of economic dislocation and popular unrest fostered similar alarm at *Blackwood's*, and the anarchically reckless manner of the magazine's opening numbers was mitigated over the course of the first few years by a gathering nervousness about popular radical protest. Where the second volume launched Lockhart's infamous series "On the Cockney School of Poetry" with a withering notice of the poetry of Leigh Hunt as the reservoir of a "crude, vague, ineffectual, and sour Jacobinism" (*BEM* 2 [1817–1818], 39), ensuing developments on the hustings and in the street seemed to present a more effectual version of the old specter of revolution. The otherwise unremarkable news department, "Domestic Politics," became an increasingly important venue for alarmist observations on national affairs, and it was here that radical parliamentary reform was identified as a program for "subversion, total excision and overthrow, – the substitution, not of one order of polity for another, but an utter destruction of the present state of things" (*BEM* 8 [1820], 329). Yet political events never constrained the formal development of *Blackwood's*, so that its heterogeneous magazine format (quite unlike the ponderous *Quarterly*) continued to accommodate everything from conventional reviews and parliamentary reporting to theatrical notices, fiction, essays, poetry, history, translations, and boxing reports – and perhaps most distinctively, the festive recapitulation of all these discursive strands and more in the fictionalized conversations of the "Noctes Ambrosianae."

Within the contrapuntal magazine order of *Blackwood's* as a whole, a programmatic response to the threat of radical reform ("this crisis") was articulated in "The Warder," a series of linked political commentaries that extended through eight parts from November 1819 to March 1821. The point of departure for the series was the event that became in radical memory the "Peterloo Massacre," when the Manchester yeomanry fired on a huge crowd of perhaps 60,000 reform protesters gathered in St. Peter's Field in August 1819, killing more than ten people and injuring hundreds. In the months that followed, "The Warder" brought the whole structure of extreme conservative feeling into sharp focus through a vivid and uncompromising narrative of "plebeian insolence and profligacy" met with salutary government repression (*BEM* 6 [1819], 208). The periodical emplotment of "The Warder" recapitulated a constitutive tension within *Blackwood's* between heterogeneous local energies and a more comprehensive periodical design. For while the device of a serial department arguably served to contain the impact of radical agitation, a sense of alarm was clearly spilling over into other portions of the magazine. And in a phase of the magazine's development that chastened the freewheeling satirical spirit of the earliest numbers, departments oriented towards the news – "Proceedings of Parliament," "Register," "British Chronicle" – were energized by an alarming present history of the threat of revolution: mass meetings, sporadic outbreaks of violence, reform petitions, radical electioneering, trials for seditious and blasphemous libel, and Cobbett's ongoing production of the *Weekly Political Register* during his self-imposed exile in America. Just as the *Anti-Jacobin* framed its own enterprise in relation to other reviews, so "The Warder" objected to "the base arts, of delusion, concealment, misrepresentation, exaggeration, calumny, and falsehood" by which the Whig and radical press was forging the myth of Peterloo – "the Manchester massacre – the bloody butchery" – from an event that seemed to *Blackwood's* a legitimate and overdue government response to the threat of revolution. "A foreigner, imperfectly acquainted with our language, would have believed from some of the newspapers and gazettes of Manchester, that England was in a civil war, that a great battle had been fought, and that the one army had been totally destroyed" (*BEM* 6 [1819], 336). This corrosive analysis extended from misleading news reports to the underlying radical demand for parliamentary representation that would be responsive to print expressions of public opinion, and in this sense "The Warder" laid bare the political stakes of the wider development of counter-revolutionary periodical expression as a critical review of other periodicals.

PERIODICAL VARIETIES OF ANTI-JACOBINISM

This tension between immediate crisis-oriented intervention and a more sustained periodical development opened out upon the larger paradox of a flexible and enterprising counterrevolutionary defense of established powers. In a world in which a French republican government had provocatively ushered itself in with a new calendar, the "steady onward clocking of homogeneous, empty time" that Benedict Anderson has identified with the form of the daily newspaper was suddenly not quite so homogeneous or empty.[43] Sylvanus Urbanus' congratulatory assessment of an editor's ability to continue publishing "under the fairest and most promising Auspices," despite a revolutionary "new Æra in the History of the World," suggests how a periodical might itself offer a reassuring experience of continuity in difficult times. The resourcefulness with which counterrevolutionary expression moved through a range of formats and intervals of appearance was nowhere more evident than in the array of "anti-Jacobin" titles and compilations that ran from the first introduction of the *Anti-Jacobin; or, Weekly Examiner* in November 1797 through the termination of the *Anti-Jacobin Review* in December 1821. Though not directly related to one another as publishing concerns, these successive projects were aligned in their purposes, and they offer a revealing case study of the way periodical form coordinated a range of critical and political objectives.

To capture the distinctive historical inscription of these print forms, it is worth beginning at the margins of periodical anti-Jacobinism, with a relatively ephemeral title. Through the period of mounting public war-weariness that led up to the Peace of Amiens in March 1802, and the subsequent cessation of hostilities until May 1803, committed anti-Jacobins were left feeling betrayed by their government and by their fellow Britons, while still urging vigilance in the face of enemies at home and abroad. The sense that peace would turn out to be a brief and misguided interruption in a more protracted campaign against revolution informed the appearance in late 1802 of an ambitiously titled annual digest of reactionary letters, *The Spirit of Anti-Jacobinism for 1802: Being a Collection of Essays, Dissertations, and Other Pieces, in Prose and*

Verse, on Subjects Religious, Moral, Political, and Literary; Partly Selected from the Fugitive Publications of the Day, and Partly Original.[44] In gathering a range of otherwise ephemeral material in the permanent form of an annual volume, material that paradoxically embodied and transcended the year of its appearance, *The Spirit of Anti-Jacobinism* assumed a distinctive position within a sequence of dialectically conceived "Anti-Jacobin" periodical enterprises. Much of its content was derived from the monthly *Anti-Jacobin Review*, itself established in 1798 as a way of extending into the terrain of the monthly and quarterly reviews a polemical campaign first waged by the weekly *Anti-Jacobin; or, Weekly Examiner* against the oppositional and reformist daily papers. *The Spirit of Anti-Jacobinism* wasted no time in distinguishing itself from its ancestors by identifying a particular antagonist, styling itself an "antidote" to the "poison" promulgated by *The Spirit of the Public Journals* (*SAJ*, iii), an annual compilation brought out by the notoriously opportunistic and often radical pressman James Ridgway. At the same time underlying continuities in the migration of periodical enterprise through time and format, signaled by the publication of *The Spirit of Anti-Jacobinism* at the "Anti-Jacobin Office, No. 3, Southampton-street, Strand,"[45] were reinforced by a stern insistence upon maintaining the established terms of counterrevolutionary political warfare. "As JACOBINISM has *demolition* for its *object*, and *depravity* for its *means*," the prefatory Advertisement declared, "so is the object of ANTI-Jacobinism *preservation*, and its means *purity*" (*SAJ*, iii). An aspiration to polite letters in *The Spirit of Anti-Jacobinism* was certainly conditioned by the experience of peace, and by a similar disposition of *The Spirit of the Public Journals*, which promised a "selection of the most exquisite essays and jeux d'esprits . . . that appear in the newspapers and other publications."[46] Yet the aim throughout *The Spirit of Anti-Jacobinism* was to remind readers who might be inclined to resort to the pleasures of the imagination during peacetime that there could be no relief from the threat of subversion at home and republican empire abroad.

Any shift in the attention of *The Spirit of Anti-Jacobinism* from the immediate threat of insurrection to subversive efforts "to corrupt the morals, and to vitiate the taste" should be understood as reinforcing and organizing, rather than decisively introducing, a literary and cultural front in the campaign against revolution.[47] As we have already seen, a similar transition was implicit in the 1799 Preface to the second volume of the *Anti-Jacobin Review*, in the treatment of a Jacobinism driven underground and into children's literature by the detection of open conspiracy. The historian Robert Hole has suggested that already by end of the year 1793 the public controversy triggered by the French Revolution was discernibly shifting "from predominantly political, constitutional, philosophical arguments to predominantly social ones of control and social cohesion, of morality, individual belief and restraint."[48] With this in mind, the unfolding sequence of "anti-Jacobin" weekly, monthly, and annual titles – with newspapers, reviews and magazines, and annual compilations successively identified as targets of critical attention – can be understood as an ongoing effort to negotiate existing relations and distinctions within the periodical organization of print culture. To be sure, the sublime terrors of a conspiratorial Jacobinism that insinuated itself into the minds of magazine readers and into the books of their children did generate demands for a seamless campaign against subversion, which would effectively transform the cultural landscape. Yet in practice such aspirations were invariably compromised by, and accommodated to, uneven and haphazard existing conditions. And while the development of periodical forms can certainly assist in tracking the transmission of counterrevolutionary impulses across distinct moral, literary, and cultural registers, it is important to keep in mind the priority that counterrevolutionary activists finally placed upon political stability and social hierarchy: reviews were worth reviewing because they sought "to undermine our civil and religious establishments." It is tempting to assign counterrevolutionary movements a distinctive vocation in the larger historical process (often said to pivot on the romantic period) by which the literary and the aesthetic emerged as discrete categories of human experience, but the record of the conservative periodical reviews is distinctly uneven in this regard. If an anxious attention to the movement of radical subversion through every area of social and cultural life yielded synthetic conceptions, this was typically offset by an analytical tendency to reinforce distinctions by referring matters of taste and aesthetic form back through morality and social structure to their ultimate bearing upon the survival of the established Church and the unreformed constitution.

The first *Anti-Jacobin; or, Weekly Examiner* is instructive for the way it accommodated heterogeneous content to an antagonistic periodical form that closely targeted the existing newspapers press. Commemorated in literary history for the satirical verse of George Canning, John Hookham Frere, George Ellis, and William Gifford, the *Anti-Jacobin* assumed its weekly interval and its critical mission through Gifford's regular editorial commentary on "the Jacobin Daily Papers of the Metropolis," a denomination that included such leading opposition newspapers as the *Morning Chronicle*, the *Morning Post*, and the *Courier* (*AJ* No. 27 [May 14, 1798], 210).[49] A rigorous campaign against any hint of sympathy with France or with domestic radicalism was pursued in three separate weekly sections entitled "Lies," "Misrepresentations," and (more charitably) "Mistakes," each of which was soon subsumed in a comprehensive department, "Weekly Examiner." Just as a weekly period of appearance was dictated by the need to shadow daily newspaper production, so content was organized under these three headings as a vigilant critical practice of reading, reviewing, and contemptuous commentary. "Our Jacobins improve upon us hourly. To exchange the Lie of to-day for that of to-morrow, and call it *correcting*, has long been familiar to them; but to go through this process in the same page of the same Paper, and almost in the same column, is an improvement that must give their Readers a high opinion of their ingenuity; – and still higher of their impudence" (*AJ* No. 7 [December 25, 1797], 50). A mediated orientation towards the news of the day was reinforced by a determination, announced on the masthead of each weekly number, that the project was "To Be Continued Every Monday During the Sitting of Parliament." Here, the corrective representations of the counterrevolutionary press were advanced as a respectful supplement to legitimate parliamentary representation. And in this sense the project was strictly occasional, terminating as promised after less than eight months with the close of the 1797–8 parliamentary session.[50]

At the same time the *Anti-Jacobin* was on its own terms a distinctive coterie production, its brash confidence and recklessly satirical manner the work of a brilliant and energetic group of young men gathered around George Canning, whose experimental handling of periodical form anticipated the later achievement of *Blackwood's Edinburgh Magazine*. Consistency of tone and manner was complicated by an overlapping and interfering set of chronological frameworks – a single meeting of parliament, unfolding weekly commentary on the daily press, the serial appearance of satirical poems across several numbers, and above all else the supervening crisis of a "tremendous Revolution . . . which has confounded all things human and divine" (*AJ* No. 1 [November 20, 1797], 1). As in *Blackwood's*, however, such rifts came to serve the purposes of a freewheeling contrapuntal form. The disparaging purpose of a satirical poem like "The Progress of Man," a burlesque of the primitivism of Richard Payne Knight's *The Progress of Civil Society*, was shrewdly reinforced by virtue of its appearance alongside more reportorial headings: "Foreign Intelligence," "Finance," "Ireland," "Mr. Fox," "Treaty of Pilnitz," "Neutral Navigation," and "Prisoners of War." The thirty six numbers of the *Anti-Jacobin* sold well enough in their first serial appearance to justify several one-volume octavo editions, in which news and parliamentary reporting became retrospection. A sorting process then began in 1799 with *The Beauties of the Anti-Jacobin*, a generous selection of "every article of permanent utility" and "the whole of the excellent poetry."[51] The familiar guise of the project for subsequent generations was the more selective 1799 volume, *Poetry of the Anti-Jacobin*, which went through several editions in these early years, and has since been reprinted throughout the nineteenth and twentieth centuries.[52] If there are distinct aesthetic pleasures to be had in returning to the original periodical sequence, the principles of selection at work in these later iterations of the *Anti-Jacobin* vividly demonstrate the way the content of the paper was unevenly contained by its weekly interval. The patriotic poems and satirical verse assaults on Jacobin optimism, sensibility, and philanthropy were consistent with the savage critical manner of Gifford's "Weekly Examiner," even as they often transected its weekly numbers, and had an enduring impact on British literary culture through the winnowing and reprinting that yielded first "Beauties" of "permanent utility" and then a discrete volume of poetry revealing few traces of the paper's first orientation towards daily newspaper misrepresentation in a single parliamentary session.

While any direct editorial connection between the two major "Anti-Jacobin" periodical titles remains obscure, and may have been concealed, the later monthly *Anti-Jacobin Review and Magazine* was anticipated with a favorable notice in the last number of the weekly *Anti-Jacobin*.[53] And in his Prospectus for the review, the editor John Gifford (a pseudonym for John Richards Green) invoked the example of his predecessors in identifying the new project's distinctive inscription within a periodical order:

The *daily* and *weekly* vehicles of Jacobinism have, for some time past, been subjected to an *examination*, the beneficial effects of which have been universally felt and acknowledged. Our object is to subject its *monthly* and *annual* publications to a similar process; and to those who have attended to the principles and conduct of modern critics, during the course of the last ten years, few arguments will be requisite to demonstrate the utility, and even the necessity, of such an undertaking. That the channels of criticism have long been corrupted; that many of the Reviews have been rendered the mere instruments of faction; that the Reviewers, sinking the critic in the partisan, have insidiously contributed to favour the designs of those writers who labour to undermine our civil and religious establishments . . . is a fact which may easily be established by an attentive perusal of their works since the year 1788. To counteract the pernicious effects of this dangerous SYSTEM, and, by a necessary consequence, to restore criticism to its original standard, will constitute the grand, the prominent feature of the present publication. For this purpose, we shall frequently *review* the *Monthly*, *criticize* the *Critical*, and *analyse* the *Analytical*, *Reviews*, on the principle already adopted by the WEEKLY EXAMINER, in its comments on the daily prints. (*AJ* 1 [1799], 2–3)

The shift in critical attention from "*daily* and *weekly*" to "*monthly* and *annual* publications" contributed to the less unruly contours of this second *Anti-Jacobin*. In comparing the two projects, Emily Lorraine de Montluzin has observed that there was "a refocusing of staff attention away from day-to-day parliamentary politics and toward a comprehensive critical survey of current literature."[54] While "literature" here should be understood in broad terms, as the sum total of every new publication that came under review, some of the historical pressures conditioning a narrower application of the term to imaginative fiction and poetry are visible in the way that verse tends to lie at one end of an implicit spectrum of reviewing content, removed from news reports and political commentary that more closely track the fortunes of Church and state.[55] The major monthly section titled "Original Criticism" was initially comprised of a numbered sequence of reviews, and later reorganized under distinct departments and subheadings, including "Politics," "Divinity," "Political Economy," "Education," "Law," "Poetry," and "Novels and Tales," all followed by a final section of "Miscellanies" to gather up stray matter – police reports, letters, poems and songs, extracts, theatrical notices, descriptions of prints. If there is a haphazard mapping of distinctions within the range of print culture here, the second *Anti-Jacobin* deployed its faculties of critical surveillance in a way that seemed to exclude very little, echoing its predecessor's fierce determination to let no subversive Lie, Misrepresentation, or Mistake pass unnoticed.

Synthetic ambitions that were roughly evident across the *Anti-Jacobin Review*'s various categories of "Original Criticism" were still more emphatically registered in a smaller and more distinctive monthly department titled "The Reviewers Reviewed," identified by the editors as "the most useful, and indeed, the most necessary part of our plan"

(*AJR* 1 [1798], 55). Here, within a hybrid monthly publication that bridged the magazine as miscellany with the review as guide to all new publications, the omnivorous operations of periodical criticism were themselves made the subject of a fluid and mobile form of counter-revolutionary meta-commentary. It was in "The Reviewers Reviewed" that the *Anti-Jacobin* retrospectively assessed Thomas Paine's *Age of Reason* by way of its reception, undertaking to show through detailed extracts how "the publication of this *malignant and blasphemous* pamphlet furnished the Editors of three Reviews with an opportunity of manifesting their religious and moral tenets," which ranged from Deism at the *Monthly* and Unitarianism at the *Critical* to the more outrageously "irreligious trash" of the *Analytical Review* (*AJR* 3 [1799], 338–41). A first-order critical response was not excluded from this department, since the editors explained that they would sometimes "begin by analyzing the work ourselves, in a manner that might entitle it to be placed under the head of 'Original Criticism,'" before advancing to a notice of "the observations of the Reviewers on the same." The result was "to blend original criticism with our comments on the criticism of others" (*AJR* 1 [1798], 62), often with vertiginous effect, as secondary transgressions escalated an initial sense of outrage. Over time, "The Reviewers Reviewed" became a forum for letters from outraged former readers of other reviews, and there were even letters from authors seeking redress from the abuse they had suffered in other periodicals. And as "The Reviewers Reviewed" became embroiled in ongoing public controversies, the work of criticism grew more intertextually embedded. For example, an 1802 translation of Juvenal's satires by William Gifford, veteran of the first *Anti-Jacobin* and future editor of the *Quarterly Review*, was first assessed by way of a negative notice in the *Critical Review*, which made an issue of the translator's ministerial connections; the matter was picked up in the next volume with a densely mediated review of Gifford's pamphlet response to his reviewers, *An Examination of the Strictures of the Critical Reviewers on the Translation of Juvenal*, and then again several volumes later with an account of Gifford's supplement to his first pamphlet *Examination* and a survey of further responses.[56] While there was little in the monthly *Anti-Jacobin Review* to match the slashing brilliance of its weekly predecessor, the most vigorous and distinctive writing did appear in "The Reviewers Reviewed," fuelled by a relish for controversy and a withering contempt for subversive political principles and literary taste. A sober concern for the importance of the critical work done in this department tended to dictate against any recognition of the potential absurdities of periodical meta-commentary. One rare exception to this rule came from a correspondent, who composed a "serio-comic" letter "to the Most Learned, the Most Loyal, and Most Orthodox, My Lords Anti-Jacobins, in Their High Court of Criticism Most Illustriously Assembled," seeking redress from abuse in other quarters: "The Anti-Jacobins being judges *en dernier resort*, (for who shall review the Reviewing Reviewers?), have a right to be addressed as peers of the realm of – CRITICISM" (*AJR* 20 [1805], 309).

That reviews of other reviews and periodicals were a common feature of "anti-Jacobin" critical practice did not prevent later editors and reviewers from making the case for the special urgency and even the novelty of their enterprise. From *Blagdon's Political Register* in 1809 through *The Gridiron; or, Cook's Weekly Register* in 1822, a series of anti-radical weeklies offered grim assessments of the revolutionary consequences that would immediately follow if the weekly sedition being promulgated by Cobbett, William Hone, T.J. Wooler, and Richard Carlile was not regularly detected and refuted. When *Blackwood's* was launched in 1817 with a department entitled "Periodical Works," devoted to regular notices "of the articles contained in the most celebrated periodical publications" as well as "a list of the contents of the minor journals," the editors claimed never to have "seen any attempt of the kind made, or at least persevered in, either by their predecessors or contemporaries."[57] Nor did they themselves persevere, though once the department itself lapsed the impulse to include critical reviews within the scope of reviewing was picked up in the "Timothy Tickler" papers, and in a range of articles and notices: "Strictures on the Edinburgh Review," "Remarks on the Quarterly Review," "Remarks on the Periodical Criticism of England," and "Reflections Occasioned by Some Late Sins of the Public Prints."[58] Although *Blackwood's* set out on its maverick course by characterizing the editor of the *Quarterly* as "a mighty bigot, both in religion and politics" (*BEM* 2 [1817–18], 673), a gathering sense of alarm at radical protest contributed to a hardening of the magazine's political outlook. The relatively neutral summary of the major reviews in its early "Periodical Works" department gave way to a more concerted assault on the *Edinburgh Review* for betraying the standards of legitimate opposition by colluding with skepticism, infidelity, and subversion. This line of attack on its northern neighbor culminated in late 1818 and 1819 in such articles as John Wilson's tendentiously titled, "Is the Edinburgh Review a Religious and Patriotic Work?"[59] If news departments and "The Warder" series worked imperfectly to contain the threat of popular radical protest, the assault on the *Edinburgh* as "an infidel review" (*BEM* 3 [1818], 36) was manifestly everywhere at once, and helped set the political tone of the magazine in these years. Even the series "On the Cockney School of Poetry" derived from the contest with the *Edinburgh Review*, as Lockhart first took offense at William Hazlitt's favorable treatment of Leigh Hunt's poetry in the pages of the *Edinburgh*: "Mr. Jeffrey does ill, when he delegates his important functions into such hands as those of Mr. Hazlitt. It was chiefly in consequence of that gentleman's allowing Leigh Hunt to pass unpunished through a scene of slaughter, which his execution might so highly have graced, that we came to the resolution of laying before our readers a series of essays on *the Cockney School*" (*BEM* 2 [1817–18], 41).[60] In this sense, a celebrated case of romantic literary reception was itself an episode in the counterrevolutionary history of reviewing the reviews.

There were of course longstanding precedents for conceiving periodical expression in terms of literary or social oversight. The canonical emergence of the eighteenth-century periodical essay was governed by the visual idiom of the literary Spectator, Observator, and Examiner, as well as by the more disciplinary figures of the Monitor and Censor.[61] A decade before the establishment of *The Anti-Jacobin*, while he was still a student at Eton, George Canning participated in a weekly satirical paper modeled on *The Spectator*.[62] Yet earlier instances of the periodical figure of observation were often calculated to signal leisure and detached perspective. What distinguished counterrevolutionary periodical surveillance in this period was not only its more systematic and coercive nature, the *Quarterly*'s "regular inspection of a strict literary police" (*QR* 2 [1809], 146), but also the catastrophic consequences that were felt to result from any neglect or perversion of the critical enterprise. Rather than simply review Mary Hays' *The Victim of Prejudice* on its first appearance in 1796, the *Anti-Jacobin Review* devoted the lead article of "The Reviewers Reviewed" to a coordinated treatment by the Rev. William Heath of the critical reception of the novel and of Hays' earlier fiction, *Memoirs of Emma Courtney* (1796). Setting out from the *Monthly Review*'s claim that *Emma Courtney* distinguished itself from "vulgar novels" of the day by transcending "an irksome attention to the daily occurrences and trivial incidents of real life," Heath insisted that this domestic attention was precisely what "nature, situation, and sex" assigned to "the female mind."[63] He found even less to like in the suggestion that Hays raised sincere feeling above "common *delicacies and hypocrisies*," and responded with a full-scale assault on female radical sensibility:

Setting aside this slang of modern philosophy, the plain question is – whether it is most for the advantage of society that women should be so brought up as to make them dutiful daughters, affectionate wives, tender mothers, and good Christians, or, by a corrupt and vicious system of education, fit them for revolutionary agents, for heroines, for Staels, for Talliens, for Stones, setting aside all the decencies, the softness, the gentleness, of the female character, and enjoying indiscriminately every envied privilege of man? (*AJR* 3 [1799] 54–5)

That two scant extracts from the *Monthly Review* could lead directly to the specter of British women become "revolutionary agents" was evidence of the extent to which counterrevolutionary reviewers conceived subversion as a conspiracy of authors and reviewers.

Of course the savageness of this review had everything to do with Hay's notoriety as a Dissenting controversialist on matters of education and women's rights, and with the unleashing of female sensibility and sexual desire in her novels. Yet the coordinated critical treatment of the work of another reviewer should not be considered secondary or derivative. The saturation effect created by the successive accumulation of weekly, monthly, and annual anti-Jacobin titles unfolded within a horizon of political expectations that treated periodical range and frequency as powerful elements of political control. Radical ambitions and conservative anxieties took shape within a self-reinforcing framework of periodical reception, in which the next month's court scandal, the next week's mass meeting, or the next day's military defeat or victory might turn the tide in a potentially catastrophic struggle. This exaggerated climate of political expectation informed the periodical enterprises of radical editors and publishers from Thomas Spence, Daniel Isaac Eaton, and John Thelwall to William Cobbett, John and Leigh Hunt, T.J. Wooler, and Richard Carlile. Yet it was Edmund Burke in his 1791 *Thoughts on French Affairs* who first decisively theorized periodical frequency as a precondition for Jacobin revolution, in a discussion of the newspaper press that serves as a formal elaboration of his earlier and more general theory in the *Reflections* of the rise of "the political Men of Letters" as a discontented French cabal:

What direction the French spirit of proselytism is likely to take, and in what order it is likely to prevail in the several parts of Europe, it is not easy to determine. The seeds are sown almost every where, chiefly by newspaper circulations, infinitely more efficacious and extensive than ever they were. And they are a more important instrument than generally is imagined. They are a part of the reading of all, they are the whole of the reading of a great number . . . The writers of these papers indeed, for the greater part, are either unknown or in contempt, but they are like a battery in which the stroke of any one ball produces no great effect, but the amount of continual repetition is decisive. Let us only suffer any person to tell us his story, morning and evening, but for one twelvemonth, and he will become our master.[64]

As this anxiety about opportunistic writers using periodical forms to shape malleable readers spilled over beyond the newspaper press, it became a persistent theme of counterrevolutionary argument, nowhere more clearly than in the periodical press. It resurfaced in *Blackwood's* in John Gibson Lockhart's claim that "the periodical press of England is, for the most part, fed by men vulgar in birth, in habits, and in education – needy adventurers – shallow, superficial, coxcombs – puny creatures," but dangerous creatures nonetheless because they were no more attached to principle than to land or status, and because their claims quickly passed into commonplace: "The lie that we read with a shudder to-day, is repeated to-morrow and to-morrow, for weeks, for months and for years, till the eye and the mind learn to glance over it with unconcern" (*BEM* 4 [1818–19], 355). It was evident too in Southey's *Quarterly Review* account of the impact of the radical press upon tavern and factory reading audiences, an account that implicitly referred back to Burke's notorious "swinish multitude" through Thomas Spence's radical periodical of 1793–5, *Pig's Meat*: "The lessons are repeated day after day, and week after week. If madder be administered to a pig only for a few days, his bones are reddened with its dye; and can we believe that the bloody colouring of such 'pig's meat' as this will not find its way into the system of those who take it for daily food?" (*QR* 8 [1812], 342).[65] Southey was easily the most insistent theorist of periodical hegemony in the early decades of the nineteenth century, and his expansiveness and figural extravagance when set upon this topic exposes a consistent irony about the way conservatives assigned incalculable effects to periodical discourse precisely because it arrested, through its routine production and habitual reception, the reader's normal defensive faculties of calculation. As Lockhart put it, "newspapers are not studied, they are simply read" (*BEM* 4 [1818–19], 355). In this sense, radical periodicals stimulated the counterrevolutionary imagination and generated antithetical forms because they were found to be, as Burke put it, "a more important instrument than generally is imagined."

As if to confirm the pivotal importance of a theory of periodical subversion to the development of counterrevolutionary reviewing, the entire seminal passage on "newspaper circulations" from *Thoughts on French Affairs* was reprinted in the first issue of the *Anti-Jacobin Review*, immediately after the headnote launching "The Reviewers Reviewed" as "the most necessary part of our plan." Curiously, though, the authority of Burke was invoked as part of an evasive and even playful internal dialogue, more appropriate to the coterie sensibilities of *Blackwood's* than the doggedly partisan *Anti-Jacobin Review*. Having announced an original intention "to prefix some remarks to this division of our work," the editors went on to explain that the intended preface was rendered superfluous by the reception of a letter from an "intelligent friend" adequately explaining the need to subject criticism to critical oversight. Signing himself "Metellus," this friend was in fact the Reverend John Brand, soon to become a regular contributor to "The Reviewers Reviewed" department of the *Anti-Jacobin Review*, and introduced here as a partner in an earlier scheme for an anti-Jacobin newspaper, said to have been abandoned only when its aims were successfully taken up by Canning and his collaborators (*AJR* 1 [1798], 55). Under the title "Prefatory Observations on Reviewers," Brand's letter was serially published over the course of the first four numbers, serving as an extended introduction to the meta-reviewing department within which it was contained. And it was in making the case for a regular "critical examination" of "the monthly publications of the opposition" that Brand himself applied the "reasoning of Mr. BURKE" to the critical reviews: "It is thus the principles of a popular Review will form those of the populace of readers" (*AJR* 1 [1798], 58).

The social conditions for this anxiety about efficient periodical subversion are familiar from other dimensions of conservative discourse, and from our own histories of literacy and print culture: the rise of the lending library and the Sunday school movement, the feminization and popularization of authorship and reading, the commercialization of publishing, and the application of longstanding popular habits of shared reception and reading aloud to radical organization. As "The Reviewers Reviewed" suggests, periodical reviews were felt to be a privileged point from which to intervene in this expanding network of social and material relations, but the work of intervention could not end with critical pronouncements on the printed page. In a 1798 notice under the heading, "Book Clubs," the *Anti-Jacobin Review* claimed that the book clubs of the disaffected middle-class fell just short of "the mischievous exertions of the Corresponding Society" in their capacity to undermine the constitution. The notice then went on to argue that radical and oppositional reviews were pivotal in the activities of such clubs: "Few publications are purchased until the lords paramount of literature, the Reviewers, have fixed on them the seal of their approbation" (*AJR* 1 [1798], 473, 475). The skeptical spirit governing the rise of a polite and sociable culture of reading and enquiry over the course of the eighteenth century had allowed infidelity to infect the taste and opinions of the "ministers of the established church," and it was here that the meta-critical practices of a High Church review could become something more than a readerly exercise. The *Anti-Jacobin* drew "the attention of all clergymen, who are members of Book Clubs" to the usefulness of its "Reviewers Reviewed" department in renovating the tenor of polite society: "We must express a hope, that after our exposure of the profligacy of the *Jacobin Reviews*, they will never henceforth be referred to as *authority*, in matters of religion or politics" (*AJR* 1 [1798], 475). Attended with ominous reports of subversive reading societies in Lincolnshire and the north of England, the core of the "Book Club" notice was a reprinted paper, "Hints for the Prospectus of the Plan of the proposed Book Society, in Maidstone, and its Vicinity," that was presented as a template for the formation of similar associations throughout provincial cities and the countryside. Loyal gentry and Anglican clergy were enjoined to recover their traditional ascendancy by directing the book club enterprise, first purging their own ranks through "a strict scrutiny" of "the religious and political principles of every person proposed as a member," then turning to their inferiors, and exercising "a peculiar degree of vigilance in attending to the publications that are circulated, by means of subscription, among the lower class of people; tradesmen, labourers, and artisans" (*AJR* 1 [1798], 473-7). While loyalist book clubs and reading societies of this kind were a feature of anti-radical mobilization in this period, they achieved nothing like the coordinated efficiency and seamless extension envisioned by the *Anti-Jacobin Review*. What such schemes confirm is that counterrevolutionary reviewing did not imagine that its work could be fulfilled as an abstract transaction between reader and writer over matters of individual preference or taste.

The practical and worldly critical orientation that motivated this kind of recruitment scheme was evident too in the relentlessly antagonistic aims of these periodicals. If the "anti-Jacobin" sequence was paradigmatic, other mastheads and title pages bristled with similarly antithetical conceptions – anti-infidel, antileveler, anti-Gallican, anti-Cobbett – and prefaces, prospectuses, and introductions worked through a shared lexicon of counter-conspiracy: "contradict," "combat," "refute," "antidote," "exposure," "counteract."[66] The constitutive relationship between the first *Anti-Jacobin* and the opposition daily press, and between the second *Anti-Jacobin Review* and the major Whig and Dissenting reviews, returned in the era of anti-Cobbetting, and then again with the establishment of the *Quarterly Review* and *Blackwood's Edinburgh Magazine* as responses to the ascendancy of the *Edinburgh Review*. If antithetical design is a common feature of the politics of literature in any era, its development in these periodicals involved distinctive counterrevolutionary assumptions. A subversive conception of the enemy yielded a dialectic that was not disposed to negotiation or resolution. Returning to the language of the *Anti-Jacobin Review*, this was not a contest "between two opposite parties," but rather "between property and no property, law and no law, justice and no justice, government and no government." *Blackwood's* envisioned a similar struggle, insisting that the skepticism and French sympathies of the *Edinburgh* had undermined its credibility as an organ of legitimate opposition, in ways that precisely mirrored a shift from "moderation" to "sedition" in the conduct of the Whig party.[67] Of course this kind of argument was itself a common enough feature of partisan pleading, but when guided by conservative assumptions that the monarchy, the Church, and the unreformed parliament comprised a political order that could bear no compromise, the tendency to conceive political controversy in catastrophic terms should not simply be dismissed as a cynical Tory effort to discredit the Whig competition by association with phantom conspiracies.

Another feature of the antithetical design of counterrevolutionary periodicals was a sense that disaffection was somehow the prevailing and even inherent disposition of the periodical press. In assessing its campaign against the daily newspapers in a July 1798 closing address to its readers, the first weekly *Anti-Jacobin* claimed some success but insisted that print subversion was by no means put to rest. "The nature of a Jacobin is restless," and with revolutionary designs exposed, the next step would be a campaign of "fallacies and lies": "For this purpose, the Press was engaged, and almost monopolized in all its branches: Reviews, Registers, Monthly Magazines, and Morning and Evening Prints sprung forth in abundance" (*AJ* No. 36 [July 9, 1798], 281). The *Anti-Jacobin Review* developed a similar case in a scathing "Reviewers Reviewed" notice of the generous reception afforded by the monthly *Critical Review* to the *New Annual Register* for 1793. Both titles, the reviewer observed, issued from the publishing and book-selling operations of George Robinson, who was also responsible for the works of William Godwin and Mary Hays and had actually been convicted for distributing the second part of Paine's *Rights of Man*. Such a notorious instance readily yielded a general theory of print dis-affection: "It is a political and religious truth, that the members of a state disaffected to the government, and the sectaries in religion that are enemies to the establishment, are always more active, virulent, and indefatigable, in the cause they espouse, than the persons constituting the majority of the people, or those that are invested with power" (*AJR* 3 [1799], 461–2).[68]

The irony of these concerns about the inherent disaffection of the press was that they were expressed in periodicals that were conceived in antagonistic terms. Despite a refusal to negotiate political terms, the counterrevolutionary critical reviews were inherently dialectical forms, brought into being by a dynamic interplay of antagonisms and affiliations, of critical and reconstructive aims. If their fierce commit-ment to the perfection of the unreformed British constitution reveals a kind of utopian impulse, so too does their unwavering faith in the renovating potential of a politics of resistance, exercised through a relentless critical parsing of subversion. In this sense counter-revolutionary periodical forms seem to move in two directions at once, driven to fierce critical negation as the only way to counteract the spread of subversion and infidelity, but opening out simultaneously onto a fantastic critical conversation that promises to restore social stability, loyalty, and piety by repairing the politics of literary trans-mission. At times, the competing impulses were explicitly worked through in a sequential fashion, with critical dissolution yielding creative reconstruction, as in the book club scheme of the *Anti-Jacobin Review*: "Where disaffected men are actually members, let the club be dissolved, and a new one formed" (*AJR* 1 [1798], 475). Systematically organized in this way, local book societies promised to restore the ascendancy of the clergy and gentry over the lower orders on a national scale. Striking evidence of the utopian impulse running through a welter of political antagonisms was the counterrevolutionary desire to preserve and sustain elements of print culture that were at risk of being lost to history, a desire that vividly frames the essential "conservative" dilemma with respect to print culture: how an active present campaign could prepare the future to receive the past. In a frankly promotional notice of one of its own publications, the *Anti-Jacobin Review* suggested that the distinctive annual "design" of *The Spirit of Anti-Jacobinism for 1802* originated in a "desire of rescuing from oblivion many pieces of merit which appear in the fugitive publications of the day" (*AJR* 12 [1802], 131–3). Ironically, this particular rescue mission turned out to be short-lived, as "permanent utility" eluded the new project: the monumental *Spirit of Anti-Jacobinism* did not survive its inaugural year, while the *Anti-Jacobin Review* continued for nearly two decades to go about its more "fugitive" monthly business.

Just as the successive sifting out of "beauties" from the weekly numbers of the first *Anti-Jacobin* left a single volume of poetry, so *The Spirit of Anti-Jacobinism* proceeded from a conventional sense of verse as a privileged site for literary merit that exceeded periodical oblivion. Yet beyond this there was little concern for any hierarchy of aesthetic content: epigrams, acrostics, satirical squibs, and pseudo-popular songs were gathered within the pages of the annual volume alongside more ambitious odes, "heroic" verse, an imitation of Martial, and a Spenserian "Vision of Liberty" (*SAJ*, 291, 355). In prose, the belletristic cast of the volume was achieved through a host of polite essays on literary, aesthetic, and philosophical topics. These included a series "On Literary Composition" reprinted from the daily *Public Advertiser*, surveying the achievement of late eighteenth-century letters and attacking its skeptical dimensions; a defense of the principles of "nature and truth" in landscape design and appreciation, as evinced in William Mason's anti-picturesque didactic poem, "The English Garden" (1772–82), rather than "the spirit of innovation, the aversion to authority, the jealousy of a high reputation" found in the upstart "democratic" theories of Richard Payne Knight and Uvedale Price (*SAJ*, 278, 291);[69] and elementary political essays on topics ranging from "Natural Rights" and "Liberty and Slavery" to "Equality" and "Religious Establishments," all opposed to reform, though to some extent relieved of the intense polemic that characterized weekly and monthly anti-Jacobin expression. While a mitigation of political urgency in peacetime certainly informed the volume's aesthetic cast, the point was to insure that leisure and pleasure contributed to the national vigor that would be required when conflict resumed. Insofar as *The Spirit of Anti-Jacobinism* possessed a topical periodical plot, it was to be found in a series of prose and verse reflections on the dangers of national complacency during a "premature and dishonourable Peace" (*SAJ*, 391). This may help account for the project's failure to survive its first year. The comparative ease of the volume's miscellaneous full title – "Being a Collection of Essays, Dissertations, and Other Pieces, in Prose and Verse, on Subjects Religious, Moral, Political and Literary; Partly selected from the Fugitive Publications of the Day, and partly original" – hardly accorded with the aggressive "Spirit" of periodical anti-Jacobinism.

Yet it would be easy to exaggerate the distinctiveness of *The Spirit of Anti-Jacobinism*. After all, polite literary content was largely drawn from other conservative periodicals, where it first appeared in a more miscellaneous framework of news, commentary, and reviewing. Other conservative literary annuals did achieve longer runs, though sustained success remained elusive. In conceiving his *Flowers of Literature* (1801–9) as a "useful, instructive, and amusing repository of the *Belles Lettres*" or "*Annual Register of Literature*," Francis Blagdon did not allow belletristic aspirations to preclude vigorous attacks on "the haughty insolence of an invading foe" and on the "spirit of insubordination and revolutionizing propensity, which prevails in modern times."[70] And of course the first *Anti-Jacobin* weekly had established the prototype for a mixed campaign against subversion, resting on verse satire as well as prose commentary. In this respect, unsettling conjunctions in *The Spirit of Anti-Jacobinism* – between politics and letters, politeness and partisanship, "*preservation*" and improvisation, patriotic fervor and wounded national feeling – can be considered broadly characteristic of counterrevolutionary expression. Indeed, in its laudatory notice, the *Anti-Jacobin Review* reprinted the volume's entire prefatory Advertisement and particularly recommended the exemplary definition of Jacobinism it contained. If the reviewer's gesture is narrowly self-promotional, the extract itself is remarkably expansive. A prefatory anatomy of Jacobinism for the year 1802 contains, in dialectical fashion, the entire justification for a counterrevolutionary mobilization that extended beyond narrow constitutional concerns into "religious, moral, political, and literary" topics:

JACOBINISM, then, is not merely a political, but an anti-social monster, which, in pursuit of its prey, alternately employs fraud and force. It first seduces by its arts, then subdues by its arms. For the accomplishment of its object it leaves no means unemployed which the deep malevolence of its native sagacity can devise. It pervades every department of literature and insinuates itself into every branch of science. Corruption is its food, profligacy its recreation, and demolition the motive of its actions, and the business of its life – This "foul fiend" flourished both in France and Germany long before it received its present appellation. Its hideous features may be plainly discovered, and will be easily recognized, in the multifarious works, profound and superficial, serious and comic, historical and scientific, in the poetry and prose, of the numerous philosophists who deluged both countries with their publications, during the latter half of the last century. Its perseverance is only to be exceeded by its malice. And, at no period, were its progress and its influence more to be dreaded, for reasons too obvious to require a specification, than at the present. Consequently never were the efforts of ANTI-JACOBINISM more necessary to check that progress and to counteract that influence. To this object and to this end, will the vigilance and care of the Editor of the *Spirit of Anti-Jacobinism* be invariably directed; most anxious to preserve the religious and civil establishments of his country, with the character of his countrymen for purity of taste, depth of knowledge, correctness of judgment, and integrity of mind. (*SAJ*, iv)

Present necessities aside, the subversive shift from "arms" to "arts" was endlessly perceived and repeated throughout the period. And again, analysis here seems to move in two directions at once, with operative distinctions (literature and science, poetry and prose) taking shape within the framework of a single overriding critical project, comprehensive in its scope, and conceived less as a way of recovering some original condition than as a necessary response to an enemy that insidiously "pervades every department of literature and insinuates itself into every branch of science."

The activation of taste and judgment within a protracted revolution controversy itself serves as a forceful reminder that conservative movements contributed actively and constructively to the historical development of the cultural field in the early nineteenth century. And yet it must be admitted that anti-Jacobin critical discourse insisted upon limits to that contribution. The sheer range and miscellaneousness of the idiom applied to Jacobinism in the passage just quoted and in the rest of the prefatory Advertisement seems to defy clear organization: key terms and distinctions include "morals," "taste," "information," "amusement," "instruction," "knowledge," "judgment," "serious and comic," "historical and scientific," "literature" and "science," "poetry and prose" (*SAJ*, iii–iv). And the willingness of *The Spirit of Anti-Jacobinism* to trace its own enterprise to Jacobin incursions into "every department of literature" and "every branch of science" betrays a broader counterrevolutionary tendency to treat critical practices as negative ("to counteract") or corrective ("to preserve"), and to blame revolutionary movements for introducing politics into matters of taste and judgment. In an 1822 *Quarterly Review* essay on

William Hazlitt's *Table Talk*, John Matthews held Hazlitt's digressive radical style responsible for his own digressive tribute to William Pitt as the "illustrious statesman" who saved Britain "from the designs of Jacobins, Spenceans, [and] Radicals." The elliptical and unpredictable movements of the *Table Talk* essays demonstrated "the truth of a remark often made, that the disciples of the Radical School lose no opportunity of insinuating their poison into all sorts of subjects; a drama, a novel, a poem, an essay, or a school-book is in their hands an equally convenient vehicle" (*QR* 26 [1822], 104). The endlessly repeated event of a shift from revolutionary arms to arts tended to reinforce the same argument. Like the earlier *Anti-Jacobin Review* and the later *Quarterly Review, The Spirit of Anti-Jacobinism* claimed to be reacting to radical initiative when it knit together a range of idioms and materials in order to combat a dangerous national feeling that the threat of revolution was "nearly extinguished": "Our only hope . . . is not in supposing Jacobinism to be destroyed, but in being convinced it is more powerful, more extended, more dangerous both in its views and means, than ever" (*SAJ* 409, 412). The intensity of this conviction meant that the arts, subversive or otherwise, were typically approached as a matter of practical political efficacy.[71] A routine recourse to politics insured that periodical anti-Jacobinism remained a mixed, flexible, and opportunistic discourse, its habits of retrospection mitigated by present necessities, and its nostalgia for an untainted cultural inheritance qualified by the conviction that a revolutionary crisis had been prepared by a century of creeping skepticism and infidelity.

The "Prefatory Address to the Reader" in the first volume of the *Anti-Jacobin Review* offers a vivid glimpse of the combination of immediate critical and editorial resourcefulness and overarching political intransigence that fuelled counterrevolutionary periodical expression. In reaffirming a core commitment to "religion, morality, and social order, as supported by the existing establishments, ecclesiastical and civil of this country," the editors treated those establishments as preordained, through a (barely) qualified adherence to "the *Divine Right*, or rather, *Divine Origin* of GOVERNMENT" (*AJR* 1 [1798], iv, vi) that would have been controversial even among opponents of reform. The terrain of print was evidently more fluid and open to intervention, and in undertaking a potentially compromised address to readers as political agents the editors moved easily across a range of legitimating assumptions and affiliations, from promotional appeals to their own rising circulation figures (over three thousand copies per month), to the "marked approbation" of "some of the most distinguished ornaments of the Established Church, and of the first Legal Characters in the country," to the redundant antagonism evident in a commitment by the review to withstand "the determined hostility of those whose principles and whose efforts it was its avowed object to combat and counteract" (*AJR* 1 [1798], i, iii–iv). This eclecticism suggests that counterrevolutionary periodical expression was to some extent licensed by its resistance to radical assumptions about the close relationship between print culture, public opinion, and political reform: since government derived its authority from God, the supporters of government in the press were free to proceed in any manner that seemed effective. And after just six months of work the editors of the *Anti-Jacobin Review* were prepared to take credit for substantial effects, including the demise of the *Analytical Review*, and a more moderate tone at the *Monthly* and *Critical* reviews (*AJR* 1 [1798], iv–v, vi). Yet where shifting circulation figures and editorial dispositions indicated a dynamic understanding of print culture and critical exchange, political impact was carefully construed in terms that avoided any suggestion that British public opinion had to be argued into its attachment to established institutions. The success of the *Anti-Jacobin Review* "clearly demonstrates, not so much, indeed, the improvement or melioration of the public mind, as the existence of an innate rooted attachment to sound principles, religious and political, which only requires to be called forth, in order to shine with transcendent luster, to bear down all resistance, and to establish its triumph over *every* foe" (*AJR* 1 [1798], ii). At the same time, editorial self-promotion did not mitigate the need for repressive state action: already in this first volume the *Anti-Jacobin Review* was urging legal action against radical clubs in London and endorsing sedition charges occasioned by Gilbert Wakefield's 1798 pamphlet, *A Reply to Some Parts of the Bishop of Landaff's Address to the People of Great Britain* (*AJR* 1 [1798], 83–6, 478). From a liberal perspective, the willingness to consider state repression the appropriate fulfillment of critical procedure is as inconsistent as it is deplorable. Yet the collaborative premises underlying the interpenetration of counterrevolutionary print expression, civic association, and criminal prosecution have long figured in the history of the political public sphere and its literary institutions. To acknowledge this is to resist our own tendency, as nominal heirs of critical traditions of independence and disinterestedness, to treat state influence as an aberration or corruption of the normal course of historical development.

Revising Terry Eagleton's decisive declaration that "modern European criticism was born of a struggle against the absolutist state,"[72] the print culture of anti-Jacobinism reminds us that critical institutions emerged with equal vigor and determination on both sides of an ongoing debate over the legitimacy of the old regime in Britain.

IMAGINED SOCIABILITY

A willingness to cultivate loyalist book clubs while also encouraging "the due administration of police" (*AJR* 1 [1798], 478) suggests some of the ways in which the work of counterrevolutionary criticism was fulfilled beyond the printed page. In this respect the radical challenge was as compelling as it was disturbing, particularly through the heady post-war years, when the unstamped weeklies of Cobbett, Wooler, and Hone became vividly social print forms, shaping even as they were shaped by the ongoing development of parliamentary election campaigns, mass meetings, political clubs, and subscription and petition drives. If counterrevolutionary periodicals were more circumspect about figuring forth a worldly supplement to their own work of writing and publishing, this was in part because they considered the promiscuous activation of public opinion to be an erosion of legitimate constitutional procedures. In this sense, reports of parliamentary debates can be considered a preeminent loyalist counterpart to radical treatments of extra-parliamentary organization, and Robert Southey went so far as to argue that even parliamentary reporting was a democratic innovation that served to justify countervailing ministerial practices of political influence.[73] Beyond a direct periodical representation of parliamentary proceedings, there were clear efforts to manage the sociable energies of the public sphere. The *Anti-Jacobin Review* provided limited space for correspondence in its "Miscellanies" department, though it clearly preferred (or contrived) letters that opened upon civic enterprise as a direct fulfillment of editorial policy. So for example in 1799 "Clericus" picked up on the book club schemes of the first volume of the *Anti-Jacobin Review* when he narrated the exemplary history of a local reading club of Anglican clergymen, who had cause to regret the "liberal reception" they once afforded the *Monthly Review* and therefore resolved to rely exclusively on the *Anti-Jacobin* and the *British Critic* in selecting books for their collection. The letter made it clear that clerical readers were exemplary because their "sphere of action" offered "opportunities of rendering extraordinary service to the general cause of the establishment" within an established framework of hierarchical social relations, particularly where "fortifying the minds" of the lower orders against infidelity was concerned (*AJR* 3 [1799], 79–81).[74]

While an overriding commitment to the conventional review format in the *Anti-Jacobin Review* limited this kind of representation, other counterrevolutionary periodicals achieved greater flexibility, though not always with clear success. In the winter of 1810, George Manners devoted a substantial portion of his loyalist miscellany, *The Satirist, or Monthly Meteor* (1807–14), to the wave of criminal proceedings against radical journalists and leaders, to the point where regular updates required a new department, ominously titled "Newgate."[75] If the dominant tone was that of withering contempt, there was room for festive satire as well. An underlying conservative ambivalence about public opinion was vividly dramatized when *The Satirist* delivered a savagely burlesque account of a public debate in which Manners and his periodical were impugned at the British Forum, the notorious Poland Street debating club of John Gale Jones.[76] Published as a letter to the editor, "The Satirist and the Debaters" worked to contain the grotesque spectacle of "incoherent" radical oratory and "violent" democratic applause within a secure epistolary frame. The breezy familiarity with which the fictional correspondent, "Cives," addressed "Mr. Satirist" effectively defused any real concern about the force of radical deliberation, even as it modeled a more privileged and confident manner of social exchange: "It is all over with you, friend Sat; you may shut up shop, and go to sleep: The Privy Council of the British Forum have ordered that an embargo be laid on your wit" (*S* 7 [1810], 273). Yet in actual fact, the hazards of *The Satirist*'s reckless and multivalent style of loyalist attack were brought home when the radical Irish pressman Peter Finnerty successfully prosecuted *The Satirist* for libel, an event that precipitated the sale of the paper and a dramatic moderation of its tone.[77]

By contrast William Roberts developed a restrained strategy of detached observation in *The Looker-On*, a deliberately modest and nostalgic weekly periodical essay and miscellany of 1792 and 1793. The announced aim was to align the model of polite literary intercourse and reflection established by Addison and Steele with a politically stabilizing preference for "ancient and prescriptive rules" over pretended "modern discoveries in morals" (*LO* 1: x).[78] But Roberts wound up staging with an almost allegorical precision the historical pressures brought to bear upon periodical sociability in an age of revolution and counterrevolution. For nearly a year the diligent weekly effort of the Reverend Simon Olive-Branch of Northamptonshire, Roberts' moderately Evangelical alter ego, to breathe some life into residual literary sociability played itself out through an innocuous (if tedious) portion of occasional verse, fictional correspondence, club meeting reports, and essays on such topics as the uses of solitude and the pleasures of country life, sharpened from time to time by faint attacks on Paine and Wollstonecraft. But the acute pressure of "Revolutions, Regenerations, and Conventions" (*LO* 2: 173) suddenly broke in upon the project in the first week of 1793 with the appearance of the thirty-seventh number. The retiring persona and rural sociability of the essayist was abruptly dissolved, so that the entire periodical "design" could be enlisted instead in a more urgent and actual public correspondence over the course of four weeks with John Reeves' newly constituted London Association for Preserving Liberty and Property against Republicans and Levellers (*LO*, 2: 126–8, 158). The probative authority of conventional periodical correspondence turned out to be inadequate to the threat of revolution. While *The Looker-On* soon reverted to its original format and played out its nostalgic purposes for the rest of the year, the brief eruption within its pages of an emerging national network of loyalist association during a memorable winter of alarm remained its most striking episode.

If Roberts' method of imitating past models under unfavorable present conditions brought to an end one line of periodical development,[79] the collaboratively edited *Blackwood's Edinburgh Magazine* achieved a more compelling supplement of quasi-fictional sociability by building instead on the coterie sensibilities of the hybrid *Anti-Jacobin* weekly. In September 1819 *Blackwood's* assembled more than its usual range of miscellaneous material – with contributions from Lockhart, John Wilson, and Archibald Alison, and poetry, songs, and toasts in addition to essays, lectures, speeches, and correspondence – within an original narrative framework of convivial conversation among an editor and his contributors. The number was collectively titled "The Tent" because, as the publisher William Blackwood indicated in a letter to John Wilson Croker, "the Editor proposes to represent himself and his coadjutors as writing the whole of the Number during a wet day in the Tent of Braemar."[80] In one particularly vivid sequence, the ongoing attacks on the Cockney School were reinforced by a sense of

Blackwood's own very different coterie organization, as a cigar-smoking John Ballantyne was regaled with – and tellingly put to sleep by – a stinging "sermon" on the debased aesthetics, politics, and social habits of the Hunt circle. The timing of "The Tent" in the immediate aftermath of Peterloo made radical mass meetings and political violence a volatile third term in any consideration of print sociability, and the attack on the Cockneyism of Leigh Hunt was itself sharpened by the discovery of a "family" relationship with the popular radical leader Henry "Orator" Hunt. An account of Leigh Hunt's display of a lock of Milton's hair to John Keats provided evidence that the poetic tradition of "Chaucer, Spenser, Shakespeare, and Milton" was debased by the Cockney School as surely as the line of "Hampden, Sydney, and Russell" was travestied in the triumph of Henry Hunt as the "White-hatted" hero of St. Peter's Field (*BEM* 5 [1819], 639–42).

If these convivial reflections on debased sociability made "The Tent" a literary tour de force, it remained a singular intensification of the miscellaneous organization of *Blackwood's* rather than an ongoing framing device. That fictional or semi-fictional representations of the social terms of periodical communication were not more central to conservative periodical expression again suggests an underlying resistance to the authority of public opinion as it was increasingly assembled in an associational world of taverns, public houses, shops, clubs, and debating societies.[81] Despite the achievement of the loyalist Association and the rise of the Pitt Clubs, contempt for that world still outstripped a desire to match it on its own terms. Although "The Satirist and the Debaters" was rhetorically framed by a distinction between radical and reactionary versions of public exchange (the debating society of John Gale Jones against the familiar correspondence of "Cives"), the underlying tension was between unruly radical leaders and the criminal justice system that would confine them to Newgate prison. And while the discovery that John Ballantyne fell asleep in "The Tent" satirically punctuated a sermon on Cockney School pretense, it also betrayed the limited threat of the case under review. In this sense, editorial attention to "Hampstead Hunt" came as some relief from the more "dry dogged plebeianism" of "Bristol Hunt" and his "bony and sinewy constituents" (*BEM* 5 [1819], 639–40). As an experimental representation of the dialogic conditions for periodical communication, "The Tent" came to fruition in *Blackwood's* after the immediate crisis of 1819 in the collaboratively produced familiar conversations of the "Noctes Ambrosianae" (1822–35), a project that was distinctly less political and that corresponded with a reining in of the magazine's early slashing style of criticism.[82]

A deferential orientation towards parliament remained the most appropriate way for counterrevolutionary periodicals to figure forth a sense of legitimate political deliberation, in part because this was by itself a challenge to emerging liberal and radical conceptions of the press as a (constitutionally ambiguous) fourth estate in its own right.[83] Such an orientation was consummately expressed in the appearance of the first *Anti-Jacobin; or, Weekly Examiner* within a single (1797–8) session of Parliament, a founding commitment that guided the paper in its allegiance to power as surely as the assault on "the Jacobin Daily Papers of the Metropolis" guided its critical mission. A final "Review of the Session" in the penultimate number paid lavish tribute "to the Vigour of Government, to the Firmness and Wisdom of Parliament, and to the good Sense and Spirit of the Nation" (*AJ* No. 35 [July 2, 1798], 273–4) for successfully negotiating the threat of revolution, and prepared the way for a less deferential farewell to the reader in the final number. The *British Critic* reinforced this conception in its review of the fourth edition of the *Anti-Jacobin*, crediting the periodical for "the good it has done; and the evil it has prevented," but reserving higher praise for a higher authority: "The great mass of good was doubtless effected, as it always must be, by the prudence and vigour of parliament" (*BC* 13 [1799], 49–50).

If subsequent projects did not make their own periodical career a dramatic sign of deference to legitimate representation, they remained committed to parliament as the appropriate institution for bringing public opinion to bear upon government. Where the radical press undermined parliamentary credibility, and opened up a presumptive reserve of political authority for itself, by attacking ministerial corruption and the inordinate political influence of land and new wealth, the counterrevolutionary press deliberately aligned itself with the same controversial features of the old regime. In his *Quarterly Review* essay "Parliamentary Reform," the poet laureate Robert Southey boldly orchestrated a defense of government support for well-disposed writers with a tribute to the way unreformed electoral procedures brought men of talent and men of property together in a House of Commons that "truly represented the complicated and various interests of the community" (*QR* 16 [1816–17], 255), in ways radical analysis could not possibly understand. *Blagdon's Political Register* hazarded a more outrageous defense of "*rotten boroughs*" in an age of revolution as "the true palladia of the Constitution; the instrument which repels the power of the people, and enables the ministry to maintain the dignity and reputation of the state." Yet despite this ostensibly good service the editor Francis Blagdon was not fortunate in his own search for adequate patronage from the social and political foundations of the old regime. After launching the paper with a promiscuous distribution of the Prospectus "to every Peer of the Realm, to every Member of the House of Commons, to every Baronet in the United Kingdom, and to every Merchant in the Metropolis," he went on to hector the Liverpool administration with demands for a return to William Pitt's more generous treatment of friendly writers and editors. In the end, he was reduced to using the failing pages of his *Register* to promote another unsuccessful venture, a scheme to combat the opposition press by recruiting "a dozen characters of rank and influence" to establish a fund of no less than five thousand pounds in support of an anti-radical "WEEKLY NEWSPAPER FOR THE PEOPLE."[84]

Ever resourceful, and more securely established by its publisher William Blackwood on market rather than patronage considerations, *Blackwood's Edinburgh Magazine* presented what may be the most vivid and compelling alignment of anti-radical periodical expression with unreformed parliamentary representation. The launching of "The Warder" series in November 1819, on the heels of "The Tent" and in a political climate still dominated by the furor over Peterloo, proved that vigorous polemic could be accommodated within an experimental, multivalent magazine format. "The Warder" followed established counterrevolutionary conventions, contending directly with the radical press as a leading source of popular discontent, and blaming moderate political opposition for facilitating subversion. The opening number held that "the *gentlemen*" of the Whig *Edinburgh Review* were in league with the ostensibly more radical "Black Dwarfs and Yellow Dwarfs" of T. J. Wooler and John Hunt, particularly where matters of religious belief and Church establishment were at issue. The skeptical spirit of Francis Jeffrey and his cohorts in the *Edinburgh* had long been "at open war with our national faith," and now sought "the destruction of the national character, in regard to both religion and politics" (*BEM* 6 [1819], 209). From its privileged perspective in the north, "The Warder" expressed a tentative confidence that "ancestral piety" and the "calm natural face of things" still subsisted beneath "the clamours of public meetings – the noise, and the music, and the dissonance – and the brawlings of orators and the applauses of multitudes" in

England's distressed manufacturing distances (*BEM* 6 [1819], 210–11). More uncertain, and perhaps more telling in the long run, was the disposition of treacherous elites:

The worst of all the features in the present convulsed countenance of the affairs of our country, is, to our mind, the behaviour not of the Reformers, but of the Whigs. There are no doubt many, very many individual adherents of that Party who have behaved nobly and well – but as a Party, we think their conduct has certainly been utterly unworthy of the name they bear, and the principles they profess to inherit. The worst of it is, that they have been studious in expressing their horror for the madness of the reforming sect; and yet . . . in the midst of these very expressions of horror they have been lending themselves to the popular outcry, and increasing, by every means in their power, the difficulties of the born and chosen guardians of the state. (*BEM* 6 [1819], 208, 210–11)[85]

This attempt to find the Whig party guilty by radical association was a conventional enough piece of Tory rhetoric in the period.[86] Yet actuated here in "The Warder" (as in an earlier programmatic *Blackwood's* essay "State of Parties, and the Edinburgh Review") by the critical impulse to grasp essential political developments through a review of the reviews, the analysis argued that a credible threat of revolution reconfigured the underlying relationship between press and government, so that legitimate opposition became a failure to support the government that amounted to revolutionary conspiracy. The *Edinburgh Review* could no longer indulge in dissident traditions of party organization and print expression without implicating itself in political violence.

Having drawn a direct line from a Whig elite through "the language of its party prints" (*BEM* 6 [1819], 211) to the postwar radical platform and the mob outrages in St. Peter's Field, the first number of "The Warder" drew to a close by respectfully deferring to parliament and government in its own attack on the character of the Whig opposition: "Parliament is about to assemble – and it is there that the true appeal, in regard to their character, must soon be made to the collective wisdom of the nation" (*BEM* 6 [1819], 211–12). By another well-worn convention of political journalism, this appeal was held to dissolve the very conditions for opposition through a catastrophic dissolution of party distinctions: "It is not now who is a Tory? – who is a Whig? But it is, who is a Briton? – who is a Christian?" Not since "the dark days of the French Revolution" had there been a period "so pregnant with danger," but the very gravity of the threat heralded a reunification of "all ranks of society" in support of repressive measures that would alone protect "order, liberty, and religion" from the designs of "the Anarchist and the Atheist" (*BEM* 6 [1819], 212).

In the event, there would be little comfort for *Blackwood's* in the unrepentant tenor of the *Edinburgh Review*. But the Liverpool ministry and the parliament that assembled on November 23, 1819 did not disappoint, and before the year was out the passage of the Six Acts provided the British government with unprecedented authority against political protest. Broad prohibitions on training and drilling addressed the worst fears of violent insurrection, yet it was the more closely targeted provisions of the Seditious Meetings Prevention Act and the Blasphemous and Seditious Libels Acts that combined to dismantle the postwar radical movement by neutralizing the potent coordination of popular organization and mass assembly with regular communication in the weekly press. The second number of "The Warder" opened by acknowledging the new laws, and recalling its earlier closing gesture towards parliamentary representation and ministerial initiative: "When we last addressed our readers on the state of Public Affairs, and on the symptoms of the diseases of the times, the country was looking forward with strong and high hopes – which have not been disappointed – to the meeting of Parliament" (*BEM* 6 [1819], 323). This conjuring of the reader was a significant pivot for the magazine. Jon Klancher and Mark Parker have shown that, despite its antidemocratic principles, *Blackwood's* was among the most sophisticated contemporary periodicals in terms of its capacity to project and engage a knowing and hermeneutically active reading audience.[87] If the political risks of this kind of periodical communication escalated as *Blackwood's* advanced from its founding in April 1817 to the crisis of late 1819, "The Warder" series can be considered timely insurance, since it worked to conscript readers to the magazine's own insistence upon a strict constitutional framework for any political activation of public opinion. To be sure, as in other campaigning counterrevolutionary periodicals, an orientation towards the authority of the ministers of the crown in parliament was not simply a matter of deference. After briefly indicating its approval of the new legislation, the second number of "The Warder" was substantially devoted to a more extensive attack on the devastating moral and political effects of "the crime of Blasphemy" (*BEM* 6 [1819], 323–1), clearly registering impatience with insufficient government action on a matter that had long been a special obsession at *Blackwood's*. In this sense, the serial narrative that ran from anticipation to satisfaction over the course of the first two numbers of "The Warder" was by no means complete. The reluctance of the periodical heirs of the first *Anti-Jacobin* to follow its example of deliberate self-suspension indicates a gathering realization that the threat of revolution had become an enduring condition. Within the routines of magazine production, "The Warder" lurched intermittently and uncertainly from one crisis to the next, and the series extended through an eighth occasional number in 1821, devoted to a vigorous defense of the popularity of the King in the face of radical agitation on behalf of Queen Caroline (*BEM* 8 [1821], 690),[88] before terminating abruptly and without explanation.

Before its demise, however, "The Warder" brilliantly confirmed its orientation towards parliamentary authority rather than extra-parliamentary opinion by devoting its entire sixth number to the "Speech of the Right Hon. George Canning, At the Liverpool Dinner, given in Celebration of his Re-election." A founding figure in both the *Anti-Jacobin* and the *Quarterly Review*, Canning had securely held the Liverpool seat since 1812 but was at this point in a difficult phase of his political career, out of favor with George IV and embroiled in factional disputes with leading members of the Liverpool administration, though he still held a minor government position as President of the Board of Control for India.[89] His widely reprinted speech was remarkable for its contemptuous dismissal of radical challenges to the representative status of the House of Commons, and for its vigorous defense of the recent Six Acts. It provided "The Warder" with an opportunity to represent within a magazine format the compelling spectacle of a member of the House of Commons convening with his electors to celebrate the mechanisms of an unreformed constitution through the public rituals of parliamentary electioneering.[90] A short headnote praised Canning's eloquence and integrity, and expressed the editor's pleasure in lending "additional circulation" to an oral performance that promised to "contribute signally and speedily to the re-establishment of sober reflection and mutual confidence among all orders of the people." There was no mistaking the calculated attachment of reading and periodical communication to public sociability and parliamentary representation, in a manner that remained deferential while perhaps suggesting that print supplementation had itself become an indispensable feature of the old regime, a notion that Canning could himself be considered to embody in his own career. "Our readers, we are sure, will be grateful to us for pressing into service an entire Speech delivered by Mr. Canning, at the dinner given in celebration of his re-election as Member for Liverpool" (*BEM* 7 [1820], 11).

Beyond the brief headnote, the speech itself effectively suspended the formidable powers of "The Warder," and the major framing device for this sixth number was Canning's own complex framing of his speech: a historical appeal "to the recollection of every man who now hears me" (a category that escalated through subsequent newspaper, pamphlet, and periodical redactions) to validate the Six Acts by considering "whether any country, in any two epochs, however distant, of its history, ever presented such a contrast with itself as this country, in November, 1819, and this country in January 1820," a chronology that nicely coincided with the history of "The Warder." Through a sequence of contrasting questions – "Do I exaggerate when I say, that there was not a man of property who did not tremble for his possessions?" "Is there a man of property who does not feel the tenure by which he holds his possessions to have been strengthened?" – Canning urged his audience to join him in endorsing those measures that restored political stability, "domestic tranquility," property rights, and the "moral and religious sense" of the nation (*BEM* 7 [1820], 12). This elaborate appeal to even "the most indifferent spectator of public events" (*BEM* 7 [1820], 12) set the terms for an increasingly pointed attack on radical protest, in which Canning boldly linked a defense of the new repressive measures with a defense of the unreformed parliament from which they issued. The preliminary spectacle of historical difference (November 1819 / January 1820) was soon reinforced by a striking appeal for aesthetic contemplation of the mechanisms of state repression. "It may be said of them, as has been said of some of the most consummate productions of literary art, that though no man beforehand had exactly anticipated them, no man, when they were laid before him, did not feel that they were such as he would himself have suggested" (*BEM* 7 [1820], 13).

Throughout the speech, distancing appeals for historical recollection and aesthetic contemplation unfolded alongside a more immediate sense of the festive occasion upon which a government minister and member of parliament undertook to address his Liverpool electors. Looking back on the "last short session of Parliament," dissolved for the accession of George the Fourth, Canning expressed his warm feeling "that it is my duty, as your representative, to render to you some account of the part which I took in that assembly to which you sent me." Ratified at the recent poll and now celebrated at the present dinner, the relationship between speaker and audience extended back through the passage of the Six Acts and served to justify the electoral procedures of an unreformed parliament:

Upon the occasions of such trying exigency as those which we have lately experienced, I hold it to be of the very essence of our free and popular Constitution, that an unreserved interchange of sentiment should take place between the representative and his constituents: and if it accidentally happen, that he who addresses you as your representative, stands also in the situation of a responsible adviser of the crown, I recognise in that more rare occurrence, a not less striking or less valuable peculiarity of that reviled Constitution under which we have the happiness to live; by which a minister of the crown is brought into contact with the great body of the community; and the service of the king is shown to be a part of the service of the people. (*BEM* 7 [1820], 11–12)

If the periodical republication of this argument about a vivid and "unreserved" sentimental "interchange" between parliamentary member and enfranchised audience opened the pages of *Blackwood's* to the social life of the old regime, Canning's identification of his electoral audience as propertied, privileged, enfranchised, and male (characteristics that were explicit in the terms in which listeners were enjoined to compare their experience in January 1820 with November 1819) offered vivid evidence of the constitutional restrictions that made the political nation dramatically smaller than the reading nation. In this sense, while the republication of the "Speech of the Right Hon. George Canning, At the Liverpool Dinner, given in Celebration of his Re-election" played into the authority of the press by projecting an oral and occasional appeal to enfranchised listeners outward for a more abstract reading audience, it did so in terms that reinforced the political exclusions that Canning, "the Warder," and *Blackwood's Edinburgh Magazine* were concerned to defend against the threat of radical reform.

By comparison with the contemptuous burlesque of vulgar democratic assembly in the "The Satirist and the Debaters," or the listless resurrection of outmoded periodical correspondence in *The Looker-On*, the publication of Canning's Liverpool speech stands out as a compelling counterrevolutionary representation of the social life of the old regime and the periodical expression that developed in its support. The festive occasion for the speech opened briefly upon a promise of social and affective reconciliation that was appropriate to the capacious and pleasurable form of *Blackwood's Edinburgh Magazine* as a whole. At the same time there was no losing sight of the narrow polemical purposes of "The Warder." As a calculated representation of a speech that itself urged "recollection" upon the event of a "re-election," this sixth number of "The Warder" effectively distinguished itself from radical mass meetings, cheap weekly periodicals, and democratic reform programs. The same volume of *Blackwood's* that closed "The Warder" series also printed Henry Matthews' "Thoughts on the Present Political Aspect of the Times," a closely argued rejection of radical principles of political delegation and "numerically considered" representation, and of any "scheme of election, however equal and universal," in which members of parliament were considered "a reflecting mirror of the people they represent" (*BEM* 8 [1820–1], 488–9). "The Warder" may have been pursuing a similar logic in the print arena when it undertook simply to reprint a political speech that was presumably not susceptible being to represented or condensed in any other way. Canning himself responded to rationalized theories of political representation when he invoked the numerical results of the poll within a framework of affective interchange and identification with a sympathetic listening audience:

We were loudly assured by the Reformers, that the test throughout the country by which those who were ambitious of seats in the new Parliament would be tried was to be – whether they had supported those measures. . . . To me, indeed, it was not put as a test, but objected to as a charge. You know how that charge was answered: and the result is to me a majority of 1300 out of 2000 voters upon the poll. (*BEM* 7 [1820], 13)

While this kind of electoral dinner would have been raucous enough in its own right, the austere text does not register audience applause or interjection, and in this sense it plays into Canning's own framing historical contrast between an intimidating radical regime of mass meetings and the legitimate parliamentary mechanisms that delivered the Six Acts. There was no correspondence between the outrages of "St George's-fields" and "an orderly meeting, recognized by the law, for all legitimate purposes of discussion and petition": "How monstrous is it to confound such meetings with the genuine recognized modes of collecting the sense of the English people!" (*BEM* 7 [1820], 13–15). By characterizing radical public assembly as a mere "aggregation," a "multitude of individuals having no permanent relation to each other, no common tie, but what arises from their concurrence as members of that meeting," Canning shrewdly recapitulated the terms in which the Seditious Meetings and Assemblies Act prohibited public meetings that were not limited in number and circumscribed by parish boundaries. And he provided himself as speaker with an occasion to acknowledge the sanctioned character of his own political audience: "To bring together the inhabitants of a particular division, or men sharing a common franchise, is to bring together an assembly, of which the component parts act with some respect and awe of each other" (*BEM* 7 [1820], 15). *Blackwood's* and "The Warder" in turn worked to enlist the support of a potentially more abstract and aggregate reading audience for Canning's sentimental yet polemically uncompromising defense of the representational premises of the old regime.

CHAPTER 4

Subverting fictions: The counterrevolutionary form of the novel

The anti-Jacobin novel can seem by turns a curiously disengaged fictional enterprise or the most vexed and compelling of counter-revolutionary forms of expression. Disengaged, because by comparison with periodical and pamphlet literature the novel did not address popular radical protest in a sustained way, nor was it significantly integrated with counterrevolutionary organization. This is partly a matter of timing since, as M. O. Grenby has shown in an impressively detailed study, the anti-Jacobin novel was a relatively late entry in the controversies precipitated by the French Revolution, coming into its own towards the end of the 1790s and in the first decade of the nineteenth century with the appearance of dozens of titles with substantial counterrevolutionary themes, including works by Isaac D'Israeli, Elizabeth Hamilton, and Jane West, but then abating well before the intense radical reform agitation of the late 1810s.[1] While programmatic loyalism was by no means absent in these years, and the rise of Napoleon Bonaparte and the emergence of a new generation of parliamentary reformers yielded acute new concerns, the first major phase of the controversy had clearly passed. In identifying the novels treated in this chapter as "anti-Jacobin," I follow the common practice of recent scholarship, justified in part by the counterpoint between such fictions and the "Jacobin" novels of William Godwin, Thomas Holcroft, Mary Wollstonecraft, and Mary Hays, although I am sympathetic to scholars who object to both categories for sustaining a conservative tendency to mark all protest as foreign and extreme, and for eliding important distinctions among conservative novelists in particular.[2] If the novel came relatively late to political controversy in this period, neither was it a significant vehicle for subsidy by the government nor by counterrevolutionary civic associations. Booksellers and publishers who were active in loyalist pamphleteering showed some interest in the novel, as when John Hatchard brought out Mary Anne

Burges' *The Progress of the Pilgrim Good-Intent, in Jacobinical Times* (1800), a fiercely anti-French redaction of Bunyan that sought to align the language of Adam and the nominalizations of allegory with Church and state.[3] But for the most part anti-Jacobin fiction did not revert to outmoded narrative devices. Instead, allowing for a bias towards political satire and against sensibility and sentiment, these novels tended to unfold within reasonably current narrative conventions. And they found their way to market through such mainstream commercial publishing firms as the Robinsons, John Murray, Cadell and Davies, Longman and Rees, Hookham and Carpenter, and William Lane's Minerva Press.

There is sufficient evidence of the alignment of anti-Jacobin fiction with anti-Jacobin critical reviewing to justify Grenby's charge of "collusion between authors and critics,"[4] particularly where personal attacks on prominent radicals were concerned. In reviewing Elizabeth Hamilton's *Memoirs of Modern Philosophers* (1800), for example, the *British Critic* noted with approval that the novel followed George Walker's *The Vagabond* (1799) in satirizing principles already "exposed by us with some care" (*BC* 16 [1800], 439) in a hostile review of Godwin's *Political Justice*. Yet as Grenby indicates, the close-knit complicity evident in the career of Robert Bisset – the prolific contributor to the *Anti-Jacobin Review* whose first novel, *Douglas; or, the Highlander* (1800), was published by the Anti-Jacobin press and whose second novel, *Modern Literature* (1804), was promoted in advance by the *Anti-Jacobin Review* and then favorably noticed for its assault on Paine and Godwin – was exceptional rather than typical.[5] And if this kind of coordination was politically motivated, it can also be traced to commercial arrangements that linked reviewing with publishing and bookselling.[6] At the same time, even the campaigning *British Critic* was to some extent prepared to acknowledge the strengths and weaknesses of both radical and conservative publications, condemning for example the excessive "scenes and circumstances of horror" in *The Vagabond* (*BC* 15 [1800], 432), and allowing with regret in paired reviews of Godwin's *Caleb Williams* and Thomas Holcroft's *Hugh Trevor* that "the opposition to revealed religion and to civil society can boast of two very amusing novelists" (*BC* 4 [1795], 70–1). And while pleased to see its own strictures on *Political Justice* bear fictional fruit in *Memoirs of Modern Philosophers*, the same review complained that the female philosopher Bridgetina Botherim, a parody of the novelist Mary Hays and her heroine Emma Courtney, was "such a caricature as exceeds all probability, and almost all patience" (*BC* 16 [1800], 439).

The anti-Jacobin novel also seems to fall outside the main stream of counterrevolutionary argument by virtue of an attenuated topicality that afforded surprisingly little in the way of close social observation. The later social problem novels of Charles Dickens, Elizabeth Gaskell, and others were fantasies in the sense that they enlisted the synthetic powers of narrative romance to resolve pressing economic and political concerns, but they did at least centrally represent the ominous figure of the urban factory laborer, and indicate the remedial social work to be done by benevolent industrialists and enterprising middle-class women.[7] By contrast, anti-Jacobin fiction was inclined to represent radical protest in ways that were satirically distorted beyond recognition, and at the same time it tended to relegate "the lower orders" to a pastoral frame of representation, where their disruptive political desires were easily overcome by facile reassertions of social hierarchy and government authority. There is surprisingly little in anti-Jacobin fiction to match even Hannah More's stylized rendering of the vernacular dialogue of Jack Anvil and Tom Hod over the challenge of Paine's *Rights of Man*. The fact that most anti-Jacobin novels take shape instead as "personal satires against leading English Jacobins,"[8] with courtship plots outrageously distorted by the supposed sexual transgressions of Godwin, Wollstonecraft, and Mary Hays, is itself a strategic deflection rather than a direct assault on political organization. As distilled by the anti-Jacobin novel in the preposterous "new philosophy" of the Godwin circle, the threat of revolution becomes a wholly ideational concoction of atheism, anarchism, free love, sentimental self-absorption, and selective disregard for the property rights of others. Critical fictions can dispense with social realism because this radical philosophy has no material foundation beyond the burlesque existence of the characters by whom it is advanced – characters who are themselves invariably confused, vain, hypocritical, and incapable of learning from experience.

And yet it was precisely this narrow and distorted focus that lent the anti-Jacobin novel its distinctive intensity and contrarian energy. Familiar literary conventions rigorously limited the possibilities for expressing and for resolving social conflict. To be sure, the tendency to reduce nearly every male vector of radical desire to the stock type of the libertine seducer was certainly a concerted political slander, and Nicola J. Watson has observed the "strenuous seduction schedules" of "philosopher-villains" who were embroiled in "all manner of undesirable activities – from Irish rebellion to Illuminati meetings, from Methodism to methodical spying-for-the-French, from reading German literature to overthrowing Christianity."[9] Yet for all its manifest distortions, this tendency to superimpose immediate political threats on residual literary vices suggests just how powerfully the form of the novel served to organize a sense of what had gone wrong with the world and how it might be made right. In anti-Jacobin domestic romance, the normative framework of the marriage plot promises to neutralize the threat of revolution as well as libertine seduction. If anti-Jacobin novels did not effectively engage radical protest, this is in part because they did something else, testing subversion and its ideological residue ("the new philosophy") against available norms of popular fiction which themselves entailed elements of ordinary life felt to be under siege in an age of revolution: marriage, domesticity, gender difference, social hierarchy, and generational transmission. An instrumental approach to narrative form helps account for the fact that anti-Jacobin fiction did not significantly influence the development of the novel: the point was to operate within and upon available literary conventions.[10] And yet these were *experimental* fictions in the sense that they grasped literary form as a kind of theater within which radical principles could be safely activated and played out, so that their consequences could be explored and discredited. Again, to proceed in this way was often to challenge the script of the Jacobin novel, and one common strategy was simply to rework episodes and characters from Godwin's *Caleb Williams* or Holcroft's *Hugh Trevor* within a more strictly observed framework of moral regulation and social convention.

In his preface to *The Vagabond* (1799), George Walker intimated a theory of the counterrevolutionary narrative experiment that traced the errors of Jacobin philosophy and fiction back to an imaginative defect that fuelled revolutionary desire. The aim of his own fiction was to rehabilitate the claims of the real, understood as the reality ordained by the British constitution, through a narrative that set "in a *practical* light, some of the prominent absurdities of many self-important reformers of mankind, who, having heated their imaginations, sit down to write *political romances*, which never were, and never will be practical" (*V* v). In fashioning his own spectacularly cruel and destructive Jacobin naïf, Frederick Fenton, after Voltaire's Candide, and similarly modeling the speculative tutor Stupeo after Pangloss (with a dose of Paine and Godwin), Walker slyly allowed the contamination of his own counter-Enlightenment fiction by the narrative methods of Enlightenment critique. And *The Vagabond* was among the most philosophically dense of anti-Jacobin fictions, composed of a network of allusions to Voltaire, Rousseau, "the fashionable Hume," Godwin, Wollstonecraft, Paine, Holcroft, and Priestley.[11] According to Walker, "so inimical are the doctrines of Godwin, Hume, Rousseau, &c. to all civil society" that the novelist can simply activate those doctrines within the disciplinary framework of the real, and transcribe the consequences that follow: "The inferences I have drawn from *their* texts naturally result" (*V* vi) . If the emphatic adjective ("*their*") registers an antithetical purpose, the term it modifies ("texts") suggests just how fully the anti-Jacobin novelist wound up engaging the subversive imagination within its own privileged sphere of language and print expression. The most vivid example within *The Vagabond* of the kind of narrative experiment Walker describes comes in a parody of a notorious utilitarian moral argument from *Political Justice*. According to Godwin, an individual faced with the choice of saving the esteemed author Fénelon or his valet from a fire must choose the more valuable life of Fénelon, even if the valet is a close relative.[12] Confronted with a fire that threatens the life of his mistress Amelia and her father, the Jacobin Frederick pauses to reflect upon the similar admonition of his tutor Stupeo (a footnote credits Godwin), with the result that mistress and father alike are left to perish in the flames (*V* 32).

The wayward moral course of picaresque fiction made it the preferred vehicle for this kind of fictional exploration of the worldly consequences of Jacobin theory, particularly for male novelists. Marilyn Butler has deftly summarized one strand of the anti-Jacobin rogue's tale that characteristically yields social reintegration: "The hero – often, Quixote-like, deluded by revolutionary ideas – travels the country, meeting grotesque groups of troublemakers, and eventually learning to see society as it is . . . . [He] is made aware of his presumption and learns to take his place in the world as it actually is."[13] In comparing this with the dominant pattern of oppression by external social forces in the Jacobin novel, Butler observes a further contrast with the anti-Jacobin domestic romances of Jane West. Home virtues do enter the anti-Jacobin picaresque as counterpoint, but the masculine designation of the hero-villain tends to prevent any sustained engagement with domestic experience. After fleeing the tragic consequences of the fire, Frederick Fenton later teams up with Doctor Alogos (a savage parody of Joseph Priestley) for a disastrous career as parish reformer, from which the two men escape to America in search of primitive republican virtue. The Doctor's virtuous niece Laura accompanies them and continues to attend to domestic responsibilities on this disenchanting picaresque circuit, but she remains wholly immune to Jacobin tutelage and to Frederick's sexual advances. In the end she achieves a romantic fulfillment that is denied even to the repentant hero when she marries Vernon, the childhood friend from whom Frederick first seduced the mistress who was then consigned to the fires of Godwinian justice. In *Memoirs of Modern Philosophers* (1800), Elizabeth Hamilton achieved a more complex form of anti-Jacobin picaresque experiment by conceiving the rogue adventurer as a woman, Bridgetina Botherim, distinguished for never having "read any thing but novels and metaphysics" (*MP* 38) and for acting without restraint on the impulses these yield. The novel's ambitious triple plot offers two other heroines: Harriet Orwell the pious daughter of an Anglican clergyman, and Julia Delmond the tragic victim of a Jacobin seducer. Yet contrary to the strictures of the *British Critic* Bridgetina remains the more original creation, living out through her own deformed body, degraded sensibilities, and misguided erotic expectations the brutally comic collisions that follow from a feminine activation of the new philosophy.[14] Having placed herself beyond the laws of romance through her rejection of sexual difference, this "ostensible heroine" (*MP* 378) is denied even the debased erotic fulfillment she imagines for herself, in the form of elopement with Henry Sidney (reserved for Harriet Orwell) and primitivist retirement among the Hottentots of Africa. The narrative is calculated to prove that there can be no Jacobin liberation of female desire, and in this sense Hamilton achieves her satirical ends through a rigorous resistance to picaresque outcomes. Unlike the peripatetic Frederick Fenton, Bridgetina is regularly thwarted in the routine act of rising from a chair or crossing a village lane, and Hottentot Africa remains a distant fantasy.[15]

Hamilton's complex reworking of the gendered terms for anti-Jacobin narrative experiment is evident in a memorable scene that finds Bridgetina deliberately falling behind a group of walking companions, so that she can persuade herself that Henry's reluctance to accompany her does not imply a lack of affection, and that decorum should not prevent her ("forbid it philosophy! forbid it love!") from indulging "the sweet sentiments of nature" he has inspired. This comic lapse into self-communion is a typical feature of anti-Jacobin narrative, and so too is the rude collision with the material world that abruptly brings it to an end:

> Here the soliloquy of Bridgetina was unfortunately interrupted; and never did the soliloquy of a love-sick maiden receive interruption from a more indignified source. While pouring out the effusions of her tender heart in the middle of the highway, she was too much occupied by her *feelings* to observe the approach of a drove of pigs, which at length advanced upon her so fast as to prevent the possibility of retreat. She was surrounded on all sides in a moment. The obstreperous and unmanageable animals, not contented with terrifying her by their snorting and grunting, (a species of music very little in unison with the tender feelings) pushed her from side to side in a most ungentle manner. She, however, contrived for some time to keep her ground, calling out to the pig-drivers for assistance. Alas! the pig-drivers were no less deaf to her supplications than were the pigs they drove. Both seemed wickedly to enjoy her distress; nor was the grunting of one species of brutes more unpleasant to her ears, than the loud laugh which was set up by the other. At length a violent push from a huge untoward beast laid her prostrate on the ground, and completed the climax of her misfortunes. (*MP* 157–8)

As so often in *Memoirs of Modern Philosophers*, the errors of the philosophical heroine disclose some of the author's most complex and original literary designs. The emblematic descent of an aspiring fallen woman among "unmanageable animals," whose features and "snorting and grunting" echo her own physical deformity and croaking voice, lays bare the crude animal desire that a new philosophy wants to elevate into a "tide of tenderness" (*MP* 157–8). Where the pigs reduce radical sensibility to lust, their drivers extend the implications of mock-epic leveling into matters of social hierarchy. The episode is framed by two distinct sociolects: on the one hand, the political jargon that dominates Bridgetina's erotic soliloquy in the moments just before her fall ("Shall a false regard for the debasing and immoral institutions of a corrupt society deter me from making a suitable return to his enchanting tenderness?"); and on the other hand, the vernacular in which the drovers defend their actions ("The pigs were goying peaceably along the way, when she run her nose into the very midst o'em. Gin a had been as blind as a buzzard, a might ha' heard un squeak.").[16] The distance between these two idioms allows for a second fall, as Bridgetina unwittingly exposes the gap between Jacobin ideology and the common people it pretends to represent. In expostulating with the pig drovers, she sets out from a merely conventional radical formula for addressing the oppressed ("Miserable and unhappy wretches!"), then goes on to vent her wounded pride in a way that exposes the hypocrisy of democratic as well as primitivist impulses: "Ye have indeed the shape of men, but ye want all the more noble distinguishing characteristics of the species. As far as relates to any intellectual improvement, ye might as well have been born in Otaheite" (*MP* 158). This comic unraveling of erotic meditation in contemptuous radical elitism is made possible by the usual anti-Jacobin fictional engagement with a distortion of Godwin rather than Paine. Yet there remain unresolved contradictions. For in staging the collision of radical sexual and political desire with the material world as a fall among "a drove of pigs," Hamilton identifies her solid "ground" of fact with Edmund Burke's notorious remark about the debasement of clerical learning "under the hoofs of a swinish multitude," a phrase that made its way out from the *Reflections on the Revolution in France* to become, in Don Herzog's account, "one of the day's cant phrases." It was ironically picked up and displayed as a badge of honor by radical pressman like Thomas Spence in *Pig's Meat* (1793) and Daniel Isaac Eaton in *Politics for the People; or, a Salmagundy for Swine* (1793–4), and then endlessly disclaimed and reclaimed as a conception of the common people in an age of revolution.[17] The allusion may reinforce Bridgetina's contempt for unimproved humanity, but Hamilton seems to be involved in a more ambiguous allegory of her own entanglement as a novelist with compromised literary material. For by contaminating the "ground" as material opposite of Bridgetina's metaphysical and erotic extravagance with a widely recognized semantic controversy, the novelist suggests that fictional representation cannot render fact in an unmediated way. It is less clear whether there is a more complex act of appropriation here, with Hamilton reclaiming from the likes of Spence and Eaton the original attempt by Burke to rescue exclusive knowledge from vulgar degradation. Having assigned the unwitting elitism to Bridgetina, the author is free to indulge a wicked delight in an episode that confuses the common man as well as the female philosopher with swine. In this sense, the "unenlightened rustic" from whom Bridgetina finally turns as she bursts into tears at the close of the encounter is ambiguously a creature of the heroine and the novelist, although he himself takes the novelist's part when he avenges the contempt with which he has been treated by dismissing Bridgetina as "a little, ugly, rickety witch" (*MP* 158). If some polemical strands remain unresolved, it is clear that with her semantically contaminated ground Hamilton has joined Hannah More and other enterprising conservatives in conceding that the campaign against revolution cannot rest its case on the inherent resistance of social or material facts to subversive refashioning.

This brilliantly negotiated concession betrays an essential and I think saving ambiguity about the way counterrevolutionary writers went about experimenting upon the novel as a narrative instrument for deflating revolutionary expectation. As Grenby has argued, when the anti-Jacobin novel made the Jacobin novel, rather than radical principles or radical organization as such, its *"raison d'etre* and its vindication," it aligned itself with longstanding doubts about the morality of popular fiction, intensified in this period by broadly conservative anxieties about foreign cultural influence, the rise of sensibility and gothic horror, and the feminization and popularization of print culture. "Except in the case of their own work," Grenby writes, "anti-Jacobin authors clung to the notion that all modern novel-writing was intrinsically Jacobin."[18] As a result, when Walker and others took up the novel as a fictional instrument for testing new philosophical speculation, they were working with contaminated instruments in a contaminated environment. Even without Hamilton's ambiguous allusion to Burke, the firm "ground" of the real was not easily identified within the unruly conventions of popular romance. Everything that committed enemies of revolution knew about the novel suggested that it was given over to subversive pathologies – sexual license, emotional extravagance, self-gratification, religious skepticism, resistance to parental authority, disregard for gender and class distinctions, and an apparently boundless appetite for French, German, and Italian cultural influences. The commercial networks and reading habits involved in the reception of popular fiction only compounded the problem. When the much-maligned Poet Laureate and occasional *Anti-Jacobin* reviewer Henry James Pye turned his modest talents to counterrevolutionary fiction in the 1799 novel, *The Aristocrat*, he employed a common rhetorical device of threatening readers who shared radical sympathies with banishment, but did so a way that consigned his own novel along with such readers to the most degenerate of literary conditions: "I would advise them to proceed no further, but immediately to shut the volume, and send it back to the circulating library."[19] For a fiction already constituted in political antagonism, this distaste for the form of the novel generated competing fields of interference, as the debased conventions of popular romance were set to work animating redemptive virtues as well as subversive vices. To some extent it is possible to distinguish relentlessly satirical fictions like Walker's *The Vagabond* from the works of Jane West and Elizabeth Hamilton, which represent what Catherine Gallagher calls "productive fictions" in the sense that they attempt to redeem compromised literary conventions.[20] Yet the distinction is not absolute, and the anti-Jacobin novel consistently struggled with more and less credible means of representing more and less virtuous characters and conditions.

A comparison with the tract literature of moral reform is instructive. The ballad and prose narratives of the Cheap Repository represented virtue and vice within a comprehensive social framework that encouraged the lower orders to attach themselves to middle-class activists who worked to reform and regularize the haphazard channels of elite provision. More critical and satirical in its orientation, the counterrevolutionary novel did not consistently concern itself with redemptive agency, nor did it pretend that its picaresque sequences were an adequate map of the world. There were exceptions, and while not strictly speaking an anti-Jacobin fiction, Jane West's *The Advantages of Education, or, The History of Maria Williams, A Tale for Misses and Their Mammas* (1793) provides the salient model of a transcription of conduct book morality into novel form.[21] Yet even here threats to feminine virtue are increasingly mediated by such familiar literary devices as concealed identity, libertine seduction, and a harrowing revenge plot. Fiction itself becomes an operative concern as the narrative rigorously averts the danger of being "deceived . . . by a fictitious tale" (*AE* 2: 53) or lured into "a fictitious celebration" of marriage (*AE* 1: 232). If more strenuously anti-Jacobin novels were not innocent of the tendency to narrate conduct book morality, they did tend to privilege a more disenchanted narrative line, relegating the treatment of moral "advantages" to the status of subplot or emblematic episode. Virtue occupied a domestic refuge from public vice and subversion, rather than underwriting the kind of pervasive social enterprise associated with the literature of moral reform. Where Cheap Repository tracts and anti-Jacobin novels were both expressions of an enterprising conservatism, they tended to complicate the elusive promise of an existing loyalist inheritance in different ways. Hannah More made it clear that resistance to subversion would be the product rather than the precondition of her own literary enterprise. By contrast anti-Jacobin novelists were willing to identify pockets of embedded virtue unrelated to the work of fiction, even as they pursued an ambiguous literary project that was potentially compromised by its own devices at every turn. Distracted by the rarified new philosophy, Bridgetina falls upon contested and compromised ground. In this respect, the division of anti-Jacobin fiction against itself affords a narrative complexity beyond what one might reasonably expect of a literature driven by polemical and didactic concerns.

To approach the anti-Jacobin novel in this way is not to deny its grotesque misrepresentations of revolutionary desire.[22] The modern reader with any interest in Paine, Godwin, and Wollstonecraft can only be dismayed by the failure of anti-Jacobin fiction to address radical claims, and by the predictability with which a compelling political movement gets reduced to an opportunistic gang of thieves, murderers, seducers, prostitutes, and idiots. In her ground-breaking early discussion of Jane West and Elizabeth Hamilton in *Jane Austen and the War of Ideas*, Marilyn Butler has poignantly contrasted the "vast and shadowy demons" projected by narrative satires of Godwin with "the small figure of a retiring man of letters known to live a frugal and well-ordered life in the St. Pancras district."[23] And even Grenby as the most thorough recent student of the form grows exasperated with the "war of shadows."[24] My aim in this chapter is not to vindicate counterrevolutionary fiction from well-deserved charges of exaggeration and slander, but rather to see what can be learned from the distinctive ways in which political subversion was hunted down in the pages of the novel. Even where the more sophisticated of these novels explicitly represented the process by which available literary conventions were reworked and supplemented in order to comprehend the unprecedented threat of revolution – as when Hamilton developed her picaresque villain Vallaton as a familiar street urchin ("*the funny vagabond*") before projecting him through the London Corresponding Society and the "higher region" of Godwinian speculation, so he could emerge a polished Jacobin seducer (*MP* 51–2, 56–60) – there was a double concession at work. First, that counterrevolutionary narrative could not help but enlist literary devices that had long catered to more salacious popular tastes, and second, that revolutionary desire was itself an elaboration of traditional vices, so that imported French principles turn out to be very much at home in the streets of London.

Given its relative distance from the front lines of political mobilization, the anti-Jacobin novel can be considered experimental in the further sense that it explored more freely than other counterrevolutionary forms the range and possibilities of conservative literary enterprise. In particular, within narratives structured by the competing claims of picaresque political satire and moralizing domestic romance, there was a desire to somehow close the gap between loyalist renderings of public and private life. Recent scholarship on eighteenth and early nineteenth-century British culture has tended to confirm the historical presence of gendered public and private realms while insisting upon the fluidity and contestation of such distinctions.[25] The tendency for anti-Jacobin fiction to insulate private virtues from public threats of revolution, while allowing political subversion to become the subject of domestic conversation, betrays an effort to police distinctions that could no longer simply be assumed. Under the pressures of global counterrevolutionary war, home became a fantastically resonant figure for nation. And the anti-Jacobin novel, for all its manifest aesthetic limitations, represents a kind of national fantasy, fueled by the desire for liberation and reconciliation as well as by a more disciplinary defense of inherited hierarchies and established institutions. It is worth recalling Fredric Jameson's compelling insistence that "the effectively ideological is also, at the same time, necessarily Utopian."[26] If Hannah More had a fantasy life, so too did the counterrevolutionary novelist. Profoundly marked at every turn by its narrow ideological purposes, the anti-Jacobin novel managed nevertheless to transcend its constitutive antinomies and consider the ways in which freedom from subversion might unleash individual and collective human potential.

ADVENTURES IN THE COUNTERREVOLUTIONARY PICARESQUE

Nancy Johnson has recently argued that the anti-Jacobin novel was centrally concerned to represent a "French Threat" in terms of sexual desire, an obsession she suggestively links with conservative anxieties about exaggerated individual development in the absence of inherited family and property relations.[27] The case is compelling, yet it is worth insisting that the seduction plot by no means exhausted the astonishing range of transgressions canvassed in these novels. Nor was picaresque narrative simply a convenient device for unleashing the Jacobin sexual predator upon as many victims as possible. On the contrary, the restless mobility and resourcefulness of the Jacobin rogue crystallized a range of distinct fears: about the power and appeal of dislocated new forms of wealth, knowledge, and subjectivity; about the ease with which character and consciousness could be uprooted from local circumstance; about the vulnerability of rural England to incursions from London and from abroad; and about the limited ability of private virtue and public authority to stop the spread of ideological contagion. With a relentlessness that betrayed fascination as well as fear, the

anti-Jacobin novel staged the threat of revolution not as a single cataclysmic event, but as an endless sequence of local episodes in which
subversion found innumerable ways into the established order of
things. A preference for villains incapable of learning from their own
misguided experience was a deliberate political slander, but it also
suggested that Jacobin agency would not respond to normal means of
correction and control. And in another important adjustment of literary convention, picaresque misadventure tended to issue in these
novels less from youthful exuberance or comic naiveté than from the
particular kind of political education that transformed Vallaton from
the *"funny vagabond"* who swept a crossing at Bloomsbury Square into a
monstrous Jacobin predator whose devastation extended across two
continents and through revolutionary movements in France, Britain,
and North America.[28]

The particular derivation and development of the subversive rogue
conditioned distinct polemical claims. One of the least compromising
narrative designs was to import a foreign agent whose tale of subversion remained merely serial because indigenous virtue somehow
resisted his overtures, driving him onward from one comically inhospitable reception to another. In *The Democrat* Henry James Pye offers
Jean Le Noir who, for no better reason than that he "drew his first
breath" in France, abandons a peasant's traditional faith in "the
bounty of the Seigneur" and "the charity of the neighbouring mon-
astery" and sets out instead on a reckless criminal career (*D* 1: 1–2). He
proceeds along familiar lines – pilfering from friends, seducing inno-
cents, enlisting in the army, deserting at the first opportunity – until he
arrives in revolutionary Boston and becomes conspicuous for "violent
declamations in favour of universal liberty" (*D* 1: 10). If character
development is not a leading consideration in these novels, it is
important that in this case criminal tendencies precede radical sympathies. Le Noir exemplifies a more specious type of Jacobin rogue
who, as Gary Kelly has written, tends to mouth "liberty, equality, and
philanthropy" while pursuing "personal ambition, desire, lust, and
passion."[29] At the same time, conventional picaresque incidents
become infinitely more dangerous in revolutionary Boston after the
petty criminal's "practical" commitment to an "equalization of property" has been infused with "speculative" Jacobin theory (*D* 1: 3–4).
Pye may admire the old thief no more than the new subversive, but he
requires the first in order to represent the second, and in this sense his
novel is as disenchanted as it is disenchanting.

This is not to say that the anti-Jacobin novel never staged more direct clashes between radical argument and the recalcitrant facts of the world, in ways that recall an early loyalist pamphleteer's suggestion that ordinary subjects should prefer a steady diet of English "beef and pudding" to French revolutionary speculation (*AP* II, 8: 14). This approach was particularly evident in the narrative handling of print culture. The reckless mobility of revolutionary agency in *The Democrat* is consistently identified with the circulation of newspapers and pamphlets, and with the promiscuous sociability afforded by bookshops, coffee houses, coaches, and taverns. After his successful revolutionary career in America, Le Noir returns to France where he joins the Jacobin Club and becomes a close associate of Marat, Robespierre, and Paine, but he is soon distracted by the "misrepresented and exaggerated reports" of British discontent that arrive daily through the medium of "disaffected newspapers," and he secures French government credentials and passage to Southampton in order to introduce "a system of equalization and fraternity" between Britain and France (*D* 1: 14–16). With the exception of the "Story of the Count de Tournelles, and the fair Adelaide," an embedded narrative of the tribulations of an exiled French nobleman, the rest of *The Democrat* is given over to a serial quest narrative in which the hero struggles to apply his revolutionary credentials to the disaffection he read about in the British press: he is frustrated at every turn, but his hopes are perpetually renewed by "fictitious representations" that are "retailed from the mouth of every coffeehouse orator, and the pen of every newspaper scribbler" (*D* 2: 10). To fulfill the narrow ideological purposes for which he was brought into being, Le Noir must remain both a shrewd predator whose crimes expose the hollowness of radical philanthropy, and a naive adventurer who cannot possibly comprehend the disenchanting fable he enacts. Were he capable of learning from experience, disillusionment would coincide with his first arrival at Southampton, where the absence of "that gloomy fog, which he had so often been told was always hovering over the British Islands," prefigures every subsequent disappointment: the clearly visible countryside around Southampton is richly cultivated, and the town itself is flourishing and prosperous, with "no trace of the dull splenetic race he was taught to expect, whose sole business was Sedition" (*D* 1: 21). Le Noir symptomatically renews his mission from time to time by burying his head in a newspaper or retreating to the hothouse atmosphere of a bookshop, coffee-house, or debating club, but even here success proves elusive as indigenous disaffections turn out to be limited, fleeting, or hopelessly compromised by partisan contention. If there is any sense of progress about the serial disappointments that conduct the novel from Portsmouth to London, it lies in the way that Le Noir learns to calibrate his mode of travel and his political overtures to audiences that potentially answer to his own disruptive mobility – drunken sailors in a country ale-house, the reckless hunting party of a Whig squire, and the "loungers and politicians" who populate the taverns, stage coaches, coffee houses, and debating societies strung out along the route to central London. Yet in each case the hapless agent provocateur is undone by the hypocrisy and selfishness of his victims, or by his own comic misunderstanding of the local idiom, as when he disastrously mistakes a Jacobite for a kindred spirit. If it is immediately evident that picaresque narrative will not yield an organized revolutionary plot, what remains surprising is the depth and range of the novel's satirical disillusionment with British society. Resistance to French revolutionary overtures does not come from indigenous virtue, but rather from the debased character types and broadly comic situations that this kind of novel richly supplies. In this sense *The Democrat* is a self-regulating fiction: discontent is anarchically undone from within. In one paradigmatic episode of Menippean satire, a radical debating society met to consider parliamentary representation degenerates rapidly from the rights of man to the rights of idiots and infants, and from orderly deliberation to the "chaos" and "confusion" of a "thousand discordant systems of reform," until a disgusted landlord enlists a watchman to expel the unruly members (*D* 2: 122–3, 131, 135). Oddly disconnected from the world through which he passes, Le Noir has at least the virtue of consistency, but there is little to admire in the haplessly contradictory forces that protect Britain from the threat of revolution. Even the disgusted landlord who finally expels the debating society, and voices a loyalist directive by swearing to admit no such clubs in the future, is motivated more by the damage done to his property than by any sense of civic virtue.

Given this pervasive disenchantment with British public life, it is significant that the most impressive rejection of Le Noir's insinuating Jacobin address comes in the novel's most radically dislocated episode, a central set-piece chapter entitled "Conversation in a Stage Coach." The rebuke is delivered by a modest American Quaker, who takes the coach's miscellaneous assembly of social types – "an old maid who was a great politician, a London rider, a young country Attorney, a sea officer" – to task for inviting Le Noir's French overtures by indulging the English national habit of complaining about government, commerce, agriculture, and social status (*D* 2: 25–26). It is a measure of Pye's unwillingness to activate indigenous virtue against subversion that this alien and nameless figure of religious dissent becomes the novel's most authoritative voice. The tendency elsewhere in the novel for uncivil discourse to degenerate into promiscuous discord is rhetorically reversed in the Quaker's long uninterrupted monologue, and in his concern to reassert social distinctions that the travelers have systematically violated by pretending "to argue on subjects which they do not understand" (*D* 2: 38). In dramatically confronting Le Noir *en route* with a virtuous antitype of his own subversive mobility, the novel boldly stages its dependence on the very dislocations it would correct. While this episode is unusually explicit, the pattern of a dislocated rebuke to revolutionary dislocation is surprisingly common in anti-Jacobin fiction, and it extends from figures of correction to figures of a virtue worth protecting. When Thomas Williams, the English Jacobin villain of Mrs. Bullock's 1801 novel, *Dorothea; or, A Ray of the New Light*, finds his initial efforts to "reap the harvest of confusion" frustrated "by the wise precautions of government" (*DR* 1: 190), he flees England and enters upon his own version of a subversive picaresque career in Ireland.[30] The Irish periphery becomes the occasion for the novel's most spectacular atrocity, a sexually charged assault on feminine cottage virtue that confounds geographical expectations by projecting the "domestic comfort" of a "happy and cheerful fire-side" (*DR* 1: 218–19) onto a Waterford farmhouse which is then ravished by monstrous English Jacobin desire. The emblematic significance of the episode is reinforced at the end of the novel when the only female survivor of the assault on the farmhouse, a mother driven mad by the slaughter of her family, reappears to admonish the dying Williams for his role in the Irish rising of 1798.

As a way of addressing one of the essential dilemmas of anti-Jacobin fiction, how to monitor the itinerant agents of subversion without replicating their restless energy, Pye's austere American Quaker is a memorable innovation, though not a decisive one. The stagecoach travelers are abashed by his harangue, and the reader is no doubt improved, but Le Noir is unrepentant and continues in his further course to meet no end of disaffected English subjects. *The Democrat* finally looks beyond its own narrative devices to purge a Jacobin infection. In a climactic sequence that begins soon after his arrival in London, Le Noir reverts to criminal type and falls in with an elegant group of gentleman pickpockets who possess "the real spirit of equalization" (*D* 2: 158, 162). When the gang is apprehended at a masquerade and brought before an examining magistrate, Le Noir is recognized and denounced as an infamous Jacobin by yet another virtuous antitype to his own revolutionary mobility, the French émigré aristocrat Chevalier Florenville, who is in court to secure a residency certificate under the provisions of the Alien Act, and who turns out to be the adopted son of one of Le Noir's early victims, the hero of the embedded "Story of the Count de Tournelles." His harrowing tale of "many hairbreadth escapes from death or imprisonment, and many dreadful scenes of devastation and bloodshed" offers a compressed inversion of the Jacobin rogue's tale, and his denunciation of Le Noir sets up the novel's final distribution of punishments and rewards. A sympathetic English nobleman who overhears the proceedings grants Florenville a "comfortable subsistence," allowing him to enter the restorative world of comic romance and marry "the fair Adelaide" (*D* 2: 171, 176, 184). No worse than the conventional rogue's tale they embody, the gentleman pickpockets are transported to Botany Bay.

But in a final reassertion of the difference between traditional theft and new model subversion, Le Noir is singled out by the court and "compelled under the authority of the Alien Bill" to return to France. The provisions of the Alien Act of 1793, a controversial early element of Pitt's legislative response to the French Revolution, were designed to expel French spies and republican agents while providing for the free movement of displaced émigrés. *The Democrat* undertakes a shrewd apology for the Act by invoking it in this climactic courtroom scene as a measured device for coordinating the incorporation of Florenville and the expulsion of Le Noir. Far from betraying any embarrassment about his *deus ex machina*, Pye offers a fulsome tribute to a legislature that "wisely armed the executive government, with a power of sending away such active citizens of a neighbouring nation, as migrate hither for the purpose of imparting to us the same liberal system they have established at home" (*D* 2: 187–8). It is worth observing that, by contrast with its sustained satirical treatment of coffee-house politics and fictitious newspaper reporting, the novel makes no effort to represent the deliberative and representational procedures that "wisely armed" the government in this way. In the end the gesture of reaching beyond narrative

The counterrevolutionary form of the novel

to state authority seems to betray the dependent status of a writer who was appointed Poet Laureate in 1790 as a reward for his unwavering loyalty to the Pitt ministry while he was a member of parliament. Yet other anti-Jacobin novels also resort to criminal justice to terminate a picaresque series, and in *Vaurien; or, Sketches of the Times* (1797) Isaac D'Israeli invoked the same Alien Act to expel a French revolutionary agent. That novel closed vividly upon the comic spectacle of the subversive hero bound for Holland, engrossed in speculative debate with a shipload of "patriots and philosophers, whom the o'erpressed stomach of England had disgorged with a violent, but a salutary effort."[31]

The peculiarly decentered and even cosmopolitan anti-Jacobin logic that would invest an American Quaker or a deranged Irish mother with authorial powers of admonition, in a narrative ostensibly designed to expel alien threats to native virtue, was evident as well in anti-Jacobin novels centrally concerned with the arrival in Britain of refugees from political violence. The French revolutionary émigré was an ambiguous figure in British culture in this period: aristocratic émigrés were susceptible to sentimental representation, and Edmund Burke in particular urged accommodation; yet national prejudices endured, particularly where the arrival of expelled French clerics elicited a wave of anti-Catholic feeling.[32] The generous acceptance that Pye encouraged in rewarding Florenville with a wife and a legacy became the central narrative strand of Ann Thomas' *Adolphus De Biron* (1795), a remarkable epistolary *counter*-picaresque that follows the providential convergence upon British soil of a dizzying array of Continental refugees and erstwhile British expatriates. The novel provocatively wrests home loyalties from cosmopolitan experience, as it ranges from Zurich, Italy, and the South of France to St. Petersburg and India, and presses into the service of a bloodthirsty French revolutionary regime every conceivable literary device of frustrated courtship, besieged virtue, denied inheritance, concealed identity, and discovered paternity. In orchestrating the complex interplay of over a dozen international correspondents for a political fantasy of ideological and geographical convergence, the novel challenges what Nicola J. Watson has identified as the prevailing movement of contemporary epistolary fiction towards disintegration and dispersal, with misdirected and deceptive letters suggesting a breakdown of political consensus and a tension among competing social discourses.[33]

Epistolary convergence is just one element of an array of strategies by which *Adolphus De Biron* reworks popular narrative convention in order to neutralize its radical or disruptive associations. A key embedded tale, "The Narrative of Madame Villeroi," revisits the sensational *ancien regime* expose, complete with "Lettres de Cachet" and imprisonment in the Bastille, in a paradoxical effort to harness enduring English suspicions of French absolutism for a new era of political reaction to French republican tyranny. For the novel's essential play of converging ideological forces, the pre-Revolutionary setting of the tale yields a crucial distinction in the historical forms of political exile that helps account for Britain's present absorption of foreign nationals. When the hero of the "Narrative," Monsieur Villeroi, finally escapes the nefarious Monsieur Le Fort and flees the "Horrors of the Bastille" for London, his conventional apostrophe to Britain's mixed constitution and "mild and equitable Laws" is premised on a limited conception of political exile: "Here I shall find an Asylum from the unjust Persecution which has constrained me to quit my native Country" (*ADB* 1: 119, 122, 124). Temporary "Asylum" turns out to be inadequate for later victims of the French Revolution, who must irrevocably renounce their birthright and elect to become British. Indeed, as the horrors of the Terror and the atrocities of Continental warfare mount over the course of the narrative, which roughly covers the years 1791 through 1795, it becomes clear that national distinctions are no longer salient in a world divided between revolutionary "Spectacles of Horror" (*ADB* 1: 3) and an embattled (though explicitly imperial and potentially global) British sphere of civility, hierarchy, and constitutional monarchy.

Though not subject to the same catastrophic pressures that make French identity untenable for men and women of virtue, British character is also significantly reframed in the novel. To begin with, such an identity is British rather than English, and therefore explicitly hybrid. This is established at the outset by a central strand of correspondence between the Scottish Alexander Bruce and the French-born Adolphus De Biron, whose maternal Scottish ancestry ultimately facilitates his own post-Revolutionary repatriation: "Britain, I must now wholly claim thee for my Country" (*ADB* 1: 41-2). National prejudices that once attached Britons to their native soil but now risk obstructing a romance of convergence are refined in their transmission, rather than being repudiated or ignored. The "contempt" felt by Alexander's worthy uncle, the retired navy officer Captain M, for the French as "the natural enemies of his Country" is treated with indulgence by a younger generation with good reason to cherish the liberties his naval career helped transmit. Furthermore, the passionate "Temper" and "Zeal" of the Captain proves that he is "a Philanthropist in the full sense" (*ADB* 1: 14, 161) of the word, rather than the cold and calculating Jacobin sense. The Captain's strong passions betray a national tendency to place feeling above reason, manifest in the present generation as a resistance to Jacobin speculation and as a generous "pity" and "sympathy" for the wave of revolutionary refugees. "The Situation of the Emigrants is greatly to be pitied," according to the normative Anglican clergyman Mr. Stanley, and "Britain with her native Generosity must extend her sheltering Arms for their Protection" (*ADB* 1: 162). The novel is remarkably precise about its redistribution of the affective resources of popular literature: if sympathy and sensibility welcome those who have fled in horror from gothicized political violence, then enthusiasm becomes the appropriate register for a series of late epistolary effusions ratifying the decision to become British.[34] In this respect, *Adolphus De Biron* is more concerned than other anti-Jacobin novels to recuperate heightened emotional states that many conservatives had come to associate with a literature of sexual transgression, individual self-fulfillment, and political subversion.[35] Indeed, the erotic energies of popular fiction are almost entirely redeployed here for a bizarre new romance of global political convergence. Courtship plays some role in achieving the fantasy of counterrevolutionary union, notably in the marriage of Adolphus to an expatriated Frenchwoman, but there is little real concern for the desires involved here. Instead, the novel consumes itself with the epistolary energies that bring passionate French disavowals of national identity together with effusive British gestures of acceptance and incorporation.

As ingenious as Ann Thomas may be in reworking the diffusive play of picaresque energies, there is a sense in which *Adolphus De Biron* fails even more spectacularly than most anti-Jacobin fictions to address the threat of revolution. The greatest challenge that seems to face British culture in the 1790s is to absorb a wave of foreign nationals who have already been ideologically tested and found hostile to subversion. The usual anti-Jacobin fear of foreign infiltration is replaced by a fantasy of the global superabundance of counterrevolutionary feeling. Yet in attending closely to the emotional relations at work in a recoil from revolutionary violence, *Adolphus De Biron* suggests one way in which anti-Jacobin picaresque fiction did come to terms with subversive agency. For if these novels tended to avoid representing the ordinary business of radical organization, except as a matter of burlesque, they were nevertheless deeply concerned with revolutionary psychology in the only way they were prepared to imagine it, as an incomprehensible and apparently boundless appetite for violence. In this sense what troubled the anti-Jacobin picaresque was not so much the radical desire for a different kind of social order (democracy, equality, infidelity), but rather the more ominous emergence under Paineite and Godwinian tutelage of a new personality type that found perverse comfort in disorder. Nowhere is this new Jacobin personality more monstrously embodied than in Frederick Fenton, the hero of George Walker's novel *The Vagabond*, who has learned from his Godwinian tutor Stupeo to "unhinge all society" and seek "a complete triumph over all regular order" (*V* 25, 66). By a striking anachronism, the opportunity to do so presents itself when he arrives in London during the Gordon Riots of 1780 and is recruited by its shadowy leadership to instigate mob violence. Though harrowing enough in itself, the subsequent narrative of the Gordon Riots falls well short of Frederick's Jacobin desire, expressed as a frustrated and sexually charged fantasy after the militia has intervened to quell the violence. "It would have been . . . like the fermentation of anarchy, which from all the rage of lust, of revenge, of murder, or cruelty, of rapine, and unheard of distress, sinks into a glorious and heart-soothing calm" (*V* 69). The historical slippage that allows Frederick to proceed from a Godwinian education to the Gordon Riots and cries of "No Popery" betrays a concerted effort, familiar from Hamilton's *Memoirs of Modern Philosophers*, to deny contemporary political protest any connection with coherent principle or a credible experience of injustice.

Walker's exuberant replaying of the Gordon Riots as the frenzied occasion for blocked Jacobin desire is a literary and polemical *tour de force*, and among the most impressive single episodes in anti-Jacobin fiction. Yet its ambiguities extend well beyond the problem of anachronism. For by fictionalizing one of England's most alarming recent experiences of urban violence,[36] the novel suggests that the threat of revolution cannot simply be traced to foreign contagion, a point reinforced early on by allusions to Cromwell and seventeenth-century civil unrest. Documentary footnotes to periodicals from the period of the riots and a close account of Frederick's insurrectionary progress ("the New-river water," "the Museum," "the toll-houses on the bridge," "the East-India warehouses and the Custom-house," "the Tower and the Bank") make this among the most rigorously situated versions of an anti-Jacobin picaresque (*V* 66–7, 72). At the same time, Walker makes no attempt to account for a presumptive link between "No Popery" and the new philosophy, and his documentary treatment of the Gordon Riots accords uneasily with a more categorical footnote tracing Stupeo's absurd theories to "Paine and Godwin on Revolutions and Anarchy" (*V* 69). The aggressive uprooting that is required to activate "Paine and Godwin" within the Gordon Riots recalls the novel's prefatory theory of anti-Jacobin fiction as a willful experiment upon radical principles. And because *The Vagabond* begins *in media res*, the entire foray into historical fiction comes as a retrospective narration by Frederick for the benefit of Alogos and his niece: narrative framing reinforces historical dislocation and the sense of distance created by the essential conception of mob violence as a consummate type of urban political spectacle. Again, Walker wants us to understand all this as the symptom of an underlying Jacobin pathology, as Frederick seems to derive pleasure less from doing violence than from instigating and observing the violence done by others, and becomes increasingly frustrated in London by his recognition that the urban mob is an imperfect instrument for his own speculative self-realization.

In this sense, the retrospective narration for Alogos and Laura of a feverishly anticipated revolutionary climax that did not come to pass ("it would have been . . .") suggests an aesthetic as well as historical problem. I have already cited the strictures of the *British Critic* about this novel's excessive indulgence in "scenes and circumstances of horror." Walker was far more willing than most anti-Jacobin novelists to indulge a voyeuristic pleasure in grotesque spectacle, so that the reader follows with unabated fascination as Frederick advances from memories of "the different conflagrations of the Fleet Prison, King's Bench, [and] Toll-houses on Blackfriar's-bridge" to lurid Jacobin fantasies of what might have been:

How much greater must have been the sight, amidst which even the soul of a modern philosopher might tremble, would it have been to see the flames chasing the distracted people from street to street; to see the enemies of liberty perishing in heaps before the burning sword of retributive justice; to see the rage of lust despoiling those disdainful beauties, whose love heretofore was only to be won by cringing; to see trembling tyrants biting the dust, and drinking their own blood as it mingled in the kennels; to hear amidst all this uproar the thunder of canons, the whistling of bullets, the clashing of swords, the tumbling of houses, the groans of the wounded, the cries of the

conquerors; and see, amidst the blazing and red-hot ruins, the sons of Freedom and Liberty waving the three-coloured banners dropping with the blood
of their enemies, and hailing the everlasting Rights of Man!!! (*V* 69–70)

If the spectacle of the tri-color raised over the embers of the Gordon
Riots represents the novel's most vivid anachronism, the historically
inevitable suppression of the riots accounts for the literary license taken.
Frederick Fenton himself draws a reassuring conclusion about political
conditions in England: "So long as what is called civil order and police
exists, I very much fear the people will never unanimously rise" (*V* 68).
And yet at this early stage in the novel legal containment has to remain
flawed if the narrative is to pursue its picaresque course. In this sense,
the obvious and disturbing alignment of Walker's counterrevolutionary
literary achievement with Frederick's revolutionary desire turns out to
be less revealing than the more subtle alignment of picaresque narration with an indulgent British government that never decisively
suppresses the Frederick Fentons of the world. Unlike Pye, Walker was
engaged in the strand of the anti-Jacobin novel that sought integration
rather than expulsion: his chastened hero returns gratefully to British
shores after exhausting himself in a Jacobin version of the new world
adventures of Voltaire's Candide. And in pursuing this course, Walker
was more willing than other novelists to concede the literary and legal
co-production of a radical recidivism, by linking the obvious delight he
himself takes in narrating Frederick's misadventures with the supposed
lenience of the British state towards domestic political threats.

A dialectic of subversion, in which counterrevolutionary narration
unfolds in the space between radical desire and government indulgence, is perhaps clearest in the novel's development of a corrective
antitype to Frederick in the figure of the loyal nobleman Lord B——,
whose capacity to ordain plot outcomes lends allegorical precision to
an otherwise unruly fiction. We first encounter the shadowy young
Lord B—— on a stagecoach that carries Frederick to London, and if this
aristocratic man of property is not so alien a figure as Pye's American
Quaker or Bullock's mad Irish mother, his unaccountable habit of
traveling under the guise of anonymity yields similar effects. The scene
in the stagecoach firmly links geographical and social mobility with
political error. Traveling conversation is triggered by a glimpse of the
socially resonant labor of hedge mending, and the detached perspective and miscellaneous social composition of the stagecoach contrasts
unfavorably with the productive hierarchy of labor and supervision in

a stable agricultural landscape. When conversation degenerates from idle speculation to subversive controversy, the otherwise reticent Lord B— intervenes to defend agriculture, commerce, and civil society from the primitivist "political romances" spun by Frederick and a republican merchant, suggestively named Adam, who compounds his misunderstanding of the American war with symptomatic errors about new world geography (V 51–2). Picaresque misadventure then briefly passes into allegory after the coach overturns: Lord B— joins some willing farmhands in setting the vehicle right, while Adams betrays his political hypocrisy by refusing to descend to the task, and Frederick merely wanders off on foot to pursue the absurd metaphysical reflections the experience has triggered.

Agricultural production similarly conditions a subsequent encounter with Lord B— in his proper person as a landlord and an embodiment of local government. At this point Frederick is involved in a primitivist walking tour, and has taken to encouraging rural laborers to reject "aristocratical enclosures" in favor of a return of wasteland to the "state of nature" (V 91–2), until he is seized in the act of fomenting rebellion by a group of gentlemen improvers. Lord B— apprehends the hapless *provocateur* in terms of a conservative theory of radical itinerancy that fuses legal and picaresque conceptions of disruptive agency: "We have here one of those seditious imposters that go about the country destroying its peace, and telling palpable lies in a flowery language, which warms the passions, and runs away with sober reason" (V 94).[37] Yet rather than lend his social status to a decisive criminal prosecution, Lord B— defuses any expectation of a trial, and instead undertakes an examination that pits his own authoritative voice (manifestly the novelist's own) against radical responses that are distinguished by the bad eminence of a footnote to Godwin. As novelistic conversation passes into catechism, the particular sense of place and status established by Lord B—'s intimacy with the farmhands yields to a more abstract framework for counterrevolutionary address: "I would ask one sober question, and would to God the whole world could hear me. If simple nature, poverty, and equality is the natural state of man, why do reformers wish to deprive the rich of their wealth, to render the poor unhappy?" (V 96). The gesture confirms a curious sympathy between the Jacobin rogue and the anti-Jacobin aristocrat, since Lord B— is in effect correctively retracing the movement by which Frederick sought to foment rebellion by rejecting particular boundaries ("fences," "hedges," "highways," "canals") in favor of nothing less than the theoretical right of an entire people "to the whole surface of the earth" (*V* 91–2). And if Lord B— recalls similar figures of mobile surveillance in the Cheap Repository, the shift from realism to catechism unleashes a fantasy of reconciliation worthy of Hannah More, as the abashed workers vow to return the next day "to replace the hedges they had thrown down" (*V* 98), and therefore retreat from Frederick's radical promise of common land to the agricultural improvements that will ensure they remain dependent laborers in enclosed fields.

The novel does not close upon this fantasy only because Lord B— enacts his homage to British liberty by generously releasing the prisoner (and the reader) from the rigors of catechism back into the endless possibilities of the picaresque: "'And to conclude this adventure,' said the young nobleman, 'let this unfortunate man be liberated; and I hope he will yet be convinced of the folly of destroying one system, which has *some faults*, with *many beauties*, and in its place proposing another, which has not one single *practical beauty*, but is pregnant with the most detestable and dreadful evils'" (*V* 98). Frederick is briefly reduced to silence, but as he wanders off he wastes no time in recovering his criminal and subversive bearings, first by lapsing into the kind of self-actualizing interior monologue that stands for new philosophical dialogue in these novels, and then by emerging from silence to an apostrophe that parodies the sentimental literary device of psychic repair through solitary expression. His speech is occasioned by the moonlight spectacle of a gibbet, and therefore blithely ignores the indulgence with which he has just been treated: "'O property! . . . this is one of thy blessed effects – what a dreadful exhibition of injustice glares upon the thinking mind, that death shall be the fate of the man who by force exerts the rights of nature'" (*V* 98–100). As if to confirm that the Jacobin rogue is a co-production of literary and social codes, the interlude of solitary recuperation becomes a hinge between the indulgence shown by Lord B— and the novel's most clichéd picaresque episode. Won over by his own case against private property, Frederick turns highwayman and winds up assaulting and (apparently) killing his mother, only to be apprehended and released by his father after a harrowing scene of discovered paternity. In this way the Vagabond reclaims his social nature the only way he knows how, by violently reinserting himself into an endless serial narrative of moral transgression and political subversion.

Frederick Fenton's solitary reconversion in the aftermath of a public humiliation evinces a broader effort within counterrevolutionary narrative to expose the ways in which Jacobin monologue and debased dialogue try to pass themselves off as deliberative intercourse. In a set-piece chapter of D'Israeli's *Vaurien* entitled "A Philosophical Conversation," the Godwinian philosopher Mr. Subtile presents his latest treatise, "Prejudices Destroyed, or Paradoxes Proved," to a gallery of radical caricatures, including the gentleman reformer Lord Belfield, the Dissenting minister Dr. Bounce, and the firebrand orator Mr. Dragon. The novelist warns us that the episode "will have more the appearance of a monologue than of a dialogue," but insists that it is "a faithful representation of the conversations of some great philosophers."[38] Elizabeth Hamilton applies similar assumptions to radical courtship each time Bridgetina Botherim lapses into soliloquy to secure in imagination the affections of an indifferent Henry Sydney. Yet these satirical deflations do not exhaust the possibilities for anti-Jacobin fictional conversation. On the contrary, the novel is distinctive within the field of counterrevolutionary literature for its detailed rendering of domestic conversation as a way of securing commitment to government and social order.

The limits of such representations are clear: on the one hand, the results of household conversation are not brought to bear upon a countervailing radical network of taverns, coffee-houses, theaters, and debating societies; on the other, domestic expressions of loyalty are not linked with public association and civic enterprise, let alone with the constitutional procedures of parliamentary deliberation and representation these novels are concerned to defend. A conceptual split between public and private realms is symptomatically reinforced even as it is challenged. Yet despite these limits, fictional episodes of domestic conversation about the forces of revolution do represent a concerted effort to meet the force of subversion through the development of collective habits of criticism, reflection, and deliberation. Where radicals argued that corrupt government could not withstand critical scrutiny, and therefore had to resort to repressive mechanisms, the anti-Jacobin novel suggested that loyalty was sustained rather than compromised by judicious habits of critical reflection and exchange. In her 1799 novel, *Translation of the Letters of a Hindoo Rajah*, Elizabeth Hamilton went so far as to reverse the radical challenge by concluding an attack on religious

skepticism with the principle that "where freedom of discussion is permitted, there skepticism and infidelity will be but little known."[39]

A commitment to the household as both a refuge for embattled
virtue and a dynamic social space in its own right conditioned the
distinctive anti-Jacobin narrative interplay between domestic romance
and picaresque misadventure: the assignment of well-disposed families
to secure homes and villages offered a counterpoint to the circulation of
disaffected individuals through restless social networks. The "happy and
cheerful" Waterford farmhouse in *Dorothea* epitomizes the simplest type
of anti-Jacobin domestic representation within a picaresque framework:
it exists to be assaulted. More compelling representations emerge
where the home is explored as an arena for the development of
complex, collective, and outward looking practices of critical deliberation, available (with some qualifications) to women as well as men,
and opening out (at least as far as topic of conversation is concerned) to
the wider public world of newspapers, books, fashion, theater, and
government. This engaged domesticity is broadly consistent with what
Claudia Johnson has identified as a late eighteenth-century female
tradition of political fiction that refused to "draw the line between
public and private at the threshold of an Englishman's home and then
assign women to that apolitical space within its doors." Although
Johnson considers such narratives "distinctively flexible, rather than
ferociously partisan, in their sympathies," the anti-Jacobin novel made
its professed flexibility about the politics of home an occasion for partisan comment.[40] Historically, this construction of a mixed and fluid
arena for domestic conversation can be considered an effort to retrieve
and reform social conditions that have long been associated with the
canonical origins of the English novel, in particular, the "audience-
oriented subjectivity" Jürgen Habermas identifies with "the intimate
sphere of the conjugal family" as a kind of "training ground" for the
development of the political public sphere.[41] To be clear, the tendency
to assign virtuous habits of conversation and critical reflection to the
home should not be taken to indicate an unrelieved politics of nostalgia,
and loyalist attacks on radical primitivism often involve a defense of
commercial society and the newer social hierarchies it sustained. But the
generally disapproving treatment of newspapers, political clubs, circulating libraries, theatrical performances, and debating societies in these
novels does betray a suspicion that, in their actual development over the
course of the eighteenth century, the institutions of middle-class civility
amounted to a destabilizing precondition for revolution.

In making interior scenes of domestic conversation available for public consumption, the anti-Jacobin novel in effect mobilizes private life as an alternative form of publicity, dissident with respect to public radical culture, but committed to reinstating hierarchies of gender, rank, education, and generation that can be represented as a matter of easy civility within the home. Where these novels relegate the normative household to a rural frame of representation, beyond the reach of urban vice and subversion, they can be said to participate in a wider process whereby the national tale and other romantic-period developments in popular fiction tend increasingly to privilege rural life.[42] Yet for this reason it is significant that loyal conversation does often take place in London, as a proximate response to urban radical protest and the corruption of public manners. Here again, it is worth insisting that these novels mobilize the home in a dialectical fashion, as a way of countering individual as well as collective vices. Family structure and parental authority were felt to be particularly effective in offsetting unruly habits of self-reflection conditioned by sentimental fiction, and here counterrevolutionary writers contended directly with Rousseau and his impact upon English narrative romance.[43] Where the rise of the novel over the course of the eighteenth century has been broadly identified with individualism and psychological realism, anti-Jacobin fiction was notably spare in its rendering of interior consciousness, preferring the exterior relationships afforded by domestic realism.[44] Tellingly, the obvious exceptions to this preference for the social responsibilities afforded by domestic realism, evident in satirical treatments of new philosophical self-absorption, are not in themselves an authentic register of individual dispositions, since such episodes are typically punctuated by references to Godwin or Paine. The errors of Frederick Fenton and Bridgetina Botherim are not errors of self-possession, but of allowing oneself to be possessed by others.

While anti-Jacobin novels are committed to private conversation about public matters, their engagement with compromised popular literary convention tends to reinforce a sense that the domestic sphere cannot sustain morality, property, and personality through a revolutionary crisis. No less than other fictions of the period, anti-Jacobin novels are littered with broken families, irresponsible parents, and neglected children, and such figures of domesticity gone astray are not exclusively identified with corrupt or subversive outcomes. For every Ellinor Stanley, who passes unscathed though London's moral hazards in Thomas Harral's *Scenes of Life* (1805) because her mind "had been too well formed by the instructions of her aunt, to fear contagion" (*SOL* 1: 198), there are more curious figures who challenge prevailing conservative assumptions about the importance of household education: on the one side, the orphaned Laura in *The Vagabond*, who preserves virtue and common sense despite having been systematically misinformed by her uncle Doctor Alogos; on the other, Geraldine Powerscourt in Jane West's *A Tale of the Times* (1799), who falls prey to Jacobin seduction despite having been raised in virtue and piety by a father who embodies the social ideal of the landed patriarch as "conscientious guardian" (*TT* 1: 28). *A Tale of the Times* heightens the sense of a gap between education and outcome through a dramatic split in the narrative form of a novel that aims to recapitulate "the penalty of Adam" (*TT* 2: 9) as domestic tragedy. At the opening of the second volume, the narrator Mrs. Prudentia Homespun advises us that a narrative so far devoted to the strength of "filial and conjugal ties" must now take up "the disgusting task of describing systematic villany mining the outworks which decorum and religion have placed around female virtue, while the unsuspecting heart becomes entangled by satanic guile and inbred vanity" (*TT* 2: 6). And *The Vagabond* indicates just how far anti-Jacobin fiction was prepared to stray from assumptions about the natural or unconscious transmission of morality by treating Laura's feminine virtue in remarkably unsentimental terms, and making her resistance to her uncle's subversive tutelage and Frederick's "brothel doctrines" (*V* 115) and sexual advances the result of an orphan's calculated determination to transmit a specific set of legal rights and social privileges to her own legitimate offspring.

Given Claudia Johnson's argument that Burke's *Reflections* bequeathed to the conservative literary imagination a patriarchal family romance that worked its way through many of the underlying narrative elements of popular fiction, especially those having to do with the transmission of property and the conditions for generational continuity,[45] it is all the more remarkable that anti-Jacobin novels were prepared to make the virtuous child of vicious parents a central character type for exploring reversals and disruptions in the normal course of transmission. At the same time, the development of the disturbing new figure of the subversive parent, epitomized in Jane West's novel *The Infidel Father* (1802), allowed novelists to safely activate objectionable literary conventions by marking them as Jacobin pathologies: to escape the influence of the infidel father becomes a counterrevolutionary response to revolutionary patriarchy. In *The*

Citizen's Daughter, or What Might Be, an anonymous novel of 1804, the young heroine Marianne Norton manages, despite her father's corrupt moral and political influence, to negotiate a courtship plot that requires her to reject the intended seducer Charles Denham so she can instead marry the virtuous Lord Morden. A potentially disturbing gap between domestic origins and romance outcomes is reinforced by a cautionary subplot that traces the opposite fate of Marianne's childhood friend Fanny Worthington, the carefully nurtured daughter of a country parson who dies after being seduced and ruined by the same Denham. When Fanny's parents themselves die of their distress, Lord Morden and Marianne collaborate to raise "an elegant tablet" in their memory, an act of filial devotion to failed virtuous parenthood that vividly challenges expected patterns of inheritance and transmission. The citizen's daughter has become a proxy for the clergyman's daughter. And it is in this collaboration that Marianne and Morden begin the process of negotiating their future together as a conspiracy against her corrupt father, so that the *"plain and moral lesson"* inscribed upon the tablet uneasily instantiates a public discourse of moral example within a novel whose troubling discontinuities undermine the idea that private virtues are adequate for the transmission of piety and loyalty.[46]

By stressing the unpredictability of domestic outcomes, and granting the vulnerability of "the outworks" of "decorum and religion," anti-Jacobin domestic romance contributes to the development of a conservatism that was interventionist rather than simply defensive or retrospective. At their most engaging, these are remedial if not overtly reformist fictions. Their deliberate reconsideration of the home as a social space for critical and judicious conversation about public matters is better evidence of the political threat they perceived than any number of Godwinian caricatures. And while never as systematic as the Cheap Repository in their representation of reading and publishing as a way of securing social order, these novels did supplement their reluctant use of debased literary conventions with a more constructive effort to make didactic political fiction an instrument for securing public order. As a modest but confident and unyielding figure for the author Jane West, Mrs. Prudentia Homespun does not idly come by her name: she is both the product and the producer of household virtues, and in that capacity she contends mightily with an irreverent new philosophy that is "sufficiently powerful to overturn governments, and to shake the deep-founded base of the firmest empires" (*TT* 2: 274). Of course it is in their relentless didacticism that these novels tend to lose modern readers, and it easy to discover a failure of the literary imagination in their reversion to conduct book morality and political catechism. Yet tensions between static precept, the *"plain and moral lesson"* inscribed upon a memorial tablet, and the uncertainties of human experience do sometimes allow a more complex and dynamic approach to narrative form. And even where precept routinely prevails, it is not always easy to decide whether we are witnessing a disciplinary campaign against the refractory tendencies of popular fiction, or a more interesting reengagement of domestic realism with some of the heterogeneous and pragmatic discourses (spiritual biography, conduct book) from which the novel emerged over the course of the eighteenth century.[47]

The Advantages of Education, or, The History of Maria Williams, A Tale for Misses and Their Mammas is a useful case in point, morally straightened in its didactic purposes yet still somehow formally resourceful and engaging. As a Prudentia Homespun tale that aims frankly "to enstruct, rather than entertain,"[48] this novel falls somewhere between West's aggressively anti-Jacobin novels, *A Tale of the Times* and *The Infidel Father*, and her gendered pair of conduct books, *Letters to a Young Man* (1801) and *Letters to a Young Lady* (1806). The doubling of the heroine figure as mother and daughter follows from a didactic concern, broached in the novel's subtitle, to transmit moral precepts simultaneously to their ultimate target ("Misses") and to a crucial point of further transmission ("Mamas"). If such a design recalls the many different implied readers of the Cheap Repository tracts, the effect in *The Advantages of Education* is quite different, shifting the narrative burden from moral precepts as such to the complex subjective and intersubjective conditions under which they take effect. A single marriage plot is fluidly developed to accommodate the shared experience and unusual physical intimacy of a pair of heroines, Maria Williams and her widowed mother Mrs. Williams. Rather than departing from the compromised devices of popular fiction in order to secure conduct book morality, the novel mobilizes its overlapping mother-daughter consciousness in order to avert all the familiar literary hazards of seduction plots, concealed identities, and fraudulent marriage ceremonies. When Maria is compelled to renounce a deceptive but appealing suitor, she announces her self-disciplinary decision to dictate the letter of rejection to her mother, so that it will be infused in its inscription by a maternal style that is "more firm than passionate" (*AE* 2: 69).[49] Intense intersubjective sympathy certainly allows an astonishing level of surveillance in this novel, through what Nicola J. Watson suggestively terms "the mother's policing eye."[50] But the result is that the novel compels the daughter to acquire moral agency through a perpetual opening out of self to scrutiny and intervention, rather than through any mechanical internalization of moral advice. And despite Mrs. Williams' authority, the term "agency" can be applied to Maria since her female virtue is put at risk within a Christian scheme of redemption that requires the daughter to assume "the power of acting" for herself (*AE* 1: 201), through a difficult and ongoing maternal process of selective disengagement. In this sense, there are ample precepts here for Mamas and Misses alike. The same Christian framework sustains a pervasive figure of gardening and cultivation: maternal surveillance turns out to be just one component of the intensive acculturating labor that is involved in domestic life.[51] As we later learn through retrospective narration, Mrs. Williams is herself paradoxically the product of the very fictional conventions she is concerned to prevent in her daughter, having endured early assaults on her virtue, a loveless marriage to a libertine gambler, and traumatic widowhood in the West Indies. In undertaking the reciprocal discipline of domestic education, Mrs. Williams and Maria effectively challenge any facile assumption that print transmission – whether through conduct books or lurid popular romances – can by itself either sustain or undermine virtuous character in a world beset with moral hazards.

If the intimate surveillance of *The Advantages of Education* was unique, other novels found distinctive ways to handle domestic experience. In *Scenes of Life*, published in 1805 but set in London in the 1790s, Thomas Harral extends the critical range of domestic romance in part by reconfiguring the anti-Jacobin picaresque through the familiar patterns of voyeuristic underworld exploration. The subversive rogue yields here to a more sympathetic urban tourist, for whom the home serves as a pivotal site of departure and return. And while the naive adventurer Sir Frederick Stanley is clearly the hero of *Scenes of Life*, the novel signals its commitment to the experience of his sister Ellinor through an early chapter praising their father's decision to educate her – a liberal position that Harral then qualifies by repudiating Wollstonecraft's grotesque "extension of female prerogative," and orienting female education instead towards an "accomplished elegance" that yields "sensible" marriage partners (*SoL* 1: 22, 24–5, 27). After their father's heroic death in battle against French Revolutionary forces, the two orphaned children set up household in Harley Street under the domestic supervision of their virtuous aunt, Miss Eliza Burton, and the equally sure public hand of Frederick's worldly friend, Henry Maitland. Frederick is committed to "any opportunity of *seeing life*" in London, and a crucial early chapter finds him and Maitland "induced to pass an evening at one of our metropolitan schools of disputation," to which they are drawn by "the large bills which appeared posted at every corner" (*SoL* 1: 155). The predictable if well-handled satire of public radical assembly that follows yields two important themes. First, given the novel's preliminary commitment to female education as a way of cultivating marriage partners without confounding "distinctions of sex" (*SoL* 1: 24), this underworld excursion must leave Ellinor and Miss Burton behind. And yet the debased conditions of radical sociability – "a motley group of males and females," vulgar and elite, "huddled promiscuously together" – are best registered by imagining and approving a virtuous female response. "Had the timid Ellinor been present, she must at first have recoiled from the heterogeneous commixture"(*SoL* 1: 156–7). The topic of the evening's debate reinforces a concern for gender roles, and suggests the disciplinary force of the novel's otherwise routine marriage plots: "*At the present enlightened Era, the close of the Eighteenth Century, ought Marriage to be considered as a Divine Ordinance, as a Civil Institution; or, as a mere Piece of Priestcraft, invented as a cover for Illicit Amours?*" (*SoL* 1: 158). By underscoring matters of decorum Ellinor's imagined recoil plays into a second important thematic concern: the radical debating society turns out to be incapable of conducting a meaningful conversation, and therefore fails on matters of procedure as well as principle. Furious harangues against wedlock and an equally misguided defense of marriage by an enthusiastic Dissenting minister are routinely interrupted by the raucous and increasingly violent audience. Yet when the reigning "indecorum" shocks Frederick into attempting to intervene, he is prevented not by the overbearing chairman of the debate or the unruly crowd, but rather by the firm corrective hand of Maitland. In enforcing "silent" observation, Maitland registers the prevailing skepticism of the anti-Jacobin novel about intervening in radical public affairs. And restraint here is possible in part because radical protest once again founders on its own divisions. As intoxicated controversy degenerates into a "confusion of tongues" and outright violence, the two friends can "hardly refrain from laughing aloud at the exhibition of so grotesque a scene" (*SoL* 1: 171–2), and they make their escape before the great question of marriage has been decided.

Although the episode closes decisively upon this elite masculine ridicule, the next chapter dramatically resurrects the Jacobin threat with an epigraph warning about the "alarming" and "dangerous" nature of radical organization. From here, Harral develops a powerful narrative coda to his debating club parody. "On the following morning, Maitland was an early visitor to his friends in Harley Street; where, over the breakfast table, he and Sir Frederick detailed the amusement of the preceding evening" (*SoL* 1: 173). A mixed sphere of domestic conversation becomes the appropriate venue for polite critical reflection upon vulgar public radical assembly, conceived here ambiguously as both entertainment and subversive challenge. Breakfast-room conversation enforces limits and constraints that were conspicuously absent in the debating society. Reintroduced at this point as a mature woman "fully acquainted with the moral, religious, and civil duties of a good subject," and therefore aware that "the arcana of politics" is "the proper sphere of man," Miss Eliza Burton boldly initiates a critical assessment of the previous evening's controversy by regretting the decline of London's civic culture. Yet her gesture is doubly qualified, since she concedes that she was not an eyewitness to the proceedings ("Had I been present . . ."), and wishes that some male "friend of social order" had stepped forward "as a partisan and defender of propriety" (*SoL* 1: 174–5). Since this last sentiment echoes Frederick's attempt to rise at the meeting, Maitland can now account for his earlier gesture of prevention. He allows that the London political clubs were once a training ground for some of "our principal senators and barristers," including "the great Mr. Burke," but insists that they have "dreadfully degenerated" since "Paine's political and theological trash" and Sunday school education have conspired to transform "every dapper apprentice" and "illiterate labourer" into a self-styled political genius (*SoL* 1: 175–6). When Miss Burton presses her point, wondering whether "men of real knowledge" might yet "silence" arrogant popular claims, he repeats his essential argument about historical difference: "That, Madam, in the present state of things, would be a difficult task" (*SoL* 1: 177). If this claim accounts for the retreat of elite civic deliberation from its earlier eighteenth-century masculine public forums to a private breakfast room, open to women as well as men, it is issued with a decorum that is calculated to respect even as it enforces gender difference. More than anything else in the novel, Maitland's generous commitment to persuade and explain within a differentiated domestic framework prevents political exchange from degenerating

into mere catechism. Of course, in a fiction rigorously structured by
the alternate rhythms of underworld exploration and domestic retirement, authority rests on the resourceful mobility that is a male privilege, and Miss Burton can neither answer nor even question to full
effect. When Maitland illustrates a point with a short biographical
sketch of his briefly radicalized friend Wingfield, and she expresses her
surprise that cultivated minds fall prey to *Rights of Man*, she tactfully
allows that as a virtuous woman she has not actually read Paine
and must therefore reason at second hand: "I have been told, and
indeed believe . . ." (*SoL* 1: 181). Again, Maitland politely answers the
objection by demonstrating Paine's specious plausibility. The same
gendered restrictions upon public access that set the chapter in motion
with Miss Burton's vivid counterfactual ("Had I been present . . .")
ensure that Henry Maitland will remain the master of domestic
ceremonies.

Yet for all its restrictions, the Harley Street conversation about the
threat of radicalism is a more distinctive piece of counterrevolutionary
writing than the debating-society burlesque it punctuates, and *Scenes of
Life* evinces a limited willingness to revise the lines of authority in public
as well as private life. In opening the novel with a tribute to Frederick's
father, the elder Sir William Stanley, Harral first proposes a hierarchical ethics of social regard that is evident again in the life of
Wingfield, who recovers from his radical delusion only after he
becomes ashamed that elite acquaintances have discovered him in
earnest political conversation with a common tinker or "a deplorably
ragged brother citizen" (*SoL* 1: 189). This embarrassment serves as a
further justification for the retirement of the Stanley breakfast room as
window upon the spectacle of public radical assembly. A similar moral
concern for the regard of others rests securely on hereditary rank when
it is first advanced in tribute to the counterrevolutionary hero Sir
William Stanley. As the scion of an ancient family declined in wealth
but not in pride, Sir William sets out to distinguish himself through a
military career, and his decision to do so yields a defense of inherited
privilege that somehow wants to accommodate talent and personal
accomplishment. "The true use of hereditary honour is to invigorate
individual virtue," Harral argues, since "pride of ancestry" fosters
a vigilant concern to avoid the "one ignoble action" that would
extinguish the memory of a noble line. Whatever their merits, "children of obscure birth have no such incentive to virtue" (*SoL* 1: 2–3).
Yet this career vividly ends in the opening pages of the novel in

counterrevolutionary martyrdom. Henry Maitland is a more dominant and resourceful figure, and through the narrative rhythms of urban exploration and domestic conversation he sustains, the novel pursues a distinctly post-revolutionary defense of social hierarchy that rests less on inherited virtue than on the active exercise of reason and critical reflection. Where the example of Sir William Stanley explicitly had nothing to offer "children of obscure birth," Wingfield's embarrassment in the streets of London presents a transferable and communicable "incentive to virtue" that is appropriate to the didactic aims of fiction.

As *Scenes of Life* pursues its cycles of masculine public exploration and mixed private conversation, it becomes an unusually comprehensive anti-Jacobin fiction, engaging and commenting critically on everything from novel reading, foreign drama, and extravagant fashion to Methodist worship and the alarming introduction of pikes and drilling at radical meetings. An extended series of episodes involving Joanna Mountford (destined to marry Frederick) in her career as a translator of German drama affords a particularly rich treatment of the late eighteenth-century world of publishing, reviewing, and the theater, and here Harral is concerned to show the ways in which men ought to mediate and facilitate new public opportunities open to women. Through it all, the home is less a separate refuge than a fluid contact zone between public and private realms: its routines and habits create an orderly interior framework within which public risks of corruption and subversion can be safely assessed. Yet there is little to challenge the sense, established early on by Maitland's gesture of prevention, that polite critical perspectives do not yield strong counterrevolutionary agency. Like other anti-Jacobin novels, *Scenes of Life* finally turns to government and the law to suppress the threat of revolution, though in doing so it establishes a particularly complex (even ironic) set of relations between its own narrative devices and the repressive authority of the state. This is clear late in the novel, after Ellinor and Miss Burton have gained qualified access to the radical underworld through an invitation from their Paineite landlord, Mr. Smith, to attend a "democratico-methodistical" (*SoL* 2: 180) worship service and the ensuing festivities in his own home. The difference between breakfast with the Stanleys and dinner with the Smiths yields a sequence of comic episodes, which only draw to a close when Harral begins to invoke state power as a way of contriving his denouement. A sudden uproar in the Smith household reveals that it has been targeted for repressive action when, "for the purpose of checking the progress of jacobinical principles, government deemed it prudent to institute a search among those who were suspected of disaffection" (*SoL* 3: 99). After a low comic scene in which Mr. Smith conceals himself in the chimney while his leveling preacher Wilson is dragged from the pantry covered in flour, both men are arrested and escorted to prison, leaving Miss Burton to discover a stray piece of evidence, Mr. Smith's personal record of his activities "in the form of a journal, not much unlike that of the Citizen, in the Spectator; or, of the Idler, in Dr. Johnson's work of that title" (*SoL* 3: 109), which Henry Maitland is then asked to read aloud for entertainment and instruction.

Just as degenerate radical organization was measured against the defunct London civic culture associated with the rise of Edmund Burke, so the private record of Smith's political and domestic affairs is presented here as the debased afterlife of an esteemed eighteenth-century literary form. Gathered within doors under Maitland's supervision to read the radical journal, the Stanley household reasserts its status as a hybrid arena for conversation and critical reflection upon public matters, antithetically framing even as it neutralizes through comic ridicule a similarly mixed private record of public subversion. Smith's diary is calculated to expose the venality, drunkenness, and hypocrisy of the typical republican citizen, but there is within its burlesque contours an unusually circumstantial rendering of London radical culture, including celebratory dining and toasting rituals, meetings of the London Corresponding Society, speeches by John Thelwall and John Gale Jones, and a formal radical debate at the Falcon Tavern in Fetter Lane. Given the novel's underlying skepticism about well-intentioned loyalist efforts to intervene in a radical under-world, it is striking that the censorious decision to burn the journal after Maitland's closet performance turns out to be the limit here of any private assistance to government repression.

The precise intersection of legal and literary codes (seized evidence, discovered diary) that makes Smith's private writing available for public consumption returns in the novel's crowded denouement, when the wayward course of the picaresque is abruptly supplanted by the narrower teleology of romance, in the form of a triple marriage: a Mr. Seabright is reintroduced so that Aunt Burton can join Frederick and Joanna and Henry and Ellinor at the altar. To achieve these satisfying unions the novel must first dispatch its versatile if incidental Jacobin villain Huntley, a gambler, swindler, subversive pamphleteer, abusive reviewer, and "dabbler in every thing that is infamous" (*SoL* 3: 74), who compounds other crimes by plotting to abduct and ruin Joanna with the assistance of her malignant stepfather Berrington. A falling out among villains leads to mutual recriminations, with Huntley exposing Berrington as a fraud and forger, and Berrington charging Huntley "with holding a secret correspondence with the French, with the rebels in Ireland, and with the *illuminati* in Germany" (*SoL* 3: 141). Huntley is tried, convicted, and sentenced to death, and his prison repentance scene becomes the occasion for a harrowing discovery plot, with Berrington driven to madness and attempted suicide when he realizes he has informed on his own lost illegitimate son. Huntley's execution and Berrington's deranged attempt on his own life register the sterility and incestuous violence of revolutionary desire, while Joanna is with the assistance of the law extricated from the Jacobin seduction plot so that she can join Frederick and the rest of the Stanley household in "holy bonds of matrimony" (*SoL* 3: 214).

In retreating from the Jacobin ruins of urban civic culture to an orderly arena of mixed domestic conversation and critical judgment, *Scenes of Life* recapitulates within a narrative framework some of the central problems of counterrevolutionary culture. How can loyal opinion be produced, and should it be brought to bear upon the threat of Jacobin subversion? What is the role of state repression? And how can women contribute to the anti-Jacobin cause without risking Wollstonecraft's grotesque "extension of female prerogative"? While Harral's strictures on gambling, libertinism, religious skepticism, Italian opera, and German drama are broadly consistent with the tenets of moral reform, his willingness to assign Sunday schools a portion of the blame for the decline of London's elite civic culture, and his failure to enlist the charitable energies of the novel's abundant supply of loyal and intelligent women, suggests that he did not approve contemporary extensions of female social enterprise beyond the domestic sphere. In this sense, the figure of Maitland can be considered a challenge to Hannah More as well Thomas Paine, a challenge mitigated only by the fact that the restrictions applied to Miss Burton in the breakfast room extend to Frederick Stanley in the debating society. The novel's ambiguous episode of book (or manuscript) burning epitomizes its reluctance to make domestic conversation and critical judgment a source of political agency. Though discretely read aloud in private before being consigned to the flames, Mr. Smith's journal is never a credible threat, since its author is already in state custody, and his claims enter neutralized by the familiar devices of counterrevolutionary satire: self-exposing entries in the diary include "Reform is a very good mask for revolution," and "Wish I could get rid of my wife altogether. They manage these things better in France" (*SoL* 3: 115, 119). If Harral rescues domestic virtue from being a mere target of Jacobin assault through his impressive reworking of the picaresque, he continues to insulate domestic romance from the threat of revolution though judicious applications of the satirical lash as well as the final resort to government initiative.

The revealing gesture by which Miss Burton announces the gendered limits of her own competence even as she contributes to a conversation about public matters ("Had I been present . . . ," "I have been told . . .") becomes far more complicated and troubling in the hands of anti-Jacobin women novelists. Claudia Johnson has remarked that "authorial self-styling" in this period was "a sticky business for a woman publicly committed to championing female subordination," and representations of domestic conversation were invariably a matter of female authorial self-styling.[52] Harral managed gender roles at the difficult interface between private loyalty and public radicalism through his proxy Maitland. By contrast, women novelists tended to advance similar claims about female political deference in the absence of clear and direct male supervision, with results that were at once more challenging and more ambiguous. In a key sequence addressing the threat of revolution in *Adolphus De Biron*, Ann Thomas tended to dissociate gender roles even as she rehabilitated the letter as a stabilizing medium of communication. The issue is triggered in the first instance by the emblematic decision of the Frenchman Eugene Villeroi to abandon a projected journey through Italy and undertake instead a tour of Britain, in such a way as to forge a new national identity for himself even as he validates the plenitude of a British nation reconstituted globally as the sole alternative to French subversion. The Reverend Mr. Stanley opens his congratulatory letter to Villeroi with a compressed treatise on the glories of the British Constitution ("you know it is the Admiration and Envy of the whole World"), followed by an attack on those who would undermine its "beautiful and well compacted Fabric" and a damning biographical sketch of Thomas Paine (*ADB* 2: 64). The scurrilous life of Paine was already by 1795 a well-worn polemical convention, but it assumes distinctive force here within a centripetal counter-picaresque, as Paine's outrageously subversive misadventures on two continents come to be measured against Villeroi's virtuous determination to limit his horizons to Great Britain.

In picking up the anti-Paineite strand of argument, the next letter in the novel's epistolary sequence, from Adolphus' younger sister Matilda D— to her English correspondent Maria Henley, involves a calculated shift from the public idioms of the revolution controversy to the private terms of female confession. In this sense, Thomas assigns distinct idioms and conventions to masculine and feminine strands of correspondence. Matilda couches her political sentiments as private disclosure, and invokes a political crisis to justify her transgression of female modesty:

> I must entreat you to hear me on a Subject which has for two whole Hours employed my Thoughts. Now, I suppose you are ready to ask what important Subject could have so much Power over your giddy Friend; I answer Politics: Yes, Maria, Politics; and, as I do not think it proper to deliver my Opinions in Public, I must insist upon your giving me proper Attention on a Matter, which I think, concerns every body, high, and low, rich, and poor. (*ADB* 2: 76)

The same revolutionary crisis that makes British loyalty available to an international community of exiles provides qualified female access to political deliberation. And just as *Scenes of Life* developed its mixed domestic conversations to frame the radical subversion of gender roles, so this epistolary expression of female decorum reflects critically on its degenerate antithesis, as Matilda complains that "the Revolution has made not only the Men, but the Ladies also profound Politicians." Her account of the feminization of political literacy and controversy in France leads directly into an attack on *Rights of Man* as one of the "diabolical Publications" recently canvassed in mixed company (*ADB* 2: 77). At this point, despite an announced commitment to private correspondence, Matilda (like her "authoress") revisits the public polemical conventions that inform Mr. Stanley's preceding letter, embellishing an attack on Paine's contempt for "Distinctions of Rank" with a sketch of his origins as a stay-maker, and defending social hierarchy on the firm historical and constitutional grounds that "the House of Peers . . . has been found by Experience to be the most effectual Barrier against the Tyranny of the Crown, and the Madness of the People" (*ADB* 2: 77–8).[53] It then falls to Miss Henley in her reply to revert to a more profound attitude of female reticence by disavowing her French correspondent's familiarity with the idioms of print culture. "I have not seen (nor ever wish to see) the Publication you mention. I have however, heard enough about it to despise and hate the wretched Production and its Author" (*ADB* 2: 82). This English persistence of distinct gender roles may account for Villeroi's eventual acquisition of an English wife as part of his British grand tour and repatriation. Though Miss Henley's gesture recalls the similar disavowals of Miss Burton in *Scenes of Life*, the distinct narrative trajectory of *Adolphus De Biron* (convergent rather than cyclical) prevents female circumspection from operating within any sustained scheme of mixed conversation. Instead, the movement is inexorably back from Matilda's shocked experience of republican conversation to Miss Henley' climactic repudiation of a challenge she cannot comprehend: "There is no Appellation in all the Vocabulary of English Titles, so hateful to my Ears as the Name of Paine" (*ADB* 2: 82). It is only in the common loyalist pun on the word "pain" that the novel preserves some trace of its female author's own sustained engagement with public political idioms.

Though not intended to trouble readers, the distinction between two poles of epistolary resistance to subversion in these letters – calculated male refutation and uninformed female disavowal – suggests how a vigorous reinstatement of gender privileges could serve to compromise the development of a critical perspective on subversion from within the framework of domestic romance. And while Ann Thomas seems content to recommend female characters who, unlike herself, despise what they cannot understand, other anti-Jacobin women writers allowed for a more complex interplay between their own narrative voices and gendered political expression within the novel. In *Memoirs of Modern Philosophers*, Elizabeth Hamilton advances fuller intellectual capacities for women while still distinguishing loyal conversation from the debased heterogeneity of Jacobin democracy. In a crucial episode of Rousseauian pastoral courtship, staged as a spontaneous picnic "beneath the shade of a spreading elm" with camp stools and a portable "tea equipage," the radical freethinker Bridgetina Botherim enacts her incompetence in matters of romance by interrupting other courtships:

[Julia Delmond] and Harriet Orwell had just finished decorating a basket of strawberries with a wreath of flowers which Henry had gathered, and were with light and graceful steps bearing it betwixt them to the table, while Henry, keeping his seat upon the grass, was with eyes of rapture following every motion of the lovely pair, when the small shrill voice of Miss Botherim accosted his ears, and drew his attention from these engaging objects. (*MP* 98–9)

After identifying one source for her erotic confusion (and for this episode) by alluding to Rousseau's *Nouvelle Héloïse*,[54] Bridgetina brings the conversation around to Wollstonecraft and then vigorously attacks gender distinctions and the degrading influence of "household cares." Harriet Orwell proves herself the daughter of an Anglican clergyman by responding with a defense of the "dignity in domestic employment" in her own life (*MP* 101–2), though her interjection is significantly framed by a pair of male assertions, based on textual authority rather than personal experience. The first is Henry's account of *A Vindication of the Rights of Women* as the work of "a sensible authoress" betrayed by an excess of feeling into arguments that mislead "superficial readers" into thinking it is "her intention to unsex women entirely," a provocatively moderate judgment that is broadly consistent with Elizabeth Hamilton's own views, though it is ironically cut short by Bridgetina's habit of interruption. The second is Dr. Orwell's similarly moderate scriptural case for a Christian ethic that enjoins "no sexual virtues" but allows the providential assignment of "peculiar duties" to men and women (*MP* 101–3). Taken together these pronouncements mitigate a commitment to patriarchy while vividly sustaining male authority within a mixed sphere of domestic conversation.

Later in the novel Harriet comes into her own as a controversialist, in a more intimate and exclusively female encounter with the radicalized yet still redeemable Julia Delmond, who occupies the role of tragic heroine in Hamilton's triple-plotted romance. Recovering from injuries sustained during a bungled assignation with the Jacobin Vallaton, and unsure whether to return to her parents, Julia is impressed by Harriet's energetic case for Christian piety and filial duty. But without herself undertaking a refutation she suggests that her orthodox friend would fare less well in Jacobin company: "You argue so well, that I should like to hear you enter into a debate with some of my learned friends: upon the necessity of repentance, for instance. Ah, Harriet, you have no notion how soon that sweet eloquence of yours would be put to silence" (*MP* 165). Rather than rise to this challenge, Harriet embraces female reticence in a way that paradoxically sustains the discussion:

If indeed I were bold enough to enter into a debate, from the hope that my eloquence could possibly convince a person skilled in argument, I should deserve the mortification I should probably meet with. But take notice, that my reasons for declining the colloquial combat arise from a knowledge of the weakness of my weapons, not from any distrust of the goodness of my cause. (*MP* 165)

With this principle of decorum secured, Hamilton then freely stages the controversy occasioned by Julia's suggestion that the two women might appropriately argue in private with the limited instruments at their disposal:

> Well, but as your weapons are certainly at least equal to mine, suppose I give you a challenge? Let us take the ground upon the wisdom and efficacy of repentance. Which, dropping my gauntlet, I here aver to be the most mistaken notion in the world;—a mere prejudice, and a prejudice very inimical to the progress of virtue. (*MP* 165)

Harriet takes up this second challenge in the same ironic terms of masculine chivalry in which it is delivered, and a sophisticated debate about faith and repentance ensues. As in *Adolphus De Biron* female controversy remains an intimate exercise, though Hamilton is clearly more ambitious than Ann Thomas, allowing Harriet Orwell to develop logical propositions, refine terms, consider and resolve paradoxes, illustrate by example, and refute thoughtful objections. The mock-epic gesture by which Julia's challenge to debate was first accepted – "I . . . only wish I had one of my father's wigs to equip me for the solemnities of the field" (*MP* 165) – does not seem wholly self-diminishing, since it expresses the genuine desire of an educated young woman for a fuller recognition and consecration of her abundant intellectual powers, evident in the very capacity to handle mock-epic devices. Still, masculine authority patrols the boundaries of a conversation that advances inexorably towards an avowal of Christian piety, as Harriet consistently reverts from Bridgetina's transgressive example to precepts laid down by her own father. In its consequences, the debate clearly enjoins submission to patriarchy:

> The impression it made upon the mind of Julia was not to be easily effaced. After a few struggles with false shame and romantic tenderness, she adopted the resolution of throwing herself at her father's feet, as soon as she should be able to appear before him, and by a free and ingenuous acknowledgment of all that passed between her and Vallaton, make an atonement for her past offence, and regain that confidence which she was miserable in having forfeited. (*MP* 168)

The irony of this "resolution," that Julia can only accede to female intellectual influence by submitting to male authority, is consistent with Hamilton's ambiguous handling of her own situation as a women writer on political matters. The utopian opening to a fuller activation of female intellectual powers finally bends to a narrative concerned to reinstitute more conventional hierarchies and controls.

Jane West vividly frames the challenge posed by anti-Jacobin domestic conversation when she concludes *A Tale of the Times* with a qualified defense of female participation in public controversy. Her closing discussion of "the misfortunes under which literature now labours" ranges from the degenerate condition of the novel to the fashion for "female letter-writers" such as Helen Maria Williams and Mary Wollstonecraft to presume to "teach us the arcana of government" (*TT* 3: 384, 387). This stricture sets in sharp relief her apology for the engagement of her own novel in matters of religious controversy that were often proscribed to women by authorities on proper conduct:

> She feels it necessary to add an apology to the lovers of propriety and decorum, for her frequent allusions to religious subjects, and her intermixture of serious truths with fictitious events. It is not from any vain desire of throwing her feeble gage in the crowded fields of controversy, much less from a want of heartfelt reverence for sacred themes, that she adventured to make these digressions; but as the most fashionable, and perhaps most successful way of vending pernicious sentiments has been through the medium of books of entertainment, she conceives it not only allowable, but necessary, to repel the enemy's insidious attacks with similar weapons. (*TT* 3: 386–7)[55]

It is hard to know what to make of the implicit distinction between a proper "intermixture" of "sacred truths" with narrative fiction and the more pernicious radical effort to convert "books of travels" into "vehicles of politics" (*TT* 3: 387). The redeeming difference cannot credibly lie in a distinction between religion and politics. Far from restricting itself to matters of faith, *A Tale of the Times* helped secure anti-Jacobin narrative convention by distilling a host of moral, religious, and political vices into a single villain, Fitzosborne, who enters the novel directly from revolutionary Paris and "the sublime spectacle of a great nation emancipating itself from the fetters of tyranny and superstition," an experience he ominously considers the best education for a British legislator (*TT* 2: 97).[56] Certainly West joined other female loyalist writers and activists by making fiction a tactful route into public controversy. But in the end it is clear that the cautionary domestic tragedy of *A Tale of the Times* requires the politics of revolution as much as it requires sexual transgression, filial disobedience, and religious infidelity.

The clearest narrative account of the appropriate terms for a domestic discussion of religious belief comes in the third volume of the novel, set in rural Wales in Powerscourt House. Now married and become Lady Monteith, Geraldine Powerscourt has been pursued to this ancestral mansion by her intended seducer Fitzosborne, and here she and her father's household must contend with his fashionable deism and with the more dangerous atheism and radicalism it masks. The villain is "peculiarly careful" to conceal his principles in this idyllic rural setting in part because he recognizes in Mr. Evans, the Anglican chaplain of Powerscourt House, and his daughter Lucy a pair of "formidable opponents" to his own designs (*TT* 3: 19–20). Matters come to a head when Sir William Powerscourt turns to his chaplain for clarification of some uncharacteristically indiscrete remarks Fitzosborne has made in favor of relaxing divorce law, an issue that is explicitly taken to challenge the British constitution as "palladium of justice" (*TT* 3: 19). Evans is sufficiently shocked to suspect some misunderstanding, but decides to open a domestic inquiry by sounding out his daughter for her impressions of Fitzosborne. She is wary of his "mysterious air," but when pressed on the outrageous possibility of deism insists that she would not even recognize the type.

Conventional enough in itself, her modest disavowal entails a more interesting theory of domestic transparency that promises to insulate the home from Jacobin disguise as well as overt Jacobin assault. It seems there may be a middle way between unbecoming religious controversy and an awkward silence about matters of faith:

"Thank God," returned Lucy, "none of my acquaintances are deists; therefore I do not know in what manner they would act. But surely, my dear sir, when religious truths are impressed deeply upon a cultivated mind, they must give a tincture to our ordinary conversation. Subjects which we esteem sacred are not dragged into table-talk controversy; and the narratives of holy writ are not degraded by being drawn into a ludicrous parallel with the light events of the passing moment." (*TT* 3: 24–5)

This preference for implicit piety rather than open "table-talk controversy," strikingly advanced by a daughter who understands the threat posed by the villain well before her father, becomes a gendered dispensation in a series of further domestic conversations with and about Fitzosborne. Mr. Evans raises the stakes of the affair when he tells Lady Monteith that an apparently "harmless singularity" in matters of faith can threaten "the general destruction of all that is dear and valuable in society." At the same time, he warns her not to join his ongoing investigation of Fitzosborne, on grounds that recall Harriet Orwell's qualified reticence in *Memoirs of Modern Philosophers*.

Imperfectly educated women will only be bewildered by the "thorny paths of theological controversy," since the "metaphysical deductions, and philological learning, by which we defend our faith against its assailants, require a severe course of study, and more intense thought than your habits, or perhaps the peculiar tendency of your intellectual powers, will afford." Lady Monteith is best advised to meet skeptical overtures with "a dignified silence, or an indication of displeasure," to show a respect that will not "enter lightly on the sacred theme" (*TT* 3: 60–2). The women of Powerscourt House are typically present as observers rather than participants once Mr. Evans concludes his investigation and enlists the support of Henry Powerscourt, Lady Monteith's exemplary cousin, in a series of direct disputes with Fitzosborne. Rather than seeking conversion, these debates are meant to make Powerscourt House inhospitable and to alert Lady Monteith to the danger at hand. In this sense, while the novel anticipates *Scenes of Life* in staging domestic conversations that bear upon public matters, it more clearly restricts the aim of those conversations to the terms of domestic romance: protecting female virtue within the marriage plot.

Of course any reader who has failed to notice that a female novelist composes the male as well as the female parts in a narrative bent on achieving "the triumph of manly sense and sound principle over sophistry" (*TT* 3: 147) will be reminded of that paradox in the closing apology for female fictional controversy. More troubling still is the way the unraveling seduction plot seems at every turn to compromise the effectiveness of a gendered framework for theological authority. When Lady Monteith goes so far as to enquire of Fitzosborne whether he was moved by Henry Powerscourt's defense of revealed religion, the narrator feels compelled to intervene, though not to censure her for violating Mr. Evans' strictures about female decorum. Instead "cowardly lady Monteith" is condemned for not further pursuing the questions of faith that are raised by Fitzosborne's evasive answer: "Why fear to drive the mean dissimulator from the affected decency of deism into the bold audacity of atheism, by asking, how animated dust and ashes can presume to question the power which called it into existence?" (*TT* 3: 144–5). And since Mrs. Prudentia Homespun has ostentatiously foreshadowed the tragic course of the novel, the reader is aware that even with their "Ithurial spear of biblical literature" (*TT* 3: 61) the phalanx of Mr. Evans and Henry Powerscourt can do nothing to secure the heroine's virtue. More importantly, Fitzosborne readily adapts his satanic wiles to the strategies meant to expose him. This is comically evident in the case of the Reverend Evans, a once "elegant tutor" who has declined into a "rural divine" and derives his "knowledge of the great world" from "the limited information of books and newspapers" (*TT* 3: 21). His preening self-importance makes him an easy mark for Jacobin villainy, and Fitzosborne even manages to make a radical critique of Church corruption palatable by exempting present company (*TT* 3: 28–9). If clerical authority turns out to be just another type of innocence, vulnerable to Jacobin seduction, it is hard to know what to make of the gendered regulations that frame Lucy Evans' modest disavowal of "table-talk controversy." Learned and informed conversation in *A Tale of the Times* is doubly framed as a feminine production, first through the fictional device of Mrs. Prudentia Homespun, and then again through the closing defense of anti-Jacobin fictional controversy as a necessary counterweight to the radical travel-writing of Wollstonecraft and Helen Maria Williams.

CHARITABLE ENTERPRISE AND THE REPAIR OF FICTION

Ambiguities about the role of women in a reconstituted sphere of domestic conversation sustain striking complexities in anti-Jacobin narrative. And yet while there may be competing directives about who is entitled to make the case against subversion and infidelity, the more telling outward bound upon counterrevolutionary agency in these novels remains the one vividly figured by Henry Maitland's gesture of prevention. Critical faculties refined in private conversation are not meant to contest the threat of revolution; the aim instead seems to be to secure existing loyalties, to assess corrupt public conditions from a safe interior distance, and to challenge radical assumptions that loyalty and piety are incompatible with critical reflection. For decisive action against subversion, these novels consistently revert to government and the law. The hasty dispatch of the Jacobin villain in *A Tale of the Times* is instructive. Having succeeded in his designs upon Lady Monteith's virtue, Fitzosborne finds himself scorned by his repentant victim and pursued by the law. He escapes a conventional literary demise at "the sword of an injured husband" by fleeing to Paris, only to meet a more ironic form of "retributive justice" when his British identity raises French government suspicions: faced with death by guillotine he resorts to "the unbeliever's last resource" and takes his own life (*TT* 3: 372–5). If this political revision of the rogue's destiny seems merely circumstantial, West is more concerned in her handling of the repentant heroine to show that female domestic reflection must proceed on a separate track from "retributive justice." Having decided not to prosecute Fitzosborne on the grounds that this would require an immodest public declaration before the law, Lady Monteith is afforded a private opportunity to recount her seduction when she defends her decision to a dubious Lucy Evans. "Suppose me now . . . repeating this narrative in a court of justice; every eye fixed upon me with offensive curiosity; insulted (at least in my own opinion) by that cross-examination, which impartial justice will require to discover whether I was not the willing partner of the crime. . . . No! Lucy; I must be silent. I have been too culpable to talk of innocence." The spectacle of intimacy that emerges when a courtroom defense yields to countervailing private "reasons" is then intensified when the illicit private correspondence of the lovers becomes a topic of conversation between the two women, and Lucy in turn undertakes to transmit Lady Monteith's modest defense to her father and Henry Powerscourt (*TT* 3: 299, 302, 309).

These novels did consider that domestic reflection might issue in social agency through the traditional female responsibility for charity, education, and the relief of the poor. Yet conservative doubts about the wisdom of institutionalizing such responsibilities, and about the hazards of personal vanity and sentimental excess, tended to sustain underlying ambiguities about female domestic agency. Jane West, who herself ventured on moral enterprise in two conduct books, explores an acute version of the problem when she narrates Lady Monteith's ambitious project of village economic reform in the second volume of *A Tale of the Times*. The episode is pivotal, occurring before the climactic seduction but after its elaborate anticipation by Prudentia Homespun, and during Lady Monteith's final struggles to save her faltering marriage by removing with her husband from the moral hazards of London to his ancestral Scottish estate. The estate is rendered in imperfectly Burkean terms as an emblem of neglected ancestral responsibilities, as the heroine responds with astonishment to the "the cruel ravages which time and negligence" have exacted on the "venerable pile" of Monteith (*TT* 2: 9). If there is a "dangerous approximation of vanity" (*TT* 2: 11) in some of her more ostentatious schemes for renovation, she at least avoids the gross errors of an earlier generation of wholesale improvers, traced at the beginning of the novel in her own mother's career as a picturesque improver of Powerscourt House. When the female desire for reform spills out from the neglected fabric of Monteith Castle to the surrounding countryside, the novel is prepared to credit the "social and benevolent spirit" that yields a "neat little model village" and a scheme for moral reform of the poor. There seems to be no irony about the progressive and imperial language that traces the rescue of the "melancholy highlander" from a rude and "uncivilized" state so that he can be incorporated into a "colony" devoted to his improvement and industry (*TT* 2: 16, 23). Against her husband's casual commitment to the traditions of occasional relief "at the castle gate," Lady Monteith insists that the poor must learn through education and a scheme for simple manufactures to "eat the bread of industry," even as she announces a deference to patriarchal authority by naming the village James-town "in honour of her lord, to whose liberality she properly referred every improvement of which she was the directing soul" (*TT* 2: 19, 30).

The novel proceeds briskly and unsentimentally from the rise of the village through its steady decline in cottage jealousy and open village factionalism, with narrative judgments on the project as such largely restricted to familiar conservative observations about "the power of local attachment" preventing Highland assimilation to the "sheltered cultivated valleys" around Monteith Castle (*TT* 2: 33–5). What does come into focus as a matter of critical concern for domestic romance is not the course of experiment in a model village, but its role in the moral development and tragic fall of the heroine. When trivial cottage feuds lead Lady Monteith to question human virtue, the narrator intervenes with a pious reminder that "all the good of this world must be blended with evil," and begins to implicate the heroine of "one-and-twenty" in errors of Godwinian perfectibility. "Dispassionate experience would have taught lady Monteith, that the very circumstances of the villagers' complaints argued comparative comfort . . . Her liberal mind would then have added to the certain satisfaction of a pure intention the exhilarating enjoyment of that moderate success to which all sublunary schemes can alone aspire" (*TT* 2: 36–38). Far from challenging the premises of moral reform, these critical reflections suggest that the village experiment might well have thrived if its "directing soul" had met minor setbacks with Christian humility rather than Jacobin ambition. In this way the course of village reform is suggestively aligned with the historically conditioned Christian framework that informs the novelist's own campaign to reform popular fiction. Immediately before Lady Monteith arrived at an ancestral house in need of repair, Mrs. Prudentia Homespun undertook to defend the upcoming shift in the course of her narrative from domestic virtue to "satanic guile" as the faithful representation of a fallen world now further compromised by "the unchristian morals of the present age" (*TT* 2: 6), signaling the sense in which her romance of "the penalty of Adam" is strictly speaking a "Tale of the Times."

It is within this mixed historical and theological framework that Lady Monteith's village experiment becomes a determined transition to Jacobin seduction, rather than a distinct utopian interlude at its brink. The "inbred vanity" that alienates Lady Monteith from her husband and makes her vulnerable to the "satanic guile" of Fitzosborne is vividly dramatized in the series of self-actualizing speculations through which she first envisions her enterprise: "I will build a neat little village . . . I will frequently visit [the tenants]; I will be their legislator, their instructor, their physician, and their friend" (*TT* 2: 10–11). And Fitzosborne detects the flaw that will allow him to seduce Lady Monteith in a conversation that pits his own radical primitivism against her reformist desire to improve rural conditions. When he later secures his triumph by luring Lord Monteith into aristocratic degeneracy, the James-town experiment winds to its ignominious close in a marital feud, with Lord Monteith blaming his wife's charitable expenses for the ruin of a fortune he has himself squandered on gambling and a costly mistress. In a pivotal scene that echoes her first response to the degenerate conditions around Monteith Castle, the heroine betrays her increasingly radical sensibilities and foreshadows her fall by looking out "from the proud heights of Monteith castle on the subject vale" and mistakenly imagining a landscape rich with miseries that no mere village experiment can address: "*There* exists pining penury; *there* destitute sickness suffers, and wasting infancy declines . . . O Fitzosborne! how strongly do such situations demonstrate the truth of your opinion, that the present order of things requires the bold hand of some intelligent reformer!" (*TT* 3: 207–9). It is worth insisting that what the novel finally condemns is this distinctively Jacobin fusion of disenchantment and utopian speculation, not the "social and benevolent spirit" that actuates the James-town experiment. At the same time, any distinction between Mrs. Prudentia Homespun's pious acceptance of human impairment and Lady Monteith's bold struggle against it rests on an underlying sense of the alignment of their roles as female moral entrepreneurs. One of the narrator's most explicit challenges to corrupt literary convention comes at the opening of the rift between husband and wife over James-town, in a warning to "young female readers" not to censure the couple on the basis of exaggerated notions of "nuptial felicity" drawn from "the delusive pages of a circulating library" (*TT* 2: 24–5). This resistance to a supposed popular taste for idealized marriages is consistent with the role of the James-town scheme in the downward spiral of tragic romance. The heroine is condemned not for wanting to improve the world, but for impiously considering anything short of perfection to be failure; she does not display full-blown Jacobin symptoms until she allows her frustration to issue in an exaggerated sense of popular distress that enlists wholesale radical reform.

If James-town and female moral enterprise remain to some extent unresolved factors in *A Tale of the Times*, it is because they figure prominently in the moral ruin of the heroine but not in the novel's impressively rich exploration of its aftermath. Mrs. Bullock's *Dorothea; or, A Ray of the New Light* suggests how a similarly qualified skepticism about female moral enterprise could be worked through the whole trajectory of anti-Jacobin narrative romance. Alienated from her husband by her own new philosophical desire for independence and by a variety of subversive devices, Dorothea (or Lady Euston as she has become by marriage) retires to the rural Welsh village of Llantrussent for a primitivist revival of "the golden age," but finds little satisfaction in "clothing of sheep-skin, and a meal of pulse and spring water" (*DR* 2: 141–2). Self-indulgent primitivism gives way to a more enterprising "scheme of usefulness" in the form of a village school for girls. It turns out that the now neglected cottages of Llantrussent were the work of "a benevolent owner of the adjacent manor-house" (*DR* 2: 138) in a previous generation, so that Lady Euston like Lady Monteith before her provocatively fills a gap left by failed patriarchal provision. Yet in this case the educational scheme is hopelessly compromised by a radical curriculum. Pastoral idyll gives way to anti-Jacobin burlesque as the classroom of well-disposed girls deteriorates under Lady Euston's democratic tutelage to the point were one particularly receptive student acts upon her newly acquired leveling impulses by robbing and nearly murdering her teacher. It is only after the chastened heroine has recovered from her injuries and returned to her husband that she exchanges the deceptive "new light" of Jacobinism for the inherited wisdom of "the old school," though it turns out that the regular "performance of her duty as a wife and mother" allows for modest charitable provision within "the gentle bonds of domestic cares and pleasures" (*DR* 2: 240). From this point on Lady Euston employs herself, "not in awakening discontent and rebellion amongst her poorer neighbours, but in ameliorating their situation, and as far as her cares and assistance can go, in striving to remove every cause of regret and complaint" (*DR* 2: 237). If these are strict limitations, prohibiting any independent or institutional enterprise, they nevertheless indicate that here as in *A Tale of the Times* the critique of female charitable provision is not absolute. Animated by something less than personal vanity, and tempered by a Christian acceptance of human impairment, James-town could be a worthy experiment, just as the extinguished wife and mother that emerges from the embers of the "new light" in *Dorothea* has a role in ameliorating neighborhood distress. And by unleashing misguided female enterprise in the gap left open by lapsed patriarchal provision, both novels suggest the urgency of some renewed custody of the poor.

Given the extensive charitable work that she herself undertook after settling in Edinburgh, it is not surprising that in *Memoirs of Modern Philosophers* Elizabeth Hamilton offers the most cogent anti-Jacobin fictional account of female social enterprise. Still, it is telling that such enterprise seems to fall just beyond the boundaries of narrative romance. In a novel organized around the didactic interplay of three courtship plots – the comic erotic quest of Bridgetina Botherim, the tragic seduction of Julia Delmond, and the normative marriage of Harriet Orwell – the work of charity is associated instead with two older women, Mrs. Martha Goodwin and Mrs. Fielding, who are themselves either past or imperfect subjects of romance. In the present revolutionary generation these unmarried women assume a corrective and enabling role with respect to courtship, and their handmaiden's tales are developed in part through the exercise of charitable agency. Mrs. Martha, the unmarried sister of Dr. Orwell and Harriet Orwell's favorite aunt, first establishes the terms for female enterprise within the same Rousseauian episode of pastoral courtship and conversation that establishes a gendered framework for domestic controversy. The fields surrounding the impromptu picnic yield idealized representations of rural life in part because their owner, the Dissenting minister Mr. Sydney (the father of Henry Sydney, Harriet Orwell's destined husband), refuses to pursue the supposed improvements of "more scientific farmers" and instead generously employs more hands than are necessary. When Mr. Sydney decisively closes the controversy about gender distinctions by suggesting that the Christian principles he has just invoked against Wollstonecraft should be enacted by distributing cheese and ale to the haymakers, his daughter Maria and her friends Harriet and Julia become ladies bountiful, "advancing in gay procession with a profuse supply of refreshments" until "every face wore the appearance of cheerfulness and contentment" (*MP* 105). As in domestic conversation, only Bridgetina strikes a note of discord, apostrophizing the laborers as "miserable wretches" despite their own vernacular professions to the contrary: "What d'ye say, Miss . . . about any one's being miserable?" (*MP* 105).

At this point the authority to refute a Jacobin challenge through domestic conversation shifts dramatically from Mr. Sydney as male landlord to Mrs. Martha as female purveyor of charity. Delivered in the familiar idioms of pious moral reform, her response to Bridgetina may lack credibility as lived experience, but this is itself striking evidence of Hamilton's willingness to invest her female conversationalist with a kind of public authority:

> I have the comfort of assuring you that you are very much mistaken. In the dwellings of the poor I am no stranger. As fortune has not put it in my power to do much toward removing their wants, I consider myself doubly bound to do all I can towards relieving their afflictions. For this purpose I make it my business to enquire into them; and in the course of these enquiries I have found frequent cause to admire the order of Providence, in distributing the portion of happiness with a much more equal hand than on a slight view we could possibly imagine. I question, whether any lord in the land enjoys half the share of content and satisfaction that falls to the lot of that industrious labourer to whom you spoke. You shall, if you please, accompany me some evening to his cottage, which is one of the neatest and pleasantest little habitations you ever visited in your life. You may there, towards sun-set, see the poor man sitting in his nicely-dressed little garden, and perhaps singing some old ballad for the amusement of his children, while their mother is preparing supper. (*MP* 105–6)

Needless to say Bridgetina ignores the invitation, since her speculative radicalism has nothing to do with practical relief, and her apparent address to the laborer was in fact nothing more than a misguided attempt to flirt with Henry Sydney. If Mrs. Martha does not have the last word in her Christian defense of "active benevolence" (*MP* 107), this is because the episode does finally revert to the gendered framework for conversational authority established early in the chapter. Intervening in support of his sister's case, Dr. Orwell turns the discussion to a comparison between English and Scottish economic conditions, and the chapter closes with an invitation to Henry Sydney to read aloud from his manuscript journal of a recent Scottish tour. If political economy and travel suggest male privileges, Hamilton continues to some extent to sustain mixed familiar conversation by punctuating Henry's oral performance with audience commentary and discussion.

Where Jane West refined the narrative voice of *A Tale of the Times* by aligning and distinguishing the revisionist social work of Mrs. Prudentia Homespun and Lady Monteith, Hamilton increasingly commits her own fiction to the didactic possibilities afforded by Mrs. Martha Goodwin. This pattern of identification culminates in the untimely but powerfully instructive death of Mrs. Martha in the second volume of the novel, and in this sense ambiguity returns not through any skepticism about the value of female social work, but rather through the gap that a spinster's death seems to open between the trajectories of narrative romance and charitable provision. Revisionist authorial purposes are evident in the way the deathbed scene is calculated to refute sentimental fiction, as young Harriet Orwell watches with feelings that are "keen and lively" but free of indulgent sensibility: "She . . . neither screamed, nor fainted, nor fell into hysterics, but sat down quietly by her aunt's bedside, and attentively listened to every word she uttered, and watched every motion of her eyes, as well as the tears, which she could not restrain, but which fell in silence, would permit" (*MP* 184). With silence again registering youthful feminine decorum, authority passes first to scripture, as Harriet is asked by her aunt to read aloud from "the last discourse of our Saviour to his disciples," and then to Mrs. Martha herself in a pair of impressive deathbed admonitions. The first and more explicitly anti-Jacobin of these admonitions follows directly from the New Testament. "If ever, in the course of life, a sceptical doubt should be suggested to your mind under the false colour of philosophy," Harriet is warned, "*think of this night*" (*MP* 184–5). The second is issued the following morning, in the company of other family members, and would seem to be less concerned with the ideological purposes of the novel except that it amounts to a bold defense of the role of an unmarried and childless women within domestic romance:

Who would have thought . . . that all this concern should appear about a poor, solitary old maid? Alas! how abortive are the desires of mortals! How many . . . have married from the apprehension of a desolate old age, have had their hopes crowned by a numerous family, and yet have had their eyes closed by the unfeeling hand of a mercenary stranger. Whilst I! – O my gracious GOD! how different hast thou made my lot! – Yes, my children, I feel all your affection, all your tenderness; it is a cordial, a balmy cordial to my heart. (*MP* 185–6)

In one sense, the movement here beyond courtship can only be transcendental, advancing from fiction to scripture and from this world to the next. Yet in a gesture that surely involves Elizabeth Hamilton's own authority as an unmarried women writer of didactic romances, Harriet is provided with a supplementary letter from her aunt that effectively insinuates the deathbed scene back into the world of the novel and its rich play of conversations and texts.

In its content the letter is conventional enough, enjoining "the necessity of submitting the passions to the authority of reason" (*MP* 188). Yet in its form, as a written reinforcement of Mrs. Martha's oral defense of the productiveness of "a forlorn state of celibacy" (*MP* 190), the letter draws on the idioms of the conduct book, spiritual biography, and educational treatise to show how such discourses can have a decisive impact in the world. It sustains Harriet over the course of the rest of the novel through the anxious contingencies of courtship with Henry Sydney. By comparison with *Scenes of Life*, where a similarly unmarried aunt, Miss Eliza Burton, is finally integrated to domestic romance through a hastily arranged marriage, *Memoirs of Modern Philosophers* achieves some of its most explicit refutations of popular fiction through the revisionist matrilineal principle that allows a dying spinster to address her extended family as "my children". According to Mrs. Martha, and here she echoes contemporary women writers on both sides of the revolution controversy, the "whole course" of existing female education is calculated to raise "the power of imagination" over "judgment," something she has tried to prevent in her niece: "Your mind has not been suffered to run wild in the fairy field of fiction; it has been turned to subjects of real and permanent utility" (*MP* 188).[57] If *Memoirs of Modern Philosophers* concludes with the expected wedding of Harriet and Henry, their marriage will be haunted by the monitory figure of Mrs. Martha just as their courtship was protracted by Harriet's wary internalization of her aunt's admonition that she accept the possibility of a future for herself without marriage.

Where the didactic voice of Mrs. Martha Goodwin survives in the material form of the deathbed letter, her charitable impulses pass to Mrs. Fielding, a benefactress of Henry Sydney and intimate friend of the elder Mr. Sydney (to whom she was once engaged) who figures prominently in the final phase of the novel, as Bridgetina Botherim and Julia Delmond pursue their wayward erotic destinies through the streets of London. In devoting a chapter to an institutional history of Mrs. Fielding's "Asylum of the Destitute" for fallen women, *Memoirs of*

Modern Philosophers extends its treatment of female charity from Mrs. Martha's neighborhood provision to the kind of professional enterprise that became familiar to Hamilton in her own work at the Edinburgh House of Industry.[58] The sheer scale of the Asylum is impressive, eventually reaching expenses of five hundred pounds a year, shrewdly offset by Mrs. Fielding through the sale of garments from an affiliated linen manufactory. Where Mrs. Martha made a traditional case for informal relief in a dispute with Bridgetina, the novel more provocatively renders Mrs. Fielding's progress from an initial encounter with a desperate young woman to an elaborate "plan of charity" through narrative devices of interior monologue ("Surely . . . there is something wrong in this . . .") and rational deliberation ("She then began to make calculations . . .") that are, in their debased form, consistently associated with Bridgetina and other Jacobin figures in the novel (*MP* 301). And the work of the Asylum is boldly revisionist. Its challenge extends from such typical anti-Jacobin targets as the sentimental but ineffectual Lady Mary Mildmay to the orthodox assumption that lost female sexual virtue cannot be recovered. Animated by a Christian piety that is "not disgraced by bigotry," Mrs. Goodwin refuses to "overwhelm the already broken spirit" of her charges "by aggravating the colour of past offences," and she pursues their full moral and social rehabilitation. "It was her opinion, that the support of reputation being found to be a strong additional motive to virtue, it ought not to be put out of the power of the unfortunate female, who, conscious of her error, is desirous to retrieve it by her after conduct" (*MP* 371).[59]

In its first presentation as a discrete episode, the history of the Asylum extends Hamilton's habit of revising and improving popular fiction by drawing upon other corrective discourses. She herself printed a short description of the Edinburgh House of Industry as a notice appended to her 1809 *Exercises in Religious Knowledge; for the Instruction of Young Persons,*[60] and the close account of Mrs. Fielding's experience can be considered a handbook for other enterprising independent women. In this sense *Memoirs of Modern Philosophers* recalls Hannah More's practice of fictionalizing practical and didactic matter. Any doubt about the correspondence between the work of female reformers within this novel and the work of the novel itself is put to rest when "the Asylum" appears to Julia Delmond with all the force of allegory to relieve her after she has been seduced and abandoned by the Jacobin villain Vallaton. And yet narrative convention still seems to impose inexorable limits, as this charitable rescue work can only be fulfilled within the tragic strand of romance. If Hamilton does more than West or Bullock to allow female social enterprise to operate freely and productively throughout her novel, Mrs. Fielding's bold case for "the power of the unfortunate female" to retrieve her reputation has little impact on the unforgiving logic of the anti-Jacobin seduction plot. In the penultimate chapter of the novel, Julia dies within the Asylum in the act of uniting the hands of Harriet and Henry, and she therefore joins Mrs. Martha and Mrs. Fielding in becoming a handmaiden to other courtships.

It is hard to know what to make then of Hamilton's delivery of the anticipated marriage in her final chapter as a merely conventional device: "But how could we have the heart to disappoint the Misses, by closing our narrative without a wedding?" (*MP* 384). At the very least there is an ironic trace here of a resistance to readerly expectation, which gets reinforced when Mrs. Fielding is numbered among those (mostly barren Jacobins) who do not marry in the final chapter. If her spinster condition is not pursued in the pointed terms of Mrs. Martha'a didactic celibacy, she is afforded an opportunity to decline a marriage proposal from the widowed Mr. Sydney in terms that invoke her charitable work: "From the day I heard of his marriage, I have devoted myself to a single life. I have endeavoured to create to myself objects of interest that might occupy my attention, and engage my affections. These I have found in the large family of the unfortunate" (*MP* 388). Here the novel wants to argue what it does not represent, since this "large family" has been largely reduced to the tragic and now deceased person of Julia Delmond. Despite the incorporation of Mrs. Martha's deathbed letter and the history of the Asylum, in the end *Memoirs of Modern Philosophers* cannot match the narrative range and heterogeneity of the Cheap Repository tracts. The eager deference of Mr. Sydney's hay-makers epitomizes the failure of the anti-Jacobin novel to represent the lower orders with any detail or complexity. In this sense, Hamilton's development of female moral enterprise is consistent with a general reluctance to combat the threat of revolution from within the terms of domestic romance. Charitable provision is powerful work, but it is applied here to the repair of fiction and to the courtship plot as a narrow and stylized arena for the play of subversive energies.

CHAPTER 5

Southey, Coleridge, and the end of anti-Jacobinism in Britain

Robert Southey and Samuel Taylor Coleridge came into their own as vigorous public critics of radicalism and as defenders of the established Church and unreformed constitution during a sustained revival of radical fortunes that began in the first decade of the nineteenth century with the emergence of Sir Francis Burdett's Westminster reform organization and the radicalization of William Cobbett, and then culminated more threateningly in the post-war era of the unstamped weekly press and mass public agitation for parliamentary reform. If the "cry about Jacobinism" was arguably outmoded by the end of 1790s, sporadic outbreaks of political violence continued right through the era of Luddism and Peterloo, and flexible new practices of popular organization and expression clearly drew on the example of Paine and the London Corresponding Society. In taking up the public campaign against subversion, Southey and Coleridge joined their "Lake School" friend and collaborator William Wordsworth in repudiating early radical sympathies, and drew the scorn of a younger generation of more liberal poets and essayists including Shelley, Keats, Byron, Hazlitt, and Leigh Hunt. The generational rifts that emerged here still shape British romantic studies, particularly where the timing and intensity of a retreat from radicalism remain matters of critical concern.[1] In closing this study of writing against revolution with the conservative careers of Southey and Coleridge, I am less concerned about the contrast with early radicalism than about the way both writers sought to revise and extend established patterns of counterrevolutionary expression, in order to establish more secure conditions for their own combative literary enterprise.[2] To reimagine the conditions for writing in defense of the established political order was also inevitably to reimagine that order, and Southey and Coleridge were both prepared to advance a reformist attack on radical reform. In doing so they were concerned to distance themselves from the anti-Jacobinism of the 1790s as well as from their own early radicalism, and while their arguments in this regard may not always be reliable, they should not simply be dismissed out of hand.[3] The effort to remodel counterrevolutionary expression in the 1810s and 1820s was also an effort to put the antinomies of the 1790s to rest.

In retrospect both Southey and Coleridge considered the Treaty of Amiens of 1802 to be the watershed event dividing themselves and the nation from the compromised political terms of an earlier era. This necessary though failed experiment in negotiating with the French regime served to expose the treachery of Napoleon Bonaparte and to reunite loyal British public opinion around a more justified subsequent military campaign against revolution. Writing in the *Quarterly Review* in 1816 in defense of "the popular character of the war" after its resumption in 1803, Southey distinguished the "deep, though mistaken principle" motivating those (like himself) who questioned the earlier "anti-jacobine war" from the more suspect and self-interested motives of later advocates for peace in the face of blatant Napoleonic aggression (*QR* 16 [1816–1817], 236–37).[4] If the two writers agreed broadly about the shifting terms of subversion at home and abroad, there were clear differences in their style of political announcement, particularly where radical youth was at issue. In coming to terms with the 1790s, Coleridge often employed what Alan Liu has termed a "doubling or self divisive" dialectical rhetoric, with results that could be as misleading as they were teasingly confessional, and he had a mischievous habit of lodging traces of radical sympathy in some of his most strenuous counterrevolutionary arguments.[5] Southey was at once more decisive in taking up the case against subversion and more obstinate about rejecting charges of inconsistency, claiming that unlike other supposed advocates of liberty he had learned that its light was no longer to be found shining in the east: "I . . . altered my position as the world went round" (*SE* 2: 21–22).[6] First advanced in 1809, this claim was repeated by Southey in 1817 in response to the embarrassing controversy triggered by the unauthorized publication of *Wat Tyler*, an early dramatic poem he tried to suppress but that was seized upon by his enemies as damning evidence of a former sympathy with rebellion.[7] When Coleridge rose to his friend's defense in a pair of articles for the *Courier* newspaper, he bluntly conceded what Southey would not, that the youthful poet of *Wat Tyler* was "deluded by such writings as those of Thomas Paine into Jacobinism" (*CW* 3, 2: 451). In private, Coleridge confirmed a sense of underlying differences in strategy by criticizing the habit of "self-desertion" (*CL* 4: 713) he detected in Southey's claim that *Wat Tyler* was somehow not the seditious work it seemed.

A crucial point on which two writers came to agree was that the radical reform movement of the early nineteenth century was more vulgar in its social foundations and more explosively democratic than anything they had been involved in during the 1790s. To some extent this was a position they worked out collaboratively in the immediate aftermath of the murder of Prime Minister Spencer Perceval by John Bellingham in the lobby of the House of Commons on the evening of May 11, 1812. Although the assassin turned out to be a distressed businessman with no connection to any wider radical conspiracy, the event horrified loyal subjects and reinforced a growing sense of alarm following newspaper reports of Luddite rioting and industrial protest in Nottingham, Yorkshire, and Lancashire. In a letter written to Southey the day after the assassination, Coleridge related his own shocking encounter in a London public house with popular rejoicing at the news. He offered his journalistic services in the cause of good order to the *Courier* newspaper, and urged Southey "to write something in your impressive way" about the ominous "sinking down of Jacobinism below the middle & tolerably educated Classes into the Readers & all-swallowing Auditors in Tap-rooms &c, of the Statesman, Examiner, Cobbet, &c" (*CL* 3: 410).[8] This identification of a nexus of subversive activity linking print expression (Daniel Lovell's *The Statesman*, John and Leigh Hunt's *Examiner*, William Cobbett's *Weekly Political Register*) with popular reading habits and radical organization became a relentless theme in the work of both writers. Though hardly necessary, Coleridge's instigation was evident in some of Southey's most alarmist subsequent writing for the *Quarterly Review*. It manifested itself more immediately in a letter Southey wrote to his friend Grosvenor Bedford invoking Coleridge's public house experience to warn of an imminent "English Jacquerie, – a *Bellum Servile*," and to propose a series of measures for protecting the constitution which he hoped Bedford, a well-connected civil servant, would pass on to his own more powerful acquaintances (*SL* 196–97).[9]

Even as Coleridge and Southey joined here in mobilizing a counter-revolutionary network that was itself an antitype to the subversive speech and print that came together in the London public house, there were import differences about how they proceeded. In generously acknowledging his correspondent's "impressive" public writing, Coleridge suppressed a less flattering distinction between his own first principles and the local contingencies of popular journalism. The *Biographia Literaria* cited Southey's work for the *Quarterly Review* in esteeming him England's leading "popular essayist" (*CW* 7, 1: 63), a judgment that was more damagingly advanced in the notebooks, where Coleridge reinforced a self-castigating reflection on the "Vulgar Errors" in politics and religion that were allowed to flourish because of his own indolence – "I could supply Subjects and Thoughts, Title pages & Chapters of Contents, for half a dozen Authors" – with a later interpolation that named Southey as his own vulgar amanuensis: for authors, "I had almost said Southeys" (*CW* 10: 74, n. 3). Southey was not above returning the favor by doubting Coleridge's ability to sustain an effective voice as a public writer, notably in his critical response to the mismanagement of weekly periodical form in the first (1809–10) incarnation of *The Friend*. Coleridge had himself modeled that project on William Cobbett's increasingly radical *Weekly Political Register*, though with a concern to avoid Cobbett's debased attention to "the Events and political Topics of the Day" and instead set forth "true Principles . . . in Criticism, Legislation, Philosophy, Morals, and International Law" (*CL* 3: 143–4).[10] On this as on most matters of achievement, literary history has tended to endorse Coleridge at the expense of Southey's reputation as a man of letters, a consensus that overlooks the remarkable efficiency with which Southey sustained himself and his family (and Coleridge's too for that matter) by working effectively across a range of genres – poetry, reviewing, biography, history, travel writing, and correspondence.[11] One of the aims of this chapter will be to challenge a determination in favor of Coleridge, less by redressing the balance than by exploring the notional gap between political principle and its contingent public expression as an enduring tension within conservative literary practice, evident in the work of Southey as well as Coleridge.

The idea that early nineteenth-century radical movements were revolutionary rather than reformist, determined to produce an "English Jacquerie, – a Bellum Servile," was another point on which the two writers readily agreed. In an 1809 *Edinburgh Annual Register* attack on Sir Francis Burdett's motion for parliamentary reform, Southey repudiated the critique of government corruption that was coming to dominate radical argument in this period, and instead defended ministerial influence and the network of government pensions and places as a stabilizing counterweight to the rising influence of the press and popular opinion. In the absence of government resources to counter democratic developments, "the government of England would be virtually dissolved. . . . The direct road to anarchy is by this way of Parliamentary Reform" (*SE* 1: 10). Writing over the course of the next decade in the *Quarterly Review*, Southey brought this attack on radical reform to bear upon the periodical press, and his programmatic 1817 review essay "Rise and Progress of Popular Disaffection" maintained that "all the other confluent causes of discontent are trifling in themselves and light in their consequences compared to the seditious press" (*QR* 16 [1817], 551).[12] Coleridge was somewhat more prepared to weigh radical organization in the balance with the threat posed by the press. In the series of letters "To Mr. Justice Fletcher" that he wrote for the *Courier* newspaper in the fall and winter of 1814, offering his own most sustained account of revolutionary developments since the 1790s, he identified "the passion and contagion of club government" and "the present numberless societies and combinations of the mechanics and lower craftsmen of every description" as "the most formidable, the most intensely *jacobinical* phaenomenon that has ever appeared in great Britain" (*CW* 3. 2: 392–93), presumably outstripping anything achieved by the London Corresponding Society or the United Irishmen in the 1790s.[13] Yet the press remained for Coleridge a key reference point, and the broad terms of his assault on the political legitimacy of print culture are evident in his bemused strictures on the very idea of "a READING PUBLIC" (*CW* 6, 36–7) in *The Statesman's Manual*. Writing to T. G. Street in the wake of the publication of *Wat Tyler* he suggested that Southey's self-defense betrayed a failure to understand that the "real evil" lay in "the *publication* of the thing." Coleridge's own axiomatic assessment of the *Wat Tyler* affair effectively summed up his grasp of the post-war crisis: "The root of the Evil is *a Public*" (*CL* 4: 713–14).

Though in some sense Coleridge issued his axiom against Southey, the rhetorical tensions at work in a prose campaign against public opinion were abundantly evident in the work of both writers. To set their own literary practice on more secure foundations, both writers advocated reforms, primarily having to do with the Church and with education, meant to secure the state from subversion without the need for extraordinary print campaigns in its defense. Of course there was nothing new about this kind of effort to resolve the contradictions of an enterprising counterrevolutionary discourse. The integrated print and educational campaigns of Hannah More reflect a similar concern to institutionalize the conditions for securing social order. And yet

Southey and Coleridge distinguished themselves by the purity of their ambition, as they avoided the kind of institutional supplementation associated with Evangelical moral reform, and sought instead to return (at least in their own conception) to more essential constitutional methods for offsetting the threat of revolution. Paradoxically, the more they reverted from immediate print conditions to pre-Reformation history, and to priestly conceptions of public authority, the more clear it was that they were discovering idealized versions of their own ordinary literary practice. They both wrote against subversion with nearly unabated vigor and determination right up through the late 1820s and early 1830s, recognizing that the reforms of these years essentially challenged their political vision by undermining the constitutional position of the Church and by extending the democratic premises of the House of Commons. Their work can be considered an end to anti-Jacobinism in Britain in the sense that it lodged a late protest against the erosion of the old regime in Britain, but also in its strikingly utopian effort to overcome the antinomies of the 1790s and achieve something else: a more stable foundation for the intellectual and literary enterprise by which the political establishment would be secured.

POLICY IN WRITING

A counterrevolutionary prose that holds the press and public opinion substantially responsible for creating a revolutionary situation would seem to enlist some account of its own public agency. As far as writing down the radical press was concerned, Southey proceeded as if there were little he could do. Surveying economic and political conditions in a *Quarterly Review* essay of 1812, he dismissed the liberal view that the press "furnishes always its own remedy, and conveys the antidote as well as the bane," and insisted instead on vigorous government action: "the anarchists must be silenced, and the associations of their disciples broken up" (*QR* 8[1812], 350–51). Elements of his case for repression were actually cut by the *Quarterly Review*'s editor, William Gifford, who often moderated Southey's more provocative and alarmist writing, particularly where there was an implicit critique of government inaction. A paragraph restored by Southey for his 1832 collection, *Essays, Moral and Political*, laid out a program for the "coercion which self-preservation renders necessary" in a revolutionary situation. The law of seditious and blasphemous libel adequately identified offenses, but it was not consistently applied, and the usual sentence of "fine and imprisonment" had to be enhanced in a way that recalls the anti-Jacobin novelist's climactic fantasy of expulsion: "The law . . . as it stands at present, punishes, but has little or no effect in lessening the frequency of the offence. Transportation would be the proper and efficient penalty" (*SE*, 1: 139–40).[14] Where Southey wrote often and with fierce determination about enhancing press controls, Coleridge was clearly more concerned to preserve the appearance of respecting English liberty. At the same time, he responded with characteristic intellectual energy and creative indirection to the challenge of using the press to make the case for press controls, and the problem of censorship elicited some of his most suggestive renderings of his own agency as a public writer.

In revising and rearranging *The Friend* as a three-volume essay collection of 1818, Coleridge set a libertarian epigraph from Milton's *Areopagitica* at the head of his own tenth essay, on "The Liberty of the Press," and drew upon Milton and other historical sources to reject licensing in advance of publication as a method of press control.[15] Such an argument was also a defense of the English constitutional tradition of prosecuting offensive works after the fact, and the next essay, on "Libel," provocatively returned to competing uses of Milton to make the case for price, format, and potential audience as key considerations in assessing criminal responsibility, an approach consistent with contemporary legal practice:

A passage, which in a grave and regular disquisition, would be blameless, might become highly libelous and justly punishable if it were applied to present measures or persons for immediate purposes, in a cheap and popular tract. I have seldom felt greater indignation than at finding in a large manufactory a sixpenny pamphlet, containing a selection of inflammatory paragraphs from the prose-writings of Milton, without a hint given of the time, occasion, state of government, &c. under which they were written—not a hint, that the Freedom, which we now enjoy, exceeds all that Milton dared hope for, or deemed practicable; and that his political creed sternly excluded the populace, and indeed the majority of the population, from all pretensions to political power. If the manifest bad intention would constitute this publication a seditious libel, a good intention equally manifest can not justly be denied its share of influence in producing a contrary verdict. (*CW* 4, 1: 81)

If this attack on misleading radical appropriations of Milton reflects an intention to use *The Friend* to establish philosophical principles and rescue the weekly periodical format from immediate (radical) topicality, it does so by paradoxically insisting upon considerations of "time, occasion, state of government." In this sense, Coleridge's fit of authorial "indignation" shrewdly facilitates his emerging argument about the law of libel as *in principle* a law of particulars. Against radical concerns that prosecutions for seditious and blasphemous libel were particularly burdensome because the vagueness of the law made criminal complaints difficult to anticipate, Coleridge insists that in this case the state can neither offer in advance a comprehensive definition of the law nor alleviate the rigor with which it is applied against particular offenses. Libel is said to be the only crime in which questions of degree and circumstance strictly *"constitute"* the offense, rather than discriminating its various degrees, as for example in distinctions between manslaughter, justifiable homicide, and murder (*CW* 4, 1: 78–81). The difference between *The Tenure of Kings and Magistrates* "in a cheap and popular tract" distributed to factory laborers and "in a grave and regular disquisition" is the difference between sedition and no crime at all. This discovery of a legal principle in the material facts of a particular case recalls Coleridge's distinction between the unpublished manuscript of *Wat Tyler* and the pirated editions that proliferated in 1817, further glossing the principle that emerged for him in that publicly contested case: "The root of the Evil is a Public."

The sequence of essays on the press and free expression in *The Friend* went on to consider hazards on the other side of the law, notably endorsing republican martyrology with a denunciation of the "murder" of Algernon Sidney, and then perversely incriminating the author himself, whose anti-Napoleonic journalism for the *Morning Post* during the peace of Amiens is offered as an example of criminal libel left unpunished (*CW* 4, 1: 81–2, 92). To draw matters to a close and secure the restrictive burden of his case under present conditions, Coleridge returns to his argument about the insusceptibility of libel to strict definition. "How shall we solve this problem?" The answer is said to lie in "that spirit which, like the universal menstruum sought for by the old alchemists, can blend and harmonize the most discordant elements," and with it Coleridge again challenges radical tradition by identifying the jury in its management of the press, rather than the press itself, as the privileged national organ of public opinion:

Its solution . . . is to be found in the spirit of a rational Freedom diffused and become national, in the consequent influence and controul of public opinion, and in its most precious organ, the jury. It is to be found, wherever Juries are sufficiently enlightened to perceive the difference, and to comprehend the

origin and necessity of the difference, between libels and other criminal overt-
acts, and are sufficiently independent to act upon the conviction, that in a
charge of libel, the degree, the circumstances, and the intention, constitute
(not merely *modify*) the offence, give it its Being, and determine its legal name.
(*CW* 4, 1: 91–2)[16]

Gratuitously unhelpful alchemical formulas aside, Coleridge's treatment of libel has become in effect a primer for "sufficiently enlightened" and "sufficiently independent" jurors, suggesting the
orientation of *The Friend* towards a reading public disposed to manage
and restrict rather than extend the political authority of public opinion.
In this sense, the law provides not only the topic of these essays but also
their imagined rhetorical occasion, framing the relationship between
author and reader.

In conceiving his weekly periodical essay as a critical alternative to
the *Weekly Political Register*, Coleridge had in mind not only Cobbett's
haphazard news content and increasingly radical politics, but also his
debased relationship with a vulgar reading audience, evident in his
willingness to fill the pages of the *Register* with "stupid makeweights
from Correspondents" of "the very lowest order" (*CL* 3: 144) who
could do no more than recapitulate the limitations of the editor.[17] As
he explains the law of libel Coleridge assumes the more magisterial role
of the judge in a criminal trial, improving potential jurors by guiding
them through the proper application of the law to particular cases and
conditions. Given the tendency to obscure and complicate causal
relationships in his own work, it may come as a surprise that the
"leading principle, the Pole Star" in any determination of criminal
responsibility is said to be the "more or less remote connection" of a
published work "with after overt-acts, as the cause and occasion of the
same" (*CW* 4, 1: 91–2). For the reader as potential juror, a dutiful
reminder that "the subversion of government and property" is not a
frequent consequence of political argument would seem to mitigate on
the side of caution, but it also enjoins a close scrutiny of material
circumstances and a predisposition against vulgar political idioms. "An
enlightened Jury . . . will require proofs of some more than ordinary
malignity of intention, as furnished by the style, price, mode of circulation, and so forth; or of punishable indiscretion arising out of the
state of the times, as of dearth, for instance, or of whatever other
calamity is likely to render the lower classes turbulent and apt to be
alienated from the government of their country" (*CW* 4, 1: 93).[18]
Milton and Sidney aside, Paine and the vernacular radicalism of the

1790s provided *The Friend* with an appropriate historical frame of reference for present (1809, 1818) conditions, as Coleridge went on to gloss the observation that "overt-acts" are of "incomparably greater mischief" where libels on government are concerned: "as for instance, the subversion of government and property, if the principles taught by Thomas Paine had been realized, or if even an attempt had been made to realize them, by the many thousands of his readers" (*CW* 4, 1: 93). Though slyly contained within a parenthetical, this remark further refines Coleridge's claim to have discovered "the Evil" in "a Public" by ominously converting a radical reading audience multiplied and organized by vernacular Jacobin address into an insurrectionary force.

Whatever the inherent ironies of a public political discourse recommending the suppression of another public political discourse, its aspirations here are inevitably conditioned by Coleridge's difficulties in bringing *The Friend* out to an adequate number of readers in an adequate format, first as a precarious weekly essay published by subscription in 1809–10 and 1812, and then again as a revised and rearranged three volume collection in 1818.[19] It is not easy to see how a prolific radicalism and its "many thousands" of readers would be contained by a project that numbered (at best) around 600 subscribers in its first periodical appearance, and that later sold around 250 copies in book form before the publisher's bankruptcy forced Coleridge to buy back remaining unsold copies.[20] In this sense, the rhetorical construction of the reader of *The Friend* as a notional juror, mindful of a personal interest in the stability of government, and alert to "mode of circulation" as a factor in "overt-acts," is itself a challenge to radical conceptions of readership as political organization and incipient constituency. And the figure of the reader as juror was not Coleridge's only effort to structure literary influence to his advantage in hierarchical terms. Writing in December 1808 to Humphry Davy, he conceded the degenerate "moral Taste of the present Public" to the likes of the *Political Register* and the *Edinburgh Review*, and reserved "widely different" purposes for *The Friend*: "I do not write in this Work for the *Multitude*; but for those, who by Rank, or Fortune, or official Situation, or Talents and Habits of Reflection, are to *influence* the Multitude" (*CL* 3: 143–4).[21] The sense of indirection here recalls an enduring touchstone of Coleridgean political address, the imperative to plead on behalf of rather than directly to the poor. In its early radical formulation in the *Conciones ad Populum* (1795), this imperative has been identified by E. P. Thompson as a vivid rendering of "the self-isolation of a utopian intellectual revolutionary."[22] But in later years it tended increasingly to involve a commitment to constitutional exclusions on political participation, a process that can be traced through the pages of *The Friend.*

In a crucial early sequence of essays on government that measured the distance between 1792 and 1809, between French Republicanism and British constitutional monarchy, Coleridge took the venerable parliamentary reformer John Cartwright to task for implicitly subscribing to a discredited "French Code of revolutionary principles," but then invoked his own favorite principle in order to exempt Cartwright from charges of catering to "the *fury* of the multitude": "He knows and acts on the knowledge, that it is the duty of the enlightened Philanthropist to plead *for* the poor and ignorant, not *to* them" (*CW* 4, 2: 110, 137). An acerbic note to the 1818 edition then responded to Cartwright's ongoing role in the development of popular radicalism by intimating that the concession of 1809 should now be revoked (*CW* 4, 1: 209–10). For Coleridge, *The Friend* was the first in what became a series of mediated counterrevolutionary addresses to select audiences about the dangers of radical reform and plebeian discontent: these included the two "lay sermons" of 1816 and 1817, *The Statesman's Manual* and *A Lay Sermon*, addressed respectively to "the higher classes" and "the higher and middle classes," and then culminated in 1830 with *On the Constitution of the Church and State*. A third Lay Sermon addressed to "the Lower and Labouring Classes of Society" would presumably have entailed vulgar conservative address, and rounded out what Jon Klancher calls Coleridge's habit of organizing the cultural field according to "'classes' of readers," but the projected volume made no appearance beyond an unfulfilled advertisement on the back wrapper of *The Statesman's Manual*.[23] A political rhetoric of widening and descending influence was sufficiently important to merit that highest of Coleridgean tributes, a neologism, coined in a request to Thomas Hurst, the publisher of *On the Constitution of the Church and State*, for copies to present to those "who might be effectually influencive on the 'Reading Public'" (*CL* 6: 824).[24] Mediated address here is no longer structured by the binary terms of a plea to the privileged on behalf of the poor, but instead spills over hierarchically through distinct circles of influence and impact. In a political crisis in which "the root of the Evil" was "*a Public,*" the conception of the "influencive" reader allowed Coleridge to imagine achieving effective leverage upon the "Reading Public" without actually descending to address it.

Measured against the complexities of a political address to potential jurors and "influencive" readers, Southey's bold case for enhanced criminal penalties would seem to bear out Coleridge's account of his friend as an altogether less sophisticated public writer. Southey was prepared to entertain such a comparison on his own terms, and in correspondence he implicated *The Friend* in a pattern of rhetorical complexity that similarly compromised the work of Edmund Burke: "So it is with C.; he goes to work like a hound, nosing his way, turning, and twisting, and winding, and doubling, till you get weary with following the mazy movements. My way is, when I see my object, to dart at it like a greyhound" (*SL* 176). And yet for all his directness Southey was also prone to mediated conceptions of literary impact. A June 1812 letter to his brother conceived a projected *Quarterly Review* essay on Patrick Colquhoun's *Treatise on Indigence* as a kind of indirect address to the government: "To-morrow I go, tooth and nail, to the *Quarterly*, for the purpose, if possible, of making our men in power see the imminent danger in which our throats are at this moment from the Luddites" (*SL* 202). And despite his relentless alarmism, it is not always easy to see how such a "tooth and nail" campaign would take effect.

Indirection was particularly evident where Southey undertook to supplement the case for repressive measures with paternalist Tory policies of economic reform and social provision. In the long conclusion to his 1816 *Quarterly Review* essay on "The Poor," an announced conviction that "the age for enacting Utopias is gone by" guided a departure from the strenuous rhythms of radical prophecy in favor of a more modest sequence of remedial exhortations:

> Let there be a system of parochial schools, connected with the church establishment, where every child may receive the rudiments of necessary knowledge, and be well instructed in his moral and religious duties. Let the temptations to guilt be lessened by a prohibition of those brutal sports which harden the heart, and by an alteration of the Game Laws, which are absurd, pernicious, and abominable. Let us multiply farms, instead of throwing many into one. Let the labourer, wherever it is possible, have his grass plot and his garden. Let the inducements of industry be further strengthened by the universal institution of Savings Banks. (*QR* 15 [1816], 233–4)

Though the commitment to national elementary education is a bold stroke, and the agricultural measures entail a willingness to urge reform upon recalcitrant elites, it is hard to escape a sense that this is a reformist language of diminished expectations, with the unmotivated shift back and forth from "let there be" to "let us" suggesting that these injunctions are directed at no one in particular. This follows in part from a calculated effort to redeem a rhetoric of Tory reform from misguided radical appeals to popular opinion. "They who exert themselves in promoting these objects, and such as these, are the genuine patriots, the true reformers, the real friends of the people" (*QR* 15 [1816], 234). Interestingly, in the conclusion to a related essay in the previous volume of the *Quarterly Review*, Southey conjured what he suggestively termed "a *vis conservatrix* in the state" through the same rhetorical formula:

> Let the sheriffs and magistrates refuse to call such meetings as manifestly tend and certainly are intended to agitate the people. Let the civil power be strengthened wherever it is needful, by swearing in as constables every man who is a known good friend to good order, mobs would then be so speedily suppressed that the turbulent and misguided would not venture to invade the property of their neighbours and disturb the peace of the country. Arm the sound part of the people then with the law . . . Let it but be made known that "*England expects every man to do his duty*" and the sense of duty will be found as strong in men who are thus armed and called upon, as it proved at Trafalgar and at Waterloo. (*QR* 15 [1816], 573)

The sense of agency is certainly more vivid here than in the syntactically similar passage from the essay on "The Poor." Where repression rather than reform is at issue, an abstractly conceived "us" gives way to the impressive phalanx of sheriffs, magistrates, and constables. Yet this concern for the legitimate offices of local government itself dictates that rhetorical impact should remain mitigated, since "the sound part of the people" does not become "a *vis conservatrix*" by virtue of civic enterprise set in motion by Southey's public writing. A concern for constitutional sanction becomes explicit later in the same paragraph: "When the well disposed are thus combined under the law, for the protection of peace and order, we shall cease to hear of depredations which have too long disgraced the country"(*QR* 15 [1816], 574).[25] If the principle of repressive enterprise "under the law" is explicit enough, the attenuated series of exhortations ("Let . . .") still risks diffusing political initiative into a static rhetorical formula, betraying Southey's inability or unwillingness to articulate within the pages of the *Quarterly Review* the terms in which counterrevolutionary public writing might contribute to achieving what it can manifestly envision.

It may be that Coleridge's faintly damning praise of his friend as a consummate "popular essayist" itself suggest a rudimentary process by which the *Quarterly Review* addresses loyal readers who then bring pressure to bear upon members of parliament and government ministers. Yet such a theory involves liberal assumptions about public opinion that Southey treated with some wariness. And if his public writing can be impersonal, his private correspondence was remarkably intimate, suggesting a deliberate reluctance on his part to activate the periodical reader as a collaborative social agent. One striking exception turns out to be instructive in this regard. In his 1812 *Quarterly Review* essay on poverty, Southey briefly conjures a privileged reader taking coffee and a newspaper at "his breakfast table," but does so in order to demonstrate that polite habits of reception inevitably fail to appreciate the dangers of the radical press. "Casting his eyes over its columns while he sips his coffee," such a reader perhaps "smiles at its blunders, or at most vents a malediction, more in wonder than in indignation, at the impudent villainy of its falsehoods." The point of this exercise in literary self-consciousness is not finally to model the reader of the *Quarterly Review*, but rather to impress upon that reader the very different and alarming habits of reception through which "the diatribes of the anarchists" take effect among impoverished laborers already grossly debilitated by "the manufacturing system":

Where one who can read is to be found, all who have ears can hear. The weekly epistles of the apostles of sedition are read aloud in tap-rooms and pothouses to believing auditors, listening greedily when they are told that their rulers fatten upon the gains extracted from their blood and sinews; that they are cheated, oppressed, and plundered . . . . These are the topics which are received in the pot-house, and discussed over the loom and the lathe: men already profligate and unprincipled, needy because they are dissolute, and discontented because they are needy, swallow these things when they are getting drunk, and chew the cud upon them when sober. (*QR* 8 [1812], 342)

A debased plebeian radical reading audience – suffering variously from ignorance, delusion, deprivation, and intoxication – is a far more familiar collective figure in Southey's work than the individual loyal reader at his breakfast table, suggesting that the underlying rhetorical relationships in his prose are those of provocation and antagonism rather than sympathy or identification. Like other apologists for the existing constitution, Southey rejected the radical approach to parliamentary reform as a misguided project of political delegation or descriptive representation, with members crudely answerable to constituent expectations.[26] Where print representation was at issue, this attitude carried over into a resistance to conceptions of literary authority that implied a straightforward correspondence between writer and reader, whether that correspondence was considered the precondition or consequence of political communication.

In the heady period leading up to the establishment of the *Quarterly Review*, Southey's private letters were unusually frank about matters of government influence ("in plain English, the ministers set it up") and financial motive ("the pay will be as high as the *Edinburgh*"), but they also betrayed a conception of himself as a maverick conservative who wrote against the grain of audience expectation and editorial policy. What he termed his own "Robert Southeyish" contributions to the new review should be rescued from Gifford's "pruning knife" because "a sprinkling of my free and fearless way of thinking" would have the effect of challenging public expectations that the new review was a predictable "ministerial business" (*SL* 151–3). Where Coleridge turned to the radical *Weekly Political Register* and the Whig *Edinburgh Review* as instances of a periodical discourse that simply met degenerate audience expectations, Southey was willing (at least in private correspondence) to distinguish his own projected work for the *Quarterly Review* from the redaction of existing opinion by other conservative periodicals: "The high orthodox men, both of Church and State, will always think as they are told: there is no policy in writing to them; the *Anti-Jacobin* and *British Critic* are good enough for their faces of brass, brains of lead, and tongues of bell-metal" (*SL* 153). To be sure, his own claim to reach "better hearts and clearer understandings" (*SL* 153) begs the same question about the "policy in writing," since we are not told how such hearts and understandings might be otherwise disposed if the *Quarterly* went unseasoned by "Robert Southeyish" prose. Yet it seems fair to allow that visionary incantations of modest reform ("Let us multiply farms. . . . Let the labourer . . . have his grass plot and his garden") represent the weak end of a political rhetoric of internal Tory resistance that is more powerfully evinced in making the case for the threat of revolution: going "tooth and nail, to the *Quarterly*" to expose for complacent government ministers "the imminent danger in which our throats are at this moment."

As he grew increasingly dismayed over the effective production of popular discontent by "Anarchist journalists" (*SL* 213), Southey was if anything less concerned about the relationship between his own writing and "the sound part of the people," since acute threats of revolution could only be put down by government and the law. His account of "a *vis conservatrix* in the state" came in an 1816 *Quarterly Review* essay on foreign travel writing about Britain, and was occasioned by the claim of the French-born American merchant Louis Simond, in his *Journal of a Tour and Residence in Great Britain, during the Years 1810 and 1811* (1815), that the threat of revolution in England was "more apparent than real." In the years since Simond's tour, Southey argued, the situation had deteriorated to the point where British political conditions now corresponded with those in France "at the commencement of the Revolution" (*QR* 15 [1816], 565, 574). Rather than any publication under review, these conditions became the major concern of the essay, which was significantly retitled "On the Accounts of England by Foreign Travellers, and the state of Public Opinion" when it was reprinted in Southey's *Essays, Moral and Political* (1832), where it joined two other *Quarterly Review* essays of 1816 – "On the State of the Poor," and "On the State of Public Opinion, and the Political Reformers" – as a compelling three part sequence on the postwar development of a more aggressive and dangerously proletarian radical reform movement. The final essay in the sequence originally listed the *Weekly Political Register* among the publications under review, and it was the first of Southey's published writings to address the cheap unstamped version of the *Register* Cobbett launched in November 1816 with his Address "To the Journeymen and Labourers of England, Wales, Scotland, and Ireland."[27] Here Southey confronted the most disturbing case of a political discourse that engaged and aroused its audience as aggrieved political constituency, and his extracts from Cobbett included an incendiary approval of the "bustle and noise" and "*action*" by which the American colonies had gained their independence and a provocative vindication of a reform meeting at Spa Fields that ended in rioting (*QR* 16 [1816–17], 273–4). In concluding his review, Southey twice reminded the reader that the motto of sedition was a claim about the ascendancy of opinion ("*Vox Populi, Vox Dei*"). Cobbett's terrifying ability "to irritate and inflame" his readers clearly dictated against any countervailing loyalist campaign:

> The press may combat the press in ordinary times and upon ordinary topics, a measure of finance, for instance, or the common course of politics, or a point in theology. But in seasons of great agitation, or on those momentous subjects in which the peace and security of society, nay the very existence of social order itself is involved, it is absurd to suppose that the healing should come from the same weapon as the wound. (*QR* 16 [1816–1817], 275–6)

The burden of the essay finally fell on "what it behoves the Government to do," namely, to "curb sedition in time; lest it should be called upon to crush rebellion and to punish treason" (*QR* 16 [1816–17], 276).[28] A few months later, in the essay "Rise and Progress of Popular Disaffection," this concern for state initiative became a political maxim. Individuals might "do much in their respective spheres" towards ameliorating distress, but government alone could save the nation from the threat of revolution: "The laws, and nothing but the laws, can preserve us from this catastrophe" (*QR* 16 [1816–17], 552).

In this same period Southey grew increasingly frustrated with what he considered the lethargy of the Liverpool government. His early remark to his brother about "making our men in power see the imminent danger" of Luddite violence suggests an indirect communication with government ministers, similar to Coleridge's address in *The Friend* to men of "Rank, or Fortune, or official Situation, or Talents and Habits," though more narrowly oriented towards the government and not embellished by a sense of secondary influence upon "the Multitude." Even after radical attacks upon him as a hired government pen mounted after his appointment as Poet Laureate in 1813, Southey continued to operate with an acute sense that he possessed nothing like ministerial authority. The conditional mood governing his correspondence in the wake of the Perceval assassination – "If I knew the ministers, I would urgently press upon them . . . " – was more painfully registered in another letter to Bedford, written at the unpromising outset of the Peninsular campaign against the French: "Spain! Spain! were the resources of the nation at my command, I would stake my head upon the deliverance of that country, and the utter overthrow of Bonaparte. But, good God! what blunders, what girlish panics, what absolute cowardice are there in our measures!" (*SL* 153). Friends such as Bedford and Charles Watkin Williams Wynn (a schoolmate who went on to become a member of parliament and a Tory cabinet minister) offered access to the inner circles of power, and Southey's correspondence with them often condenses and relays arguments more fully developed in his public writing for the *Edinburgh Annual Register* and *Quarterly Review*.

In this sense, the extraordinary memorandum that Southey composed for Lord Liverpool in March of 1817, recommending more vigorous repressive measures than the government was prepared to adopt, represents a rare case in which he dispensed with intermediaries and took the case directly to a Prime Minister.[29] While there is every reason to be skeptical about his claims to political consistency over the course of his career, this brief (five paragraph) memorandum suggests an admirable consistency across a range of reading audiences. Notwithstanding his own caution that these are "private" reflections, there is little here that is not familiar from the *Quarterly* and from more intimate correspondence: a warning of "the horrors of a *bellum servile*," now so imminent that "if the fear of the military were withdrawn, four and twenty hours would not elapse before the tricoloured flag would be planted upon Carlton House"; an assault on the radical press, and especially the weekly "manifestoes" of "Cobbett, Hone, and the *Examiner*," which are routinely "read aloud in every alehouse" and disseminated "throughout the remotest parts of England"; a program for immediate measures "to secure the attachment of the army," and above all, "the main thing needful," a vigorous legal campaign against the seditious press.[30] If the message is the same, the fact that it is not issued in the *Quarterly* allows Southey to dispense with the rhetorical ambiguities of addressing an audience not fully authorized to act against subversion. The imperative to Liverpool is clear and uncompromising: "You must curb the press, or it will destroy the country." Any new ground broken in the memorandum follows from the sense of a direct address to power. Referring to the recent acquittal of the Spa Fields agitator John Hooper on charges of high treason, Southey insists that where juries "either from fear or faction" fail to discharge their duty, the government must take extraordinary measures: "I beseech you do not hesitate at using that vigour beyond the law which the exigence requires."[31] Where Coleridge made the role of the judge in instructing jurors the imagined premise for his own authority in *The Friend*, Southey registered his diminished faith in the jury system by urging Liverpool to act "beyond the law."

It may be tempting to dismiss a political program alarmist enough to expect a republican uprising in London within hours, but imprudent enough to advise the government to take the provocative course of simply ignoring unfavorable jury verdicts. And yet taken on its own terms, Southey's memorandum to Liverpool has the virtue of being animated throughout by a sober sense of his own limited authority, and it clearly and effectively summarizes positions he developed over the course of a decade at the *Quarterly Review*. In this sense the memorandum compares favorably with a more expansive letter Coleridge sent to Liverpool later in the summer of the same year. Where Southey condensed in order to insist upon repressive action beyond his own literary powers, Coleridge elaborated and embellished in order to encourage the Prime Minister to spend more time with his own published writings, and the letter was in fact accompanied by a copy of the *Biographia Literaria*. Acknowledging at the outset that "scarcely one in ten thousand is sufficiently interested in the first problems of speculative science," Coleridge then proceeds on the assumption that the Prime Minister is among the elect, advancing a favorite argument that political unrest among the lower orders is a consequence of the ascendancy achieved by "the common-sense and mechanic Philosophy" among British elites over the course of the eighteenth century, a particularly regrettable development where "our Clergy and Gentry" are concerned (*CL* 4: 758, 761–2).[32] If for Southey an address to power closed the gap between argument and action, the effect here is reversed, as the very fact that Liverpool is in a position to act seems to Coleridge to mitigate on the side of historical and philosophical reflection. Where he is not embellishing his case with Latin and Greek quotations and oblique historical examples, Coleridge takes the opportunity to hector the British people by way of a flattering address to their leader: "It is high time, my Lord! that the subjects of Xtian Governments should be taught that neither historically nor morally, neither in right nor in fact, have men made the state but that the state & that alone makes them men" (*CL* 4: 762). If this thorough rejection of radical contractualism and popular sovereignty, consistent with Coleridge's effort in this period to substitute a political language of duties for one of rights, represents a rare instance of a bold stroke in the address to Liverpool, it lends support to the view that the elusive Lay Sermon to the common people was perhaps best left undelivered.[33] In this sense the flattering letter with the gift of the *Biographia Literaria* serves as an early episode in a longer and ultimately disappointing campaign to secure patronage from the Liverpool government, which Coleridge conducted primarily through his friend (the former *Anti-Jacobin* contributor) John Hookham Frere.[34] There is evidence that Coleridge missed his mark even at this early stage. The Prime Minister endorsed the letter with a fair summary of its contents, closing with this bemused remark: "At least I believe this is Mr. Coleridge's meaning, but I cannot well understand him."[35]

Where Coleridge's letter anticipated an unsuccessful bid for government patronage, Southey's memorandum served as a kind of coda to his own difficult decision in September 1816 to decline an invitation from the ministry, delivered by way of Bedford and the Tory politician John Charles Herries, to meet with Lord Liverpool in London to consider a new periodical enterprise in support of government.[36] That the invitation came through these friends, and that it came at all, suggests that Southey's notional communication with "our men in power" by way of public writing and private correspondence was not a mere fantasy. His letters to Bedford and to John Rickman on the government overtures suggest that he was skeptical from the outset, reluctant to remove himself and his family from rural Keswick and to sacrifice his ambitions as a poet and historian to public affairs, and anxious too that in becoming an openly salaried government writer he would compromise his ongoing defense of government and social order in the *Quarterly Review*. While the *Wat Tyler* affair still lay ahead, the wounds from personal attacks by Leigh Hunt, William Hazlitt, and others after his acceptance of the Poet Laureateship were still fresh enough.[37] At first he agreed to come to London to meet with the Prime Minister, "if it be necessary," and even began to outline the terms of the project, writing to Bedford on September 8 about the possibility of contributing to, though not actually managing, "a journal with the same object in view as the Anti-Jacobin, but conducted upon better principles" (*SLC* 4: 202). Within days of this letter his scruples seem to have prevailed, and in explaining the decision not to become a "salaried writer" he reiterated his practical concern that this would "lessen the worth of my services" in the public eye (*SLC* 4: 209–10). At the same time, he intimated a more principled objection, which supports a reading of the later memorandum to Liverpool as part of a wider effort to instigate appropriate counterrevolutionary agency, beyond the press and opinion. Writing privately to Bedford and Rickman, he was prepared to criticize the government for ignoring his earlier admonitions: "It is very obvious that a sense of danger has occasioned this step. Look at my first Paper upon the Poor in the 16th Quarterly; had the ministry opened their eyes four years ago, had they seen what was passing before their eyes, the evil might have been checked" (*SLC* 4: 202). Indeed, as early as the assassination of Perceval in 1812, Southey had begun this habit of looking back in frustration over the prophetic character of his earlier alarmist writing.[38] By 1817, the need for "effective measures" far outweighed any corrective print campaign, even where the radical excesses of the press were concerned. "Less is to be done by administering antidotes, than by preventing the distribution of the poison. Make by all means the utmost use of the press in directing the public opinion, but impose some curb upon its license, or all efforts will be in vain" (*SLC* 4: 203–4).

With his own visionary powers securely committed to identifying a threat of revolution he could not prevent, Southey employed the

familiar "Let . . ." formula of the *Quarterly Review* as a way of articulating in private correspondence the limits of counterrevolutionary
public expression:

> The whole fabric of social order in this country is in great danger; the
> Revolution, should it be effected, will not be less bloody nor less ferocious
> than it was in France. It *will* be effected unless vigorous measures be taken to
> arrest its progress. . . . Let me write upon the State of Affairs (the freer I am
> the better I shall write), and let there be a weekly journal established, where
> the villanies and misrepresentations of the Anarchists and Malignants may be
> detected and exposed. But all will be in vain unless there be some check given
> to the licentiousness of the press, by one or two convictions, and an adequate
> (that is to say) an effective punishment. (*SLC* 4: 210)

It is worth observing that any pressure against public writing and
public opinion is significantly qualified here in two ways. First, Southey
makes it clear that the excesses of "the Anarchists and Malignants"
have not so compromised matters that he should give up writing "upon
the State of Affairs," and second, he confirms that repressive measures
should target the press as the critical nexus for radical transmission.
And even as he explained his decision to decline a government invitation that followed upon his own public and private lobbying, Southey
continued to invoke initiatives ("my measures") outlined in the pages of
the *Quarterly*, above all, making "transportation the punishment for
sedition" (*SLC* 4: 206).[39] In terms that recall his remark to his brother
about "making our men in power" see the danger of Luddite violence,
public writing for the *Quarterly Review* became a kind of redirected
address:

> Four years ago I wrote in the Q. R. to explain the state of Jacobinism in the
> country, and with the hope of alarming the Government. At present they are
> alarmed; they want to oppose pen to pen, and I have just been desired to go
> up to town and confer with Lord Liverpool. God help them, and is it come to
> this! It is well that the press should be employed in their favour; but if they rely
> upon influencing public opinion by such means, it becomes us rather to look
> abroad where we may rest our heads in safety, or to make ready for taking
> leave of them at home. (*SLC* 4: 205)[40]

It was here, in the capacity of *Quarterly* reviewing to reach government
ministers and condition state policy, that Southey found a credible
loyalist alternative to the subversive circuit of radical print expression
and political organization that Coleridge had discovered in a London
public house on the day of Perceval's assassination. As he grew more

confident about the decision to decline Liverpool's invitation, Southey scaled the project back in his own conception to a major pamphlet or perhaps a volume on the post-war crisis, and a willingness to supplement his work for the *Quarterly* with occasional contributions to any new periodical designed for a wider audience.

While Southey was prepared to imagine a government responsive to literary instigation, he confirmed his straightened and embattled conception of his own authority by shaping such fantasies less often as dreams of power ("were the resources of the nation at my command") than as nightmares of victimization ("the imminent danger in which our throats are at this moment"). His reluctance to accept the ministry's invitation in 1816 treaded ominously on these terms: "If they would but act as I will write, – I mean as much in earnest and as fearlessly – the country would be saved, and I would stake my head upon the issue, which very possibly may be staked upon it without my consent" (*SLC* 4: 206). And given the responsibility he assigned "Anarchist journalists" in precipitating a crisis, it is not surprising that the imagined threat to his own head and throat came less often from the mob than from the literary agents of a prospective revolutionary regime. The fearsome prospect that his enemies might someday be authorized "to pass sentence upon me as a counter-revolutionist" was vividly expressed in an October 1816 letter to Bedford: "I know very well what I have at stake in the event of a Revolution, were the Hunts and Hazlitts to have the upper hand. There is no man whom the Whigs and the Anarchists hate more inveterately, because there is none whom they fear so much" (*SLC* 4: 212, 217). It is evidence of his resistance to secure or positive constructions of his own literary-political authority that he becomes a particular kind of agent here – "a counter-revolutionist" – not by virtue of his work for the *Quarterly*, but through an imagined sentence brought down upon him by his literary enemies. The central paradox of Southey's writing against revolution lies in his capacity to sustain an acute and even paranoid sense of his own embattled significance even as he insists upon the limited role of the press in combating subversion.

Given that Coleridge's letter to Liverpool anticipated a bid for patronage, it is worth noticing that the fall of 1816 was for Southey a period of financial uncertainty and heightened professional self-consciousness. Even as he communicated his decision to decline the ministry's offer, Southey pressed Bedford for a loan, with assurances that payment due from the *Quarterly* "will float me" (*SLC* 4: 215, 218).

Within weeks he then moved to settle a debt with another friend, the wine merchant John May, by sending a draft of £100 upon his publisher Longman, along with a close account of his "highly advantageous" circumstances, notably as a poet, over the course of the previous year (*SL* 269–70).[41] Any prospective role in a new government periodical played into these concerns by necessitating a costly move to London, and by requiring editorial responsibilities that he considered beneath his dignity as an author. In declining, he reminded Bedford that he lacked the resources by which clerics, lawyers, and other civil servants typically supplemented the vagaries of government patronage (*SLC* 4: 203, 212). Postwar disruptions in trade and manufacturing also figured in his correspondence and his *Quarterly* reviewing in this period, as he advanced a linked critique of political economy, commercial society, and "the manufacturing system" that went back as far as his pseudonymous 1807 *Letters from England, by Don Manuel Espriella*, and conditioned his tentative interest in Robert Owen's socialist experiments at New Lanark.[42]

Yet for all his concern about supporting himself and his family through uncertain economic times, it would be a mistake to interpret his negative response to the Liverpool overture as a declaration of professional independence or a high-minded rejection of state patronage. On the contrary, he was determined to continue at the *Quarterly*, whose government origins he confirmed even as he declined any new responsibilities: "I can exert myself only in one place at a time, and Government would gain nothing by transferring me from the Quarterly to anything else which they might be willing to launch" (*SLC* 4: 203). And he made it clear to Bedford that his doubts about political patronage were limited to the unmerited "suspicion" and "discredit" that would fall upon an already demonized Poet Laureate in a climate of furious radical attacks on corruption:

It would be superfluous to assure you that in declining any immediate remuneration, I act from no false pride or false delicacy. Proof enough of this is, that at first I was willing to accept it. But I feel convinced that it would (however undeservedly) discredit me with the public. Every effort, even now, is making to discredit me, as if I had sold myself for the Laureateship. While I am as I am, these efforts recoil upon the enemy, and I even derive advantage from them. (*SLC* 4: 209–10)

He went on in this same letter to distinguish the "really independent" status that he felt was consistent with a government salary from the more "ostensible independence" at stake in his concern to protect his reputation from undeserved radical attacks (*SLC* 4: 211). For all its ambiguity, "ostensible independence" seems a plausible way of conceiving the professional practice of a pragmatic writer who was capable of declining one government salary so that he could continue writing for another ministerial publication, and who responded to attacks on his reputation as Poet Laureate in part by supplementing the meager income provided by the laureateship with the profits of a work like *The Poet's Pilgrimage to Waterloo* (1816), in which his own self-styling rested on the possession of "the laurel which my master Spenser wore."[43]

More precarious in his professional circumstances, Coleridge found his own ways to resolve literary integrity with government patronage. In rising to Southey's defense in the pages of the *Courier* during the Laureate controversy, he set state provision for literature against the threat of revolution, insisting that the legitimate "honour" and reward represented by Southey's position could not possibly be understood by "those who hate the Government in Church and State" (*CW* 3, 2: 452). Yet he too drew distinctions among various channels and conditions of government support, and while his own professional quest for security was typically vexed and irresolute, one episode from late in his career helps clarify his grasp of the "honour" that eluded radical critics of corruption. Upon his election to a fellowship at the Royal Society of Literature in the spring of 1824, Coleridge was awarded one hundred guineas annually from the crown, and if the stipend fell short of his sense of his needs and merits, it did answer his ideal of state patronage in its dispensation as a crown reward for literary achievement.[44] And when he was denied the fellowship by the termination of the royal endowment in 1831, personal honor was at stake along with financial security. Negotiations through William Sotheby and the Lord Chancellor Henry Brougham to make up his loss yielded the promise of an immediate award of £200 from Lord Grey at the treasury, but Coleridge declined this on principle: "I cannot but find a most essential difference between a private donation from Lord Grey, and a public honor and stipend conferred on me by my Sovereign in mark of approval of the objects and purposes to which I had devoted and was continuing to devote the powers and talents entrusted to me" (*CL* 6: 863).[45]

Interestingly, Southey was also reflecting on the conditions for state patronage in the same year, and when Brougham requested his thoughts on the topic he responded with a tentative scheme for a national academy of letters with "literary or lay benefices" of up to £500 per year, to be distributed by the government. The benefit of such a system "as a political measure" would in his view lie less in its creation of a body of paid pamphleteers and journalists than in its prevention of that "hostility to the established order of things" to which "men of letters, as a class" were always at risk (*SLC* 6: 134–5). By contrast, Coleridge was always concerned to stipulate that grants for literature should flow from the crown rather than the ministry, and should be assigned to a certain kind of writer rather than to "men of letters, as a class." In a gesture that was as principled as it was self-serving, he accounted for his decision to decline the compensatory grant from Lord Grey by citing a theory of subsidy that he had advanced in his 1824 election address to the Royal Society. This linked the insistence upon royal provision with a distinction between popular and unpopular writing, reminiscent of the distinction between Southey and himself. According to Coleridge, most writers simply worked "to distribute and popularize the stores of knowledge already existing," and could therefore without hazard be left to "look for their own remuneration to the Public in whose service they labour." Royal Society membership properly belonged to a more exclusive enterprise:

> In every age and country there is, or ought to be, a smaller class, consisting of those who labor in the service of Science itself, for the enlargement of it's precincts or the deepening of it's foundations: and who must needs narrow the circle of their immediate influence and diminish the number of their readers in exact proportion to the success of their attempts. And to whom shall such men look for support and patronage, but to the lawful Representative of THE NATION, contra-distinguished from the People, as the Unity of the Generations of a people organized into a State – that is, to the King, or the Sovereign. (*CL* 6: 864)

In advancing this idealized account of his own literary practice under crown patronage in terms of a higher conception of "the Nation" that was more fully developed in *On the Constitution of the Church and State*, Coleridge showed just how closely matters of literary production and patronage were at stake in his distinctive understanding of the constitution. It may have been that Southey ("Southeys") served him as a kind of shorthand for the kind of writer who found adequate provision in the marketplace, but in fact in his own negotiations over state patronage Southey was himself engaged in a similar enterprise, working to institutionalize an idealized version of his own practice as a literary agent of political stability, in ways that promised to resolve some of the inconsistencies and tensions involved in public writing against revolution. While the conceptions of both writers were by no means innocent of material self-interest, the fact that both proved capable of declining incomes on principle suggests that their defenses of patronage and of ministerial expenditure should not be considered merely opportunistic.

As Southey and Coleridge worked through from their own practice to a sense of the appropriate constitutional framework for state provision, a leading concern remained the need, as Southey put it in his sketch of an Academy for Brougham, to give writers "something to look for beyond the precarious gains of literature; thereby inducing in them a desire to support the existing institutions of their country, on the stability of which their own welfare would depend" (*SLC* 6: 135). But it was not enough to secure the production of literature. In order to effectively challenge radical mobilizations of extra-parliamentary public opinion, and to achieve a wider stabilizing effect, the reciprocal attachment of "men of letters" to "the existing institutions of their country" had to be somehow conditioned by those institutions. Both Southey and Coleridge came to identify their highest ambitions for their own work with the acculturating functions of a revitalized Anglican Church and national schools under its auspices. Such a Church and its schools would require extensive economic support, and one reason both writers felt that the radicalism of the early nineteenth century was more dangerous than anything in the 1790s was that the more focused radical critique of excessive taxation and "Old Corruption" mounted by William Cobbett, Henry Hunt, John Wade and others seemed to them to undermine a crucial efficiency of the British constitution: the capacity of the state to recruit and finance those in the Church, as well as in government and the military, who served to secure its long-term survival. For Southey the historical forces at work were precisely counterposed, with "the increased power which has been given to public opinion by the . . . prodigious activity of the press" threatening to overwhelm any supposed increase in ministerial influence, and dictating against economical reforms that would simply "exclude talents from the Government" (*QR* 16 [1816–1817], 272). Coleridge was perhaps more skeptical about the efficiency with which state dependence actually rewarded talent and virtue, but he similarly criticized the radical view that "Poverty is the consequence of

Taxation" (*CW* 4, 1: 228), and he developed natural figures of evaporation and circulation to account for government expenditure as a means of healthy redistribution rather than corrupt appropriation or exploitation.[46] Judiciously applied, taxation could serve to reward active virtue and punish the creeping "indolence of the wealthy" by means of "its continual transfer of property to the industrious and the enterprizing" (*CW* 6: 157). In this sense his attack on the radical critique of corruption was conceived as a defense of social mobility and historical change. And it was where such accommodation seemed inadequate, either because historical developments had eroded an original provision, or because escalating threats of subversion demanded broader state powers of self-preservation, that both Southey and Coleridge set about imagining how an idealized form of their own vigilant resistance to subversion might be consolidated and made permanent within the old regime.

In the campaign to formalize counterrevolutionary agency, a rehabilitated Anglican communion and a new national system of education might seem to mark opposite poles of inheritance and invention, reality and fantasy. Yet for both Southey and Coleridge, reactionary and revisionist impulses were in fact more thoroughly interfused in the development of what Marilyn Butler has termed a conception of the intellectual as "the champion of the old order but in an ideal form."[47] Coleridge was never more rhapsodically unconstrained by the mere facts of the historical record as when he developed his constitutional idea of a national Church. And while Southey advocated national education within the framework of the Church, and vigorously defended the "Madras system" of monitorial instruction put forth by the Anglican clergyman Andrew Bell against the more doctrinally neutral system of the Quaker Joseph Lancaster,[48] his expectations for Anglican renovation clearly hinged on the success of educational reform. Bell's Madras system was an "intellectual steam-engine" (*QR* 15 [1816], 227), but it also promised to fulfill Reformation-era intentions, since its incorporation of the Anglican catechism within parish schools would enforce a scandalously neglected directive by "the fathers of the English Church" that curates regularly "instruct and examine" youths on the articles of faith.[49] For both writers, the pursuit of a more secure endowment for the Church's spiritual and educational mission rested on a critical history of the mismanagement of Church property during the English Reformation, an event that Coleridge identified with "the first and deadliest wound inflicted on the constitution of the kingdom" (*CW* 10: 72).[50] If Burke's attack on Richard Price helped make the Glorious Revolution of 1688 a key historical reference point through the early phases of a Revolution controversy, in reverting to the Reformation Southey and Coleridge pursued a line of enquiry more characteristic of debates over poor law reform and the controversies triggered by Robert Malthus' *Essay on the Principle of Population* (1798).[51]

A critical reinterpretation of the English Reformation entered Southey's prose in response to Napoleonic-era economic distress among the lower orders. In gauging the "physical and moral" condition of the poor to be worse than "at any former time since the shock of the Reformation," his 1812 *Quarterly Review* essay on poverty linked the two high water marks of popular distress, and maintained that the sixteenth-century transfer of Church property into secular hands served to degrade ordinary English subjects "not only by depriving the poor of that eleemosynary support which the monasteries afforded when there was no other constant source of relief, but because men who shared the plunder of the church in the vile way in which it was lavished, became hard landlords" (*QR* 8 [1812], 328–9). A sharply dualist rendering of the historical forces at work in the Reformation seems to betray an effort to manage his own critical and polemical energies. "Never was there a good work so wickedly effected as the Reformation in England. It is at once our chief blessing and our foulest reproach" (*QR* 8 [1812], 328–9).[52] In revisiting the English Reformation in later *Quarterly Review* essays, and in the *Life of Wesley* (1820), *The Book of the Church* (1824), and the *Colloquies on the Progress and Prospects of Society* (1829), Southey increasingly sorted out the paradox of "a good work . . . wickedly effected" by demonizing the lavish distribution of Church property by Henry VIII and the shrewd management of spiritual affairs by Elizabeth, while casting Edward VI as "the spotless Tudor" and "the Angel of the English Church" who appeared to the visionary poet in *The Lay of the Laureate* (1816).[53] Though less willing than Coleridge to present his own idea of the Church as its authentic constitutional form, Southey did draw from Edward's early death – "probably the greatest misfortune that England ever sustained" – a sense of unfinished national business, in effect authorizing a more speculative reconstruction of how the Church fathers might have proceeded if allowed "to complete the edifice" they first "raised from the ruins" left by earlier zealots.[54] Edward was himself said to have envisioned "a thorough reformation of the people," including "sound instruction for all, wholesome chastisement for the dissolute, [and] wholesome encouragement for the well-disposed" (*QR* 19 [1818], 87), an approach that accords readily enough with Southey's own early nineteenth-century agenda. By the time he returned to Church history in the *Life of Wesley*, Southey was prepared to advance the present legislative measures necessary to repair the social mission of the clergy as a fulfillment of historical precedent. "Three measures then were required for completing the Reformation in England: that the condition of the inferior clergy should be improved; that the number of religious instructors should be greatly increased; and that a system of parochial education should be established and vigilantly upheld."[55]

Although Southey never entirely abandoned the concern for material deprivation that first animated a critical history of the English reformation in the 1812 essay on poverty, he increasingly stressed the moral, spiritual, and political advantages that would follow from a repair of the Anglican communion through a national system of elementary education. "No proposition in geometry" was more certain, "no inference . . . more inevitable," than the one that linked political stability with education under Church auspices: "If governments are secure in proportion as the great body of the subjects are attached to the institutions of their country, it necessarily follows that national education ought to be conducted in conformity to those institutions" (*QR* 15 [1816], 226).[56] To be sure, his 1818 *Quarterly Review* essay "On the Means of Improving the People" sought to avoid the mistake of "the quack in politics" who "prescribes one remedy for all the maladies of the commonweal," and to this end Southey recommended such ancillary measures as the suppression of public houses and the establishment of savings banks for the poor. Yet in the end he came remarkably close to recommending education as "the one thing needful" to correct an inherited constitutional imbalance and avert the threat of revolution:

Give us an educated population, – fed from their childhood with the milk of sound doctrine, not dry-nursed in dissent, – taught to fear God and honour the king, to know their duty toward their fellow-creatures and their Creator, – the more there are of such people, the greater will be the wealth and power and prosperity of a state: for such a people constitute the strength of states. (*QR* 19 [1818], 94, 96–7)

Though he was violently opposed to Catholic emancipation, Southey pursued his critical history of the English Reformation to the point where he felt the need to disavow any supposed sympathy for Rome.[57]

And his sharp distinction between the destructive "expenditure of Henry VIII" and the unfulfilled plans of "his saintly son" was conditioned by a qualified sympathy for the educational mission of the Roman Catholic clergy, as a model for what the Reformation might have achieved:

Such as the instruction of the Romish church is, it was amply provided by the Romish establishment: its outward and visible forms were always before the eyes of the people; the ceremonials were dexterously interwoven with the whole habits of their usual life; the practice of confession, baleful as it is, and liable to such perilous abuses, had yet the effect of bringing every individual under the knowledge of his spiritual teacher, while a faith, blind indeed, and grossly erroneous, was kept alive in the most ignorant of the populace by superstitious observances, the scaffolding and the trappings, the tools and the trinkets of popery. . . . Under that state of things, every person in the kingdom was instructed in as much of Christianity as his teacher, erring himself and ignorant of its true nature, thought necessary for salvation. (*QR* 19 [1818], 87–8)

In searching for ways to reconstruct a social world in which the devotion of the common people was "dexterously interwoven with the whole habits of their usual life," and their conscience open to elite scrutiny, Southey went so far as to regret the wholesale suppression of the monastic orders in Britain, wondering whether it would have been possible "to reform the regular clergy, instead of abolishing them altogether" (*QR* 19 [1818], 89).

If this particular reflection on the unfinished business of the Reformation seems to test the limits of loyalist nostalgia, it is hard to know what Southey had in mind, since specific proposals for new measures did not follow. *The Book of the Church* offers an intriguing clue when it suggests that the religious houses at Cambridge might have been converted "into colleges for students and teachers," and sets Henry's plundering of the monasteries against a proposal (credited to Hugh Latimer) that scattered monasteries might have been preserved, "not in Monkery, . . . but as establishments for learned men, and such as would go about preaching and giving religious instruction to the people."[58] Taken together with his complaint in the *Life of Wesley* that the abolition of the monasteries made "the clerical profession" less attractive to the talented children of ambitious parents,[59] this willingness to seed a critical history of the English Reformation with alternative possibilities for Church endowments suggests just how closely Southey's case for popular education was linked with his concern for literary professionalism and patronage. In the terms of his own historical vision, Southey was writing against revolution imperfectly, situated as he was between a flawed English Reformation and its deferred fulfillment. A renewal of the social mission of the clergy became the permanent and legitimate form of own remedial literary practice, with the disciplinary framework offered by Church doctrine and Church hierarchy promising to resolve ambiguities about audience and literary agency that were left open by his reluctance to operate within a compromised arena of public opinion. Southey could imagine narrowing the audience for his *Quarterly Review* essays to a select company of "men in power" because he expected such men to legislate a system of parochial education that would institutionalize the vulgar conservative address to which he would not himself descend, even when invited to do so by the Liverpool government.

The 1817 *Quarterly Review* essay "Rise and Progress of Popular Disaffection" offered Southey's most visionary yet narrowly retrospective account of literary production within the confines of the Church. Nominally a review of a February 1817 parliamentary enquiry into the Spa Fields riots,[60] the essay was haunted throughout by the terrifying impact of the cheap *Weekly Political Register*. Cobbett's "act of moral suicide" became a kind of fall into the modern world of radical letters, in which journalists cast off established institutions and moral codes in order to pander to "the worst passions of man's corrupted nature," making a trade of "scandal, sedition, obscenity, or blasphemy" (*QR* 16 [1817], 538–9). Setting out from a familiar attack on seditious journalism and unruly popular reading habits, the essay closed decisively with the demand for educational reform. Along the way, without fully recapitulating the English Reformation, Southey sketched the longer historical process by which literary men were first denied their traditional home in the Church and forced to "exist as a separate class" of "mere men of letters," inevitably reaching a point where they declared war, "open or secret, against the established order of things" (*QR* 16 [1817], 541). More profoundly lapsarian than Burke's paradigmatic account of the rise of the political men of letters in France, the argument was suffused with an overwhelming sense of regret for the development of alienated literary labor, "without any other profession or means of subsistence." There was a notable adjustment of Southey's usual period scheme, since ample patronage and college endowments were said to combine with a limited supply of learned men to leave the way open for advancement through the ranks of church and state "long after the Reformation": "during the

seventeenth century, every man had his place in society, and none of
the ways of life were crowded" (*QR* 16 [1817], 537–8). To postpone
the fall of the man of letters in this way was to more fully stigmatize the
Enlightened eighteenth century. There is then an almost Coleridgean
deviousness about the way progressivist historical assumptions
get reversed in the title of the essay, "Rise and Progress of Popular
Disaffection."

Yet Southey still reserved his purest expressions of yearning for pre-
Reformation conditions, in a passage that is as acutely utopian and
anti-modern as anything in his prose:

When literature was confined to colleges and convents, it may safely be
affirmed, that men of letters were at the same time the happiest and the most
useful of their generation. They had no cares for the morrow; they wrote from
the fullness of the mind, or from the impulse of strong desire: some to collect
the scattered memorials of past times, or record the events of their own; others
to exert the whole force of their intellect on the subtlest or the highest problems which could be proposed to human understanding. If they obtained
celebrity, it was well; and if they failed, the labour had been its own reward.
The schoolmen will not now be spoken of with derision, as they have often
been by writers "too ignorant to be humble;" enough is known of their real
merits to ensure the acknowledgment that their powers of mind were com-
mensurate with their Herculean industry; and that characters more truly
venerable, or on whom it is more consolatory and delightful for the imagination to dwell, than Bede, William of Malmsbury, and many of the monkish
historians, are not to be found in the annals of mankind. Great as have been
the advantages of printing, it was a lamentable change, when literary composition and that exercise of reason which should be, as till then it had been,
the noblest of human occupations and the highest of human enjoyments,
became a trade – a mere trade, to be pursued not from aptitude or choice, but
from necessity and for daily bread. (*QR* 16 [1817], 538)

If the structure of feeling here seems overwhelmingly nostalgic, what
Philip Connell has termed a "narrative of 'the world we have lost,'"[61]
it is worth observing that a similar desire for "confined" yet independent conditions informed Southey's more bracing and pragmatic
decision to preserve his own remote professional circumstances at
Keswick rather than accept an invitation to become a paid ministerial
writer and editor in London. And the particular relevance of this
utopian meditation to his own circumstances may be signaled by the
respectful account of the schoolmen's effort "to collect the scattered
memorials of past times, or record the events of their own." In conjunction with his work for the *Quarterly*, Southey was in this period very

much a chronicler of his own and past times, and the appearance of "Rise and Progress of Popular Disaffection" in 1817 was framed by an array of multi-volume works of history that included *The Life of Nelson* (1813), *The History of Brazil* (1810, 1817, 1819), *A History of the Peninsular War* (1823, 1827, 1832), and *The Book of the Church* (1824). And for all their remoteness, secure "colleges and convents" wound up bearing directly on immediate polemical purposes, as Southey brought this paragraph around to a furious attack on the avarice and moral recklessness driving "our present race of libelers" (*QR* 16 [1817], 539).

The counterrevolutionary pastoral of Hannah More and William Paley suggests a counterpart along the axis of literary reception to this regret for monastic production, although Southey's reluctance to address ordinary readers in political terms tended to limit his engagement with the process by which the common people would be "fed from their childhood with the milk of sound doctrine." The 1812 essay on poverty does explicitly idealize rural cottage life as a refuge for "local attachments" under alienating industrial conditions, and Southey interestingly suggests that, even where "his religious education is neglected," the peasant requires no outside intervention to secure his loyalty and piety. Rural habits are themselves sufficient: "Sunday is to him a day of rest, not of dissipation: the sabbath bells come to his ear with a sweet and tranquillizing sound; and though he may be inattentive to the service of the church, and uninstructed in its tenets, still the church and church-yard are to him sacred things" (*QR* 8 [1812], 337–8). Later Southey enlisted Wordsworth's celebration of "low and rustic life" in support of his own view that, "in the natural course of things," the peasantry is "strongly attached to a government which protects them" (*QR* 15 [1816], 200–1).[62] And yet as the manufacturing system seemed to him to erode inherited economic and social relations beyond repair, he grew less willing to rest the case against revolution on the "natural course of things," and instead aligned his regret for the passing of rural loyalties with a bitter reformist campaign against the "infectious" vices of "idleness, drunkenness, gambling, and cruelty" to which the lower orders were supposedly prone (*QR* 19 [1818], 86). Here he parts company from Wordsworth and from Coleridge to directly engage the traditions of moral reform. In an explicitly utopian "picture of what might be the condition" of a reformed parish, the 1818 essay "On the Means of Improving the People" develops something like Hannah More's interventionist variety of pastoral, with "a zealous clergyman" and "a few worthy and intelligent parishioners" joining with "the steady administration of good laws" to correct the moral and political irregularities of the poor (*QR* 19 [1818], 100–1). To be sure, beyond his strenuous support for Bell's Madras system, Southey did not develop a systematic moral reform agenda, and tended instead to endorse an array of initiatives – from savings banks and the suppression of public houses to a program of road improvements to employ the indigent – as these came his way in reviews and in commentary upon the moral enterprise of others. He was particularly fond of the work of the Society for Bettering the Condition of the Poor and the writings of its founder, Sir Thomas Bernard, and enthusiastically endorsed Bernard's claim "that no plan for the improvement of the condition of the poor will be of any avail, unless the foundation be laid in the amelioration of their moral and religious character" (*QR* 15 [1816], 206). The 1816 *Quarterly Review* essay, "The Poor," was in part a favorable review of Bernard's 1814 digest of the Society's annual reports,[63] and it was through such publications rather than his own experience that Southey's prose accrued the moral reformer's usual stock of improving facts and exemplary cases. Here too his idealized representations of a rural peasantry were conditioned by experiment and elite provision rather than historical retrospection. In recounting the expenses, methods, and acreages involved in a series of "experiments" undertaken by Lord Winchelsea and others on behalf of the Society for Bettering the Condition of the Poor, Southey endorsed Bernard's supposed proof that while the "possession of arable land is hurtful to the cottager," his condition might be "materially improved" by the limited provision of "a garden and grass-land for one or two cows" (*QR* 15 [1816], 207). Rather than thoroughgoing land reform, the framework for rural stability remained that of labor under traditional landowners and close moral and spiritual supervision by the parish clergy.

As Southey undertook to promote the work of the Society for Bettering the Condition of the Poor, utopian glimpses of cottage plenitude – children "educated to husbandry," fathers engaged "in hopeful and therefore willing occupation," mothers guaranteed the domestic pleasure "which, in the right order of things, has been appointed by a benevolent Creator" (*QR* 15 [1816], 208) – took shape within a dual framework of cultivation by other hands. The *Quarterly* reviewer assisted moral entrepreneurs and patrons who were finding new ways to discharge elite responsibilities for the common people. The same essay on "The Poor" tentatively advanced a revisionist theory of social organization, according to which "the different classes of men" were no longer remotely connected as separate "links in a chain," but were instead "now more artificially and intimately combined," so that the modern state came to resemble "a spider's web, in which the slightest impact upon any one of the threads is felt throughout the whole" (*QR* 15 [1816], 191). And yet Southey never imagined that his own literary intervention in this complex web of relations could be the final or framing term in any response to the threat of revolution from below. On the contrary, his remarkable commitment to what Raymond Williams has termed "the positive functions of government" guaranteed that his social vision never came to rest on pastoral nostalgia infused with reformist experiment: in provision as in repression, the state remained the primary agent.[64] Over the course of the 1820s, this approach became a protest against emerging "Liberal Tory" views that the government should not intervene in the economy to correct the effects of industrial and commercial development.[65] If Southey's emphasis on state responsibility was consistent with his account of educational reform as a way of completing the unfinished business of the Reformation, it followed too from his dismal assessment of the absolute "moral deterioration" of the family and the local community under industrial and urban conditions (*QR* 19 [1818], 81). In a passage Gifford excised from the essay "On the Means of Improving the People," Southey went so for as to recommend a policy of transporting neglected children to the colonies, on the grounds that "authority devolves upon the public" in cases where parents are irredeemably corrupted by social conditions (*SE* 2: 141–42).[66] In this sense, counter-revolutionary pastoral lost its critical force for him where pastoral conditions no longer obtained. An enterprising clergyman and a few worthy parishioners might reform a country parish, but "the diseases of crowded civilization require a stronger interference," and it becomes "the paramount duty of government" to repair the moral, spiritual, and political condition of the urban poor (*QR* 19 [1818], 85, 100).

For students of canonical romanticism, there is much in Southey's approach to redressing a flawed Reformation that recalls Coleridge's celebrated theory of the clerisy as a "a permanent, nationalized, learned order" (*CW* 10: 69), committed to mediating social difference and moderating historical change. My concern here is not to settle a question of influence, though it seems clear that Southey's case for national education under church auspices was sufficiently bound up with his own sustained interests – poverty and population, the rise of

Methodism, the impact of industrial society – to dictate against endorsing Coleridge's view of Southey as a mere point of popular transmission.[67] At the same time, it is worth approaching Coleridge's clerisy in relatively narrow terms. While it is easy to understand why his theory has often been treated as a comprehensive theory of the intellectual class, to do so is to overlook not only its specific and restrictive features (which can be highlighted by a comparison with Southey), but also the peculiar combination of fantasy and anxious self-compensation by which Coleridge sought to fulfill his own literary labors in a revitalized and expanded clerical function. Specific institutional and polemical contexts for the theory are vividly registered in the full title of the work in which it was fully articulated, _On the Constitution of the Church and State, According to the Idea of Each; with Aids Toward a Right Judgment on the Late Catholic Bill_ (1830). As a response to the bill for Catholic emancipation that had passed through both Houses of Parliament in March 1829, the main argument of the volume was that the Roman Catholic priesthood should not benefit from wealth and property reserved for a national church. At the same time, Coleridge was developing an account of the Church of England that he first projected in 1825 as part of Frere's efforts to obtain for him some kind of state patronage,[68] and the concerns about literary authority that conditioned his distinctive understanding of the clergy's constitutional position stretched back through the two Lay Sermons to the first version of _The Friend_.

Southey's concern for the debilitating effects of the Reformation upon popular education can seem among the most Coleridgean features of his thought. Yet it is worth noting that while Coleridge certainly identified the expropriation of Church property as "the first and deadliest wound inflicted on the constitution of the kingdom" (_CW_ 10: 72), he did not restrict his treatment of the decline of education and the historical dislocation of the man of letters to Reformation history. No less regrettable to him was the attachment of the clergy and the gentry to mechanical philosophy, an essential development that was then expressed "_extrinsically_, by all the causes, consequences, and accompaniments of the Revolution of 1688" (_CW_ 10: 108).[69] A main concern of his 1817 letter to Liverpool was to trace popular radical discontent and political violence back to this remote intellectual source. And where Southey discovered an ideal type of the man of letters in the figure of the medieval chronicler, Coleridge articulated his own narrative of decline through a kind of conjectural history, redeemed from suspect Enlightenment associations by being recast as the history of "the idea" or "ultimate aim of an Institution" rather than its mere "fact" or accidental temporal form (*CW* 10: 56, 82). Unencumbered by distracting questions of evidence, *On the Constitution of the Church and State* was able to trace the distinctive form of national property that Coleridge termed the "Nationalty" – manifest in English tradition as Church property, and vested in the national Church as the third estate of the realm – back to the reserve made "for the nation itself" rather than for any individual or corporate proprietor in a primitive and therefore pre-Christian "division of the land into hereditable estates among the individual warriors or the heads of families (*CW* 10: 35).

This argument about the specifically *national* character of church property was crucial to Coleridge because it dictated against Catholic claims, inevitably compromised by allegiance to Rome. And again, he complicated his history of constitutional corruption beyond the single shock of the Reformation by identifying an earlier phase in the perversion of the Nationalty, when a "self-expatriated and anti-national" (that is, Roman Catholic) priesthood extended its holdings by appropriating heritable property from individual landowners and confounding it with the legitimate Nationalty "under the common name of church property" (*CW* 10: 51). This meant that some part of the expropriation of Church property during the Reformation could be excused as a corrective redistribution of merely Roman Catholic holdings. The historical opportunity missed by Henry VIII, which would have made his name "outshine that of Alfred," was to have "righted the balance on both sides," shedding inappropriate Roman Catholic additions to the Nationalty but directing what was left back to its original purpose: "the maintenance, – 1, Of universities, and the great schools of liberal learning: 2, Of a pastor, presbyter, or *parson* in every parish: 3, Of a school-master in every parish" (*CW* 10: 52–3). Understood in these terms, a secure endowment for the National Church was not merely a matter of retrenchment. Like Southey, Coleridge brought conservative and revisionist impulses together within a single vision of educational reform meant to ensure future prospects for social mobility and historical change. In his specialized political idiom, this meant assimilating the work of the clerisy to the purposes of a state conceived around the two opposite interests of "Permanence" and "Progression," the former identified with the landed classes and represented in both houses of parliament, the latter identified with "the mercantile, the manufacturing, the distributive, and the professional" classes and represented in the House of Commons alone (*CW* 10: 24–5, 29). The clerisy secured its status as "the third remaining estate of the realm" by virtue of its ability to mediate and sustain these competing forces, as it worked "to secure and improve that civilization, without which the nation could be neither permanent nor progressive" (*CW* 10: 44).[70]

Coleridge shared Southey's commitment to Bell's Madras system and to Anglican doctrine as a necessary component of any national system of education, and he was if possible more savage in his response to indiscriminate Lancastrian schemes, which he termed "a species of Jacobinism, proceeding from the same source, and tending to the same end, the rage of innovation, and the scorn and hatred of all ancient establishments" (*CW* 3, 2: 396).[71] At the same time, in elaborating the role of the clerisy he was concerned to move beyond the primary education provided for by the Madras system, and even beyond the specific functions of the Anglican clergy, to a more broadly conceived civilizing mission, while still insisting upon the disciplinary framework of Church establishment. At the outset, *On the Constitution of the Church and State* insists on the "primary acceptation" of the term "clerisy" in relation to "clerk" as well as "clergy," and makes available a generous conception of the work of this class, encompassing "the learned of all denominations; – the sages and professors of the law and jurisprudence; of medicine and physiology; of music; of military and civil architecture; of the physical sciences; with the mathematical as the common *organ* of the preceding; in short, all the so called liberal arts and sciences, the possession and application of which constitute the civilization of a country, as well as the Theological" (*CW* 10: 46). And yet succeeding chapters are concerned to refine the idea of this permanent, national order of learning within the contours of the national Church, and to remind readers that the social work of the clerisy must involve the dissemination of Anglican doctrine. Against claims for any accommodation of Dissent within a national system of education, and against provision for the Roman Catholic clergy, the right idea of the clerisy remains in a strict sense "the right Idea of the National Clergy, as an estate of the realm" (*CW* 10: 74).[72]

The concern to include and to exclude (many functions, one institution) sustains a characteristically wayward Coleridgean dialectic throughout *On the Constitution of the Church and State*, and the extent to which this is felt in a strict division of labor *within* the ranks of the clerisy remains one of the most telling ambiguities about Coleridge's constitutional theory of intellectual labor. On the one hand, in his list of the three functions underwritten by the Nationalty, it is clear that the two parish elements overlap, with worthy schoolmasters succeeding to become pastors, and both very much involved in the wider task of extending and preserving a cultural patrimony:

So that both should be labourers in different compartments of the same field, workmen engaged in different stages of the same process, with such difference of rank, as might be suggested in the names pastor and sub-pastor, or as now exists between curate and rector, deacon and elder. Both alike, I say, members and ministers of the national clerisy or church, working to the same end, and determined in the choice of their means and the direction of their labours, by one and the same object – namely, in producing and reproducing, in preserving, continuing and perfecting, the necessary sources and conditions of national civilization; this being itself an indispensable condition of national safety, power and welfare, the strongest security and the surest provision, both for the permanence and the progressive advance of whatever (laws, institutions, tenures, rights, privileges, freedoms, obligations, &c. &c.) constitute the public weal. (*CW* 10: 53)

And yet Coleridge is less clear about functional mobility with respect to the first of his three terms, the "universities, and the great schools of liberal learning." In a passage that captures the strange blend of memory and fantasy that counts as historical method in *On the Constitution of the Church and State*, and that recalls the distinction between intellectual discovery and distribution in his Royal Society address, Coleridge outlines some of the ways in which the work of the clerisy at every rank would originally have been discharged:

A certain smaller number were to remain at the fountain heads of the humanities, in cultivating and enlarging the knowledge already possessed, and in watching over the interests of physical and moral science; being, likewise, the instructors of such as constituted, or were to constitute, the remaining more numerous classes of the order. This latter and far more numerous body were to be distributed throughout the country, so as not to leave even the smallest integral part or division without a resident guide, guardian, and instructor; the objects and final intention of the whole order being these – to preserve the stores, to guard the treasures of past civilization, and thus to bind the present with the past; to perfect and add to the same, and thus to connect the present with the future; but especially to diffuse through the whole community, and to every native entitled to its laws and rights, that quantity and quality of knowledge which was indispensable both for the understanding of those rights, and the performance of the duties correspondent. (*CW* 10: 43–4)

The idea that under the original terms of the Nationalty a "certain smaller number" assumes responsibility for training the "more

numerous classes" of the clerisy certainly suggests a hierarchical relationship between cultivation and distribution, between university and
parish. Yet there remains a calculated ambiguity about the division of
labor, since Coleridge does not want to reserve progressive responsibilities for an elite, nor does he restrict ordinary parsons and schoolmasters to the mundane work of preservation. The university and the
parish share "one and the same object," and the dialectical labor that
binds "the present with the past" and "the present with the future"
must take place at every level.

This said, Coleridge was clearly more interested than Southey in
pursuing a higher order of educational reform than parish schools
could afford. In his biography of Coleridge, Richard Holmes
acknowledges that a certain elitism results: "revolutionized national
education" does not become "democratic in the fullest sense." Yet
Holmes regrettably diminishes Southey's own sustained interest in
popular education, arguing that Coleridge rescued himself from his
friend's merely "reactionary Toryism" through his commitment to
educational reform.[73] On the contrary, Southey's writing was
refreshingly free of the stubborn defensiveness about cultural privilege
that suffused *On the Constitution of the Church and State*, nowhere more
clearly than in Coleridge's scathing address to "Liberalists and Utili-
tarians" on the effects of "Lancasterian schools":

> But you wish for *general* illumination: you . . . begin, therefore, with the attempt
> to *popularize* science: but you will only effect its *plebification*. It is folly to think of
> making all, or the many, philosophers, or even men of science and systematic
> knowledge. But it is duty and wisdom to aim at making as many as possible
> soberly and steadily religious; – inasmuch as the morality the state requires in
> its citizens for its own well-being and ideal immortality, and without reference
> to their spiritual interest as individuals, can only exist for the people in the
> form of religion. (*CW* 10: 69–70)

In his own case for the Church catechism as a pedagogy of the dispossessed, Southey was certainly concerned to secure social hierarchy,
but he was not haunted by this acute anxiety about the "*plebification*"
of knowledge. An acknowledgment of the exclusionary cast of Coleridge's approach to education should not obscure the fact that
he considered a reform of elite learning indispensable to any correction
of the lapses of the poor. "I am greatly deceived," he wrote in
The Statesman's Manual, "if one preliminary to an efficient education of
the laboring classes be not the recurrence to a more manly discipline of
the intellect on the part of the learned themselves, in short a thorough

recasting of the moulds, in which the minds of our Gentry, the characters of our future Land-owners, Magistrates and Senators, are to receive their shape and fashion" (*CW* 6: 42). Where Southey turned to the experimental language of moral reform and to the power of the state, in part out of a sense of despair at the breakdown of natural loyalty, Coleridge was more willing to trust the authority that would revert to traditional elites if the gentry and clergy would cast off their debilitating commitment to an experimental philosophy.

Of critical importance here was another hierarchical principle, the downward movement of linguistic and cultural influence that Coleridge proposed in chapter seventeen of the *Biographia Literaria*, in response to the excessively democratic implications of Wordsworth's 1800 Preface to *Lyrical Ballads*. The "best parts of language" were not the work of "clowns or shepherds," as Wordsworth seemed to suggest, but were instead originally "transferred from the school to the pulpit," and from here "gradually passed into common life" and vernacular speech (*CW* 7, 2: 40, 53–4).[74] Conditioned by this theory, Coleridge's version of a counterrevolutionary pastoral in the *Biographia* pivots not on the cottager but on the Anglican clergyman himself, as a figure of intercession and social reconciliation:

> That to every parish throughout the kingdom there is transplanted a germ of civilization; that in the remotest villages there is a nucleus, round which the capabilities of the place may crystallize and brighten; a model sufficiently superior to excite, yet sufficiently near to encourage and facilitate, imitation; *this*, the inobtrusive, continuous agency of a protestant church establishment, *this* it is, which the patriot, and the philanthropist, who would fain unite the love of peace with the faith in the progressive amelioration of mankind, cannot estimate at too high a price. . . . The clergyman is with his parishioners and among them; he is neither in the cloistered cell, nor in the wilderness, but a neighbour and family-man, whose education and rank admit him to the mansion of the rich landholder, while his duties make him the frequent visitor of the farmhouse and the cottage. He is, or he may become, connected with the families of his parish or its vicinity by marriage. (*CW* 7, 1: 227)

The concern here for the parish as a principle of geographical extension partly qualifies Terry Eagleton's judgment that Coleridge was complicit in a process by which vertically structured theories of intellectual activity replaced the more horizontal relations of the classical public sphere.[75] Yet it is clear enough that the point of horizontal extension is to sustain vertical relations. Within a clerisy that is itself susceptible to hierarchical conception, the parish clergy secures the privileges and exclusions of hierarchical society by virtue of its reassuring capacity to achieve relationships of apparent equality at every social rank and through every portion of the kingdom.[76]

This argument about the "inobtrusive, continuous agency" of the Anglican clergy in the *Biographia* was important enough to Coleridge that he reproduced it in *On the Constitution of the Church and State* as part of an account of "the beneficial influences and workings" of the National Church (*CW* 10: 71, 75–6). And in both volumes, he proceeded directly from the conception of the parish as social "nucleus" and "germ of civilization" to a spirited defense of "church property" against radical attacks on corruption, through the same organic figure of "moving and circulative" taxation that informed his defense of government places and pensions (*CW* 7, 1: 227, *CW* 10: 76). Idealized conceptions of pastoral agency were never far from immediate material and polemical concerns. For Raymond Williams, the sense of embattlement in Coleridge discloses a critical phase in the process by which conceptions of "culture" and human cultivation tended to shift from the individual and personal terms of the early eighteenth century to the more social and institutional terms of the nineteenth century. Coleridge certainly drew upon Burke's *Reflections* for his sense of cultivation as a national project, "but where Burke had found the condition satisfied, within the traditional organization of society, Coleridge found the condition threatened, under the impact of change."[77] It was this strain, the sense that writing against revolution could no longer refer to available conditions of stability beyond its own insecure procedures, that made the reconstitution of the clerisy such a critical and indispensable project.

The application of a civilizing and binding clerical role to Coleridge's own situation as a writer, evident in the first conception of an "Essay on the Church" as a bid for ministerial patronage, was reinforced in the *Biographia* by the appearance of the parish as "germ of civilization" within a chapter addressed to those who, under precarious conditions, "feel themselves disposed to become authors." The Church is said to offer "every man of learning and genius a profession in which he may cherish a rational hope of being able to unite the widest schemes of literary utility with the strictest performance of professional duties" (*CW* 7, 1: 223, 226). Yet it is not easy to see how Coleridge imagined his own provision, literally or figuratively, within the institutional framework that conditions his theory of the clerisy as a defense of Anglican establishment. The mediating yet engaged figure of the parish clergyman, "whose education and rank admit him to the mansion of the rich landholder, while his duties make him the frequent visitor of the farmhouse and the cottage," hardly corresponds to the more obscure and discriminating language of his own public writing, particularly given the elusiveness of the third Lay Sermon addressed to "the Lower and Labouring Classes of Society." Jon Klancher has cogently suggested that this paradox is precisely the point, as the movement of the theory of the clerisy "from the mind to the land, from a moral place to actual, regional places" allows "the mere writer who suffers the world of publishing" to recuperate a more perfect "union of practice and principles" in the ordinary life of the parish clergyman.[78] With respect to the common people, this shift is negotiated as a matter of implied encounter ("the frequent visitor of the farmhouse and the cottage") rather than direct address. Although Southey also shunned vulgar conservative writing, he arguably did more to fulfill Coleridge's own dictum about pleading "*for* the poor and ignorant, not *to* them," in the sense that his *Quarterly Review* essays are genuinely troubled in a sustained way by the problem of poverty.[79] If there was no outdoing Southey in sheer hostility to democracy, there is nothing in his public or private writing quite so grotesque as the sense of relish with which Coleridge, in a summary of the Fletcher letters for Daniel Stuart, claimed to have struck "at the *root* of all *Legislative* Jacobinism" by driving home the principle that the constitution protects property rather than persons: "The view, which our Laws take of robbery and even murder, not as *guilt* of which God alone is presumed to be the Judge, but as *Crimes*, depriving the *King* of one of *his* Subjects, rendering dangerous and abating the value of the *King's High*-ways, &c, may suggest some notion of my meaning. Jack, Tom, and Harry have no existence in the eye of Law, except as included in some form or other of the *permanent Property* of the Realm" (*CL* 3: 537).

It may be that the best way to square Coleridge's ordinary literary practice with his theory of the clerisy is to return to the primary conception of the clerisy as "the learned of all denominations," and count him among the "certain smaller number" who remain "at the fountain heads of the humanities." Yet it is worth recalling too his refusal of a £200 grant from Lord Grey, on the constitutional grounds that "a private donation" was no compensation for the "public honor and stipend" of a fellowship dispensed by the crown. If Grey could not repair Coleridge's loss, neither could Coleridge as a public writer repair the dispossession of the clerisy. He was not prepared to follow Southey in conceiving national education under clerical auspices as a *state* enterprise, to be ordained by parliamentary legislation, since the historical damage done to the English Church before and during the Reformation required a more essential constitutional correction. Terminology is vexed here, since Southey was not rigorous, and Coleridge allowed that there were two senses of the term "state." At a lower level of conceptualization, the state was distinguished from the National Church, and the two together formed complementary portions of the nation; but in a higher sense the term state was "equivalent to the nation," and included the National Church (*CW* 10: 73). Coleridge tended to use the term "nation" for this higher conception of the state, and in this sense *On the Constitution of the Church and State* develops its ideas of Church and state in contradistinction. This terminology becomes critically important towards the end of the second chapter, in a key transition leading from the dialectic of landed permanence and commercial progress within the state to a fuller consideration of the National Church: "In order to correct views respecting the constitution, in the more enlarged sense of the term, viz. the constitution of the *Nation*, we must, in addition to a grounded knowledge of the *State*, have the right idea of the *National Church*. These are two poles of the same magnet; the magnet itself, which is constituted by them, is the CONSTITUTION of the nation" (*CW* 10: 31).

In this understanding of the constitution, the members and property of the National Church (clerisy and Nationalty) were not subject to legislative interference. The particular manifestation of the "established clergy" might vary over time and circumstance, but the Nationalty could not properly be "alienated from its original purpose" of supporting a national learned order (*CW* 10: 50–1).[80] As David Aram Kaiser argues, by distinguishing the Nationalty as a form of property from other heritable estates, which he termed "the propriety," Coleridge effectively "separates the national church from the governance of Parliament, and gives the Clerisy, his cultural institution, an autonomous and co-equal status next to the traditional political institutions of the state."[81] This was a principle Coleridge intimated as far back as 1802, in a letter to his brother, the Reverend George Coleridge, seeking to clarify the extent to which he was prepared to give up his early radical scruples respecting church establishment: "The Clergy . . . & their property are an elementary part of our constitution, not created by any Legislature, but really & truly antecedent to any form of Government in England upon which any existing Laws can be built" (*CL* 2: 805–6). Where Southey was convinced that only parliamentary legislation could correct the imbalance left by the Reformation disposal of church property, Coleridge pursued an altogether stricter constitutional exercise: he aimed not only to reinvigorate the work of the clergy in "making as many as possible soberly and steadily religious," but also to reconstitute the property of the Church and the status of the clerisy as third estate in order to place both beyond the reach of future interference. Nothing short of this could avert the threat of revolution, and nothing short of this could dissolve the precarious rhetorical and economic conditions of writing against revolution. To make this distinction is not to suggest that education as Coleridge conceived it had nothing to do with the state. As Terry Eagleton has astutely observed, the kind of harmonizing and reconciling activity that Coleridge and others identified with cultivation could only take place within civil society if the state was already at work there, "soothing its rancour and refining its sensibilities."[82] In this sense, a verbal ambiguity about the meaning and the location of the state with respect to church and nation is an essential feature of *On the Constitution of the Church and State*. Coleridge extricates the clerisy from state interference in order to ensure its permanent and progressive role in a properly constituted state.

As it turned out, neither urgent demands for new legislation nor theoretical revisions of the English constitution managed to avert impending disaster. If there was no revolution in Britain in these years, the convergence of relief for Dissenters and Roman Catholics and an extension of the franchise, achieved against a background of dramatic extra-parliamentary protest, could not have been more precisely calculated to offend the political sensibilities of Southey and Coleridge. And by contrast, universal elementary education was not achieved until the Education Act of 1870, with no provision for an Anglican monopoly. If as Southey claimed in 1809 "the government of England would be virtually dissolved" by parliamentary reform, then government as he and Coleridge understood it was dissolved in 1832. Geoffrey Carnall has written that "with the passing of the Reform Bill, Southey found himself in an unfamiliar political world, in which the struggles of his generation were becoming extremely remote."[83] When he reprinted his *Quarterly Review* essays in the 1832 volume, *Essays, Moral and Political*, Southey registered his sense that a protracted struggle "against the growing errors of the times" (*SE*, 1: vii) had come to a head, and in subsequent years he turned his attention increasingly to economic rather than political affairs. Coleridge was particularly outraged by the press and public agitation that led up to reform, and a September 1831 letter to T. H. Green betrayed his characteristic yearning for strong legitimate authority: "The first thing the House of Lords ought to do should be, to pass and present a solemn address to the King on the system of intimidation carried on by the Journalists & Pamphleteers under the presumed protection and partially *expressed* approval of his Majesty's Ministers" (*CL* 6: 872). Ironically, the Reform Act of 1832 passed only after Lord Grey succeeded in putting down the opposition in the House of Lords by pressuring King William IV to threaten the creation of new peers. A notebook entry registers Coleridge's sense of traumatic dispossession: "I will never consent to be anything but an Englishman – and England is – no more!"[84] Of course 1832 did not terminate radical agitation for further political reform, nor conservative resistance to it. But the extent to which later antiradical movements in Britain tended to accept the need to engage the common people as a political force, and to operate within a legitimate sphere of extra-parliamentary opinion, suggests that Southey and Coleridge were correct to anticipate the subversion of their own literary enterprise. Of all the counterrevolutionary movements and forms explored in this book, Hannah More's evangelical effort to secure the subordination of the lower orders by promising them charitable provision in this world and salvation in the next turned out to be the most enduring, in part because it was the most willing to address ordinary readers. In this sense, the effort by Southey and Coleridge to resolve the contradictions inherent in writing against revolution under the unreformed constitution by shifting the burden of stability to a revitalized clerisy and national education represents the final phase in a protracted counterrevolutionary enterprise first triggered by the crisis of the 1790s.

Notes

INTRODUCTION: RECONSIDERING COUNTERREVOLUTIONARY EXPRESSION

1 Two notable exceptions are Raymond Williams, *Culture and Society, 1780–1950* (New York: Columbia University Press, 1983), which opens by complicating a pair of contrasts between radical and conservative positions, and Marilyn Butler, *Romantics, Rebels, and Reactionaries: English Literature and its Background, 1760–1830* (Oxford: Oxford University Press, 1981), which is alert throughout to the reactionary as well as radical contributions to artistic change. While both studies are highly regarded, their attention to conservatism has not been widely borne out in subsequent scholarship, although Wordsworth has been forcefully reappraised by Alison Hickey in *Impure Conceits: Rhetoric and Ideology in Wordsworth's Excursion* (Stanford: Stanford University Press, 1997), and by John Rieder in *Wordsworth's Counterrevolutionary Turn: Community, Virtue, and Vision in the 1790s* (Newark: University of Delaware Press, 1997), and Philip Connell has offered a compelling reassessment of Lake School conservatism in relation to economic discourse in *Romanticism, Economics and the Question of "Culture"* (Oxford: Oxford University Press, 2001).

2 Ronald Paulson, *Representations of Revolution (1789–1820)* (New Haven and London: Yale University Press, 1983), p. 37.

3 Nicola J. Watson, *Revolution and the Form of the British Novel, 1790–1825: Intercepted Letters, Interrupted Seductions* (Oxford: Clarendon Press, 1994), p. 15.

4 "Counter-revolution," *Oxford English Dictionary*, 1971 edition.

5 For insurrection and political violence in this period, see Roger Wells, *Insurrection: The British Experience, 1795–1803* (Gloucester: A. Sutton, 1983), and John Stevenson, *Popular Disturbances in England, 1700–1832*, second edition (London: Longmans, 1992).

6 David Simpson, "The French Revolution," in *Romanticism*, ed. Marshall Brown, Vol. 5 of *The Cambridge History of Literary Criticism* (Cambridge: Cambridge University Press, 1989–), p. 60.

7 The phrase is from Marilyn Butler, "Revolving in Deep Time: The French Revolution as Narrative," in *Revolution and English Romanticism: Politics and Rhetoric*, ed. Keith Hanley and Raman Selden (New York: St. Martin's Press, 1990), pp. 7–8.

8 William Wordsworth, *The Excursion*, in *Wordsworth's Poetical Works*, ed. Thomas Hutchinson and Ernest De Selincourt (Oxford and New York: Oxford University Press, 1936), II: 423–4, 484.

9 Jane Austen, *Northanger Abbey*, ed. Marilyn Butler (Harmondsworth: Penguin, 1995), pp. 107–8.

10 William Hazlitt, *The Complete Works of William Hazlitt*, ed. P. P. Howe, 21 vols. (London: J. M. Dent and Sons, 1930–4), 13: 38.

11 A transference of apocalyptic expectation from politics to consciousness and language was a major theme of romantic studies in the United States especially in the 1960s and 1970s; see Geoffrey Hartman, *Wordsworth's Poetry, 1787–1814* (New Haven: Yale University Press, 1964); Geoffrey Hartman, "Romanticism and 'Anti-Self-Consciousness,'" in *Romanticism and Consciousness: Essays in Criticism*, ed. Harold Bloom (New York and London: Norton, 1970), pp. 46–56; M. H. Abrams, *Natural Supernaturalism: Tradition and Revolution in Romantic Literature* (New York and London: Norton, 1971); Harold Bloom, *The Visionary Company: A Reading of English Romantic Poetry*, revised edition (Ithaca: Cornell University Press, 1971). Jürgen Habermas' 1962 study appeared in English as *The Structural Transformation of the Public Sphere: An Inquiry into a Category of Bourgeois Society*, trans. Thomas Burger and Frederick Lawrence (Cambridge, Massachusetts: MIT Press, 1989), and accounts of romantic-period literature that draw on his study include Jon Klancher, *The Making of English Reading Audiences, 1790–1832* (Madison: University of Wisconsin Press, 1987); Kevin Gilmartin, *Print Politics: The Press and Radical Opposition in Early Nineteenth-Century England* (Cambridge: Cambridge University Press, 1996); and Paul Keen, *The Crisis of Literature in the 1790s: Print Culture and the Public Sphere* (Cambridge: Cambridge University Press, 1999).

12 See David Eastwood, "Patriotism and the English State in the 1790s," in *The French Revolution and British Popular Politics*, ed. Mark Philp (Cambridge: Cambridge University Press, 1991), p. 165.

13 William Wordsworth, Preface to *Lyrical Ballads*, in *The Prose Works of William Wordsworth*, ed. W. J. B. Owen and Jane Worthington Smyser, 3 vols. (Oxford: Clarendon Press, 1974), 1: 128.

14 Hazlitt, *Complete Works*, 13: 38–9.

15 I have discussed Burke's response to popular radical protest in "Burke, Popular Opinion, and the Problem of a Counter-revolutionary Public Sphere," in *Edmund Burke's Reflections on the Revolution in France: New Interdisciplinary Essays*, ed. John Whale (Manchester: Manchester University Press, 2000), pp. 94–114.

16 The major study of Burke in relation to Wordsworth is James K. Chandler, *Wordsworth's Second Nature: A Study of the Poetry and Politics* (Chicago: University of Chicago Press, 1984); for Burke and Hazlitt, see David Bromwich, *Hazlitt: The Mind of a Critic* (New York and Oxford: Oxford University Press, 1983), pp. 288–300, and John Whale, "Hazlitt on

Burke: The Ambivalent Position of a Radical Essayist," *Studies in Romanticism* 25 (1986), 465–81.

17 Major studies in recent decades have included Steven Blakemore, *Burke and the Fall of Language: The French Revolution As Linguistic Event* (Hanover: University Press of New England, 1988); Christopher Reid, *Edmund Burke and the Practice of Political Writing* (New York: St. Martin's, 1985); Conor Cruise O'Brien, *The Great Melody: A Thematic Biography and Commented Anthology of Edmund Burke* (Chicago: University of Chicago Press, 1992); Tom Furniss, *Edmund Burke's Aesthetic Ideology: Language, Gender and Political Economy in Revolution* (Cambridge: Cambridge University Press, 1993); Frans De Bruyn, *The Literary Genres of Edmund Burke: The Political Uses of Literary Form* (Oxford: Clarendon Press, 1996); Nicholas K. Robinson, *Edmund Burke: A Life in Caricature* (New Haven: Yale University Press, 1996); John Whale, ed., *Edmund Burke's Reflections on the Revolution in France: New Interdisciplinary Essays* (Manchester: Manchester University Press, 2000); Luke Gibbons, *Edmund Burke and Ireland: Aesthetics, Politics and the Colonial Sublime* (Cambridge: Cambridge University Press, 2003); Yoon Sun Lee, *Nationalism and Irony: Burke, Scott, Carlyle* (New York: Oxford University Press, 2004); and Seamus Deane, *Foreign Affections: Essays on Edmund Burke* (Notre Dame: University of Notre Dame Press, 2005).

18 For protean radicalism in this period, see Mark Philp, "The Fragmented Ideology of Reform," in *The French Revolution and British Popular Politics*, ed. Mark Philp (Cambridge: Cambridge University Press, 1991), pp. 50–77.

19 J. G. A. Pocock, Introduction to *Reflections on the Revolution in France*, ed. Pocock (Indianapolis: Hackett, 1987), p. xl. James J. Sack has also suggested Burke's long-term rather than immediate influence; see "The Memory of Burke and the Memory of Pitt," *Historical Journal* 30 (1987), 623–40, and *From Jacobite to Conservative: Reaction and Orthodoxy in Britain, c. 1760–1832* (Cambridge: Cambridge University Press, 1993), pp. 90–2.

20 Gregory Claeys, "The French Revolution Debate and British Political Thought," *History of Political Thought* 11 (1990), 59–60. H. T. Dickinson has similarly stressed the range of conservative thought and action in this period, maintaining that "it is a mistake to think that all the leading conservative writers of the age were simply repeating or embellishing Burke's original arguments"; see "Popular Conservatism and Militant Loyalism, 1789–1815," in *Britain and the French Revolution, 1789–1815*, ed. H. T. Dickinson (London: Macmillan, 1989), pp. 104–5. For tensions between Burke and Evangelical attitudes, see Eastwood, "Patriotism and the English State in the 1790s," pp. 165–6.

21 See, for example, Isaac Kramnick, *The Rage of Edmund Burke: Portrait of an Ambivalent Conservative* (New York: Basic Books, 1977), pp. 3–11; C. B. Macpherson, *Burke*, Past Masters Series (Oxford: Oxford University Press, 1980), pp. 1–7; Furniss, *Edmund Burke's Aesthetic Ideology*, pp. 3–8.

22 Major studies of the radical dimensions of romantic-period literature include Michael Scrivener, *Radical Shelley: The Philosophical Anarchism and*

Utopian Thought of Percy Bysshe Shelley (Princeton: Princeton University Press, 1982); Nicholas Roe, *Wordsworth and Coleridge: The Radical Years* (Oxford: Clarendon Press, 1988); Jon Mee, *Dangerous Enthusiasm: William Blake and the Culture of Radicalism in the 1790s* (Oxford: Clarendon Press, 1992); Eleanor Ty, *Unsex'd Revolutionaries: Five Women Novelists of the 1790s* (Toronto: University of Toronto Press, 1993); Anne Janowitz, *Lyric and Labour in the Romantic Tradition* (Cambridge: Cambridge University Press, 1998); Martin Priestman, *Romantic Atheism: Poetry and Freethought, 1780–1830* (Cambridge: Cambridge University Press, 1999); Gregory Dart, *Rousseau, Robespierre and English Romanticism* (Cambridge: Cambridge University Press, 1999); John Barrell, *Imagining the King's Death: Figurative Treason, Fantasies of Regicide, 1793–1796* (Oxford: Oxford University Press, 2000); Michael Scrivener, *Seditious Allegories: John Thelwall and Jacobin Writing* (University Park: Pennsylvania State University Press, 2001), and Saree Makdisi, *William Blake and the Impossible History of the 1790s* (Chicago: University of Chicago Press, 2003).

23 See Dickinson, "Popular Conservatism and Militant Loyalism," pp. 103–25; H. T. Dickinson, "Introduction: The Impact of the French Revolution and the French Wars, 1789–1815," in *Britain and the French Revolution*, pp. 1–19; H. T. Dickinson, "Popular Loyalism in Britain in the 1790s," in *The Transformation of Political Culture: England and Germany in the Late Eighteenth Century*, ed. Eckhart Hellmuth (Oxford: Oxford University Press, 1990), pp. 503–33; Ian R. Christie, *Stress and Stability in Late Eighteenth-Century Britain: Reflections on the British Avoidance of Revolution* (Oxford: Clarendon Press, 1984); Robert R. Dozier, *For King, Constitution, and Country: The English Loyalists and the French Revolution* (Lexington: University of Kentucky Press, 1983); Frank O'Gorman, "Pitt and the 'Tory' Reaction to the French Revolution, 1789–1815," in *Britain and the French Revolution*, ed. Dickinson, pp. 21–37; Claeys, "The French Revolution Debate and British Political Thought," pp. 59–80; Eastwood, "Patriotism and the English State in the 1790s," pp. 146–68; Mark Philp, "Vulgar Conservatism, 1792–3," *English Historical Review* 110 (1995), 42–69; Sack, *From Jacobite to Conservative*; Don Herzog, *Poisoning the Minds of the Lower Orders* (Princeton: Princeton University Press, 1998); Emma Vincent Macleod, *A War of Ideas: British Attitudes to the Wars against Revolutionary France, 1792–1802* (Aldershot: Ashgate, 1998).

24 For loyalist violence see Stevenson, *Popular Disturbances in England*, pp. 137–42, and Alan Booth, "Popular Loyalism and Public Violence in the North-west of England, 1790–1800," *Social History* 8 (1983), 295–313. Nicholas Rogers provides a compelling account of the ritual violence involved in burnings of Paine's effigy in *Crowds, Culture, and Politics in Georgian Britain* (Oxford: Oxford University Press, 1998), pp. 203–7, and in "Burning Tom Paine: Loyalism and Counter-Revolution in Britain, 1792–1793," *Histoire Sociale-Social History* 32 (1999), 139–71.

25 There has been growing interest in recent decades in the stage and visual culture in relation to political controversy. For the theater, see Jeffrey N. Cox, "Ideology and Genre in the British Antirevolutionary Drama of the 1790s," *ELH* 58 (1991), 579–610; Marc Baer, *Theatre and Disorder in Late Georgian London* (Oxford: Clarendon Press, 1992); Gillian Russell, *The Theatres of War: Performance, Politics, and Society, 1793–1815* (Oxford: Clarendon Press, 1995); Jane Moody, *Illegitimate Theatre in London, 1770–1840* (Cambridge: Cambridge University Press, 2000). For visual representation, see Paulson, *Representations of Revolution*; M. Dorothy George, *English Political Caricature*, 2 vols. (Oxford: Clarendon Press, 1959); John Brewer, *The Common People and Politics, 1750–1790s* (Cambridge: Chadwyck-Healey, 1986); H. T. Dickinson, *Caricatures and the Constitution, 1760–1832* (Cambridge: Chadwyck-Healey, 1986); David Bindman, *The Shadow of the Guillotine: Britain and the French Revolution* (London: British Museum Publications, 1989); Diana Donald, *The Age of Caricature: Satirical Prints in the Reign of George III* (New Haven and London: Yale University Press, 1996).

26 "Counter-revolution," *Oxford English Dictionary*, 1971 edition.

27 Sack, *From Jacobite to Conservative*, pp. 1–7, 88–90.

28 Darrin M. McMahon, *Enemies of the Enlightenment: The French Counter-Enlightenment and the Making of Modernity* (Oxford: Oxford University Press, 2001), pp. 14–15.

29 Linda Colley, *Britons: Forging the Nation 1707–1837* (New Haven: Yale University Press, 1992), p. 295; Colley writes throughout about the reconstruction of the monarchy and elites, but see especially pp. 155–93, 195–236.

30 Titles in the series included *One Penny-Worth of Truth from Thomas Bull, to his Brother John; One Penny-Worth of Answer from John Bull to His Brother Thomas; Answer from John Bull to Thomas Bull; John Bull in Answer to His Brother Thomas; One Penny-worth More, or, A Second Letter from Thomas Bull to His Brother John; John Bull's Answer to his Brother Thomas's Second Letter; A Letter from John Bull to His Countrymen*; and *A Letter to John Bull, Esquire, from His Second Cousin Thomas Bull, Author of the First and Second Letters to His Brother John.*

IN THE THEATER OF COUNTERREVOLUTION: LOYALIST ASSOCIATION AND VERNACULAR ADDRESS

1 See for example E. P. Thompson, *The Making of the English Working Class* (New York: Vintage, 1966); Albert Goodwin, *The Friends of Liberty: The English Democratic Movement in the Age of the French Revolution* (Cambridge, Massachusetts: Harvard University Press, 1979); and J. Ann Hone, *For the Cause of Truth: Radicalism in London, 1796–1821* (Oxford: Clarendon Press, 1982).

2 For the emergence of the modern conservative position in this period, see James J. Sack, *From Jacobite to Conservative: Reaction and Orthodoxy in Britain, c. 1760–1832* (Cambridge: Cambridge University Press, 1993).

3 For estimates of the strength of the movement, see Austin Mitchell, "The Association Movement of 1792–3," *The Historical Journal* 4 (1961), 61–2; Robert R. Dozier, *For King, Constitution, and Country: The English Loyalists and the French Revolution* (Lexington: University Press of Kentucky, 1983), pp. 60–4; H. T. Dickinson, "Popular Loyalism in Britain in the 1790s," in *The Transformation of Political Culture: England and Germany in the Late Eighteenth Century*, ed. Eckhart Hellmuth (Oxford: Oxford University Press, 1990), pp. 517–20. For the London Association's own estimate, see *AP*, Preface, v.

4 Eugene Charlton Black, *The Association: British Extraparliamentary Political Organization, 1769–1793* (Cambridge, Massachusetts: Harvard University Press, 1963), p. 261.

5 Central expressions of this defense of the conservative position can be found in H. T. Dickinson, *Liberty and Property: Political Ideology in Eighteenth-Century Britain* (London: Methuen, 1979); Ian R. Christie, *Stress and Stability in Late Eighteenth-Century Britain: Reflections on the British Avoidance of Revolution* (Oxford: Clarendon Press, 1984); Dozier, *For King, Constitution and Country*; H. T. Dickinson, "Introduction: The Impact of the French Revolution and the French Wars, 1789–1815," and "Popular Conservatism and Militant Loyalism, 1789–1815," in *Britain and the French Revolution, 1789–1815*, ed. H. T. Dickinson (London: Macmillan, 1989), pp. 1–19, 103–25; Frank O'Gorman, "Pitt and the 'Tory' Reaction to the French Revolution, 1789–1815," in *Britain and the French Revolution*, ed. Dickinson, pp. 21–37; and Dickinson, "Popular Loyalism in Britain," pp. 503–33.

6 Dickinson, *Liberty and Property*, pp. 271–2.

7 O'Gorman, "Pitt and the 'Tory' Reaction," pp. 36–7, and Dickinson, *Liberty and Property*, p. 272.

8 J. E. Cookson, "The English Volunteer Movement of the French Wars, 1793–1815: Some Contexts," *The Historical Journal* 32 (1989), 868. For other accounts of the traditions behind loyal association, and its relative strength with respect to radicalism, see Dickinson, "Introduction," *Britain and the French Revolution*, p. 10; Dozier, *For King, Constitution, and Country*, pp. 176–7; Christie, *Stress and Stability*, pp. 36–7; and Black, *The Association*.

9 Dickinson, "Popular Loyalism in Britain," p. 517.

10 John Dinwiddy, "Interpretations of Anti-Jacobinism," in *The French Revolution and British Popular Politics*, ed. Mark Philp (Cambridge: Cambridge University Press, 1991), p. 41.

11 Dinwiddy, "Interpretations of Anti-Jacobinism," p. 47.

12 Mark Philp, "Vulgar Conservatism, 1792–3," *English Historical Review* 110 (1995), 43–5, 68. In *Poisoning the Minds of the Lower Orders* (Princeton: Princeton University Press, 1998), pp. 132–3, Don Herzog identifies the same paradox, observing that print intervention by conservatives in this period "looked self-defeating: it encouraged further reading, the corrosion of prejudice, precisely what they wanted to avoid." The major account of the events of this period in relation to the emergence of British national

identity is Linda Colley, *Britons: Forging the Nation, 1707–1837* (New Haven: Yale University Press, 1992), but see J. E. Cookson, *The British Armed Nation, 1793–1815* (Oxford: Clarendon Press, 1997), who argues for a more complicated relationship between loyalism, war with France, and national consciousness.

13 See Philp, "Vulgar Conservatism," 45.

14 A. V. Beedell, "John Reeves's Prosecution for a Seditious Libel, 1795–6: A Study in Political Cynicism," *The Historical Journal* 36 (1993), 821–2. Dickinson's wide-ranging discussion in "Popular Loyalism" underscores the difficulty: he draws together impressive evidence about the number of signatures gathered for loyalist resolutions in various towns, to show that "the Association movement often reached beyond the propertied middle classes into the humbler ranks of society" (pp. 520–1), but later suggests with regard to loyalist intimidation that "perhaps most insidious of all were the efforts of several loyalist associations to pressurize every local householder into signing their addresses and resolutions" (p. 532–3). The early claim about the Association's penetration of the lower ranks is not easy to challenge, but the questions remain: how far did this "reach" extend, and in what manner was it achieved?

15 Ian Christie uses the phrase in the subtitle of *Stress and Stability*, the published version of his 1983–4 Ford Lectures.

16 Dozier, *For King, Constitution, and Country*, pp. 82–3.

17 David Eastwood, "Patriotism and the English State in the 1790s," in *The French Revolution and British Popular Politics*, ed. Philp, pp. 149–50.

18 Thompson, *The Making of the English Working Class*, p. 82, and Dickinson, "Popular Loyalism in Britain," pp. 516–17.

19 Thomas A. Horne, "'The Poor Have a Claim Founded in the Law of Nature': William Paley and the Rights of the Poor," *Journal of the History of Philosophy* 23 (1985), 55, n. 24.

20 For Paley's ambiguous political reputation, see Horne, "'The Poor Have a Claim Founded in the Law of Nature'," 54–5, and John Gascoigne, *Cambridge in the Age of the Enlightenment: Science, Religion and Politics from the Restoration to the French Revolution* (Cambridge: Cambridge University Press, 1989), pp. 241–4. In *Stress and Stability*, Ian Christie reclaims the *Principles* as "a systematic exposition of the intellectual tradition" upon which conservatives of the 1790s drew, but he concedes that Paley would have shared some ground with the reformers of the 1780s (pp. 159–64); see also J. G. A. Pocock, *Virtue, Commerce, and History* (Cambridge: Cambridge University Press, 1985), p. 278, where Paley is treated as a "liberal and conservative" philosopher.

21 See Robert Hole, *Pulpits, Politics and Public Order in England, 1760–1832* (Cambridge: Cambridge University Press, 1989), pp. 79–81. For Evangelical criticisms of Paley, see Gascoigne, *Cambridge in the Age of the Enlightenment*, pp. 243–4, and Boyd Hilton, *The Age of Atonement: The Influence of Evangelicalism on Social and Economic Thought, 1785–1865* (Oxford:

Clarendon Press, 1988), pp. 3–5; for Coleridge, see Claude Welch, "Samuel Taylor Coleridge," in *Nineteenth-Century Religious Thought in the West*, ed. Ninian Smart *et al.*, 3 vols. (Cambridge: Cambridge University Press, 1985), 2: 3–4.

22 William Paley, *The Principles of Moral and Political Philosophy* (London, 1785), pp. 92–3.

23 See Horne, "The Poor Have a Claim Founded in the Law of Nature," p. 60, and Gascoigne, *Cambridge in the Age of the Enlightenment*, pp. 242–3.

24 See *Reasons for Contentment. Addressed to the Labouring Part of the British Public* (Newcastle, 1819), and *Reasons for Contentment: Addressed to the Labouring Part of the British Public: Together with the Fable of the Bee Hive* (London, 1831).

25 See Black, *The Association*, p. 267. The earliest edition of *Reasons for Contentment* I have seen is held at the Sutro Library in San Francisco, and has the imprint "Carlisle, / Printed by F. Jollie.–1792. / Price Two-pence."

26 See Hole, *Pulpits, Politics and Public Order*, p. 73.

27 See David Marshall, *The Figure of Theater: Shaftesbury, Defoe, Adam Smith, and George Eliot* (New York: Columbia University Press, 1986), and Philip Corrigan and Derek Sayer, *The Great Arch: English State Formation as Cultural Revolution* (Oxford: Basil Blackwell, 1985), p. 104.

28 Ronald Paulson, "Life as Journey and as Theater: Two Eighteenth-Century Narrative Structures," *New Literary History* 8 (1976), 52.

29 Henry Fielding, *Tom Jones*, ed. John Bender and Simon Stern (Oxford: Oxford University Press, 1996), pp. 284–5.

30 William Wordsworth, Preface to *Lyrical Ballads*, in *The Prose Works of William Wordsworth*, ed. W. J. B. Owen and Jane Worthington Smyser, 3 vols. (Oxford: Clarendon Press, 1974), 1: 128–30, and Edmund Burke, *Reflections on the Revolution in France*, in *The Writings and Speeches of Edmund Burke*, ed. Paul Langford *et al.*, 12 vols. (Oxford: Clarendon Press, 1981–), 8: 115. For theater and revolution in Burke, see Marilyn Butler, "Revolving in Deep Time: The French Revolution as Narrative," in *Revolution and English Romanticism: Politics and Rhetoric*, ed. Keith Hanley and Raman Selden (New York: St. Martin's Press, 1990), pp. 7–8, and Frans De Bruyn, *The Literary Genres of Edmund Burke: The Political Uses of Literary Form* (Oxford: Clarendon Press, 1996), pp. 165–208.

31 In this sense, Paley's attitudes may derive from some of the social and cultural developments which preferred private closet to public stage, and left the world as stage "a forgotten metaphor"; see J. Paul Hunter, "The World as Stage and Closet," in *British Theatre and the Other Arts, 1660–1800*, ed. Shirley Strum Kenny (Washington: Folger Shakespeare Library, 1984), pp. 271–87.

32 John Rieder, *Wordsworth's Counterrevolutionary Turn: Community, Virtue, and Vision in the 1790s* (Newark: University of Delaware Press, 1997), p. 99.

33 Elaine Hadley, *Melodramatic Tactics: Theatricalized Dissent in the English Marketplace, 1800–1885* (Stanford: Stanford University Press, 1995), pp. 34–8; Marc Baer, *Theatre and Disorder in Late Georgian London* (Oxford: Clarendon

Press, 1992), pp. 46–52; and John Brewer, *The Pleasures of the Imagination: English Culture in the Eighteenth Century* (New York: Farrar, Straus, and Giroux, 1997), pp. 351–6.

34 Adam Smith, *The Theory of Moral Sentiments* (Indianapolis: Liberty Classics, 1984), p. 61. For the spectatorial framework of this consideration in Smith, see Marshall, *The Figure of Theater*, pp. 187–8, and Stewart Justman, "Regarding Others," *New Literary History* 27 (1996), 84–5.

35 Marshall, *The Figure of Theater*, pp. 173–4.

36 For discussions of state spectacle and theater in this period, which have involved a good deal of disagreement about the precise nature and impact of public displays designed to secure popular loyalty, see Colley, *Britons*, pp. 195–236; Gillian Russell, *The Theatres of War: Performance, Politics, and Society, 1793–1815* (Oxford: Clarendon Press, 1995); Timothy Jenks, "Contesting the Hero: The Funeral of Admiral Lord Nelson," *Journal of British Studies* 39 (2000), 422–53.

37 Marshall, *The Figure of Theater*, p. 173.

38 Burke, *Reflections on the Revolution in France*, in *The Writings and Speeches of Edmund Burke*, 8: 97–8.

39 See Mitchell, "The Association Movement," pp. 72–3, for an example of the printing and free distribution of *Reasons for Contentment* by the Manchester association.

40 In this sense, the kind of political contentment promulgated by Paley, and by the association movement more broadly, confirms Linda Colley's point in *Britons* about national feeling in the period: "Active commitment to Great Britain was not, could not be a given. It had to be learnt; and men and women needed to see some advantage in learning it" (p. 295).

41 For the various government connections and positions of the committee members, see Mitchell, "The Association Movement," p. 59, and n. 17.

42 Black, *The Association*, p. 237. Beedell, "John Reeves's Prosecution," p. 801, and Donald E. Ginter, "The Loyalist Association Movement of 1792–93 and British Public Opinion," *Historical Journal* 9 (1966), 179, also suggest a government role in the founding; see Eastwood, "Patriotism and the English State," pp. 154–5, for a review of the debate as well as an interesting suggestion that there may have been *local* government inspiration for the movement.

43 See Dickinson, "Popular Loyalism in Britain," pp. 516–18; Dickinson, "Popular Conservatism and Militant Loyalism," pp. 120–2; Dozier, *For King, Constitution, and Country*, pp. 55–60, 76–7. In surveying the literature in *The British Monarchy and the French Revolution* (New Haven: Yale University Press, 1988), pp. 58–9, Marilyn Morris concludes that "it is hard to separate the activities of the government, the [Association], and independent supporters of the monarch."

44 Michael Duffy, "William Pitt and the Origins of the Loyalist Association Movement of 1792," *Historical Journal* 39 (1996), 947–8, 952–3; my account in this and the following paragraph is indebted to Duffy's analysis.

The tendency of the loyalist association movement to reflect the dynamics of radicalism has often been noticed. See for example Mitchell, "The Association Movement," p. 58; Dickinson, "Popular Loyalism in Britain," p. 526; and Black, *The Association*, pp. 267–70. For government suspicion of clubs and associations, see Sack, *From Jacobite to Conservative*, pp. 102–5.

45 Duffy, "William Pitt and the Origins of the Loyalist Association Movement," pp. 956–7.

46 Duffy, "William Pitt and the Origins of the Loyalist Association Movement," pp. 950–2, 954–5.

47 See Mitchell, "The Association Movement," pp. 64–7; Dickinson, "Popular Loyalism in Britain," pp. 519–20; Dozier, *For King, Constitution, and Country*, pp. 77–9. For a satirical treatment of the formula for a typical Association gathering, see Black, *The Association*, pp. 256–7.

48 Terry Eagleton, *The Function of Criticism, From the Spectator to Post-Structuralism* (London: Verso, 1984), p. 36. For an account of the notion of a counterpublic sphere in relation to the resurgent radicalism of the 1810s and 1820s, see Kevin Gilmartin, *Print Politics: The Press and Radical Opposition in Early Nineteenth-Century England* (Cambridge: Cambridge University Press, 1996), pp. 1–10.

49 Beedell, "John Reeves's Prosecution," p. 804.

50 Dozier, *For King, Constitution, and Country*, p. 78; J. C. D. Clark, *English Society, 1688–1832* (Cambridge: Cambridge University Press, 1985), p. 263; and Eastwood, "Patriotism and the English State," p. 157.

51 See Nicholas Rogers, *Crowds, Culture, and Politics in Georgian Britain* (Oxford: Oxford University Press, 1998), p. 199: "The creation of associations to co-ordinate and finance prosecutions was not new; similar societies had been formed throughout the eighteenth century, sometimes in response to royal proclamations. But their extension into the political sphere was novel."

52 See Mitchell, "The Association Movement," pp. 74–7. For the development of the volunteer movement, which shares a number of key features with loyalist Association, see Cookson, "The English Volunteer Movement," pp. 867–91, and J. R. Western, "The Volunteer Movement As an Anti-Revolutionary Force, 1793–1801," *English Historical Review* 71 (1956), 603–14.

53 For Ashhurst's charge in the framework of loyalist mobilization, see Rogers, *Crowds, Culture, and Politics in Georgian Britain*, p. 198.

54 *AP* I, 2: 12–16; 4: 10–15; 8: 13–16; 9: 1–8.

55 This title page is reproduced in *Political Writings of the 1790s*, ed. Gregory Claeys, 8 vols. (London: Pickering, 1995), 7: 213; for details about its publication, see Claeys' note, 7: 215.

56 Philp, "Vulgar Conservatism," p. 57; see also Mitchell, "The Association Movement," p. 70, for evidence of how the intimidation of booksellers and publicans allowed the association movement to achieve "many notable successes without ever having recourse to prosecution." For an

account of the 1790s that shifts attention away from prosecution, see Clive Emsley, "Repression, 'Terror' and the Rule of Law in England During the Decade of the French Revolution," *English Historical Review* 100 (1985), 801–25.

57 See Jürgen Habermas, *The Structural Transformation of the Public Sphere*, trans. Thomas Burger and Frederick Lawrence (Cambridge, Massachusetts: MIT Press, 1989), pp. 27, 60.

58 Olivia Smith, *The Politics of Language, 1791–1819* (Oxford: Clarendon Press, 1984), pp. 71, 76–7.

59 Philp, "Vulgar Conservatism," pp. 62–3.

60 Philp, "Vulgar Conservatism," p. 63.

61 See *The Englishman's Political Catechism* and *The English Freeholder's Catechism*, in *AP* II, 3: 13–15; 10: 1–8. The former tract was adapted from Bolingbroke's *The Freeholder's Political Catechism*. Gary Kelly has made the point about a reversion from dialogue to catechism with respect to More's Cheap Repository Tracts, in "Revolution, Reaction, and the Expropriation of Popular Culture: Hannah More's Cheap Repository," *Man and Nature/L'Homme et La Nature* 6 (1987), 152. For a suggestive treatment of the authority of a catechistic method within late eighteenth-century educational practices, see Alan Richardson, *Literature, Education, and Romanticism: Reading as Social Practice, 1780–1832* (Cambridge: Cambridge University Press, 1994), pp. 64–77.

62 For Edmund Burke's use of the almanac in order to expose the new and more volatile conditions of revolutionary era publicity, see my "Burke, Popular Opinion, and the Problem of a Counter-Revolutionary Public Sphere," in *Edmund Burke's Reflections on the Revolution in France: New Interdisciplinary Essays*, ed. John Whale (Manchester: Manchester University Press, 2000), pp. 107–8. And for suggestive remarks about the presence of the printed almanac in the making of a Protestant nation, see Colley, *Britons*, pp. 20–2.

63 William Jones, *One Penny-worth More, or, A Second Letter from Thomas Bull to His Brother John* (London, 1792), unpaginated broadsheet tract.

64 For this tradition, see David Philips, "Good Men to Associate and Bad Men to Conspire: Associations for the Prosecution of Felons in England, 1760–1860," in *Policing and Prosecution in Britain, 1750–1850*, ed. Douglas Hay and Francis Snyder (Oxford: Clarendon Press, 1989), pp. 113–70, and Peter Clark, *British Clubs and Societies, 1580–1800: The Origins of an Associational World* (Oxford: Clarendon Press, 2000), pp. 95–6, 102–4.

65 See Black, *The Association*, pp. 253–5, and Goodwin, *The Friends of Liberty*, pp. 273–4.

66 Some of these pamphlets have been collected in *The Friends to the Liberty of the Press: Eight Tracts, 1792–1793*, ed. Stephen Parks (New York and London: Garland, 1974).

67 Alan Liu, "Wordsworth and Subversion, 1793–1804: Trying Cultural Criticism," *Yale Journal of Criticism* 2 (1989), 68–9.

68 *The Resolutions of the First Meeting of the Friends to the Liberty of the Press* (London, 1793), p. 4.
69 Bowles had immediate reasons for aligning private initiative with government policy in this way, since like many Association pamphleteers he held an official position in the government, and was also secretly paid for his work; see Mitchell, "The Association Movement," p. 59.

"STUDY TO BE QUIET": HANNAH MORE AND COUNTERREVOLUTIONARY MORAL REFORM

1 The tracts were published under these titles by the Cheap Repository in March and September of 1795; in the first collected edition of her work, *The Works of Hannah More,* 8 vols. (London: T. Cadell and W. Davies, 1801), they were reprinted as *The History of Tom White the Post Boy. In Two Parts.* More's work for the Cheap Repository appeared in a dizzying array of editions and formats over the course of her life. I cite the 1801 Cadell and Davies edition for the sake of consistency, except where particular variations in content or presentation are relevant to my argument. I also refer to several Cheap Repository Tracts not written by More; since these were not collected in any uniform edition, I cite them in their original form. Such tracts were subject to More's approval and appeared under the Cheap Repository title, and can therefore be treated as integral to the project. For the authorship of the tracts, see G. H. Spinney, "Cheap Repository Tracts: Hazard and Marshall Edition," *The Library* 20 (1939–40), 310–11.
2 For the public house as "central transmitter of . . . plebian custom," see Mitzi Myers, "Hannah More's Tracts for the Times: Social Fiction and Female Ideology," in *Fetter'd or Free?: British Women Novelists, 1670–1815,* ed. Mary Anne Schofield and Cecilia Macheski (Athens: Ohio University Press, 1986), p. 272. For the tavern in radical culture, see John Money, "Taverns, Coffee Houses and Clubs: Local Politics and Popular Articulacy in the Birmingham Area in the Age of the American Revolution," *Historical Journal* 14 (1971), 15–47, and Iain McCalman, *Radical Underworld: Prophets, Revolutionaries and Pornographers in London, 1795–1840* (Cambridge: Cambridge University Press, 1988), pp. 113–27.
3 Though widely applied to Hannah More by literary critics and historians alike, "Evangelical" is in some respects an imperfect term. In using it, I accept Robert Hole's caution that, while the term usefully indicates her concern for personal salvation, and her social activism with respect to slavery and poverty, it should not obscure her dislike for Methodism, and her firm commitment to social hierarchy and the established church: "It does no harm to describe More as an Evangelical, so long as it is remembered that that is only a partial description. She was an Anglican with strong links with the orthodox mainstream of that church – influenced

by the Evangelical thinking of a wing of the church, but first and foremost a supporter of the Church Establishment." See Introduction, *Selected Writings of Hannah More*, ed. Robert Hole (London: William Pickering, 1996), pp. xx–xiv.

4 The precise circumstances of the title are glossed in later editions of More's work: "Written in 1795, the Year of Scarcity" (*WHM* 5: 244). For an account of famine through the war years, see Roger Wells, *Wretched Faces: Famine in Wartime England, 1793–1801* (Gloucester: Alan Sutton, 1988).

5 *The History of Tom White, the Postillion. In Two Parts* (London and Bath, [no date]), p. 25. In the 1801 edition of her works, the word "present" was dropped from this phrase (*WHM* 5: 261).

6 In an intriguing discussion of providential causality in the Cheap Repository Tracts, Catherine Gallagher identifies what I take to be a related gap between the moral agency of More's characters and the narrative episodes they occupy, though Gallagher's concern is finally the priority of divine providence rather than the institutional framework within which moral reform occurs. "Even though the characters are portrayed as vigilantly active, their exertions are not the motors that propel the plot. These pious characters are eventually saved through their submissiveness, but their salvation usually falls outside the compass of the story's recorded events." See Catherine Gallagher, *The Industrial Reformation of English Fiction: Social Discourse and Narrative Form, 1832–1867* (Chicago: University of Chicago Press, 1985), p. 38.

7 Dorice Elliott, "'The Care of the Poor Is Her Profession': Hannah More and Women's Philanthropic Work," *Nineteenth-Century Contexts* 19 (1995), 187.

8 See Elliott, "'The Care of the Poor Is Her Profession,'" pp. 194–5; Anne Mellor, *Mothers of the Nation*, (Bloomington: Indiana University Press, 2000), pp. 28–32; and Kathryn Sutherland, "Hannah More's Counter-Revolutionary Feminism," in *Revolution in Writing: British Literary Responses to the French Revolution*, ed. Kelvin Everest (Milton Keynes and Philadelphia: Open University Press, 1991), pp. 53–61.

9 In collected editions of More's work, the tract was renamed *A Cure for Melancholy: Shewing the Way to Do Much Good with Little Money*, emphasizing the way Mrs. Jones's introduction to Evangelical enterprise corrects her excessive grief after the death of her husband; by contrast, the earlier title, consistently used for Cheap Repository editions beginning in early 1797, calls attention to the practical guidance contained in a closing section of recipes and domestic advice, removed in the collected works.

10 Sutherland, "Hannah More's Counter-Revolutionary Feminism," pp. 27, 51. This formulation seems to me preferable to Anne Mellor's more radical suggestion, in *Mothers of the Nation*, pp. 31–2, that More "erased any meaningful distinction between the private and the broadly defined public sphere." To have obliterated this potent distinction would have

been to risk sacrificing too much of the authority that could accrue to her from the kind of calculated revisions we witness in *The Cottage Cook*.

11 The most comprehensive account of the association of virtue with the country and vice with the city is of course Raymond Williams, *The Country and the City* (New York: Oxford University Press, 1973). Given More's willingness to complicate the dichotomy (Tom White's conversion to virtue takes place in a London hospital), it is interesting that Williams, in his influential reading of the poem "London," credits one of her radical contemporaries, William Blake, with an aesthetic breakthrough that "decisively transcended" the "simplifying contrast between country and city" through a grasp of the urban experience as a comprehensive set of social relations (148–9).

12 More does take her epigraph for volume five of the 1801 collected works from "Burke on the French Revolution," but it is significant that the passage she selects from the *Reflections* involves a discussion of the established Church, and therefore presents Burke as the defender of faith rather than custom: "Religion is for the man in humble life, and to raise his nature, and to put him in mind of a state in which the privileges of opulence will cease, when he will be equal by nature, and may be more than equal by virtue." More has somewhat confused Burke's meaning, by making his claim about an established Church into one about religion generally; for the original, see Edmund Burke, *Reflections on the Revolution in France*, in *The Writings and Speeches of Edmund Burke*, ed. Paul Langford *et al.*, 12 vols. (Oxford: Clarendon Press, 1981–), 8: 149.

13 I borrow the notion of an invented tradition from *The Invention of Tradition*, ed. Eric Hobsbawm and Terence Ranger (Cambridge: Cambridge University Press, 1983). In his introduction, Hobsbawm defines the concept (in part) as ritualized practices "which seek to inculcate certain values and norms of behaviour by repetition, which automatically implies continuity with the past" (1). On this last point, More is inconsistent, sometimes legitimating the manners and habits she fabricates as a restoration of "good old" practices, at other times proposing the more frank revisionism that Tom expresses here.

14 John Belchem, "Republicanism, Popular Constitutionalism and the Radical Platform in Early Nineteenth-Century England," *Social History* 6 (1981), 4.

15 For a critical treatment of the conventional idea of a revolution controversy, see Mark Philp, "Vulgar Conservatism, 1792–3," *English Historical Review* 11 (1995), 43–4.

16 William Wordsworth, Preface to *Lyrical Ballads*, in *The Prose Works of William Wordsworth*, ed. W. J. B. Owen and Jane Worthington Smyser, 3 vols. (Oxford: Clarendon Press, 1974), 1: 120, 128–30. For a similar conjunction between Wordsworth and the female moral reformers on matters of "colloquial but 'correct' style," see Alan Richardson, *Literature*,

Education, and Romanticism: Reading as Social Practice, 1780–1832 (Cambridge: Cambridge University Press, 1994), pp. 213–14.

17 Philp, "Vulgar Conservatism," pp. 43–5, 62–3, 67–8. For the way Hannah More "distanced herself from Burke and his kind" on questions of chivalry and a romanticized gothic past, see David Simpson, *Romanticism, Nationalism, and the Revolt Against Theory* (Chicago: University of Chicago Press, 1993), p. 118.

18 Robert Ryan makes a similar point with respect to organized Anglican opposition to the campaign against the political disabilities imposed upon Dissent; see *The Romantic Reformation: Religious Politics in English Literature, 1789–1824* (Cambridge: Cambridge University Press, 1997), p. 21.

19 Joanna Innes, "Politics and Morals: The Reformation of Manners in Later Eighteenth-Century England," in *The Transformation of Political Culture: England and Germany in the Late Eighteenth Century*, ed. Eckhart Hellmuth (Oxford: Oxford University Press, 1990), pp. 60, 66–7, 75–85. Peter Clark suggests distinct phases in the development of moral reform associations, with an initial period of growth after 1688, a loss of momentum during the reign of Queen Anne, and a revival of energy in the later eighteenth century; Peter Clark, *British Clubs and Societies, 1580–1800: The Origins of an Associational World* (Oxford: Clarendon Press, 2000), pp. 64–6, 74–5, 102–9. For another account of the Evangelical attack on "French traits" as an extension of a "moral revolution" already underway before 1789, see Gerald Newman, *The Rise of English Nationalism: A Cultural History, 1740–1840* (New York: St. Martin's Press, 1987), pp. 234–5.

20 Susan Pedersen, "Hannah More Meets Simple Simon: Tracts, Chapbooks, and Popular Culture in Late Eighteenth-Century England," *Journal of British Studies* 25 (1986), 87. For the Cheap Repository as an effort to supplant existing chapbook literature, see Spinney, "Cheap Repository Tracts," p. 295; Anne Stott, *Hannah More: The First Victorian* (Oxford: Oxford University Press, 2003), pp. 171–3; and Gary Kelly, "Revolution, Reaction, and the Expropriation of Popular Culture: Hannah More's "Cheap Repository," *Man and Nature* 6 (1987), 147–59.

21 Kelly, "Revolution, Reaction, and the Expropriation of Popular Culture," p. 151.

22 Olivia Smith, *The Politics of Language, 1791–1819* (Oxford: Clarendon Press, 1984), p. 12. See also Harry T. Dickinson, "Popular Loyalism in Britain in the 1790s," in *The Transformation of Political Culture: England and Germany in the Late Eighteenth Century*, ed. Eckhart Hellmuth (Oxford: Oxford University Press, 1990), p. 527, for the view that "although they were not directly political, these tracts were designed to persuade the poor to accept the existing social order with its inequitable distribution of wealth and power."

23 For the migration of Wilberforce's Proclamation Society toward anti-Jacobinism in the late 1790s, see Innes, "Politics and Morals," pp. 100–1.

24 In a letter of January 1796 to Zachary Macaulay, More described the Cheap Repository in terms that similarly insist upon a counter-revolutionary vocation, at least with respect to the "horrid blasphemy" of infidel theory: "Vulgar and indecent penny books were always common, but speculative infidelity, brought down to the pockets and capacities of the poor, forms a new era in our history. This requires strong counter-action; I do not pretend that ours is very strong, but we must do what we can." See William Roberts, *Memoirs of the Life and Correspondence of Mrs. Hannah More*, 4 vols. (London: R. B. Seeley and W. Burnside, 1834), 2: 458.

25 Christine L. Krueger, *The Reader's Repentance: Women Preachers, Women Writers, and Nineteenth-Century Social Discourse* (Chicago: University of Chicago Press, 1992), pp. 94–7, and Philp, "Vulgar Conservatism," p. 45. In an account of More's professional and moral enterprise in *Britons: Forging the Nation 1707–1837* (New Haven and London: Yale University Press, 1992), pp. 274–5, Linda Colley also warns against "seeing her simply as a conservative figure."

26 Mellor, *Mothers of the Nation*, pp. 13–38; Krueger, *The Reader's Repentance*, pp. 85,112–15; Elliott, "'The Care of the Poor Is Her Profession,'" pp. 179–204; Sutherland, "Hannah More's Counter-Revolutionary Feminism," pp. 27–63; Myers, "Hannah More's Tracts for the Times," pp. 264–84; and Mitzi Myers, "Reform or Ruin: 'A Revolution in Female Manners,'" *Studies in Eighteenth-Century Culture* 11 (1982), 199–216. For a less sympathetic feminist response, see Elizabeth Kowaleski-Wallace, *Their Fathers' Daughters: Hannah More, Maria Edgeworth, and Patriarchal Complicity* (New York: Oxford University Press, 1991), pp. 56–93.

27 In *The Industrial Reformation of English Fiction*, pp. 37–40, Gallagher has written suggestively about the potential "friction" between More's commitment to a "rule of providential necessity" and her effort "to portray people in all conditions of life as free moral agents." If the latter concern does sometimes lend More's servants and laborers a certain moral dignity, and even autonomy, Gallagher suggests a coming together of determinism and free will that finally reinforces subordination in divine as well as human affairs: "because the events of her plots are always traced to God's will, the characters' only morally permissible free act is the act of submission."

28 Mary Alden Hopkins, *Hannah More and Her Circle* (New York: Longmans, Green, and Co., 1947), p. 213, and Myers, "Hannah More's Tracts for the Times," pp. 267–8; Stott picks up Myers point in *Hannah More*, p. 179.

29 See Sutherland, "Hannah More's Counter-Revolutionary Feminism," pp. 42–4, and Krueger, *The Reader's Repentance*, pp. 95–6. While Krueger identifies this strand in the critical response to the Cheap Repository, her own work aims to complicate our understanding of More by attending to

her early plays, and to the later conduct books and essays directed at the middle and upper classes.

30 Myers, "Hannah More's Tracts for the Times," p. 267. In *Their Fathers' Daughters*, pp. 78–9, Kowaleski-Wallace has written suggestively about the elements of "fantasy" or "dream world" that suffuse More's fiction, even where markers of the real are most in evidence.

31 The quotation is from Myers, "Hannah More's Tracts for the Times," p. 268. In *Pulpits, Politics and Public Order in England, 1760–1832* (Cambridge: Cambridge University Press, 1989), p. 130, Robert Hole offers this blunt assessment of More's "picture of a just and caring hierarchical society" knit together by Christian faith: "It was, of course, apparent to all that such an ideal society existed only in this fictional form, not in reality."

32 Arthur Young, *The Example of France a Warning to Britain* (London, 1793), p. 85. For the role of this and similar claims in conservative political practice in the 1790s, see David Eastwood, "Patriotism and the English State in the 1790s," in *The French Revolution and British Popular Politics*, ed. Mark Philp (Cambridge: Cambridge University Press, 1991), p. 149. For a comprehensive account of the long history of the confrontation between English fact and foreign theory, see Simpson, *Romanticism, Nationalism, and the Revolt against Theory*.

33 Stott, *Hannah More*, p. 190.

34 Pedersen, "Hannah More Meets Simple Simon," p. 109.

35 Critics have frequently remarked on More's ability to manage plebeian and middle-class audiences simultaneously; see for example Krueger, *The Reader's Repentance*, p. 111, and Elliott, "'The Care of the Poor Is Her Profession'," p. 184.

36 For Mrs. Jones' "social service activities" as "a fictionized account of the village welfare work of Hannah and [her sister] Martha," see Hopkins, *Hannah More and Her Circle*, pp. 215–16.

37 Hole, "Introduction," *Selected Writings of Hannah More*, p. vii.

38 Patricia Demers, *The World of Hannah More* (Lexington: The University Press of Kentucky, 1996), p. 114. For radical reading practices, see Kevin Gilmartin, *Print Politics: The Press and Radical Opposition in Early Nineteenth Century England* (Cambridge: Cambridge University Press, 1996), pp. 102–8.

39 In this sense, More offered charitable enterprise and a provisional print culture as the mediating terms for what Hole has identified as a characteristic Evangelical vision of "a Christian community in which all parts of society were bound together by mutual duty, obligation and affection." See Hole, *Pulpits, Politics and Public Order*, p. 185.

40 For early sales, see Stott, *Hannah More*, p. 176.

41 See *An Account of the Origin and Progress of the London Religious Tract Society* (London, 1803), p. 6; *Report of the Committee of the Religious Tract Society* (London, 1808), p. 5; *The Twenty-Fifth Annual Report of the Religious Tract Society* (London, 1824), p. xv.

42 Richard Altick, *The English Common Reader: A Social History of the Mass Reading Public, 1800–1900* (Chicago: University of Chicago Press, 1957), p. 76.

43 For bulk sales, and for the economic and institutional design of the Cheap Repository generally, see Stott, *Hannah More*, pp. 174–8.

44 For Hannah More's "campaign against extravagant waste," see Mellor, *Mothers of the Nation*, pp. 35–6.

45 *Hints to All Ranks of People* (Bath and London, [1795]), pp. 18–20.

46 See Spinney, "Cheap Repository Tracts," p. 303; Smith, *The Politics of Language*, p. 95, and Stott, *Hannah More*, pp. 174–7.

47 Spinney, "Cheap Repository Tracts," pp. 296, 309–10; see also Kelly, "Revolution, Reaction, and the Expropriation of Popular Culture," p. 154, and Stott, *Hannah More*, pp. 175–6. My discussion of the formal features of these tracts is indebted to Spinney's account.

48 For the Evangelical view of "a Christian community in which all parts of society were bound together by mutual duty, obligation, and affection," see Hole, *Pulpits, Politics and Public Order*, p. 185.

49 These can be found in *The Cottage Cook; or, Mrs. Jones's Cheap Dishes: Shewing the Way to Do Much Good with Little Money* (London and Bath, [no date]), pp. 14–16.

50 For a suggestive account of the shift to a non-convertible paper currency in the work of nation making, see Jerome Christensen, "The Detection of the Romantic Conspiracy in Britain," *South Atlantic Quarterly* 95 (1996), 603–27.

51 Hole, "Introduction" to *Selected Writings of Hannah More*, p. xx.

52 *Mendip Annals: Or, A Narrative of the Charitable Labours of Hannah and Martha More in Their Neighbourhood. Being the Journal of Martha More*, ed. Arthur Roberts (London: James Nisbet, 1859), p. 8.

53 This part of the discussion does not appear in the original Cheap Repository version of the tract and seems to have been introduced for the 1801 edition of More's works. It comes as an expansion of the Shepherd's response to Johnson's concern that he is perhaps "a little too cautious" (*WHM* 5: 44) in refusing to send one of his sons for a mug of beer on Sunday.

54 In *Hannah More*, p. 181, Stott notes that this self-referential detail was characteristically added for later editions of the tract.

55 *The Loyal Subject's Political Creed; or, What I Do, and What I Do Not Think* (London and Bath, [no date]), and *The Apprentice's Monitor; or, Indentures in Verse, Shewing What They Are Bound to Do* (Bath and London, [1795]). Neither of these works appeared in collected editions of More's work, although the latter tract was brought out under her characteristic signature, "Z."

56 *Mendip Annals*, ed. Roberts, p. 6.

57 Smith, *The Politics of Language*, p. 93. While it is easy to sympathize with Stott's complaint, in *Hannah More*, p. 180, that *The Shepherd of Salisbury-Plain* fails "not merely because of its complacency, but because it is an

unconvincing marriage of the realistic and the pastoral," the tract seems to me consummate evidence of More's achievement in the way every element of the narrative is finally subsumed by the project moral reform.

58 *Dame Andrews, A Ballad* (Bath and London, [1795]).

59 Of course the force of obligation moved primarily in one direction along the social hierarchy: "Indeed, the rich have been very kind," Betty Plane observes at the end of *Tom White*, as the villagers gather under Dr. Shepherd's direction to cope with the effects of the high price of provision, "I don't know what we should have done without them" (*WHM* 5: 280).

60 Dorice Elliott has written perceptively about the way that More's charitable enterprise, more broadly considered, sustained itself by generating obligations as well as further demands: "While the philanthropic act could fulfill the poor person's need, it was necessary at the same time to generate a new need, which would require another philanthropic act." See Elliott, "'The Care of the Poor Is Her Profession'," pp. 185–7.

61 For conservative anxieties about the growth of radical print culture, see Gilmartin, *Print Politics*, pp. 68–9.

62 For the importance of the fall and human corruption in More's work, see Demers, *The World of Hannah More*, pp. 77–8; Hole, *Pulpits, Politics and Public Order*, p. 142; and Hole, "Introduction," *Selected Writings of Hannah More*, p. xxv.

63 For More's role in the later revival of the Cheap Repository, see Hopkins, *Hannah More and Her Circle*, pp. 211–12, and Stott, *Hannah More*, pp. 310–11.

64 Edmund Burke, *Thoughts on French Affairs*, in *The Writings and Speeches of Edmund Burke*, ed. Paul Langford *et al.*, 12 vols. (Oxford: Clarendon Press, 1981–), 8: 348. For the serial publication of the Cheap Repository Tracts, see Spinney, "Cheap Repository Tracts," p. 302, and Demers, *The World of Hannah More*, p. 109.

65 Sarah More, *The Good Mother's Legacy* (London and Bath, [no date]), p. 2. The phrase is certainly appropriate to the domestic circle represented in this 1795 tract, as the widow Mrs. Adams gathers her whole household, family and servants, each evening and puts them to work mending family linen while she and her eldest son read scripture and sermons.

66 See Gallagher, *The Industrial Reformation of English Fiction*, pp. 36–7, for the contrast between this notion of obscure providential design and "the Deists' Watchmaker God."

67 For the authority of Allestree in the English Dissenting tradition, see Michael Watts, *The Dissenters*, 2 vols., Vol. 2, *The Expansion of Evangelical Nonconformity* (Oxford: Clarendon Press, 1995), pp. 425–7.

68 In fact, Jack associates severe censorship with the French Revolution rather than British reaction: "Why, Tom, only t'other day they hang'd a man for printing a book against this pretty government of theirs" (*WHM* 1: 336).

69 More has revised and sharpened the New Testament text: "And that ye study to be quite, and to do your own business, and to work with your own hands, as we commanded you" (1 Thessalonians 4, 11).

70 *The Village Disputants; or, A Conversation on the Present Times* (London, 1819). A more expensive edition, containing other tracts addressing recent events, appeared under the title *Cheap Repository Tracts Suited to the Present Times* (London, 1819). Material from the Cheap Repository was widely reprinted in response to the renewed radical challenges of the 1810s and 1820s, in tract form and in periodicals such as *The Cottage Magazine* (1812–23) and *The Cottager's Monthly Visitor* (1821).

71 Krueger, *The Reader's Repentance*, pp. 108–9. More's use of the dialogue form has drawn the attention of a number of critics: in "Vulgar Conservatism," pp. 62–3, Philp discovers an active exercise of plebeian judgment in the conversation between Tom and Jack, and claims this might have had unintentional radical effects; but Kelly is more skeptical in "Revolution, Reaction, and the Expropriation of Popular Culture," p. 152, and argues that More's tendentious use of dialogue tends to slip into catechism.

72 For the circumstances of the publication of *Village Politics*, see Spinney, "Cheap Repository Tracts," p. 296; Stott, *Hannah More*, pp. 138–40; and Don Herzog, *Poisoning the Minds of the Lower Orders* (Princeton: Princeton University Press, 1998), p. 130.

73 For the Blagdon controversy, see Jones, *Hannah More*, pp. 172–83; Demers, *The World of Hannah More*, pp. 106–9; Mitzi Myers, "'A Peculiar Protection': Hannah More and the Cultural Politics of the Blagdon Controversy," in *History, Gender, and Eighteenth-Century Literature*, ed. Beth Fowkes Tobin (Athens: University of Georgia Press, 1994), pp. 227–57; and Stott, *Hannah More*, pp. 232–57. For the tension between More's educational program and those who feared that "the schools were opening the door to sedition and political poison," see Hole, *Pulpits, Politics and Public Order*, p. 138.

74 Stott notes the Burkean terms in *Hannah More*, p. 141.

75 *Burke, Paine, Godwin, and the Revolution Controversy*, ed. Marilyn Butler (Cambridge: Cambridge University Press, 1984), p. 179.

76 Julie Ellison, "Aggressive Allegory," *Raritan* 3 (1984), 100.

77 For More's critique of the upper classes, see Mellor, *Mothers of the Nation*, pp. 18–21; Myers, "Hannah More's Tracts for the Times," pp. 274–5; and Beth Fowkes Tobin, *Superintending the Poor: Charitable Ladies and Paternal Landlords in British Fiction, 1770–1860* (New Haven: Yale University Press, 1993), pp. 75–6, 86–9, 108.

78 Kelly, "Revolution, Reaction, and the Expropriation of Popular Culture," p. 152.

79 See Dickinson, "Popular Loyalism in Britain in the 1790s," p. 508.

80 *A Plan for Establishing by Subscription a Repository of Cheap Publications, on Religious and Moral Subjects*, [no publication information], p. 1, In *Hannah*

More, p. 174, Stott identifies Henry Thornton as the author of the plan. An appeal to the generosity of British charitable provision was a common feature of counterrevolutionary address to ordinary readers; see for example *L*, No. 5 (1803), 90–1, and *Anti-Cobbett, or The Weekly Patriotic Register* 1 (1817), 123. For More's commitment to the "institutionalized philanthropy" represented by hospitals, schools, and orphanages, see Mellor, *Mothers of the Nation*, p. 27.

REVIEWING SUBVERSION: THE FUNCTION OF CRITICISM
AT THE PRESENT CRISIS

1 The term "pamphlet war" is the point of departure for Marilyn Butler's influential anthology, *Burke, Paine, Godwin, and the Revolution Controversy*, ed. Marilyn Butler (Cambridge: Cambridge University Press, 1984), p. 1.

2 I will omit terminal dates for periodical works that continued well beyond the scope of this study.

3 An exemplary case of a study that approaches the reviews through their response to romantic writing is John O. Hayden, *The Romantic Reviewers, 1802–1824* (Chicago: University of Chicago Press, 1968). Recent scholars have proven more willing to approach periodical expression on its own terms, notably in Mark Parker's excellent study, *Literary Magazines and British Romanticism* (Cambridge: Cambridge University Press, 2000), and in the essays collected in *Romantic Periodicals and Print Culture*, ed. Kim Wheatley (London and Portland: Frank Cass, 2003). At the same time, some of the celebrated episodes in the history of reviewing have been studied in a fuller and more satisfying cultural framework; see for example Jeffrey Cox, *Poetry and Politics in the Cockney School: Keats, Shelley, Hunt and Their Circle* (Cambridge: Cambridge University Press, 1998) and Charles Mahoney, *Romantics and Renegades: The Poetics of Political Reaction* (New York: Palgrave, 2003).

4 James J. Sack, *From Jacobite to Conservative: Reaction and Orthodoxy in Britain, c. 1760–1832* (Cambridge: Cambridge University Press, 1993), p. 12. For a detailed account of the establishment of these two papers, see Arthur Aspinall, *Politics and the Press, c. 1780–1850* (London: Home and Van Thal, 1949), pp. 78–83.

5 Aspinall, *Politics and the Press*, pp. 68, 79.

6 Aspinall, *Politics and the Press*, pp. 67–8, 74.

7 Sack, *From Jacobite to Conservative*, p. 16. For the complex political history of the *Courier*, see Aspinall, *Politics and the Press*, pp. 206–14, 218–20.

8 For the establishment of these later papers, see Aspinall, *Politics and the Press*, pp. 95, 98–9. The *New Times* was famously a result of Stoddart's personal feud with his former employer John Walter at *The Times*, but it also represented an effort by the Liverpool government to respond to the increasingly critical tone of *The Times* after 1812.

9 See Sack, *From Jacobite to Conservative*, p. 13; Derek Roper, *Reviewing before the Edinburgh, 1788–1802* (Newark: University of Delaware Press, 1978), pp. 23, 36, 180–1, 265 n. 50; Aspinall, *Politics and the Press*, pp. 166, 176 n. 2; and Emily Lorraine de Montluzin, *The Anti-Jacobins, 1798–1800: The Early Contributors to the Anti-Jacobin Review* (New York: St. Martin's Press, 1988), p. 21.

10 Though it continued irregularly under the short title, "The Rise, Progress, and Effects of Jacobinism," the series was launched under this title in the first number for July 1798 (*AJR* 1 [1798], 109–11) as an unsigned letter from an enthusiastic reader of the Prospectus, a disingenuous device because in this same opening number Bisset was already the reviewer of Holcroft's *Knave or Not?* and Wollstonecraft's *Maria or The Wrongs of Woman*. For Bisset's contributions to the *Anti-Jacobin Review*, see Montluzin, *The Anti-Jacobins*, pp. 57–9.

11 See for example *GM* 61, 1 (1790), 143; *GM* 61, 2 (1790), 1021–32, 1123; *GM* 61, 2 (1791), 737–40; *GM* 62, 1 (1792), 449–50; *GM* 64, 1 (1794), 1201; *GM* 65, 1 (1795), 413; and *GM* 66, 1 (1796), 229, 506.

12 See for example *GM* 62, 1 (1792), 30, and *GM* 62, 2 (1792), 893.

13 Signed "Simplex," Richmond's narratives ran irregularly in a second New Series of the magazine (launched in 1809 under the full title, *The Christian Guardian, and Church of England Magazine*), beginning with "The Cottage Conversation" in *CG* 1 (1809), 18–20, and continuing through the final part of the "Recollections of the Dairyman's Daughter" in *CG* 8 (1816), 138–41.

14 Identified as "C —'s W— P— R—," in *CG* 9 (1817), 168–9.

15 *Cottager's Monthly Visitor* 1 (1821), 323, and *Cottage Magazine* 2 (1813), 202.

16 George Spater, *William Cobbett: The Poor Man's Friend*, 2 vols. (Cambridge: Cambridge University Press, 1982), 1: 121–2.

17 William Wickwar, *The Struggle for the Freedom of the Press, 1819–1832* (London: George Allen and Unwin, 1928), pp. 51–2.

18 Shared content between the *Association Papers* and *The AntiGallican Songster* and *The Anti-Levelling Songster* suggests that the latter appeared under Association auspices.

19 See *BC* 17 (1801), 444–5; *BC* 18 (1801), 216–17, 437; *BC* 19 (1802), 90, 439, 663; *AJR* 11 (1802), 417–28; *AJR* 13 (1802), 199–210; *AJR* 14 (1803), 219–21; *AJR* 15 (1803), 90–3. For the best recent account of the controversy, see Anne Stott, *Hannah More: The First Victorian* (Oxford: Oxford University Press, 2003), pp. 232–57.

20 For a compelling analysis of the complicated way Shelley was treated in *Blackwood's* and the *Quarterly* as well as other reviews, see Kim Wheatley, *Shelley and His Readers: Beyond Paranoid Politics* (Columbia and London: University of Missouri Press, 1999).

21 As Paul Keen has suggested, this overdetermination of the reviewing function was by no means an exclusive province of the right: "by the 1790s, the combined pressures of political conflict, literary over-production, and the tyranny of fashion demanded that the reviews play a more important role than ever." See *The Crisis of Literature in the 1790s* (Cambridge: Cambridge University Press, 1999), p. 117.

22 Hayden, *The Romantic Reviewer*, p. 7.

23 For the innovations of the *Edinburgh Review*, see Hayden, *The Romantic Reviewers*, pp. 8–22; John Leonard Clive, *Scotch Reviewers: The Edinburgh Review, 1802–1815* (Cambridge, Massachusetts: Harvard University Press, 1957); Walter Graham, *English Literary Periodicals* (New York: Thomas Nelson and Sons, 1930), pp. 238–9; *British Literary Magazines. The Romantic Age, 1789–1836*, ed. Alvin Sullivan (Westport: Greenwood Press, 1983), pp. 139–40.

24 For a perceptive account of similarities between the *Quarterly* and the *Edinburgh* despite their political rivalry, see Hayden, *The Romantic Reviewers*, pp. 36–8.

25 For the formal character and innovations of *Blackwood's*, see Graham, *English Literary Periodicals*, pp 274–9; J. H. Alexander, *"Blackwood's*: Magazine as Romantic Form," *The Wordsworth Circle* 15 (1984), 57–68; and Parker, *Literary Magazines and British Romanticism*, pp. 106–34.

26 For the catastrophic premises of radical expression, see Kevin Gilmartin, *Print Politics: The Press and Radical Opposition in Early Nineteenth-Century England* (Cambridge: Cambridge University Press, 1996), pp. 53–64.

27 The letter appeared separately as well in a six-penny pamphlet version, titled *Letter to Lord Sidmouth* (London, 1818).

28 Sack, *From Jacobite to Conservative*, p. 28.

29 "Press," *Oxford English Dictionary*, 1971 edition.

30 For the Southey and Lockhart essays, see *QR* 16 (1816–17), 511–52 and *BEM* 4 (1818–19), 353–8. For examples of the departments mentioned here, see *AJR* 1 (1798), 99–100; *AJR* 3 (1799), 54–5; *AJR* 16(1803), 213–21, 515–23; *BEM* 1 (1817), 81–3; *National Register* No. 1 (January 3, 1808), 3; *National Register* No. 4 (January 24, 1808), 50–1.

31 These phrases are from Southey in *QR* 16 (1816–17), 551 and Lockhart in *BEM* 4 (1818–19), 354.

32 *AJR* 3 (1799), 185; *AJR* 1 (1798), 478; *AJR* 18 (1804), 70–2; *AJR* 33 (1809), 296–7.

33 For the establishment of the *Quarterly*, an event coordinated early on by Sir Walter Scott, see Walter Graham, *Tory Criticism in the Quarterly Review, 1809–1853* (New York: Columbia University Press, 1921), pp. 1–8; Hayden, *The Romantic Reviewers*, pp. 22–36; and Aspinall, *Politics and the Press*, 200. For the *Anti-Jacobin Review* see Roper, *Reviewing before the Edinburgh*, pp. 181–2; Montluzin, *The Anti-Jacobins*, pp. 27, 33–4.

34 Elsewhere, the magazine suggested from its own extended perspective that such political disturbances were not unprecedented: "We have yet again lived to see turbulent and perilous times"(*GM* 61, 2 [1791], iii).

35 I have located only one number of *The Anti-Leveller*, dated January 10, 1793, and held at the Bodleian Library (fol. DELTA 716 [1]). *The Anti-Infidel* ran through six weekly numbers in 1823.

36 The phrase appeared in a favorable notice in the *Morning Herald*, and was then quoted by *The Loyalist* among "Testimonies" in its favor (*L* No. 8 [September 17, 1803], 129).

37 In fact *The Loyalist* printed More's "Will Chip's True Rights of Man, in Opposition to the New Rights of Man" under the signature "H.M." (*L* No. 14 [October 29, 1803], 239–40).

38 Hatchard also published the pamphlet, whose content was effectively summarized in its full title: *Footsteps of Blood; or, The March of the Republicans: Being a Display of the Horrid Cruelties, and Unexampled Enormities Committed by the French Republican Armies in All Parts of the World. Containing True Accounts of Their Savage Barbarity, in the Burning and Plundering of Towns, Villages, and Farms; the Murder of Men, Women, and Children; and in Sacrilege, Rape, and Every Other Crime. Embellished with a Frontispiece, Representing the Massacre of Four Thousand Prisoners at Jaffa.* (London, 1803).

39 For a perceptive account of the way radical as well as conservative commentators regarded "the events of 1789 and thereafter as the summation of a historical tendency already fully developed in philosophical and aesthetic theory, and only awaiting the right moment to solidify into political form," see David Simpson, "The French Revolution," in *Romanticism*, ed. Marshall Brown, Vol. 5 of *The Cambridge History of Literary Criticism* (Cambridge: Cambridge University Press, 1989–), pp. 51–2. The *British Critic* took the occasion of its review of the English translation of the Abbé de Barruel's *Memoirs Illustrating the History of Jacobinism* (1797) to remind readers that while Voltaire was undoubtedly "the founder of the whole conspiracy against Christianity," he conceived his plan in England under the influence of "the deistical writers, who were in fashion when he visited this country" (*BC* 10 [1797], 160). A year earlier, the same review approved a pamphlet response to Paine's *Age of Reason* that offered a predominantly British genealogy for deism and infidelity (*BC* 7 [1796], 557), including Thomas Hobbes, John Toland, Matthew Tindal, Anthony Collins, Thomas Morgan, and Thomas Chubb.

40 Marilyn Butler, *Romantics, Rebels, and Reactionaries: English Literature and Its Background, 1760–1830* (Oxford: Oxford University Press, 1981), pp. 15, 36–7.

41 For an early instance of the phrase, which became a kind of refrain, see *Weekly Political Register* 18 (1807), 816.

42 The pamphlet under review was John Bowles' *Thoughts on the Late General Election. As Demonstrative of the Progress of Jacobinism* (London, 1802).

43 Benedict Anderson, *Imagined Communities: Reflections on the Origin and Spread of Nationalism* (London: Verso, 1983), p. 37.

44 Reprinted material came largely from *The Anti-Jacobin Review*; see the favorable notice in *AJR* 12 (1802), 131–9. For the emergence of the *Edinburgh Review* in relation to the same interlude of peace, see Jerome Christensen, "The Detection of the Romantic Conspiracy in Britain," *Studies in Romanticism* 95 (1996), 607–8.

45 This information is provided on the title page.

46 *The Spirit of the Public Journals: Being an Impartial Selection of the Most Exquisite Essays and Jeux d'Esprits, Principally Prose, that Appear in the Newspapers and Other Publications*, Vol. 1 (1797).

47 For a suggestive account of the anti-Jacobin contribution to development of literature in the 1790s, see Keen, *The Crisis of Literature in the 1790s*, pp. 50–1.

48 Robert Hole, *Pulpits, Politics and Public Order in England, 1760–1832* (Cambridge: Cambridge University Press, 1989), p. 102.

49 For a survey of the attacks on the daily press, see Emory Lee Head, "A Study of the *Anti-Jacobin; or, Weekly Examiner*," dissertation, Duke University, 1971, pp. 116–58.

50 Montluzin, *The Anti-Jacobins*, p. 25.

51 *The Beauties of the Anti-Jacobin: or, Weekly Examiner; Containing Every Article of Permanent Utility in That Valuable and Highly Esteemed Paper, Literary and Political, the Whole of the Excellent Poetry, Together with Explanatory Notes, Biographical Anecdotes, and a Prefatory Advertisement by the Editor* (London, 1799). In "A Study of the *Anti-Jacobin*," p. 219, Head suggests that this volume may not have been authorized.

52 *Poetry of the Anti-Jacobin* (London, 1799).

53 See *AJ* No. 36 (July 9, 1798), 281. For the potential connections, see Stuart Andrews, *The British Periodical Press and the French Revolution, 1789–99* (Houndmills: Palgrave, 2000), p. 97.

54 Montluzin, *The Anti-Jacobins*, p. 27.

55 For the historical development of "literature" in this period, see Raymond Williams, *Keywords: A Vocabulary of Culture and Society*, revised edition (New York: Oxford University Press, 1983), pp. 183–8; Clifford Siskin, *The Work of Writing: Literature and Social Change in Britain, 1700–1830* (Baltimore: Johns Hopkins University Press, 1998), pp. 6, 79–99; and Keen, *The Crisis of Literature in the 1790s*, pp. 1–22.

56 See *AJR* 15 (1803), 57–60; *AJR* 16 (1803), 206–13; and *AJR* 20 (1805) 95–100.

57 The notice appears on the unpaginated verso of the title page of the first number, *BEM* 1 (1817).

58 See *BEM* 2 (1817–18), 41–7, 57–65, 671–8, and *BEM* 4 (1818–19), 353–8.

59 See *BEM* 3 (1818), 715–22, and *BEM* 4 (1818–19), 228–33.

60 See also *BEM* 14 (1823), 221.

61 After the canonical appearance of *The Spectator* (1711–12) of Addison and Steele, early titles in a more disciplinary idiom include *The Censor* (1715–17),

The British Journal, or, The Censor (1728–29), and *The Monitor, or, The British Freeholder* (1755–65).

62 See Head, "A Study of the *Anti-Jacobin*," pp. 90–1.

63 In *The Anti-Jacobins*, p. 106, Montluzin observes that Heath was a particularly aggressive critic of female Jacobin expression.

64 Edmund Burke, *Thoughts on French Affairs*, in *The Writings and Speeches of Edmund Burke*, ed. Paul Langford *et al.*, 12 vols. (Oxford: Clarendon Press, 1981-), 8: 347–8; and for "the political Men of Letters" in the *Reflections*, see 8: 160. For the relation between a conservative fear of print hegemony and the development of the radical press, see Gilmartin, *Print Politics*, pp. 74, 80–3.

65 The allusion of course is to Burke's notorious phrase, "a swinish multitude," whose radical and reactionary afterlife has been traced by Don Herzog in *Poisoning the Minds of the Lower Orders* (Princeton: Princeton University Press, 1998), pp. 505–45.

66 See for example *BC* 4 (1795), iv; *AJR* 1 (1798), iii, 5, 475; *SAJ*, p. iii; *WD* No. 2 (December 6, 1817), 23; and *The Loyalist and Anti-Radical* (London, 1820), p. v.

67 See for example *BEM* 3 (1818), 715–19, and *BEM* 4 (1818–19), 231–2.

68 Similar assumptions underwrote complaints about insufficient ministerial patronage for the loyalist press; see, for example, *Blagdon's Political Register* 1 (1809–10), 808; and *The Loyalist's Magazine; Or, Anti-Radical* (January 1, 1821), 233–4.

69 For the anti-Jacobin response to Knight and the "cult of simplicity," see Marilyn Butler, *Jane Austen and the War of Ideas*, new edition (Oxford: Clarendon Press, 1987), pp. 90–1.

70 Preface and Introduction, *Flowers of Literature for 1801 and 1802* (London, 1803), no pagination, and *Flowers of Literature for 1803* (London, 1804), p. 437. Blagdon was himself a contributor to the *Anti-Jacobin Review* (see Montluzin, *The Anti-Jacobins*, pp. 59–60), and verbal correspondences in the introductory matter of *Flowers of Literature* suggest a connection with *The Spirit of Anti-Jacobinism* and with the parent review.

71 In *The Anti-Jacobins*, p. 27, Montluzin observes that "though in name a literary review," the *Anti-Jacobin Review* "always allowed political and religious concerns to dominate literary ones."

72 Terry Eagleton, *The Function of Criticism: From the Spectator to Post-Structuralism* (London: Verso, 1984), p. 9.

73 See for example *SE* 1: 10, 414.

74 For the presence of critical reviews in libraries and book clubs of the period, see Roper, *Reviewing before the Edinburgh*, pp. 25–6.

75 For an instance of the "Newgate" department, see *S* 8 (1811), 133–6.

76 For Jones and the British Forum, see Iain McCalman, *Radical Underworld: Prophets, Revolutionaries, and Pornographers in London, 1795–1840* (Cambridge: Cambridge University Press, 1988), pp. 89–90.

77 For a report of the trial and a vigorous defense of *The Satirist*, see George Manners, *Vindiciae Satiricae, or, A Vindication of the Principles of the Satirist, and the Conduct of Its Proprietors* (London, 1809). For the political and literary fortunes of the paper, see, *British Literary Magazines: The Romantic Age*, ed. Sullivan, p. 386.

78 In its original folio appearance as a Saturday weekly, the periodical ran through ninety-two numbers, from March 10, 1792, through February 1, 1794, and was then reissued in four octavo volumes. See Arthur Roberts, *The Life, Letters, and Opinions of William Roberts, Esq* (London: Seeleys, 1850), p. 19.

79 Alexander Chalmers reprinted *The Looker-On* as the final item in his forty-five volume collection of 1803, *The British Essayists*, and William Roberts' son Arthur offered the following charitable judgment in *Life, Letters, and Opinions*, p. 19: "If the Tatler led the way in this species of composition, 'The Looker-on' may be said to have put the finish to it." In *English Literary Periodicals*, p. 139, Graham more damningly identified *The Looker-On* as "only a feeble effort to preserve the *Spectator* or *Rambler* form."

80 For the letter and for the circumstances of this number see Alan Lang Strout, *A Bibliography of Articles in Blackwood's Magazine, Volumes I through XVIII, 1817–1825* (Lubbock: Texas Technical College, 1959), pp. 4–6, 57–9.

81 I take the phrase "associational world" from Peter Clark's brilliant account of its development in *British Clubs and Societies, 1580–1800: The Origins of an Associational World* (Oxford: Clarendon Press, 2000).

82 See Graham, *English Literary Periodicals*, p. 279. For dialogue and process in the *Noctes Ambrosianae*, see Parker, *Literary Magazines and British Romanticism*, pp. 106–34, and Alexander, *"Blackwood's:* Magazine as Romantic Form," pp. 57–68.

83 The OED identifies a telling early version of the phrase in William Hazlitt's remark that Cobbett was "a kind of *fourth estate* in the politics of the country." See "estate," *Oxford English Dictionary*, 1971 edition, and William Hazlitt, *The Complete Works of William Hazlitt*, ed. P. P. Howe, 21 vols. (London: J. M. Dent and Sons, 1930–4), 8: 50.

84 *Blagdon's Political Register* 1 (1809–10), 8, 294, 298, 330–2, 582, 803.

85 The pagination of the magazine is irregular at this point, and the pages 210 and 211 cited here are marked with an asterisk.

86 See for example the programmatic article on "The Opposition" by William Gifford and David Robinson, in *QR* 28 (1822), 197–219. In *His Majesty's Opposition, 1714–1830* (Oxford: Clarendon Press, 1964), pp. 448–50, Archibald S. Foord discusses this article as an effective summary of Tory views on political partisanship.

87 See Parker, *Literary Magazines and British Romanticism*, p. 106, and Jon Klancher, *The Making of English Reading Audiences, 1790–1832* (Madison: The University of Wisconsin Press, 1987), pp. 52–61.

88 Strout, *A Bibliography of Articles in Blackwood's Magazine*, p. 77, identifies the author of this final article as George Croly, but this is the only identification for the entire series.

89 For this stage in Canning's career and for the circumstances of his election (which was not contested) and speech, see Peter Dixon, *Canning: Politician and Statesman* (London: Weidenfeld and Nicolson, 1976), pp. 184–6, 196–7, and Wendy Hinde, *George Canning* (Oxford and New York: Basil Blackwell, 1989), pp. 277–8.

90 For festive electoral traditions in this period, see Frank O'Gorman, *Voters, Patrons, and Parties: The Unreformed Electoral System of Hanoverian England, 1734–1832* (Oxford: Clarendon Press, 1989), and for Canning's participation in such traditions at Liverpool, see Dixon, *Canning*, pp. 161–6, 195–6, and Hinde, *George Canning*, pp. 258–62, 278, 317. The speech received extensive periodical coverage, and John Murray printed a pamphlet version under the title *Speech of the Right Hon. George Canning to His Constituents at Liverpool on Saturday, March 18th, 1820, at the Celebration of His Fourth Election* (London, 1820).

SUBVERTING FICTIONS: THE COUNTERREVOLUTIONARY FORM OF THE NOVEL

1 M. O. Grenby, *The Anti-Jacobin Novel: British Conservatism and the French Revolution* (Cambridge: Cambridge University Press, 2001), p. 23. I am indebted to the range of Grenby's interpretive survey as well as to his bibliographical identification of anti-Jacobin novels throughout this chapter. In *Jane Austen and the War of Ideas*, new edition (Oxford: Clarendon Press, 1987), pp. 106–7, Marilyn Butler identifies two successive phases of anti-Jacobin fiction, the first associated with the "feminine female-conduct novel" of Jane West, the second and more sustained from 1796 on with the dominance of male protagonists and a picaresque narrative. Gary Kelly approaches the matter of periodization differently in *English Fiction of the Romantic Period, 1789–1830* (London and New York: Longman, 1989), pp. 59–60, suggesting that the English anti-Jacobin novel flourished in a briefly embattled phase of literary expression between a sharp turn against English radicalism after 1795 and the emergence of a new consensus in the early years of the new century. The sub-canonization of the anti-Jacobin novel continues apace with release of Pickering and Chatto's ten volume edition of *Anti-Jacobin Novels* (2005), under the general editorship of W. M. Verhoeven, an edition that began to appear as this book was being prepared for press.

2 The classic study of the Jacobin novel is Gary Kelly, *The English Jacobin Novel 1780–1805* (Oxford: Clarendon Press, 1976), supplemented more recently by Nancy E. Johnson, *The English Jacobin Novel on Rights, Property, and the Law: Critiquing the Contract* (New York: Palgrave, 2004). For the

tendency of the term "anti-Jacobin" to obscure a range of positions, see Claudia Johnson, *Jane Austen: Women, Politics, and the Novel* (Chicago: University of Chicago Press, 1988), pp. xxi–xxiii.

3 Mary Anne Burges, *The Progress of the Pilgrim Good-Intent, in Jacobinical Times* (London, 1800), v–vii.

4 Grenby, *The Anti-Jacobin Novel*, pp. 179–80.

5 *Douglas* was reviewed in *AJR* 5 (1800), 232–4, and *Modern Literature* in *AJR* 19 (1804), 44–55, following an advance notice in *AJR* 18 (1804), 220. For Bisset's reviewing, see Emily Lorraine de Montluzin, *The Anti-Jacobins, 1798–1800: The Early Contributors to the Anti-Jacobin Review* (New York: St. Martin's Press, 1988), pp. 57–9.

6 But for the suggestion that such coordination was perhaps less systematic than contemporary complaints about it would suggest, see John O. Hayden, *The Romantic Reviewers, 1802–1824* (Chicago: University of Chicago Press, 1968), pp. 10–11, and Derek Roper, *Reviewing before the Edinburgh, 1788–1802* (Newark: University of Delaware Press, 1978), pp. 29–37.

7 Major studies of the social problem novel as it developed in the mid-nineteenth century include Raymond Williams, *Culture and Society 1780–1950* (New York: Columbia University Press, 1983), pp. 87–109; Catherine Gallagher, *The Industrial Reformation of English Fiction: Social Discourse and Narrative Form, 1832–1867* (Chicago: University of Chicago Press, 1985); Christine L. Krueger, *The Reader's Repentance: Women Preachers, Women Writers, and Nineteenth-Century Social Discourse* (Chicago: University of Chicago Press, 1992); Joseph Childers, *Novel Possibilities: Fiction and the Formation of Early Victorian Culture* (Philadelphia: University of Pennsylvania Press, 1995); and Suzanne Keen, *Victorian Renovations of the Novel: Narrative Annexes and the Boundaries of Representation* (Cambridge: Cambridge University Press, 1998).

8 Kelly, *English Fiction of the Romantic Period*, p. 60.

9 Nicola J. Watson, *Revolution and the Form of the British Novel, 1790–1825: Intercepted Letters, Interrupted Seductions* (Oxford: Clarendon Press, 1994), pp. 70–1. See also Butler, *Jane Austen and the War of Ideas*, pp. 108–9, and Johnson, *Jane Austen*, p. 5, where the anxiety about seduction is traced to Burke.

10 Though see Grenby, *The Anti-Jacobin Novel*, p. 27, for the view that a part of "the new respect which the nineteenth-century novel commanded was earned … through its service during the Revolutionary crisis." While this is plausible, the process by which the novel gained moral seriousness and literary respectability seems to me to have taken place well beyond the framework of anti-Jacobin fiction.

11 See for example *V*, pp. 9, 11, 13, 30, 55, 59, 80, 118, 143, and 222.

12 William Godwin, *Enquiry Concerning Political Justice*, ed. Isaac Kramnick (Harmondsworth: Penguin, 1985), pp. 169–70. For variations in the scenario in editions of *Political Justice*, see Kramnick's textual note,

pp. 57–8, and for similar parodies in other anti-Jacobin novels, see Grenby, *The Anti-Jacobin Novel*, p. 95.

13 Butler, *Jane Austen and the War of Ideas*, p. 107.

14 For Bridgetina and Julia Delmond as a Quixote characters, whose false ideology leads them to "misread the world," see Gary Kelly, *Women, Writing, and Revolution 1790–1827*, (Oxford: Clarendon Press, 1993), pp. 145–6.

15 See Watson, *Revolution and the Form of the British Novel*, pp. 85–6, for a suggestive account of Bridgetina's imperfect body in relation to epistolary convention.

16 *MP*, pp. 157–8.

17 Don Herzog, *Poisoning the Minds of the Lower Orders* (Princeton: Princeton University Press, 1998), p. 505. Herzog devotes his final chapter to a close study of the phrase. For Burke's claim, see *Reflections on the Revolution in France*, in *The Writings and Speeches of Edmund Burke*, ed. Paul Langford *et al.*, 12 vols. (Oxford: Clarendon Press, 1981–), 8: 130.

18 Grenby, *The Anti-Jacobin Novel*, pp. 25–6. For the longer British history of anti-novel sentiment, see Joseph Bunn Heidler, *The History, from 1700 to 1800, of English Criticism of Prose Fiction* (Urbana: University of Illinois Press, 1928); W. F. Gallaway, "The Conservative Attitude toward Fiction, 1770–1830," *PMLA* 55 (1940), 1041–59; John Tinnon Taylor, *Early Opposition to the English Novel: The Popular Reaction from 1760 to 1830* (New York: King's Crown Press, 1943); Gary Kelly, "'This Pestiferous Reading': The Social Basis of Reaction against the Novel in Late Eighteenth- and Early Nineteenth-Century Britain," *Man and Nature* 4 (1985), 183–94.

19 Henry James Pye, *The Aristocrat*, 2 vols. (London, 1799), 1: 24–5. Pye's first anti-Jacobin novel, *The Democrat* (1795), was brought out by William Lane's Minerva Press, notorious for its mass distribution of sensational fiction through the circulating libraries.

20 Catherine Gallagher, *Nobody's Story: The Vanishing Acts of Women Writers in the Marketplace, 1670–1820* (Berkeley: University of California Press, 1994), pp. 279–80.

21 For this novel as "a thinly fictionalized conduct book for mothers as well as daughters," see Johnson, *Jane Austen*, p. 6.

22 See for example Kelly, *English Fiction of the Romantic Period*, pp. 62–3, and Eleanor Ty, *Unsex'd Revolutionaries: Five Women Novelists of the 1790s* (Toronto: University of Toronto Press, 1993), pp. 26–7.

23 Butler, *Jane Austen and the War of Ideas*, pp. 118–19.

24 Grenby, *The Anti-Jacobin Novel*, pp. 65–6.

25 For a survey of the literature on separate spheres and a compelling critical synthesis of the problem, see Harriet Guest, *Small Change: Women, Learning, Patriotism, 1750–1810* (Chicago: University of Chicago Press, 2000), pp. 1–14. Important studies include Dena Goodman, "Public Sphere and Private Life: Toward a Synthesis of Current Historiographical

Approaches to the Old Regime," *History and Theory* 31 (1992), 1–20; Amanda Vickery, "Golden Age to Separate Spheres? A Review of the Categories and Chronology of English Women's History," *The Historical Journal* 36 (1993), 383–414; and Lawrence E. Klein, "Gender and the Public/Private Distinction in the Eighteenth Century: Some Questions about Evidence and Analytic Procedure," *Eighteenth-Century Studies* 29 (1995), pp. 97–109.

26 Fredric Jameson, *The Political Unconscious: Narrative as a Socially Symbolic Act* (Ithaca: Cornell University Press, 1981), p. 286.

27 Nancy E. Johnson, "The 'French Threat' in Anti-Jacobin Novels of the 1790s," in *Illicit Sex: Identity Politics in Early Modern Culture*, ed. Thomas DiPiero and Pat Gill (Athens: University of Georgia Press, 1997), pp. 186, 188–9, 200.

28 In *The Anti-Jacobin Novel*, pp. 91, 104–25, Grenby identifies this new philosophical villain as the "vaurien," or "good for nothing," after the French agent of Isaac D'Israeli's 1797 novel *Vaurien: or, Sketches of the Times: Exhibiting Views of the Philosophies, Religions, Politics, Literature, and Manners of the Age*, 2 vols. (London, 1797).

29 Kelly, *English Fiction of the Romantic Period*, p. 63.

30 The novel was published anonymously, but for this attribution see *Dorothea* (1801) in *British Fiction, 1800–1829: A Database of Production, Circulation and Reception*, ed. P. D. Garside, J. E. Belanger, and S. A. Ragaz, www.british-fiction.cf.ac.uk/titleDetails.asp?title=1801A017, last accessed 10 April 2005.

31 D'Israeli, *Vaurien*, 2: 323. In the Huntington Library copy of the novel (shelfmark 357093), an early reader has offered the following vivid response to D'Israeli's closing figure: " 'tis time for another vomit."

32 For contemporary responses to the French émigré, see Emma Vincent Macleod, *A War of Ideas: British Attitudes to the Wars Against Revolutionary France 1792–1802* (Aldershot: Ashgate, 1998), pp. 27–8, 35–6, 79, 165, 185.

33 Watson, *Revolution and the Form of the British Novel*, pp. 16–17.

34 See for example *ADB* 2: 128, 185–7.

35 The cultural politics of sympathy and sensibility in this period has been a subject of extensive study and debate. See Butler, *Jane Austen and the War of Ideas*, pp. 7–28, Kelly, *English Fiction of the Romantic Period*, pp. 12–13, 63–4, 66; Watson, *Revolution and the Form of the British Novel*, pp. 1–28; Janet Todd, *Sensibility: An Introduction* (London: Methuen, 1986); Chris Jones, *Radical Sensibility: Literature and Ideas in the 1790s* (London and New York: Routledge, 1993); Markman Ellis, *The Politics of Sensibility: Race, Gender and Commerce in the Sentimental Novel* (Cambridge: Cambridge University Press, 1996); G.J. Barker-Benfield, *The Culture of Sensibility: Sex and Society in Eighteenth-Century Britain* (Chicago: University of Chicago Press, 1996). For enthusiasm, see Jon Mee, *Romanticism, Enthusiasm, and Regulation: Poetics and the Policing of Culture in the Romantic Period* (Oxford: Oxford University Press, 2003).

36 For crowd activity in the Gordon Riots, see Nicholas Rogers, *Crowds, Culture, and Politics in Georgian Britain* (Oxford: Oxford University Press, 1998), pp. 152–75.

37 For the effort to control radical protest through the containment of its vagrant forms, see Kevin Gilmartin, *Print Politics: The Press and Radical Opposition in Early Nineteenth-Century England* (Cambridge: Cambridge University Press, 1996), pp. 52–3.

38 D'Israeli, *Vaurien*, 1: 69–70.

39 Elizabeth Hamilton, *Translation of the Letters of a Hindoo Rajah*, ed. Pamela Perkins and Shannon Russell (Peterborough: Broadview Press, 1999), p. 273, and see pp. 323–4 of this edition for related material from the second edition of 1801.

40 Johnson, *Jane Austen*, pp. xix–xx.

41 Jürgen Habermas, *The Structural Transformation of the Public Sphere: An Inquiry into a Category of Bourgeois Society*, trans. Thomas Burger (Cambridge, Massachusetts: MIT Press, 1989), pp. 29, 43–51.

42 See Kelly, *English Fiction of the Romantic Period*, pp. 86–7.

43 For the presence of Rousseau and especially *La Nouvelle Héloïse* in British literary treatments of revolutionary politics, see Watson, *Revolution and the Form of the British Novel*.

44 For psychological realism and interiority in the rise of the novel see Ian Watt, *The Rise of the Novel: Studies in Defoe, Richardson, and Fielding* (Berkeley and Los Angeles: University of California Press, 1957), pp. 60–92, 174–207, and J. Paul Hunter, *Before Novels: The Cultural Contexts of Eighteenth Century English Fiction* (New York and London: W. W. Norton and Company, 1990), pp. 23–4, 40–2. For the bias against individual reflection in anti-Jacobin fiction, see Johnson, *Jane Austen*, pp. 12–14.

45 See *Jane Austen*, p. 5, where Johnson ably summarizes some of the elements of the novel that would have been reconditioned by Burke: "the retired life of the country gentleman, the orderly transmission of property, the stabilizing principle of generational continuity, the grateful deference of youth to venerable age, and of course the chastity of wives and daughters which alone can guarantee the social identity of men and heirs."

46 *The Citizen's Daughter; or What Might Be* (London, 1804), p. 125.

47 The central theoretical account of heterogeneity in the novel is of course Mikhail M. Bakhtin, *The Dialogic Imagination*, ed. Michael Holquist (Austin: University of Texas Press, 1981). Major historical studies of the heterogeneous traditions that went into the early development of the British novel include Hunter, *Before Novels;* Michael McKeon, *The Origins of the English Novel, 1600–1740* (Baltimore: Johns Hopkins University Press, 1987); and John J. Richetti, *Popular Fiction before Richardson: Narrative Patterns, 1700–1739* (Oxford: Clarendon Press, 1992).

48 The disclaimer comes in an unpaginated Preface to *AE*.

49 See Watson, *Revolution and the Form of the British Novel*, p. 75, for the way this approach prevents the epistolary hazards that ensnare West's later heroines.

50 Watson, *Revolution and the Form of the British Novel*, p. 75. In *Unsex'd Revolutionaries*, pp. 15–16, Eleanor Ty shrewdly observes that while this novel has "no obvious paternal model," Mrs. Williams significantly incorporates female deference into her advice to her daughter.

51 For the figure of cultivation, see the title page epigraph from Gilbert West, and *AE* 1: 35, 36, 125, 128, 232.

52 Johnson, *Jane Austen*, p. 18.

53 The term "authoress" appears on the title page of the novel, and a dedication page discloses the name of Ann Thomas.

54 For Hamilton's engagement with Rousseau here, see Kelly, *Women, Writing, and Revolution*, p. 145, and Watson, *Revolution and the Form of the British Novel*, pp. 85–6.

55 See Kelly, *Women, Writing, and Revolution*, pp. 11–12, for the prohibition on "Religious Controversy" in James Fordyce's influential *Sermons to Young Women* (1765).

56 The diversion of revolutionary desire into a seduction plot is consistent with novel's claim that political subversion followed from moral corruption; see for example *TT* 2: 275.

57 In *Small Change*, pp. 272–89, Harriet Guest offers a thoughtful account of areas of overlap as well as important distinctions between Hannah More and Mary Wollstonecraft on matters of female education.

58 For Hamilton's direction of the Edinburgh House of Industry, which assisted the poor rather than the morally compromised, see Elizabeth Benger, *Memoirs of the Late Mrs. Elizabeth Hamilton. With a Selection from Her Correspondence, and Other Unpublished Writings*, 2 vols. (London: Longman, Hurst, Rees, Orme, and Brown, 1818), 1: 178–9, and Kelly, *Women, Writing, and Revolution*, pp. 277–8.

59 For a compelling study of fictional reworkings of female sexual transgression in this period, see Roxanne Eberle, *Chastity and Transgression in Women's Writing, 1792–1897: Interrupting the Harlot's Progress* (New York: Palgrave, 2002).

60 Kelly, *Women, Writing, and Revolution*, p. 277, n. 9.

SOUTHEY, COLERIDGE, AND THE END OF
ANTI-JACOBINISM IN BRITAIN

1 The departure of Wordsworth, Coleridge, and Southey from their early radicalism has been related and debated many times. Assessments include E. P. Thompson, "Disenchantment or Default? A Lay Sermon" and "Wordsworth's Crisis," in *The Romantics: England in a Revolutionary Age* (New York: The New Press, 1997), pp. 33–74, 75–95; John Colmer, *Coleridge: Critic of Society* (Oxford: Clarendon Press, 1959); Geoffrey Carnall, *Robert*

Southey and His Age: The Development of a Conservative Mind (Oxford: Clarendon Press, 1960), pp. 37–120; James K. Chandler, *Wordsworth's Second Nature: A Study of the Poetry and Politics* (Chicago: University of Chicago Press, 1984), pp. 1–61, 194–206; John Morrow, *Coleridge's Political Thought: Property, Morality, and the Limits of Traditional Discourse* (New York: St. Martin's Press, 1990), pp. 11–74; Mark Francis and John Morrow, *A History of English Political Thought in the Nineteenth Century* (New York: St. Martin's Press, 1994), pp. 123–6; and Alan Liu, *Wordsworth: The Sense of History* (Stanford: Stanford University Press, 1989), pp. 27–8, 411, 416–28. For recent studies of the politics of romantic generations, see Jeffrey Cox, *Poetry and Politics in the Cockney School: Keats, Shelley, Hunt and Their Circle* (Cambridge: Cambridge University Press, 1998) and Charles Mahoney, *Romantics and Renegades: The Poetics of Political Reaction* (New York: Palgrave, 2003).

2 Although there is much in Wordsworth's poetry and prose that bears upon the issues raised in this chapter, particularly his treatment of the Church of England in *The Excursion* (1814) and *Ecclesiastical Sketches* (1822), his general reluctance after the 1809 *Convention of Cintra* pamphlet to engage in direct public and polemical expression accounts for my decision to focus instead on Southey and Coleridge.

3 A critical treatment of anti-Jacobinism can be found in *SE* 1: 26; *QR* 16 (1816–18), 228–9; and *CW* 4, 1: 214–2. For a sympathetic account of Southey's development of a language of conservative patriotism that "never simply mirrored or revived the anti-Jacobin rhetoric of the early 1790s," see David Eastwood, "Robert Southey and the Meanings of Patriotism," *Journal of British Studies* 31 (1992), 272–3.

4 See also *Selections from the Letters of Robert Southey*, ed. John Wood Warter, 4 vols. (London: Longman, Brown, Green, and Longmans, 1856), 3: 319–20; *CW* 3, 2: 38; *CW* 4, 1: 81–2, 217–18, 226, 264–6; and *CW* 7, 1: 189–90. For similar comments by Wordsworth, see his 1809 pamphlet, *The Convention of Cintra*, in *The Prose Works of William Wordsworth*, ed. W. J. B. Owen and Jane Worthington Smyser, 3 vols. (Oxford: Clarendon Press, 1974), pp. 226–7, 308.

5 Liu, *Wordsworth*, p. 422. For a contrast between the Coleridge's "evasiveness and falsification" and Wordsworth's more frank account of his radical past, see Nicholas Roe, *Wordsworth and Coleridge: The Radical Years* (Oxford: Clarendon Press, 1988), pp. 3–5.

6 See also *QR* 8 (1812), 345, and for related imagery, see Mark Storey, *Robert Southey: A Life* (Oxford: Oxford University Press, 1997), p. 180.

7 For the publication of *Wat Tyler* by Sherwood, Neely, and Jones in 1817 and the piracies, controversies, and court proceedings that ensued, see Carnall, *Robert Southey and His Age*, pp. 161–6; Storey, *Robert Southey*, pp. 253–63; Frank T. Hoadley, "The Controversy Over Southey's Wat Tyler," *Studies in Philology* 38 (1941), 81–96; Charles Mahoney, *Romantics and Renegades*, pp. 124–33, 138–42; and Ian Haywood, "The Renovating Fury': Southey, Republicanism and Sensationalism," *Romanticism on the Net*

32–33 (November 2003–February 2004) www.erudit.org/revue/ron/ 2003/v/n32–33/009256ar.html, last accessed 12 May 2005, for the text and related material see the online edition *Wat Tyler: A Dramatic Poem* (1817), ed. Matt Hill, *Romantic Circles*, ed. Neil Fraistat and Steven E. Jones, last accessed www.rc.umd.edu/editions/wattyler, last accessed 15 July 2005.

 8 Richard Holmes vividly relates Coleridge's experience on the day of Perceval's assassination in *Coleridge: Darker Reflections: 1804–1834* (New York: Pantheon Books, 1998), pp. 307–9.

 9 For the figure of the "Bellum Servile" and Southey's alarms about insurrection, see Carnall, *Robert Southey and His Age*, pp. 141–71.

10 For Southey on *The Friend*, see *SL*, p. 177.

11 For an astute treatment of the range of Southey's professional practice at an earlier stage in his career, see Brian Goldberg, "Romantic Professionalism in 1800: Robert Southey, Herbert Croft, and the Letters and Legacy of Thomas Chatterton," *ELH* 63 (1996) 681–706.

12 In "Robert Southey and the Language of Social Discipline," *Albion* 30 (1999), 648, Philip Harling observes that "it is virtually impossible to exaggerate Southey's estimate of the power of the radical press." For the role of the press in Southey's treatment of radical transmission as contagion, see Philip Connell, *Romanticism, Economics and the Question of "Culture"* (Oxford: Oxford University Press, 2001), pp. 252–3.

13 Although he produced the letters in response to conditions in Ireland, Coleridge suggested that they offered "no exaggerated picture of the predominance of Jacobinism" in England (*CL* 4: 565). While no deliberate design was attributed to the "immense fortress" these clubs formed, it is easy to sympathize with David Erdman's editorial suggestion that the Fletcher letters conducted Coleridge back to the conspiracy theories of the 1790s; see *CW* 3, 2: 383, n. 10.

14 For evidence of Gifford's severe editing and Southey's objections, see Hill Shine and Helen Chadwick Shine, *The Quarterly Review under Gifford: Identification of Contributors, 1809–1824* (Chapel Hill: University of North Carolina Press, 1949), pp. 23, 26–7, 43–5, 83, and Carnall, *Robert Southey and His Age*, pp. 98–9, 136–7, 221–3. In a December 1831 letter to Bedford, Southey described the 1832 project as a collection of essays "reprinted from the Quarterly Review, and the Edinburgh Annual Register; and with the passages restored, which poor Gifford cut out, that is, where I was lucky enough to recover either the MSS. or the proofs" (*SLC* 6: 170–1). I have cited Southey's *Quarterly* essays as they first appeared, except where passages restored to the 1832 collection are concerned. For evidence that Southey's "more extreme views" on public opinion and the press "were considerably out of step with much anti-reform argument during this period," see Connell, *Romanticism, Economics and the Question of "Culture,"* p. 255.

15 See *CW* 4, 1: 70, 72, 77; the epigraph from *Areopagitica* was provided for the three-volume edition of 1818.

16 Coleridge went on to refute another prevailing radical sentiment by endorsing "the legal paradox, that a libel may be the more a libel for being true" (*CW* 4, 1: 93–4).

17 For Cobbett's *Register* as "an important foil for Coleridge's somewhat loftier conception of political journalism," see Connell, *Romanticism, Economics and the Question of "Culture,"* pp. 147–8.

18 As part of the same discussion, Coleridge maintains that "the frequency of open political discussion, with all its blamable indiscretions," actually "indisposes a nation to overt acts of practical sedition or conspiracy" (*CW* 4, 1: 93), an argument that recalls the "Apologetic Preface" he affixed to the poem "Fire, Famine, and Slaughter" on the occasion of its publication in *Sibylline Leaves* (1817). John Barrell offers a shrewd reading of the poem and its preface in *Imagining the King's Death: Figurative Treason, Fantasies of Regicide, 1793–1796* (Oxford: Oxford University Press, 2000), pp. 646–51. For Coleridge's interest in doctrinal dissension as a premise for liberal society, see Mark Canuel, *Religion, Toleration, and British Writing, 1790–1830* (Cambridge: Cambridge University Press, 2002), pp. 86–121.

19 For the difficult publishing history of *The Friend*, see Rooke's Introduction, *CW* 4, 1: xxxv–cv; Holmes, *Coleridge: Darker Reflections*, pp. 143–4, 151–96; and Deirdre Coleman, *Coleridge and The Friend (1809–1810)* (Oxford: Clarendon Press, 1988), pp. 1, 41–62. Coleman persuasively challenges Rooke's more positive account of the first production of *The Friend*.

20 See Rooke's Introduction, *CW* 4, 1: lvi, lxviii, lxxxv.

21 Coleridge went on to insist, unconvincingly, that the contrast with Cobbett was not meant to be "depreciating," since "the style and contents of the work are perfectly well suited to the Purpose of the writer" (*CL* 3: 144).

22 E. P. Thompson, "Bliss Was It in That Dawn – The Matter of Coleridge's Revolutionary Youth," in *The Romantics*, p. 130. For versions of Coleridge's maxim and editorial remarks on its development, see Samuel Taylor Coleridge, *Lectures 1795 On Politics and Religion*, ed. Lewis Patton and Peter Mann, Vol. 1 of *The Collected Works of Samuel Taylor Coleridge* (Princeton: Princeton University Press, 1971), p. 43; *CW* 3, 2: 376 and n. 5; *CW* 7, 1: 185 and n. 2; and *CW* 6: 148 and n. 1.

23 Jon Klancher, *The Making of English Reading Audiences, 1790–1832* (Madison: University of Wisconsin Press, 1987), p. 15. For the advertised third sermon, see *CW* 6, xxxi, and n. 5. Coleridge's habit of coding audiences has drawn a range of recent critical responses: in *Religion, Toleration, and British Writing*, pp. 97–8, Canuel extends the issue from class to religion, and stresses the way Coleridgean address consolidates as it divides; and in *The Rhetoric of Romantic Prophecy* (Stanford: Stanford University Press, 2002), p. 253, Ian Balfour responds sympathetically to Coleridge's frank recognition of "the impossibility of a homogeneous readership."

24 See *CL* 6: 824, n. 1, for Griggs' suggestion that Lord Lyndhurst was probably the "GREAT Man" targeted for a finely bound copy with blank sheets for inscription.

25 In the midst of the Queen Caroline agitation in 1821, Southey expressed his doubts about a revival of the loyalist association movement on the grounds that government was charged to preserve order and that even loyalist associations risked contributing to "club law"; see *Selections from the Letters of Robert Southey*, ed. Warter, 3: 227, and James J. Sack, *From Jacobite to Conservative: Reaction and Orthodoxy in Britain, c. 1760–1832* (Cambridge: Cambridge University Press, 1993), pp. 105–6.

26 See, for example, *SE* 1: 12–13; *QR* 8 (1812), 346; and *QR* 16 (1816–17), 258–9. For descriptive representation, see Hanna Fenichel Pitkin, *The Concept of Representation* (Berkeley: University of California Press, 1972), pp. 60–91; and Catherine Gallagher, *The Industrial Reformation of English Fiction* (Chicago: University of Chicago Press, 1985), pp. 222–4.

27 See *QR* 16 (1816–17), 225, 273–4. The essay appeared in Number 31 of the *Quarterly*, dated October 1816, but not actually produced until February 1817; see Shine and Shine, *The Quarterly Review under Gifford*, p. 53.

28 Gifford may have reshaped and moderated the conclusion of the essay; *SE* 1: 421–2 prints a final paragraph protesting "great and crying evils" in the country, above all, the "seditious spirit which is fed and fostered by the periodical press" and which it is "the first duty of government" to put down.

29 See Harling, "Robert Southey and the Language of Social Discipline," pp. 650–1, for the memorandum as evidence of the fact that "Southey's own authoritarian impulse was considerably stronger than the government's."

30 Reprinted in Charles Duke Young, *The Life and Administration of Robert Banks, Second Earl of Liverpool* (London: Macmillan, 1868), pp. 298–9.

31 Young, *Life and Administration*, p. 299. Southey did omit from the memorandum his doubts about Liverpool's effectiveness as a leader; see Storey, *Robert Southey*, p. 216.

32 See David Simpson, *Romanticism, Nationalism, and the Revolt against Theory* (Chicago: University of Chicago Press, 1993), p. 82, for this "negative model of the power of ideas."

33 But see Balfour, *The Rhetoric of Romantic Prophecy*, pp. 268–9, for a more positive response, in line with Coleridge's own rhetorical principles, suggesting that the third Lay Sermon did not appear because Coleridge had "nothing to say *to* the working classes on behalf of them."

34 Matters closed unsuccessfully in 1826 when Lord Liverpool died before Frere could finalize arrangements for Coleridge to be appointed paymaster of the gentlemen-pensioners, a sinecure formerly held by Gifford; see *CL* 6: 536, 539 and n. 3, 670.

35 See *CL* 4: 757, and Young, *Life and Administration*, p. 300, n. 1.

36 Storey, *Robert Southey*, p. 250.
37 See for example his remarks in *SLC* 4: 210, 212. For the circumstances of his appointment as Poet Laureate and the controversy that followed, see Storey, *Robert Southey*, pp. 223–30; Michael N. Stanton, "'A Scourge for the Laureate': William Benbow vs. Robert Southey," *The Wordsworth Circle* 19 (1988), 45–9; and Charles Mahoney, *Romantics and Renegades*, pp. 13–16, 24–9.
38 See for example *SL*, p. 196.
39 See also *SL*, p. 265.
40 For this reason Southey expressed particular outrage at Gifford's editing of his own alarmist prose, "*in pity*, as he says, *to the* TERRORS *of Ministers!!!!*" (*SL* 277).
41 The self-accounting included payments from Longmans of £500 for three editions of *Roderick the Last of the Goths* and £215 for *The Poet's Pilgrimage to Waterloo*, and a regular income from Murray of up to £100 for each *Quarterly Review* essay.
42 See *SL*, pp. 268–9, and *SLC*, 4: 213. For Southey's qualified interest in Owen and his 1819 visit to New Lanark, see Storey, *Robert Southey*, pp. 249–50, 275–6, and Raymond Williams, *Culture and Society, 1780–1950*, new ed. (New York: Columbia University Press, 1983), pp. 22–4. For his critical response to political economy, commerce, and industrialism, see Carnall, *Robert Southey and His Age*, pp. 67–9, 179–80; Donald Winch, *Riches and Poverty: An Intellectual History of Political Economy in Britain, 1750–1834* (Cambridge: Cambridge University Press, 1996), pp. 323–5; J. R. Poynter, *Society and Pauperism: English Ideas on Poor Relief, 1795–1834* (London: Routledge and Kegan Paul, 1969), pp. 250–4; David Eastwood, "Robert Southey and the Intellectual Origins of Romantic Conservatism," *English Historical Review* 104 (1989), 317–25; David Eastwood, "Ruinous Prosperity: Robert Southey's Critique of the Commercial System," *The Wordsworth Circle* 25 (1994), 72–6; and Connell, *Romanticism, Economics and the Question of "Culture,"* pp. 244–54, 259–63, 267–71.
43 *The Poetical Works of Robert Southey* (London: Longmans, Green, and Co., 1876), p. 729. In a suggestive reading of Southey's *Colloquies on the Progress and Prospects of Society*, Philip Connell identifies a similar pattern of rhetorical ambiguity, suggesting that an inward movement "towards a Renaissance humanist ideal of dialogue in retirement" is offset by an outward orientation "towards a 'public mind' perceived quite distinctly from this ideal, and indeed defined in opposition to it"; see Connell, *Romanticism, Economics and the Question of "Culture,"* p. 266.
44 See *CL* 5: 343 and n. 1, and *CL* 6: 536, where Coleridge pitched his expectations at £200 per year.
45 See *CL* 6: 854–7 for Griggs' editorial summary of the affair.
46 See for example *CW* 4, 1: 229–30 and *CW* 6: 156. But for Coleridge's strictures on earlier anti-Jacobin defenses of "the wages of state-dependence," see *CW* 4, 1: 216.

47 Marilyn Butler, *Romantics, Rebels, and Reactionaries: English Literature and Its Background, 1760–1830* (Oxford: Oxford University Press, 1981), p. 165.

48 For Southey's support of Bell, see Alan Richardson, *Literature, Education, and Romanticism: Reading as Social Practice, 1780–1832* (Cambridge: Cambridge University Press, 1994), pp. 95–7, and for the interest of the Lake Poets more broadly in Bell and in popular education, see Connell, *Romanticism, Economics and the Question of "Culture,"* pp. 126–44. For the development of the monitorial system and the controversy among supporters of Bell and Lancaster, see E. L. Woodward, *The Age of Reform 1815–1870* (Oxford: Oxford University Press, 1949), pp. 455–60; Elie Halevy, *A History of the English People in 1815* (London: Ark Paperbacks, 1987), pp. 461–5; Carl F. Kaestle, *Joseph Lancaster and the Monitorial School Movement: A Documentary History* (New York: Teachers College Press, 1973), pp. 1–139; and Keith Evans, *The Development and Structure of the English School System* (London: Hodder and Stoughton, 1985), pp. 26–8.

49 Robert Southey, *The Origin, Nature, and Object of the New System of Education* (London: John Murray, 1812), p. 109. This volume expanded an 1811 *Quarterly Review* essay on the controversy between supporters of Bell and Lancaster; see *QR* 6 (1811), 264–304. For Coleridge's use of an industrial figure for the Madras system, see *CW* 6: 41.

50 For a compelling recent discussion of "the rise of Reformation historiography as a politically charged subject in this period," and its role in the thought of Coleridge and Southey, see Connell, *Romanticism, Economics and the Question of "Culture,"* pp. 241–7.

51 In *Riches and Poverty*, a brilliant intellectual history of the relationship between wealth and poverty from Adam Smith through Robert Malthus to the Poor Law Amendment Act of 1834, Donald Winch traces the resistance of Southey and Coleridge to political economy and to the population theories of Malthus; see especially pp. 289–90, 292–3, 295–6, 298–306, 311–14, 398–9. The Lake School response to Malthus figures centrally as well in Connell, *Romanticism, Economics and the Question of "Culture."* For poverty and poor law reform in this period, see Poynter, *Society and Pauperism*; Gertrude Himmelfarb, *The Idea of Poverty: England in the Early Industrial Age* (New York: Alfred A. Knopf, 1984); Peter Mandler, "The Making of the New Poor Law *Redivivus*," *Past and Present* 117 (1987), 131–57; Peter Mandler, "Tories and Paupers: Christian Political Economy and the Making of the New Poor Law," *The Historical Journal* 33 (1990), 81–103; Joanna Innes, "The Distinctiveness of the English Poor Laws, 1750–1850," in *The Political Economy of British Historical Experience, 1688–1914*, ed. Donald Winch and Patrick K. O'Brien (Oxford: Oxford University Press, 2002), pp. 381–407.

52 For Southey and Reformation history, see Eastwood, "Robert Southey and the Intellectual Origins of Romantic Conservatism," pp. 316–18.

53 Robert Southey, *The Book of the Church* (London: Frederick Warne, 1869), pp. 251, 277–80; *QR* 8 (1812), 332; *SE* 1: 102; *Poetical Works of Robert*

Southey, p. 760. See also *QR* 19 (1818), 86–8, and Robert Southey, *The Life of Wesley and the Rise and Progress of Methodism*, ed. Maurice Fitzgerald, 2 vols. (Oxford: Oxford University Press, 1925) 1: 223–4.

54 *QR* 8 (1812) 332, and Southey, *Life of Wesley*, ed. Fitzgerald, 1: 223; see also *QR* 19 (1818), 86–7.

55 Southey, *Life of Wesley*, ed. Fitzgerald, 1: 239.

56 This proportion was a favorite claim for Southey; see, for example, *QR* 15 (1816), 200, and *SE* 2: 25–6.

57 See for example *QR* 19 (1818), 89. In the 1832 collection, Southey presented a sequence of reviews for the *Quarterly* (1809, 1812, 1828) as three essays "On the Catholic Question" (*SE* 2: 277–443). For Southey's hostility to Catholicism, see Winch, *Riches and Poverty*, p. 343, and Harling, "Robert Southey and the Language of Social Discipline," pp. 641–3. For differences at the *Quarterly* over the Catholic question and the challenges that Southey's uncompromising views posed for Lockhart as editor in 1828, see Scott Bennett, "Catholic Emancipation, the 'Quarterly Review', and Britain's Constitutional Revolution" *Victorian Studies* 12 (1969), 283–304. As Connell astutely suggests in *Romanticism, Economics and the Question of "Culture,"* p. 244, ambiguities enter Southey's account of the Reformation when, rather than addressing the Catholic question directly, he treats its "long-term effects on English society."

58 Southey, *Book of the Church*, p. 250.

59 Southey, *Life of Wesley*, ed. Fitzgerald, 1: 226.

60 Among the other items listed for review was Percy Shelley's "Hermit of Marlow" pamphlet, *A Proposal for Putting Reform to the Vote Throughout the Kingdom. By the Hermit of Marlow* (London: C. & J. Ollier, 1817); see *QR* 16 (1817), 511. For the committee report, see "Report of the Secret Committee into the Disturbed State of the Country, February 1817," *Parliamentary Debates*, 1st Series, vol. 35, (1817) col. 438.

61 Connell, *Romanticism, Economics and the Question of "Culture,"* p. 245.

62 For the passage in Wordsworth's 1800 Preface to *Lyrical Ballads*, see *The Prose Works of William Wordsworth*, ed. W. J. B. Owen and Jane Worthington Smyser, 3 vols. (Oxford: Clarendon Press, 1974), 1: 124.

63 Society for Bettering the Condition and Increasing the Comforts of the Poor, *Of the Education of the Poor* (London, 1809).

64 Williams, *Culture and Society*, p. 24. For the "radically augmented role" assigned to the state in Southey's social vision, see Eastwood, "Robert Southey and the Intellectual Origins of Romantic Conservatism," p. 320.

65 See Francis and Morrow, *A History of English Political Thought in the Nineteenth Century*, pp. 109–12. For Southey's "Romantic Tory social discourse," see Eastwood. "Ruinous Prosperity," p. 72.

66 The argument represents a more stringent version of a policy suggested in Thomas Courtenay's *Treatise Upon the Poor Laws* (London, 1818), one of the items under review.

67 In a withering critique of Coleridge's reputation as a political writer, E. P. Thompson has observed the scholarly tendency to take Coleridge at his own valuation; see "A Compendium of Cliché: The Poet as Essayist," in *The Romantics*, p. 148. For Coleridge's claim that he influenced Southey's writing on the Madras system, see *CW* 6: 40 and n. 2.

68 For the early conception of the project and the quest for patronage, see John Colmer's introduction to *CW* 10: li–lix.

69 For a sympathetic reading of Coleridge's claims about the politics of empiricism, see Francis and Morrow, *A History of English Political Thought in the Nineteenth Century*, pp. 135–6.

70 If this seems a hopelessly abstract approach to the challenge of restoring the clerisy's constitutional role, Coleridge also advanced more practical measures, including a revived Church Convocation, and even direct parliamentary representatives; see *CW* 10: 84 and n. 1, 99 and n. 3, and *CL* 4: 711.

71 For Coleridge on Bell and Lancaster, see Connell, *Romanticism, Economics and the Question of "Culture,"* pp. 135, 139–43, and R. A. Foakes, "'Thriving Prisoners': Coleridge, Wordsworth and the Child at School," *Studies in Romanticism* 28 (1989), 187–206, as well as Foakes' revealing editorial discussion in Samuel Taylor Coleridge, *Lectures 1808–1819 On Literature*, ed. R. A. Foakes, 2 vols., Vol. 5 of *The Collected Works of Samuel Taylor Coleridge* (Princeton: Princeton University Press, 1987), 1: 96–104.

72 For the distinction between the "Church of Christ" and the National Church as a strategy for shoring up Anglicanism, see Francis and Morrow, *A History of English Political Thought in the Nineteenth Century*, pp. 133–4. In *Pulpits, Politics and Public Order in England, 1760–1820* (Cambridge: Cambridge University Press, 1989), pp. 253–4, Robert Hole considers Coleridge's views in the relation to broader tendencies to distinguish the civil and spiritual functions of the clergy.

73 Holmes, *Coleridge: Darker Reflections*, pp. 309–10. For a similar effort to vindicate Coleridge's "calm sensibility and balance" by comparison with Southey's "reactionary stance," see Francis and Morrow, *A History of English Political Thought in the Nineteenth Century*, p. 123. By contrast, and it seems to me more persuasively, Connell discerns in Southey's *Colloquies on the Progress and Prospects of Society* a "refinement of the Lake school ideal of humanistic, literary education that is lacking in comparable texts such as Coleridge's *Church and State*"; see *Romanticism, Economics and the Question of "Culture,"* pp. 271–2.

74 For a perceptive account of Coleridge's "idealist's complaint" against Wordsworth's "apparently democratic project," see Klancher, *Making of English Reading Audiences*, pp. 141–2.

75 Terry Eagleton, *The Function of Criticism: From the Spectator to Post-Structuralism* (London: Verso, 1984), p. 64.

76 In *Making of English Reading Audiences*, p. 136, Klancher frames the mediating role of Coleridge's idealized clergyman in relation to other

social forms by which romantic-period writers approached reading audiences.

77 Williams, *Culture and Society*, pp. 62–3. See also Klancher, *Making of English Reading Audiences*, pp. 150–1, for Coleridge's tendency to conceive reading and writing "in the framework of institutions."

78 Klancher, *Making of English Reading Audiences*, pp. 165–6.

79 This is not to dispute Harling's suggestion, in "Robert Southey and the Language of Social Discipline," p. 647, that Southey likely had little in the way of first-hand experience with the poor.

80 See *CL* 6: 903, for Coleridge's objection to the idea (attributed to John Wilson Croker) that the clerisy should be considered "neither more or less than Government Cooks in office, to be kept, or dismissed, by the Ministers & Majority of the Houses for the time being."

81 David Aram Kaiser, *Romanticism, Aesthetics, and Nationalism* (Cambridge: Cambridge University Press), p. 70.

82 Terry Eagleton, *The Idea of Culture* (Oxford: Blackwell, 2000), pp. 6–7.

83 Carnall, *Robert Southey and His Age*, p. 188.

84 Quoted in Colmer, *Coleridge: Critic of Society*, p. 165.

Bibliography

Abrams, M. H. *Natural Supernaturalism: Tradition and Revolution in Romantic Literature*. New York and London: Norton, 1971.

Alexander, J. H. "*Blackwood's*: Magazine as Romantic Form." *The Wordsworth Circle* 15 (1984), 57–68.

Altick, Richard. *The English Common Reader: A Social History of the Mass Reading Public, 1800–1900*. Chicago: University of Chicago Press, 1957.

Anderson, Benedict. *Imagined Communities: Reflections on the Origin and Spread of Nationalism*. London: Verso, 1983.

Andrews, Stuart. *The British Periodical Press and the French Revolution, 1789–99*. Houndmills, Basingstoke: Palgrave, 2000.

Anti-Cobbett, or The Weekly Patriotic Register (1817).

Anti-Gallican Monitor and Anti-Corsican Chronicle (1811–17).

The AntiGallican Songster (1793).

The Anti-Gallican, or, Standard of British Loyalty, Religion and Liberty (1803–4).

The Anti-Jacobin; or, Weekly Examiner (1797–8).

Anti-Jacobin Review and Magazine (1798–1821).

The Anti-Levelling Songster (1793).

Aspinall, Arthur. *Politics and the Press, c. 1780–1850*. London: Home and Van Thal, 1949.

Association for Preserving Liberty and Property against Republicans and Levellers. *Association Papers*. Part I: *Proceedings of the Association* and *Publications Printed by Special Order of the Society*, Part II, *A Collection of Tracts Printed at the Expence of the Society*. London, 1793.

Austen, Jane. *Northanger Abbey*. Ed. Marilyn Butler. Harmondsworth: Penguin, 1995.

Baer, Marc. *Theatre and Disorder in Late Georgian London*. Oxford: Clarendon Press, 1992.

Bakhtin, Mikhail M. *The Dialogic Imabination*. Ed. Michael Holquist. Austin: University of Texas Press, 1981.

Balfour, Ian. *The Rhetoric of Romantic Prophecy*. Stanford: Stanford University Press, 2002.

Barker-Benfield, G. J. *The Culture of Sensibility: Sex and Society in Eighteenth-Century Britain*. Chicago: University of Chicago Press, 1996.

Barrell, John. *Imagining the King's Death: Figurative Treason, Fantasies of Regicide, 1793–1796*. Oxford: Oxford University Press, 2000.

The Beauties of the Anti-Jacobin: or, Weekly Examiner. London, 1799.

Beedell, A. V. "John Reeves's Prosecution for a Seditious Libel, 1795–6: A Study in Political Cynicism." *The Historical Journal* 36 (1993), 821–2

Belchem, John. "Republicanism, Popular Constitutionalism and the Radical Platform in Early Nineteenth-Century England." *Social History* 6 (1981), 1–32.

Benger, Elizabeth. *Memoirs of the Late Mrs. Elizabeth Hamilton. With a Selection from Her Correspondence, and Other Unpublished Writings*. 2 vols. London: Longman, Hurst, Rees, Orme, and Brown, 1818.

Bennett, Scott. "Catholic Emancipation, the 'Quarterly Review,' and Britain's Constitutional Revolution." *Victorian Studies* 12 (1969), 283–304.

Bindman, David. *The Shadow of the Guillotine: Britain and the French Revolution*. London: British Museum Publications, 1989.

Black, Eugene Charlton. *The Association: British Extraparliamentary Political Organization, 1769–1793*. Cambridge, Massachusetts: Harvard University Press, 1963.

Blackwood's Edinburgh Magazine (1817–).

Blagdon's Political Register (1809–11).

Blakemore, Steven. *Burke and the Fall of Language: The French Revolution as Linguistic Event*. Hanover: University Press of New England, 1988.

Bloom, Harold. *The Visionary Company: A Reading of English Romantic Poetry*. Ithaca: Cornell University Press, 1971.

Bowles, John. *Thoughts on the Late General Election. As Demonstrative of the Progress of Jacobinism*. London, 1802.

Brewer, John. *The Common People and Politics, 1750–1790s*. Cambridge: Chadwyck-Healey, 1986.

The Pleasures of the Imagination: English Culture in the Eighteenth Century. New York: Farrar, Straus, and Giroux, 1997.

The British Critic (1793–).

Bromwich, David. *Hazlitt: The Mind of a Critic*. New York and Oxford: Oxford University Press, 1983.

Bullock, Mrs. *Dorothea; or, A Ray of the New Light*. 2 vols. Dublin, 1801.

Burges, Mary Anne. *The Progress of the Pilgrim Good-Intent, in Jacobinical Times*. London, 1800.

Burke, Edmund. *The Writings and Speeches of Edmund Burke*. Ed. Paul Langford et al. 12 vols. Oxford: Clarendon Press, 1981–.

Butler, Marilyn. *Jane Austen and the War of Ideas*. New edition. Oxford: Clarendon Press, 1987.

"Revolving in Deep Time: The French Revolution as Narrative." In *Revolution and English Romanticism: Politics and Rhetoric*. Ed. Keith Hanley and Raman Selden. New York: St. Martin's Press, 1990.

Romantics, Rebels, and Reactionaries: English Literature and Its Background, 1760–1830. Oxford: Oxford University Press, 1981.

Burke, Paine, Godwin, and the Revolution Controversy. Ed. Marilyn Butler. Cambridge: Cambridge University Press, 1984.

Canning, George. *Speech of the Right Hon. George Canning to His Constituents at Liverpool on Saturday, March 18th, 1820, at the Celebration of His Fourth Election.* London, 1820.

Cannon, John. *Parliamentary Reform, 1640–1832.* Cambridge: Cambridge University Press, 1973.

Canuel, Mark. *Religion, Toleration, and British Writing, 1790–1830.* Cambridge: Cambridge University Press, 2002.

Carnall, Geoffrey. *Robert Southey and His Age: The Development of a Conservative Mind.* Oxford: Clarendon Press, 1960.

Chandler, James K. *Wordsworth's Second Nature: A Study of the Poetry and Politics.* Chicago: University of Chicago Press, 1984.

Cheap Repository. *Dame Andrews, A Ballad.* Bath and London, [1795].

Hints to All Ranks of People. Bath and London, [1795].

The Loyal Subject's Political Creed; or, What I Do, and What I Do Not Think. London and Bath [no date].

Childers, Joseph. *Novel Possibilities: Fiction and the Formation of Early Victorian Culture.* Philadelphia: University of Pennsylvania Press, 1995.

Christensen, Jerome. "The Detection of the Romantic Conspiracy in Britain." *South Atlantic Quarterly* 95 (1996), 603–27.

Christian Guardian (1802–).

Christie, Ian R. *Stress and Stability in Late Eighteenth-Century Britain: Reflections on the British Avoidance of Revolution.* Oxford: Clarendon Press, 1984.

The Citizen's Daughter; or What Might Be. London, 1804.

Claeys, Gregory. "The French Revolution Debate and British Political Thought." *History of Political Thought* 11 (1990), 59–60.

Political Writings of the 1790s. Ed. Gregory Claeys. 8 vols. London: Pickering, 1995.

Clark, J. C. D. *English Society, 1688–1832: Ideology, Social Structure and Political Practice During the Ancien Regime.* Cambridge: Cambridge University Press, 1985.

Clark, Peter. *British Clubs and Societies, 1580–1800: The Origins of an Associational World.* Oxford: Clarendon Press, 2000.

Clive, John Leonard. *Scotch Reviewers: The Edinburgh Review, 1802–1815.* Cambridge, Massachusetts: Harvard University Press, 1957.

Coleman, Deirdre. *Coleridge and The Friend (1809–1810).* Oxford: Clarendon Press, 1988.

Coleridge, Samuel Taylor. *Biographia Literaria.* Ed. James Engell and W. Jackson Bate. 2 vols. Vol. 7 of *The Collected Works of Samuel Taylor Coleridge.* Princeton: Princeton University Press, 1983.

Collected Letters of Samuel Taylor Coleridge. Ed. Earl Leslie Griggs. 6 vols. Oxford: Clarendon Press, 1956–71.

Essays on His Times in the Morning Post and the Courier. Ed. David V. Erdman. 3 vols., Vol. 3 of *The Collected Works of Samuel Taylor Coleridge.* Princeton: Princeton University Press, 1978.

The Friend. Ed. Barbara E. Rooke. 2 vols. Vol. 4 of *The Collected Works of Samuel Taylor Coleridge.* Princeton: Princeton University Press, 1969.

Lay Sermons. Ed. R. J. White. Vol. 6 of *The Collected Works of Samuel Taylor Coleridge.* Princeton: Princeton University Press, 1972.

Lectures 1795 On Politics and Religion. Ed. Lewis Patton and Peter Mann. Vol. 1 of *The Collected Works of Samuel Taylor Coleridge.* Princeton: Princeton University Press, 1971.

Lectures 1808–1819 On Literature. Ed. R. A. Foakes. 2 vols. Vol. 5 of *The Collected Works of Samuel Taylor Coleridge.* Princeton: Princeton University Press, 1987.

On the Constitution of the Church and State. Ed. John Colmer. Vol. 10 of *The Collected Works of Samuel Taylor Coleridge.* Princeton: Princeton University Press, 1976.

Colley, Linda. *Britons: Forging the Nation 1707–1837.* New Haven: Yale University Press, 1992.

Colmer, John. *Coleridge: Critic of Society.* Oxford: Clarendon Press, 1959.

Connell, Philip. *Romanticism, Economics and the Question of "Culture".* Oxford: Oxford University Press, 2001.

Cookson, J. E. *The British Armed Nation, 1793–1815.* Oxford: Clarendon Press, 1997.

"The English Volunteer Movement of the French Wars, 1793–1815: Some Contexts." *The Historical Journal* 32 (1989), 867–91.

Corrigan, Philip, and Derek Sayer. *The Great Arch: English State Formation as Cultural Revolution.* Oxford: Basil Blackwell, 1985.

Cottage Magazine; or Plain Christian's Library (1812–1832).

The Cottager's Monthly Visitor (1821–).

Cox, Jeffrey N. "Ideology and Genre in the British Antirevolutionary Drama of the 1790s." *ELH* 58 (1991), 579–610.

Poetry and Politics in the Cockney School: Keats, Shelley, Hunt and Their Circle. Cambridge: Cambridge University Press, 1998.

Dart, Gregory. *Rousseau, Robespierre and English Romanticism.* Cambridge: Cambridge University Press, 1999.

Deane, Seamus. *Foreign Affections: Essays on Edmund Burke.* Notre Dame: University of Notre Dame Press, 2005.

De Bruyn, Frans. *The Literary Genres of Edmund Burke: The Political Uses of Literary Form.* Oxford: Clarendon Press, 1996.

Demers, Patricia. *The World of Hannah More.* Lexington: The University Press of Kentucky, 1996.

de Montluzin, Emily Lorraine. *The Anti-Jacobins, 1798–1800: The Early Contributors to the Anti-Jacobin Review.* New York: St. Martin's Press, 1988.

Dickinson, H. T. *Caricatures and the Constitution, 1760–1832.* Cambridge: Chadwyck-Healey, 1986.

"Introduction: The Impact of the French Revolution and the French Wars, 1789–1815." In *Britain and the French Revolution, 1789–1815*. Ed. H. T. Dickinson. London: Macmillan, 1989. 1–19.

Liberty and Property: Political Ideology in Eighteenth-Century Britain. London: Methuen, 1979.

"Popular Conservatism and Militant Loyalism, 1789–1815." In *Britain and the French Revolution, 1789–1815*. Ed. H. T. Dickinson. London: Macmillan, 1989. 103–25.

"Popular Loyalism in Britain in the 1790s." In *The Transformation of Political Culture: England and Germany in the Late Eighteenth Century*. Ed. Eckhart Hellmuth. Oxford: Oxford University Press, 1990. 503–33.

Dinwiddy, John. "Interpretations of Anti-Jacobinism." In *The French Revolution and British Popular Politics*. Ed. Mark Philp. Cambridge: Cambridge University Press, 1991.

D'Israeli, Isaac. *Vaurien: or, Sketches of the Times: Exhibiting Views of the Philosophies, Religions, Politics, Literature, and Manners of the Age*. 2 vols. London, 1797.

Dixon, Peter. *Canning: Politician and Statesman*. London: Weidenfeld and Nicolson, 1976.

Donald, Diana. *The Age of Caricature: Satirical Prints in the Reign of George III*. New Haven and London: Yale University Press, 1996.

Dozier, Robert R. *For King, Constitution and Country: The English Loyalists and the French Revolution*. Lexington, Kentucky: University of Kentucky Press, 1983.

Duffy, Michael. "William Pitt and the Origins of the Loyalist Association Movement of 1792." *Historical Journal* 39 (1996), 943–62.

Eagleton, Terry. *The Function of Criticism, From the Spectator to Post-Structuralism*. London: Verso, 1984.

The Idea of Culture. Oxford: Blackwell, 2000.

Eastwood, David. "Patriotism and the English State in the 1790s." In *The French Revolution and British Popular Politics*. Ed. Mark Philp. Cambridge: Cambridge University Press, 1991. 146–68.

"Robert Southey and the Intellectual Origins of Romantic Conservatism." *English Historical Review* 104 (1989), 308–31.

"Robert Southey and the Meanings of Patriotism." *Journal of British Studies* 31 (1992), 265–87.

"Ruinous Prosperity: Robert Southey's Critique of the Commercial System." *The Wordsworth Circle* 25 (1994), 72–6.

Eberle, Roxanne. *Chastity and Transgression in Women's Writing, 1792–1897: Interrupting the Harlot's Progress*. New York: Palgrave, 2002.

Elliott, Dorice. "'The Care of the Poor Is Her Profession': Hannah More and Women's Philanthropic Work." *Nineteenth-Century Contexts* 19 (1995), 179–204.

Ellis, Markman. *The Politics of Sensibility: Race, Gender and Commerce in the Sentimental Novel*. Cambridge: Cambridge University Press, 1996.

Ellison, Julie. "Aggressive Allegory." *Raritan* 3 (1984), 100–15.

Emsley, Clive. "Repression, 'Terror' and the Rule of Law in England During the Decade of the French Revolution." *English Historical Review* 100 (1985), 801–25.

Evans, Keith. *The Development and Structure of the English School System*. London: Hodder and Stoughton, 1985.

Fielding, Henry. *Tom Jones*. Ed. John Bender and Simon Stern. Oxford: Oxford University Press, 1996.

Flowers of Literature (1801–9).

Foord, Archibald S. *His Majesty's Opposition, 1714–1830*. Oxford: Clarendon Press, 1964.

Footsteps of Blood; or, The March of the Republicans. London, 1803.

Francis, Mark, and John Morrow. *A History of English Political Thought in the Nineteenth Century*. New York: St. Martin's Press, 1994.

Furniss, Tom. *Edmund Burke's Aesthetic Ideology: Language, Gender, and Political Economy in Revolution*. Cambridge: Cambridge University Press, 1993.

Gallagher, Catherine. *The Industrial Reformation of English Fiction: Social Discourse and Narrative Form, 1832–1867*. Chicago: University of Chicago Press, 1985.

Nobody's Story: The Vanishing Acts of Women Writers in the Marketplace, 1670–1820. Berkeley: University of California Press, 1994.

Gallaway, W. F. "The Conservative Attitude toward Fiction, 1770–1830." *PMLA* 55 (1940), 1041–59.

Garside, P. D., J. E. Belanger, and S. A. Ragaz. *British Fiction, 1800–1829: A Database of Production, Circulation and Reception*. www.british-fiction.cf.ac.uk, last accessed 10 April 2005.

Gascoigne, John. *Cambridge in the Age of the Enlightenment: Science, Religion and Politics from the Restoration to the French Revolution*. Cambridge: Cambridge University Press, 1989.

Gentleman's Magazine (1731–).

George, M. Dorothy. *English Political Caricature*. 2 vols. Oxford: Clarendon Press, 1959.

Gibbons, Luke. *Edmund Burke and Ireland: Aesthetics, Politics and the Colonial Sublime*. Cambridge: Cambridge University Press, 2003.

Gilmartin, Kevin. *Print Politics: The Press and Radical Opposition in Early Nineteenth-Century England*. Cambridge: Cambridge University Press, 1996.

"Burke, Popular Opinion, and the Problem of a Counter-revolutionary Public Sphere." In *Edmund Burke's Reflections on the Revolution in France: New Interdisciplinary Essays*. Ed. John Whale. Manchester University Press, 2000. 94–114.

Ginter, Donald E. "The Loyalist Association Movement of 1792–93 and British Public Opinion." *Historical Journal* 9 (1966), 179–90.

Godwin, William. *Enquiry Concerning Political Justice*. Ed. Isaac Kramnick. Harmondsworth: Penguin, 1985.

Goldberg, Brian. "Romantic Professionalism in 1800: Robert Southey, Herbert Croft, and the Letters and Legacy of Thomas Chatterton." *ELH* 63 (1996), 681–706.

Goodman, Dena. "Public Sphere and Private Life: Toward a Synthesis of Current Historiographical Approaches to the Old Regime." *History and Theory* 31 (1992), 1–20.

Goodwin, Albert. *The Friends of Liberty: The English Democratic Movement in the Age of the French Revolution.* Cambridge, Massachusetts: Harvard University Press, 1979.

Graham, Walter. *English Literary Periodicals.* New York: Thomas Nelson and Sons, 1930.

Tory Criticism in the Quarterly Review, 1809–1853. New York: Columbia University Press, 1921.

Grenby, M. O. *The Anti-Jacobin Novel: British Conservatism and the French Revolution.* Cambridge: Cambridge University Press, 2001.

The Gridiron, or, Cook's Weekly Register (1822).

Guardian of Education (1802–6).

Guest, Harriet. *Small Change: Women, Learning, Patriotism, 1750–1810.* Chicago: University of Chicago Press, 2000.

Habermas, Jürgen. *The Structural Transformation of the Public Sphere: An Inquiry into a Category of Bourgeois Society.* Trans. Thomas Burger and Frederick Lawrence. Cambridge, Massachusetts: MIT Press, 1989.

Hadley, Elaine. *Melodramatic Tactics: Theatricalized Dissent in the English Marketplace, 1800–1885.* Stanford: Stanford University Press, 1995.

Halevy, Elie. *A History of the English People in 1815.* London: Ark Paperbacks, 1987.

Hamilton, Elizabeth. *Memoirs of Modern Philosophers.* Ed. Claire Grogan. Peterborough, Ontario: Broadview Press, 2000.

Translation of the Letters of a Hindoo Rajah. Ed. Pamela Perkins and Shannon Russell. Peterborough, Ontario: Broadview Press, 1999.

Harling, Philip. "Robert Southey and the Language of Social Discipline." *Albion* 30 (1999), 630–55.

Harral, Thomas. *Scenes of Life.* 3 vols. London, 1805.

Hartman, Geoffrey. "Romanticism and 'Anti-Self-Consciousness'." In *Romanticism and Consciousness: Essays in Criticism.* Ed. Harold Bloom." New York and London: Norton, 1970. 46–56.

Wordsworth's Poetry, 1787–1814. New Haven: Yale University Press, 1964.

Hayden, John O. *The Romantic Reviewers, 1802–1824.* Chicago: University of Chicago Press, 1968.

Haywood, Ian. "'The Renovating Fury': Southey, Republicanism and Sensationalism." *Romanticism on the Net* 32–3 (November 2003–February 2004) www.erudit.org/revue/ron/2003/v/n32–33/009256ar.html, last accessed 12 May 2005.

Hazlitt, William. *The Complete Works of William Hazlitt.* Ed. P. P. Howe. 21 vols. London: J. M. Dent and Sons, 1930–4.

Head, Emory Lee. "A Study of the *Anti-Jacobin; or, Weekly Examiner.*" Dissertation, Duke University, 1971.

Heidler, Joseph Bunn. *The History, from 1700 to 1800, of English Criticism of Prose Fiction.* Urbana, Illinois: University of Illinois Press, 1928.

Herzog, Don. *Poisoning the Minds of the Lower Orders.* Princeton: Princeton University Press, 1998.

Hickey, Alison. *Impure Conceits: Rhetoric and Ideology in Wordsworth's Excursion.* Stanford: Stanford University Press, 1997.

Hilton, Boyd. *The Age of Atonement: The Influence of Evangelicalism on Social and Economic Thought, 1785–1865.* Oxford: Clarendon Press, 1988.

Himmelfarb, Gertrude. *The Idea of Poverty: England in the Early Industrial Age.* New York: Alfred A. Knopf, 1984.

Hinde, Wendy. *George Canning.* Oxford and New York: Basil Blackwell, 1989.

Hoadley, Frank T. "The Controversy Over Southey's Wat Tyler." *Studies in Philology* 38 (1941), 81–96.

Hobsbawm, Eric and Terence Ranger, eds. *The Invention of Tradition.* Cambridge: Cambridge University Press, 1983.

Hole, Robert. *Pulpits, Politics and Public Order in England, 1760–1832.* Cambridge: Cambridge University Press, 1989.

Holmes, Richard. *Coleridge: Darker Reflections: 1804–1834.* New York: Pantheon Books, 1998.

Hone, J. Ann. *For the Cause of Truth: Radicalism in London, 1796–1821.* Oxford: Clarendon Press, 1982.

Hopkins, Mary Alden. *Hannah More and Her Circle.* New York: Longmans, Green, and Co., 1947.

Horne, Thomas A. "'The Poor Have a Claim Founded in the Law of Nature': William Paley and the Rights of the Poor." *Journal of the History of Philosophy* 23 (1985), 51–70.

Hunter, J. Paul. *Before Novels: The Cultural Contexts of Eighteenth Century English Fiction.* New York and London: W. W. Norton and Company, 1990.

"The World as Stage and Closet" In *British Theatre and the Other Arts, 1660–1800.* Ed. Shirley Strum Kenny. Washington: Folger Shakespeare Library, 1984. 271–87.

Innes, Joanna. "The Distinctiveness of the English Poor Laws, 1750–1850." In *The Political Economy of British Historical Experience, 1688–1914.* Ed. Donald Winch and Patrick K. O'Brien. Oxford: Oxford University Press, 2002. 383–407.

"Politics and Morals: The Reformation of Manners in Later Eighteenth-Century England." In *The Transformation of Political Culture: England and Germany in the Late Eighteenth Century.* Ed. Eckhart Hellmuth. Oxford: Oxford University Press, 1990. 57–118.

Jameson, Fredric. *The Political Unconscious: Narrative as a Socially Symbolic Act.* Ithaca, New York: Cornell University Press, 1981.

Janowitz, Anne. *Lyric and Labour in the Romantic Tradition.* Cambridge: Cambridge University Press, 1998.

Jenks, Timothy. "Contesting the Hero: The Funeral of Admiral Lord Nelson." *Journal of British Studies* 39 (2000), 422–53.

Johnson, Claudia. *Jane Austen: Women, Politics, and the Novel*. Chicago: University of Chicago Press, 1988.

Johnson, Nancy E. *The English Jacobin Novel on Rights, Property, and the Law: Critiquing the Contract*. New York: Palgrave, 2004.

"The 'French Threat' in Anti-Jacobin Novels of the 1790s." In *Illicit Sex: Identity Politics in Early Modern Culture*. Ed. Thomas DiPiero and Pat Gill. Athens, Georgia: University of Georgia Press, 1997.

Jones, Chris. *Radical Sensibility: Literature and Ideas in the 1790s*. London and New York: Routledge, 1993.

Jones, William. *John Bull's Second Answer to His Brother Thomas*. London, 1792. *One Penny-worth More, or, A Second Letter from Thomas Bull to his Brother John*. London, 1792.

Justman, Stewart. "Regarding Others." *New Literary History* 27 (1996), 83–93.

Kaestle, Carl F. *Joseph Lancaster and the Monitorial School Movement: A Documentary History*. New York: Teachers College Press 1973.

Kaiser, David Aram. *Romanticism, Aesthetics, and Nationalism*. Cambridge: Cambridge University Press, 1999.

Keen, Suzanne. *Victorian Renovations of the Novel: Narrative Annexes and the Boundaries of Representation*. Cambridge: Cambridge University Press, 1998.

Kelly, Gary. *English Fiction of the Romantic Period, 1789–1830*. London and New York: Longman, 1989.

"Revolution, Reaction, and the Expropriation of Popular Culture: Hannah More's *Cheap Repository*." *Man and Nature* 6 (1987), 147–59.

"'This Pestiferous Reading': The Social Basis of Reaction against the Novel in Late Eighteenth- and Early Nineteenth-Century Britain." *Man and Nature* 4 (1985), 183–94.

Women, Writing, and Revolution 1790–1827. Oxford: Clarendon Press, 1993.

Keen, Paul. *The Crisis of Literature in the 1790s: Print Culture and the Public Sphere*. Cambridge: Cambridge University Press, 1999.

Klancher, Jon. *The Making of English Reading Audiences, 1790–1832*. Madison, Wisconsin: University of Wisconsin Press, 1987.

Klein, Lawrence E. "Gender and the Public/Private Distinction in the Eighteenth Century: Some Questions about Evidence and Analytic Procedure." *Eighteenth-Century Studies* 29 (1995), 97–109.

Kowaleski-Wallace, Elizabeth. *Their Fathers' Daughters: Hannah More, Maria Edgeworth, and Patriarchal Complicity*. New York: Oxford University Press, 1991.

Kramnick, Isaac. *The Rage of Edmund Burke: Portrait of an Ambivalent Conservative*. New York: Basic Books, 1977.

Krueger, Christine. *The Reader's Repentance: Women Preachers, Women Writers, and Nineteenth-Century Social Discourse*. Chicago: University of Chicago Press, 1992.

Lee, Yoon Sun. *Nationalism and Irony: Burke, Scott, Carlyle*. New York: Oxford University Press, 2004.

Liu, Alan. "Wordsworth and Subversion, 1793–1804: Trying Cultural Criticism." *Yale Journal of Criticism* 2 (1989), 55–100.

Wordsworth: The Sense of History. Stanford: Stanford University Press, 1989.

The Loyalist (1803).

The Loyalist; or, Anti-Radical (1820).

Macleod, Emma Vincent. *A War of Ideas: British Attitudes to the Wars against Revolutionary France, 1792–1802*. Aldershot: Ashgate, 1998.

Macpherson, C. B. *Burke*. Past Masters Series. Oxford: Oxford University Press, 1980.

Mahoney, Charles. *Romantics and Renegades: The Poetics of Political Reaction*. New York: Palgrave, 2003.

Makdisi, Saree. *William Blake and the Impossible History of the 1790s*. Chicago: University of Chicago Press, 2003.

Mandler, Peter. "The Making of the New Poor Law *Redivivus*." *Past and Present* 117 (1987), 131–57.

"Tories and Paupers: Christian Political Economy and the Making of the New Poor Law." *The Historical Journal* 33 (1990), 81–103.

Manners, George. *Vindiciae Satiricae, or, A Vindication of the Principles of the Satirist, and the Conduct of Its Proprietors*. London, 1809.

Marshall, David. *The Figure of Theater: Shaftesbury, Defoe, Adam Smith, and George Eliot*. New York: Columbia University Press, 1986.

McCalman, Iain. *Radical Underworld: Prophets, Revolutionaries and Pornographers in London, 1795–1840*. Cambridge: Cambridge University Press, 1988.

McKeon, Michael. *The Origins of the English Novel, 1600–1740*. Baltimore: Johns Hopkins University Press, 1987.

McMahon, Darrin M. *Enemies of the Enlightenment: The French Counter-Enlightenment and the Making of Modernity*. Oxford: Oxford University Press, 2001.

Mee, Jon. *Dangerous Enthusiasm: William Blake and the Culture of Radicalism in the 1790s*. Oxford: Clarendon Press, 1992.

Romanticism, Enthusiasm, and Regulation: Poetics and the Policing of Culture in the Romantic Period. Oxford: Oxford University Press, 2003.

Mellor, Anne. *Mothers of the Nation*. Bloomington, Indiana: Indiana University Press, 2000.

Mitchell, Austin. "The Association Movement of 1792–3." *The Historical Journal* 4 (1961), 56–77.

Money, John. "Taverns, Coffee Houses and Clubs: Local Politics and Popular Articulacy in the Birmingham Area in the Age of the American Revolution." *Historical Journal* 14 (1971), 15–47.

Moody, Jane. *Illegitimate Theatre in London, 1770–1840*. Cambridge: Cambridge University Press, 2000.

More, Hannah. *The Apprentice's Monitor; or, Indentures in Verse, Shewing what they are Bound to Do*. Bath and London, [1795].

The Cottage Cook; or, Mrs. Jones's Cheap Dishes: Shewing the Way to Do Much Good with Little Money. London and Bath, [no date].

The History of Tom White, the Postillion. in Two Parts. London and Bath, [no date].

Selected Writings of Hannah More. Ed. Robert Hole. London: William Pickering, 1996.

The Village Disputants; or, A Conversation on the Present Times. London, 1819.

The Works of Hannah More. 8 vols. London: T. Cadell and W. Davies, 1801.

More, Martha. *Mendip Annals: Or, A Narrative of the Charitable Labours of Hannah and Martha More in Their Neighbourhood. Being the Journal of Martha More*. Ed. Arthur Roberts. London: James Nisbet, 1859.

More, Sarah. *The Good Mother's Legacy*. London and Bath, [no date].

Morris, Marilyn. *The British Monarchy and the French Revolution*. New Haven: Yale University Press, 1988.

Morrow, John. *Coleridge's Political Thought: Property, Morality, and the Limits of Traditional Discourse*. New York: St. Martin's Press, 1990.

Myers, Mitzi. "Hannah More's Tracts for the Times: Social Fiction and Female Ideology." In *Fetter'd or Free?: British Women Novelists, 1670–1815*. Ed. Mary Anne Schofield and Cecilia Macheski. Athens, Ohio: Ohio University Press, 1986. 264–84.

"'A Peculiar Protection': Hannah More and the Cultural Politics of the Blagdon Controversy." In *History, Gender, and Eighteenth-Century Literature*. Ed. Beth Fowkes Tobin. Athens, Georgia: University of Georgia Press, 1994. 227–57.

Newman, Gerald. *The Rise of English Nationalism: A Cultural History, 1740–1840*. New York: St. Martin's Press, 1987.

O'Brien, Conor Cruise. *The Great Melody: A Thematic Biography and Commented Anthology of Edmund Burke*. Chicago: University of Chicago Press, 1992.

O'Gorman, Frank. "Pitt and the 'Tory' Reaction to the French Revolution, 1789–1815." In *Britain and the French Revolution, 1789–1815*. Ed. H. T. Dickinson. London: Macmillan, 1989. 21–37.

Voters, Patrons, and Parties: The Unreformed Electoral System of Hanoverian England, 1734–1832. Oxford: Clarendon Press, 1989.

Paley, William. *The Principles of Moral and Political Philosophy*. London, 1785.

Reasons for Contentment; Addressed to the Labouring Part of the British Public. London, 1793.

Parker, Mark. *Literary Magazines and British Romanticism*. Cambridge: Cambridge University Press, 2000.

Parks, Stephen, ed. *The Friends to the Liberty of the Press: Eight Tracts, 1792–1793*. New York and London: Garland, 1974.

Paulson, Ronald. "Life as Journey and as Theater: Two Eighteenth-Century Narrative Structures." *New Literary History* 8 (1976), 43–58.

Representations of Revolution (1789–1820). New Haven and London: Yale University Press, 1983.

Pedersen, Susan. "Hannah More Meets Simple Simon: Tracts, Chapbooks, and Popular Culture in Late Eighteenth-Century England." *Journal of British Studies* 25 (1986), 84–113.

Philips, David. "Good Men to Associate and Bad Men to Conspire: Associations for the Prosecution of Felons in England, 1760–1860." In *Policing and Prosecution in Britain, 1750–1850*. Ed. Douglas Hay and Francis Snyder. Oxford: Clarendon Press, 1989. 113–70.

Philp, Mark. "The Fragmented Ideology of Reform." In *The French Revolution and British Popular Politics*. Ed. Mark Philp. Cambridge: Cambridge University Press, 1991. 50–77.

"Vulgar Conservatism, 1792–3." *English Historical Review* 110 (1995), 42–69.

Pitkin, Hanna Fenichel. *The Concept of Representation*. Berkeley: University of California Press, 1972.

Pocock, J. G. A. *Virtue, Commerce, and History: Essays on Political Thought and History, Chiefly in the Eighteenth Century*. Cambridge: Cambridge University Press, 1985.

"Introduction" to Edmund Burke, *Reflections on the Revolution in France*. Ed. J. G. A. Pocock. Indianapolis, Indiana: Hackett, 1987. vii–lvi.

Poetry of the Anti-Jacobin. London, 1799.

Pole, J. R. *Political Representation in England and the Origins of the American Republic*. London: Macmillan, 1960.

Poynter, J. R. *Society and Pauperism: English Ideas on Poor Relief, 1795–1834*. London: Routledge and Kegan Paul, 1969.

Priestman, Martin. *Romantic Atheism: Poetry and Freethought, 1780–1830*. Cambridge: Cambridge University Press, 1999.

Pye, Henry James. *The Aristocrat*. 2 vols. London, 1799.

The Democrat: Interspersed with Anecdotes of Well Known Characters. 2 vols. London, 1795.

Quarterly Review (1809–).

Reid, Christopher. *Edmund Burke and the Practice of Political Writing*. New York: St. Martin's, 1985.

Reid, John Phillip. *The Concept of Representation in the Age of the American Revolution*. Chicago: University of Chicago Press, 1987.

Religious Tract Society. *An Account of the Origin and Progress of the London Religious Tract Society*. London, 1803.

Report of the Committee of the Religious Tract Society. London, 1808.

The Twenty-Fifth Annual Report of the Religious Tract Society. London, 1824.

Richardson, Alan. *Literature, Education, and Romanticism: Reading as Social Practice, 1780–1832*. Cambridge: Cambridge University Press, 1994.

Richetti, John J. *Popular Fiction before Richardson: Narrative Patterns, 1700–1739*. Oxford: Clarendon Press, 1992.

Rieder, John. *Wordsworth's Counterrevolutionary Turn: Community, Virtue, and Vision in the 1790s*. Newark: University of Delaware Press, 1997.

Ring the Alarum Bell! (1803).

Roberts, William. *The Looker-On: A Periodical Paper. By the Rev. Simon Olive-Branch, A.M.* Fourth edition. 4 vols. London, 1797.
Memoirs of the Life and Correspondence of Mrs. Hannah More. 4 vols. London: R. B. Seeley and W. Burnside, 1834.
Robinson, Nicholas K. *Edmund Burke: A Life in Caricature.* New Haven: Yale University Press, 1996.
Roe, Nicholas. *Wordsworth and Coleridge: The Radical Years.* Oxford: Clarendon Press, 1988.
Rogers, Nicholas. "Burning Tom Paine: Loyalism and Counter-Revolution in Britain, 1792–1792." *Histoire Sociale-Social History* 32 (1999), 139–71.
Crowds, Culture, and Politics in Georgian Britain. Oxford: Oxford University Press, 1998.
Roper, Derek. *Reviewing before the Edinburgh, 1788–1802.* Newark, New Jersey: University of Delaware Press, 1978.
Russell, Gillian. *The Theatres of War: Performance, Politics, and Society, 1793–1815.* Oxford: Clarendon Press, 1995.
Ryan, Robert. *The Romantic Reformation: Religious Politics in English Literature, 1789–1824.* Cambridge: Cambridge University Press, 1997.
Sack, James J. *From Jacobite to Conservative: Reaction and Orthodoxy in Britain, c. 1760–1832.* Cambridge: Cambridge University Press, 1993.
"The Memory of Burke and the Memory of Pitt." *Historical Journal* 30 (1987), 623–40.
The Satirist, or Monthly Meteor (1807–14).
Scrivener, Michael. *Radical Shelley: The Philosophical Anarchism and Utopian Thought of Percy Bysshe Shelley.* Princeton: Princeton University Press, 1982.
Seditious Allegories: John Thelwall and Jacobin Writing. University Park, Pennsylvania: Pennsylvania State University Press, 2001.
Shadgett's Weekly Review, of Cobbett, Wooler, Sherwin, and Other Democratical and Infidel Writers (1818–19).
Shine, Hill, and Helen Chadwick Shine. *The Quarterly Review under Gifford: Identification of Contributors, 1809–1824.* Chapel Hill: University of North Carolina Press, 1949.
Simpson, David. "The French Revolution." In *Romanticism.* Ed. Marshall Brown. Cambridge: Cambridge University Press, 2000. Volume 5 of *The Cambridge History of Literary Criticism.*
Romanticism, Nationalism, and the Revolt Against Theory. Chicago: University of Chicago Press, 1993.
Wordsworth's Historical Imagination: The Poetry of Displacement. New York and London: Methuen, 1987.
Siskin, Clifford. *The Work of Writing: Literature and Social Change in Britain, 1700–1830.* Baltimore: Johns Hopkins University Press, 1998.
Smith, Adam. *The Theory of Moral Sentiments.* Indianapolis: Liberty Classics, 1984.

Smith, Olivia. *The Politics of Language, 1791–1819.* Oxford: Clarendon Press, 1984.

Southey, Robert. *The Book of the Church.* London: Frederick Warne, 1869.

Essays, Moral and Political. 2 vols. London: John Murray, 1832.

Letters of Robert Southey. Ed. Maurice H. Fitzgerald. London: Henry Frowde, 1912.

The Life and Correspondence of Robert Southey. Ed. Charles Cuthbert Southey. 6 vols. London: Longman, Brown, Green, and Longmans, 1850.

The Life of Wesley and the Rise and Progress of Methodism. Ed. Maurice Fitzgerald. 2 vols. Oxford: Oxford University Press, 1925.

The Origin, Nature, and Object of the New System of Education. London: John Murray, 1812.

The Poetical Works of Robert Southey. London: Longmans, Green, and Co., 1876.

Selections from the Letters of Robert Southey. Ed. John Wood Warter. 4 vols. London: Longman, Brown, Green, and Longmans, 1856.

Sir Thomas More: or, Colloquies on the Progress and Prospects of Society. 2 vols. London: John Murray, 1829.

Wat Tyler: A Dramatic Poem (1817). Ed. Matt Hill. *Romantic Circles.* ed. Neil Fraistat and Steven E. Jones, www.rc.umd.edu/editions/wattyler/, last accessed 15 July 2005.

Spater, George. *William Cobbett: The Poor Man's Friend.* 2 vols. Cambridge: Cambridge University Press, 1982.

Spinney, G. H. "Cheap Repository Tracts: Hazard and Marshall Edition." *The Library* 20 (1939–40), 295–340.

The Spirit of Anti-Jacobinism for 1802: Being a Collection of Essays, Dissertations, and Other Pieces, in Prose and Verse, on Subjects Religious, Moral, Political and Literary; Partly Selected from the Fugitive Publications of the Day, and Partly Original. London, 1802.

Stevenson, John. *Popular Disturbances in England, 1730–1848.* Second edition. London: Longmans, 1992.

Storey, Mark. *Robert Southey: A Life.* Oxford: Oxford University Press, 1997.

Strout, Alan Lang. *A Bibliography of Articles in Blackwood's Magazine, Volumes I through XVIII, 1817–1825.* Lubbock, Texas: Texas Technical College, 1959.

Sullivan, Alvin, ed. *British Literary Magazines. The Romantic Age, 1789–1836.* Westport, Connecticut: Greenwood Press, 1983.

Sutherland, Kathryn. "Hannah More's Counter-Revolutionary Feminism." In *Revolution in Writing: British Literary Responses to the French Revolution.* Ed. Kelvin Everest. Milton Keynes and Philadelphia: Open University Press, 1991. 53–61.

Taylor, John Tinnon. *Early Opposition to the English Novel: The Popular Reaction from 1760 to 1830.* New York: King's Crown Press, 1943.

Tobin, Beth Fowkes. *Superintending the Poor: Charitable Ladies and Paternal Landlords in British Fiction, 1770–1860.* New Haven: Yale University Press, 1993.

Thomas, Ann. *Adolphus De Biron. A Novel. Founded on The French Revolution*. 2 vols. Plymouth, [1795].

Thompson, E. P. *The Making of the English Working Class*. New York: Vintage, 1966.

———. *The Romantics: England in a Revolutionary Age*. New York: The New Press, 1997.

Todd, Janet. *Sensibility: An Introduction*. London: Methuen, 1986.

Ty, Eleanor. *Unsex'd Revolutionaries: Five Women Novelists of the 1790s*. Toronto: University of Toronto Press, 1993.

Vickery, Amanda. "Golden Age to Separate Spheres? A Review of the Categories and Chronology of English Women's History." *The Historical Journal* 36 (1993), 383–414.

Walker, George. *The Vagabond*. First American edition, from the fourth English edition. Boston, 1800.

Watson, Nicola J. *Revolution and the Form of the British Novel, 1790–1825: Intercepted Letters, Interrupted Seductions*. Oxford: Clarendon Press, 1994.

Watt, Ian. *The Rise of the Novel: Studies in Defoe, Richardson, and Fielding*. Berkeley and Los Angeles: University of California Press, 1957.

Watts, Michael. *The Dissenters*. 2 vols., Vol. 2, *The Expansion of Evangelical Nonconformity*. Oxford: Clarendon Press, 1995.

Welch, Samuel. "Samuel Taylor Coleridge." In *Nineteenth-Century Religious Thought in the West*. Ed. Ninian Smart et al. 3 vols. Cambridge: Cambridge University Press, 1985.

Wells, Roger. *Insurrection: The British Experience, 1795–1803*. Gloucester: A. Sutton, 1983.

———. *Wretched Faces: Famine in Wartime England, 1793–1801*. Gloucester: Alan Sutton, 1988.

West, Jane. *The Advantages of Education, Or, The History of Maria Williams, A Tale for Misses and Their Mamas, By Prudentia Homespun*. 2 vols. London, 1793.

———. *A Tale of the Times*. London, 1799.

Western, J. R. "The Volunteer Movement as an Anti-Revolutionary Force, 1793–1801." *English Historical Review* 71 (1956), 603–14.

Whale, John, ed. *Edmund Burke's Reflections on the Revolution in France: New Interdisciplinary Essays*. Manchester: Manchester University Press, 2000.

———. "Hazlitt on Burke: the Ambivalent Position of a Radical Essayist." *Studies in Romanticism* 25 (1986), 465–81.

Wheatley, Kim, ed. *Romantic Periodicals and Print Culture*. London and Portland: Frank Cass, 2003.

Wheatley, Kim. *Shelley and His Readers: Beyond Paranoid Politics*. Columbia and London: University of Missouri Press, 1999.

The White Dwarf (1817–18).

Wickwar, William. *The Struggle for the Freedom of the Press, 1819–1832*. London: George Allen and Unwin, 1928.

Williams, Raymond. *The Country and the City*. New York: Oxford University Press, 1973.

Culture and Society, 1780–1950. New York: Columbia University Press, 1983.

Keywords: A Vocabulary of Culture and Society. Revised edition. New York: Oxford University Press, 1983.

Winch, Donald. *Riches and Poverty: An Intellectual History of Political Economy in Britain, 1750–1834.* Cambridge: Cambridge University Press, 1996.

Woodward, E. L. *The Age of Reform 1815–1870.* Oxford: Oxford University Press, 1949.

Wordsworth, William. *The Prose Works of William Wordsworth.* Ed. W. J. B. Owen and Jane Worthington Smyser. 3 vols. Oxford: Clarendon Press, 1974.

Wordsworth's Poetical Works. Edited by Thomas Hutchinson and Ernest De Selincourt. Oxford and New York: Oxford University Press, 1936.

Young, Charles Duke. *The Life and Administration of Robert Banks, Second Earl of Liverpool.* London: Macmillan, 1868.

Young, Arthur. *The Example of France a Warning to Britain.* London, 1793.

Index

CAMBRIDGE STUDIES IN ROMANTICISM

GENERAL EDITORS

MARILYN BUTLER *University of Oxford*
JAMES CHANDLER *University of Chicago*